PART III

ENERGY AND UTILITIES

SYSTEMS

Coordinator:
Mohammad H. Qayoumi
University of Missouri/Rolla

01/07

APPA: The Association for Higher Education Facilities Officers, 1643 Prince Street, Alexandria, Virginia 22314-2818

Printed in the United States of America
Library of Congress Catalog Card Number: 97-73729
International Standard Book Number: 1-890956-00-7

Editor: Steve Glazner

Editorial Production and Typography: Wolf Publications, Inc.
Printing: Port City Press, Inc.

Printed on acid-free paper

CONTENTS

Part III

SECTION III-C: OTHER UTILITIES

Editor: Wayne W. Kjonaas

SECTION III-A

UTILITIES MANAGEMENT

Editor:
Dr. M. Reza Karkia, C.C.P.
California State University

INTRODUCTION

Utilities Management

As the technical sophistication of utilities infrastructures and building systems increases, so must the technical sophistication of engineers, owners, managers, and operators. Without such parallel growth, it will be difficult to achieve the immense potential benefits of current technology or technology transfer at large.

Unlike the 1970s, when energy concerns were defined by shortage and higher costs, energy concerns currently are much more complex. According to long-term projections, in the 21st century energy will be readily available. However, energy will continue to consume a larger percentage of the shrinking higher education budget and will bring about many environmental implications. Energy costs of colleges and universities in the United States currently are approaching a staggering $5 billion a year. At California State University in Carson, California, energy costs are responsible for as much as 30 to 40 percent of the campus facilities operating budget. On average, about 5 percent of student tuition stems from these energy expenditures, not including environmental regulatory compliance and other related expenditures such as public health and safety. One of the major implications of environmental degradation is an increasing societal burden on public health costs. To address the current situation, the Clean Air Act Amendment of 1991 and the Energy Policy Act of 1992 have established very strict requirements for use of fossil fuel, energy generation, distribution, and demand-side management. In the long run, these requirements will increase energy costs at an unproportionally higher rate than the average inflation.

Colleges and universities must be aggressively involved in energy management and conservation efforts to ameliorate this situation. Traditional energy managers now need to develop utilities expertise and understand the legal; environmental; economic; political; and social ramifications of energy production, purchase, and use. This can be a critical success factor in the financial viability of many institutions in the future. This section covers new strategies for utilities master planning, energy conservation and management, energy control and measurement, and fuel management and regulation in view of the current conditions. The positive impact of energy conservation projects on the United States economy and environment is also demonstrated.

The objective of this section is to present the ideas and practices of energy, utilities, and environmental conservation and management in a manner that demonstrates their essential unity and collective economic impact on institutions. Considering the finite topics and issues of energy, utilities, and environment, it becomes apparent that condensing many decades worth of knowledge, experience, and know-how into one section of a book would be almost impossible. The aim of this section is to provide an overview of the energy; utilities; and environmental planning, conservation, and management issues and concerns, followed by practical conservation and management techniques applicable to our educational facilities. The range of topics varies from energy conservation and management to utilities master planning to regulations to fuel management.

Hopefully, this section will build a common vision that the consumption of energy is as much a business as its production. It must be treated and managed in a businesslike manner.

—Dr. M. Reza Karkia, C.C.P.

CHAPTER 39

Campus Utility Systems Master Planning

Joel Goss
Goss Engineering, Inc.

39.1 INTRODUCTION

Campus utility master planning is a disciplined form of self-analysis for the campus. It examines and documents existing utility systems, current needs, potential future expansion needs, when the needed services are required, the best way to meet those needs, and the cost of providing the needed services. Like all forms of self-analysis, much of what the master plan contains is already known, at least by certain individuals. Master planning takes the known information about the institution's utility systems and its needs, organizes the information, documents conditions, develops conclusions, determines an action plan, and communicates this information to others.

A good utility master plan is the institution's utility road map into the future. Without that road map, the potential problems ahead may not be recognized, nor is there any assurance that the path being taken is the best one, in view of the challenges ahead. Even if the path is the best, a formal document indicating the challenges, weighing the alternatives, and recommending the path is the best tool available for obtaining support for that proper path.

39.2 WHY MASTER PLANNING IS ESSENTIAL

Nearly 2,000 years ago, the writer Luke cited Jesus of Nazareth as pointing out the need for advanced planning. He asked, "Which of you, desiring to build a tower, does not first count the cost to see if he will be able to complete, lest the incomplete building begin to mock him?" If a similar question were posed today, it might be, "What institution would build buildings without adequate central services to support the building's needs or without the committed funds necessary for the building's operation and maintenance?" The answer would likely be, "Most institutions."

In many cases today, buildings are planned and even budgeted for construction without considering whether the central plant and/or utility mains will serve the building. Because a building must have electricity, heating, cooling, and water and sewerage service to be usable, this is more than a little short sighted. Sometimes this occurs when outside parties donate buildings but fail to provide for the services necessary for the buildings. In other cases the problems occur because the relationship between the visible buildings and the more or less invisible support infrastructure is little understood. When it is determined that adequate capacity is not available, the buildings are sometimes built anyway. Sometimes they are built with low-first-cost, high-operation-cost local systems that add to the operational cost and to the workload of an already overburdened operation staff.

A utility master plan is the tool of planning and construction and also of the facilities manager. The facilities manager uses the plan in part to define utility and energy systems needs and the associated costs for the campus. This plan guides the efforts of the facilities management department in expanding and maintaining the energy and utilities systems.

Every campus has some sort of a utility plan. The problem is that this plan is often in the heads of several key individuals rather than set down in an organized way on paper. Without the discipline of writing the plan down in an organized way, the plan may not acknowledge future problems or provide the best way to meet the challenges of the present or the future. The lack of a well-documented, written plan also makes the task of communicating the needs of the present or future virtually impossible.

This chapter describes some of the elements of a master plan. No two situations are identical, as the needs of institutions vary, but the basic concepts will apply to all needs. A good master plan should determine 1) the expansion ability of campus systems; 2) the magnitude, cost, and timing of needed campus expansion; 3) cost-effective ways to meet campus expansion needs; 4) the impact of expansion on the cost of facilities operations; and 5) whether utility systems expansion will meet expected future expanded campus needs. Furthermore, the plan should develop the political support required for the needed expansion and operations.

Determine the Expansion Ability of Campus Systems to Serve a Growing Campus   One of the primary reasons a utility master plan is necessary is to determine whether a campus has the resources to expand. Campus expansion is not just a matter of placing another building on campus. Buildings require heating, cooling, water, electrical service, gas, and storm and sanitary sewerage, as well as access for students, staff and service vehicles, fire protection, and maintenance. These factors need to be considered when first planning the siting of a building. In this way advanced planning will reduce the costs of providing services by locating the building where the services are available. Buildings, of course, are sited based not only on where utilities are available, but also on many independent variables that all must work together. All of these variables must be evaluated in site selection. Still, the cost of extending utility services to the site and the cost of providing services such as steam, hot water, chilled water, and power over the years must be considered early in the planning process.

The ability of the facilities organization to accept expansion includes variables such as the surplus capacity of the existing central plant, the location and capacity of utilities, the age and condition of the existing plant, and the cost and/or ease of adding additional capacity if needed. To determine this, the utility master plan must first determine not only the central plant capacity and plans for expansion, but the location and capacity of the existing installed utilities. These include electrical, heating, cooling, and domestic hot water systems; sewer; storm sewer; gas; and telephone and other communications systems. The methods of routing services (e.g., tunnel, utilidor, duct bank, direct bury) are also key elements in planning.

From these data the plan should estimate the ability of the system to accommodate existing and future loads. This process will pinpoint areas that need improvement to support the campus in the present and in the future.

Determine the Magnitude, Cost, and Timing of Needed Campus Expansion Another primary reason utility master planning is required is the need to know in advance the demands on the central plant and utility system so that the needed services are available when a new building comes on line. Usually the central system capacity increase and utility services expansions do not occur in conjunction with the new building. In fact, a central services expansion element often is sized for several buildings. As an example, a new chiller or electric substation may have the capacity to serve many buildings, but the capacity must be available when needed for any one new building. Also, because many specialized pieces of equipment in the central plant require long lead times to manufacture, the central plant expansion may require longer construction periods than that required for a new building. The master plan determines the magnitude of the needed central plant and utility expansion, when the expansion must occur, and the budget required for the expansion.

Determine Cost-Effective Ways to Meet Campus Expansion Needs A good master plan also evaluates the most cost-effective ways of meeting expansion needs. At Arizona State University, as an example, the staff thought a major expansion of the campus, combined with inadequate chilled water to the existing campus, would require major additional new chilled water mains. The master plan found that by increasing the chilled water temperature range (ΔT), the capacity served by the existing mains could be doubled, and variable flow modifications could eliminate many of the circulation problems. Thus, the master plan determined a cost-effective way of meeting capacity expansion needs.

At the University of Arizona, a planned major expansion located in an area remote from the existing central plant, combined with severe space restrictions around the old central plant, offered the opportunity to meet expansion needs from a new central plant site. The cost-effectiveness of this approach was determined by an evaluation method that weighed various potential plant locations by the distance to the buildings served and the capacity served.

Determine the Impact of Expansion on the Cost of Facilities Operations   Another reason utility master plans are necessary is to determine the impact of expansion and other factors on the facilities organization operational costs. In addition to capital costs, the utility master plan should contain estimates of the operation and maintenance and energy costs for each expansion or change affecting the campus energy system. Without adequate attention in the planning process, the facilities organization will have inadequate operating budget and staff.

Determine that Utility Systems Expansion Meets Expected Future Expanded Campus Needs   Without good utility master planning, utility expansion may not be sized properly for the added building; utilities may be added and/or installed without proper isolation valves and tees, manholes, or junction boxes located where future connections will be required. The mains may even be routed through a future building site, which will necessitate relocation when the future building is constructed. This is extremely wasteful of campus resources. It not only costs more to duplicate pipe runs or relocate mains, it also disrupts campus operation and sometimes takes buildings out of service for an extended period of time. Although good utility master planning cannot entirely eliminate this problem, it can reduce it.

Develop Political Support for Needed Expansion and Operations   Decisions on budgets for facilities operations and expansion are usually political or bureaucratic rather than rational or even based on good economics. Budgets and operations are often based on historic precedents, with adjustments (often downward) based on economic trends and factors such as inflation. Budgets are sometimes based on square footage served or student full-time equivalents.

All too frequently in higher education, short-term costs can drive financial decisions. Thus, lowest first cost, one-year operational costs, or similar considerations will often govern decisions, rather than life cycle costs or long-range operational and maintenance costs. Similarly, the need to curtail current costs can lead to deferral of investments needed for renewal, modernization, and expansion to meet future capacity considerations. Given the long-term nature of most campus utility system investments, these systems can be particularly vulnerable to the adverse effects of short-term financial decisions. A good utility master plan that lays out the long-term utility investment needs and a sound financial case for making these investments presented in a clear and convincing manner can do much to overcome this tendency.

39.3 RELATION OF UTILITY MASTER PLANNING TO OVERALL MASTER PLANNING

An overall campus master plan is the result of an integrated process. The principal goal of a college or university is to educate; thus, the planning process is driven by the academic master plan. Facilities master planning is related to the buildings necessary to support the academic master plan. The utility master plan in turn supports both the facilities and the academic master plans. All of these plans are related to financial planning, or what is usually called the *budget*. To succeed, all these master plans must be integrated and work together.

The focus in this chapter is on the utility master plan, but it is important for everyone to keep in mind how the academic, facilities, and utility master plans and budget relate to the overall campus master plan.

Academic Planning Campus management philosophy and projections of facilities needs begin with the academic planning process. This process determines what academic programs will be taught and the type of research that will be conducted, as well as the number of students and the physical requirements (buildings, square footage, type of space etc.). It is important that this planning be well developed and accurate to project the best possible information about campus growth and the needs for improvements or additions to the current buildings and systems. The facilities planning process provides feedback about the limitations of the plant's ability to supply the potential needs of an academic program and the costs of supporting the needed improvements.

Facilities Master Plan The academic plan drives a facilities master plan. This plan defines the square footage needed to support the academic plan and determines where and when remodeling is needed as well as where and when buildings must be added. For the new projected buildings, the size and construction have an impact on the utility needs. The type of construction also has an impact on the maintenance and operations cost to the central plant of maintaining the new construction.

Financial Planning   Facilities planning and financial planning must work hand in hand to develop and implement the overall master plan. The financial planning process, however, must take into consideration many factors other than building costs and plant operating costs. Academic salaries, administrative costs, and funding methods are among a few of the financial considerations that affect or compete with plant improvement and operating costs. In addition to the number of dollars needed, the source of the money is a major consideration in financial planning.

The utility master plan provides financial planners with the information they need on the costs of energy, operations, and maintenance. The information includes purchased energy, central plant operation costs, distribution, and general building custodial operations and maintenance. Energy-using systems are often a major part of building operational costs.

A campus utility master plan, closely coordinated with the overall campus master plan, provides the campus with the planning information, including costs, needed to set aside money for maintaining buildings in the future, as well as to meet day-to-day or year-to-year needs. By providing documentation and justification for the needed future expenditures, the plan helps ensure that these funds will be available when needed.

39.4   TYPICAL ELEMENTS OF A UTILITY MASTER PLAN

A master plan as discussed above contains many integrated elements that work together to enable managers to establish a plan of operation. By approaching master planning as a series of related steps or building blocks while keeping the big picture in mind, the process becomes much more manageable.

In its basic form the process can be broken down into the following steps:

- Determine what exists or what is available.
- Determine what is currently needed.
- Determine what will be needed in the future.
- Determine when the need will occur.
- Determine what part of the needs are or will not be met.
- Determine ways in which items that are lacking can be provided.
- Determine feasibility, construction cost, and operation and maintenance costs of potential solutions.
- Evaluate and determine the best options.
- Determine how the best option can be improved.
- Determine the best strategy to implement the best option.
- Develop and document a timetable and budget for the recommended actions.
- Keep the plan current.

Existing Campus Assets

A master plan begins by evaluating current assets. Naturally this includes the size or capacity, location, and condition of the various components of the utility systems. During this process the planner needs to also seek for other, potentially hidden, assets that may be useful, even if not presently used. Every campus has some strong existing assets that should be built upon. Some imagination is sometimes required to see the assets in certain situations, but there are usually numerous opportunities to capitalize on existing situations. Some assets are more readily recognized than others. As an example, it takes little imagination to recognize as an asset an existing central plant that was designed for expansion or a central walk-through tunnel system with room for expansion. Additional effort will likely identify other potential assets. The following are examples of actual items that have been identified as potential utility assets in utility master planning:

- Buildings with year-round cooling needs
- Room around a chiller plant for thermal storage
- A hill above the campus
- Gas below the campus
- Waste paper obtained on the campus (as an energy source)
- An abandoned water reservoir
- A lake on campus
- Good wells on campus
- A river or canal nearby
- An existing utility tunnel
- Existing piping and power distribution systems
- A second power substation near campus
- Buildings designed to use low-temperature heating water
- Utility company incentives for thermal storage
- Utility incentives for conservation

An example of an asset that is not readily apparent is the irrigation system at Oregon State University. The agriculture activities of the university include irrigating farmlands that are owned by the university and located next to the main campus. In the future this water might be used as a heating and cooling energy source before it is used for irrigation. Such use would improve the performance of a heat recovery chiller plant.

Existing Campus Liabilities

In master planning it seems as though liabilities are relatively easy to find. The challenge is to list them and then find either how to convert them to assets or how to at least neutralize them. Many of the liabilities listed in the planning process are the result of inadequate planning in the past. This underscores the need for good planning in the present. Some common liabilities from actual master plans are as follows:

- Poor or trapped central plant location
- Inadequate distribution system for expansion needs
- Failing central plant or distribution mains
- Systems and/or distribution unsuited to current technology
- Deteriorating or undersized systems and equipment

The University of Oregon central plant is located on a millrace, and the site has been desired for other uses. When the land occupied by the central plant is desired for other purposes or starts to affect the cost of plant operations, there is a specific liability that must be addressed in the master plan. This problem has not been resolved at the time of this writing, and the boiler plant has the most attractive site on campus.

At the University of Arizona, one of the largest liabilities was the central plant location. The central plant is located in the center of the original campus on what is currently the most valuable land owned by the university. Expansion in the present location would be expensive and limited. The campus is growing rapidly, but recent growth is not near the present central plant. In this case, a new satellite plant central to the added construction avoided the bottleneck of the old central plant.

Current Energy Loads, Location, and Uses

A key element of an energy or utility master plan is the analysis of campus energy use records. These records reveal how much and what type of energy is being used and, in some cases, where the energy is used. Comparing the university's energy records with those of other like institutions is a useful tool in establishing the potential for energy use savings. As an example, a comparison of Sacramento State to Fresno State showed that Fresno State—which is the same size as Sacramento State, has the same building construction type and use, and is in the same general climate—used twice the energy used by Sacramento State. The increased energy use was primarily in the summer. In the winter, both universities used about the same electricity and gas per square foot. In the summer, both universities used about the same electrical energy, but Fresno State used more gas.

The reason for this difference was determined and addressed in the utility master plan. The single-stage absorption chillers used by Fresno State required large amounts of gas in the summer. The chillers also required the operation of a large steam plant and a distribution steam system, with attendant energy losses. The oversized cooling tower, the condenser pumps, and the inefficient arrangement used as much electricity as a conventional electricity-driven chiller plant.

This conclusion was confirmed after the campus was modified to use electric chillers and thermal storage. Adjusted for square footage, the campus currently uses less electrical energy in the summer than previously, and gas use is dramatically reduced. The large central steam plant is shut down in the summer.

Other valuable planning information, not so easily obtainable, is peak load and energy use patterns. This information sometimes is available from the electrical utility for electrical energy, but similar information for other types of energy usually is not available. Likewise, there is usually little information about how the energy is used on campus. It is necessary to know the energy use of individual buildings, each building's energy use pattern, and the transport energy required to support the buildings. Individual meters on each building are ideal; however, it often is difficult to justify the costs of individual building metering and record keeping. Metering costs now are falling, especially when integrated into energy management control systems and computerized statistical energy use records.

Expansion and Replacement Needs and Schedule

As a basis for utility master planning, it is necessary to determine future loads from the predicted types, sizes, and uses of buildings. The location of these future loads must be estimated and a schedule for probable expansion developed. This is the basis for determining future expansion needs. By comparing the capability of the present production and delivery system in the area of new construction with the expanded need, the need for capacity increase or other modifications can be determined.

The need for new buildings, their locations, construction type, and probable time of construction is determined from the academic and facilities master plans. Such plans should also incorporate the needs for remodeling and the program changes that will have an impact on the utility systems. Replacement and expansion needs for the central energy plant and utility distribution systems come about as a result of the analysis of those needs and the evaluation of the current utility systems.

When planning for new or extended systems, campus utility installations should be flexible enough to respond to changing energy costs and availability and expansion needs. At the same time, budgetary constraints seldom allow large expenditures far in advance of future growth. These challenges require significant thought and input from the most knowledgeable utility people available. This is often addressed in brainstorming sessions, but whatever the solution method, careful planning is required.

Based on the projections of campus growth from the overall campus master plan, the utility master plan provides the needed guidance for expanding the energy systems. The design concepts are defined, the approximate size of equipment is selected, the location of expansions or modifications are defined, and the costs are estimated for planning purposes.

Timing of expenditure for the needed expansion is estimated based on the needs for updating existing systems and the timing of the need to support campus remodeling or expansion. The master plan must take into account the unusually long lead times typical for some components in central plants. Also, access to the campus is a key element in timing. It is necessary to schedule some work for low-activity periods such as summer. If it is necessary to suspend service to a building or the campus, there may only be certain limited times that such suspension is possible, and therefore significant advanced planning and coordination are necessary.

Potential Solutions: Central Versus Individual Building

The master plan should look at a variety of ways to meet needs. Often there are several ways in which campus needs can be met. Identifying these potential ways and evaluating them in a way that takes into account all the variables, including the uncertain developments of the future, is a significant challenge. When this challenge is met well, the master plan has served its purpose.

One typical evaluation, common in university master planning, is a comparison of the relative merits of stand-alone, or local site solutions, with service from a central campus system. Although the simple economics of first cost, energy costs, and operation costs can be compared in a reasonably straightforward way, some variables are more difficult to identify, and their value is similarly difficult to quantify. Examples include, "What will be done when the original equipment wears out?"

University buildings typically last 100 years or more, and mechanical and electrical equipment is often totally worn out in 20 years. Europe, with its longer history, demonstrates that we should think in terms of centuries. Yet time after time we see equipment buried in buildings where reasonable service or replacement is impossible. In many cases this is due to inadequate planning at the time of installation. In other cases it is due to additions, remodeling, or construction of other buildings that eliminated access. The centrifugal chillers at the *Los Angeles Times,* which were installed in 1933, are still in use—not because they should not have been replaced, but because the limited planning done at the time of their installation did not allow for actual developments and therefore did not provide a way for them to be replaced.

Many campuses that were built with low-cost modular buildings and low-cost unitary equipment currently find themselves trapped. The buildings are still in use, fuel cost is a much more important issue than when the equipment was installed, and there is no reasonable way of getting out of the situation. Buildings built today must be analyzed with respect to issues such as whether the fuel selected today will even be available 20 to

40 years from now, and if not, how will heating and cooling be provided? Is an 8-, 10-, or even 20-year life cycle cost a reasonable tool to use in measuring the costs for a building or a campus that you know will still be in use in 100 years?

Current Available Energy Sources and Systems Cost

Other elements to be considered in a utility master plan are the available energy sources, their costs, and the cost of the systems to use them. Because of variables, this is not always a simple process. As an example, a utility master plan for a California university found that an electric chiller plant expansion would have lower energy costs than a steam-driven plant, but the cost of additional power to the central plant would result in a more costly installation. An independent utility study of the same problem obtained different results, for a variety of reasons. Some of the reasons are worth consideration:

- The original master plan was based on 2,000-ton expansion increments without considering optional sizes or identifying a reason for the specific size selection.
- The original master plan comparison listed electric drive as a selected option with higher first cost and lower energy cost. Although the cost estimate for this alternative was not included in the report, the higher first cost appeared to be a result of a simple evaluation of the cost of an electric-drive chiller plus electric service compared with the cost of a steam-drive chiller. It did not appear to include adjustments for cooling tower size, condenser pump and piping, elimination of the surface condenser, and the steam and condensate piping.
- The original comparison evaluated only the chiller energy and not the entire chiller plant, which included cooling towers, condenser pumps, and variables. The electric plant used less energy for these purposes.
- Combining thermal storage and modifications to pumping resulted in lower on-peak electric energy consumption than the alternative steam-drive solution.
- The alternative of using steam to offset electric service expansion was considered in the original report as being feasible only until expansion used the available cooling tower capacity.
- The electric company was interested in providing the expanded power as well as other incentives in order to sell electricity. Such incentives have nearly all disappeared as utilities move toward deregulation of electricity.
- The evaluation was based on a size that required both steam- and electric-drive chillers to be open-drive. Slightly smaller semi-hermetic chillers are available at about half the cost per ton of

open-drive chillers. Of course, this lower cost option applies only to electric-drive options.

The existing old steam-drive chillers, which the original study recommended for replacement, had condenser piping and cooling towers that were in good condition. The existing cooling towers could each serve a 1,500-ton chiller but were not big enough for the 2,000-ton chillers, and the incremental cost was not considered. Thus, the decision to limit evaluation to 2,000-ton chillers created a major cost for cooling towers that were not needed with slightly smaller chillers or electric-drive chillers.

Therefore, there should be careful and complete evaluation of all the potential when defining the available energy sources and their costs. Only then is it safe to determine which potential energy source should be favored during the planning process. Energy sources for consideration include the following:

- Electricity
- Natural gas
- Heat recovery
- Geothermal
- Oil
- Wind
- Solar
- Coal
- Biomass
- Solid waste

In most cases the evaluation should include utilization efficiency as well as relative energy cost per Btu. As an example, an electric boiler may be considered almost 100 percent efficient. A groundwater heat pump may have a coefficient of performance (COP) of 4 to 500. A bootstrap or internal heat recovery heat pump may significantly reduce the heating need by eliminating the use of the outside air economizer cycle. This cycle usually reduces the air temperature to the heating coils and thus increases the heating need. When this occurs, the effective thermal efficiency may be twenty times better. Yet all of these concepts are based on the same energy source: electricity. A gas boiler that is 75 percent efficient may have a lower energy cost, because gas has a lower cost per Btu than electricity, and this lower cost offsets the electric boiler's greater efficiency.

In certain cases cogeneration may be a good candidate for evaluation. The primary considerations are the relative cost of electricity and gas and the percentage of the energy that is effectively used. Again, care must be taken to see what is being compared. As an example, a cogeneration plant may make it economical to use wasteful building heating systems and low-efficiency, single-stage absorption cooling, because large amounts of waste heat are available for use. However, even though this is true, the decision to use the system should be based on the best alternative to the cogeneration system that will likely not include those wasteful energy practices. With a good match of waste heat, system size, and load profile combined with high electric cost in comparison to gas, there is real potential for cogeneration, since it provides more total utilization of gas energy than power company plants that do not make use of waste heat. Under the proper circumstances, this can offset the higher first cost, operation cost, and maintenance cost of a cogeneration system.

Integrated Energy Solutions

The best solutions in a university use the principle of synergy. That is, the systems combine together to make a solution that is better than the sum of the parts. Examples include thermal storage, heat recovery chillers, strainer cycles, and cogeneration and variable volume systems.

The element to look for in a utility master plan is how to develop the best integrated energy solution for the specific campus. Often this is a unique integration that will not be found on any other campus. The best integration cannot be determined by "cookbook" engineering, even though the solutions that work on one campus often will work on others. Systems integration actually means using each energy source to its best advantage. For example, central plants that are designed to recover heat use the same chiller energy for both heating and cooling. In fact, the part of the heating energy that is used reduces the requirement of the cooling towers to dispose of heat.

Cogeneration can also be a part of an integrated system. The purchased fossil fuel energy can be used to generate power, heat buildings, do process heating, and possibly provide energy for an absorption chiller.

Another excellent opportunity is integration of chilled water and fire protection. The large mains that are required for chilled water can be also used for fire protection by connecting building fire sprinklers and fire hydrants to the chilled water system. This is particularly attractive when a large chilled water storage tank is part of the cooling system. In that case the storage tank, if properly located, can also serve as a fire protection storage tank, adding to the available city or campus water.

Integrated solutions strive to use the assets of the campus to best advantage. The goal is to give the best long-range plan, considering cost, reliability, and flexibility.

Primary Campus Energy Production Options

Keeping in mind 1) the energy sources that are available and 2) the fact that integrated solutions provide the best utilization of the energy, a number of options should be considered. Some of the combinations that have formed viable energy options for various projects are presented here.

Chillers with Heat Recovery Chillers, usually electric drive, can be designed to make the rejected heat that is normally sent to the cooling towers available for space heating on campus. Cooling energy from overheated spaces is made available to other spaces on campus that need heat. This greatly improves the heating and cooling efficiency of the campus energy system.

Boilers with Heat Recovery When energy was cheap, boiler designers allowed 20 to 25 percent of the purchased fossil fuel energy to be wasted in the form of hot stack gases expelled to the atmosphere. Currently there are devices on the market that can recover half of this energy, and more in some cases. The recovered heat can be used for heating domestic water, for process heating, or for space heating. The recovered energy allows elimination of a separate heating process that was probably either inefficient or expensive.

Thermal Storage Thermal storage allows a form of energy to be generated at one time and used at a different time. As an example, one campus in northern California was designed with chilled water storage. The required cooling capacity was 2,000 tons. By using chilled water storage, only 1,000 tons of chiller capacity was installed. This reduced the overall capital cost, reduced electrical demand charges, allowed a time-of-day electrical rate break, and reduced energy use because chilling was done at night, when cooling towers perform better. Many electric utilities have offered financial incentives through their demand-side management programs in the past. In many situations the incorporation of thermal energy storage not only reduces the need for more chillers, it also lowers the cost of generating chilled water. With deregulation, incentives may be replaced with high peak demand cost as the reason for storage.

Geothermal Geothermal energy does not have to mean 300°F. Well water as low as 50°F can be used as an energy source for a heat pump. Obviously, the warmer the water source, the less supplemental energy will be required to make it useful heating energy. The 180°F water at Oregon Technical Institute in Klamath Falls, Oregon, is a major asset, but a geothermal asset of almost any temperature should be considered in a utility master plan. Where 100 percent outside air is used, heat exchange with groundwater can temper the air. When groundwater is not hot enough to supply direct heat, a small amount of energy can raise the temperature of the water to one that is usable.

   Cold geothermal sources (i.e., groundwater below normal air conditioning temperatures) should be considered for direct cooling or precooling. By using a heat exchanger to cool returning chilled water, the load on chillers can be significantly reduced, and for parts of the year, it may not be necessary to run the chillers at all.

Biomass- or Waste Energy-Containing Materials In the future, biomass and solid waste will likely become significant sources of energy, because the conversion to energy process eliminates the purchase of new energy while performing the necessary task of processing solid waste. The technology is advancing steadily, and this option should be considered in every utility master plan. Air pollution controls and ash disposal are key concerns to be solved in the future.

Nearby Industrial Waste Heat In Springfield, Oregon, there are three industrial plants, each with enough waste heat to heat all of the large commercial customers in the city. The main reason this is not being done is that the commercial customers are spread over a wide area, making collection and distribution economically impossible. A campus has the advantage of a dense heat need and, in many cases, an existing central distribution system. Industrial waste heat is an excellent option for consideration in a campus utility master plan when available.

"Free Cooling" Concepts Cooling with the use of cool geothermal water was discussed above. The use of cooling towers or any other cooling source to avoid the use of chillers should be explored in a utility master plan.

Potential Solutions to Meet Changing Conditions

As in many situations, change is one of the "sure things" that must be anticipated when planning. Unfortunately, we are never able to know all the ways that change will occur, or even when changes will occur. A campus utility master plan must consider the effects of changing conditions and provide some guidance for responding to changing conditions. One of the challenges in utility planning is knowing the changing conditions in energy sources and energy delivery systems. The coal-burning boilers of the 1950s are still in use on many campuses. On others, the boilers are in use, but burners have been added to burn gas, oil, or wood pellets. Given the current uncertain fuel reserves, managers must recognize that over a reasonably short period, in terms of the campus building's life, the energy availability and cost picture may change dramatically. Photovoltaic systems built into roofing and window materials are quickly improving to become cost-effective. Inexpensive conversion of ocean water to a hydrogen fuel such as a pipeline gas may be near. Drilling the mantel of the earth to tap the earth's heat offers the potential for cheap, nonpolluting electricity as soon as we can develop the proper drilling and energy extraction techniques. The primary element in utility master planning is to acknowledge that change will occur and evaluate the potential solutions planned and the ability to meet change.

Changing Energy Costs   Recent history tells us that energy costs can go up or down. In the recent past, some bad energy decisions were made based on predicted upward energy costs. Even so, current plans that are based on energy costs that are increased slightly above general inflation rates will be fairly safe. Prudent plans should also consider the possibility of other developments. Plans must take into consideration the probability that costs will change, and this change will not occur across the board. The cost of electrical energy may go up faster than the cost of natural gas in some regions, but that will not be the general case. Over the long term, electricity is a more conservative selection, because almost any energy source can produce electricity. In the Pacific Northwest, gas is an international commodity, and its price and availability depend in part on good relations with Canada. Gas as a fossil fuel exists in finite amounts. Oil and gas can be manufactured from other materials but at significantly greater cost than is currently charged.

The best campus energy solution should provide methods for shifting with the current energy economics. The solution proposed may be shown to be efficient enough that the economics will not reverse within the range of reasonable energy price fluctuations. However, if a certain solution has the advantage of a fast payback and can be replaced in the future with another solution, then the university will be less reliant on the long-term economic possibilities.

Changing Available Fuel Types   The stability of supply of any fuel type used or recommended should be studied. If there is a likelihood that a fuel type will become unavailable, a backup fuel system should be provided. This is becoming more of a problem in much of the country. As an example, oil is not an acceptable backup fuel in the Los Angeles area, and compatible propane restrictions are severe because of fire dangers.

Changing Indoor Space Environment Requirements   Campus buildings are continually changing occupancy and use. In addition, indoor air environmental regulations are continually changing. The American Society of Heating, Refrigeration, and Air Conditioning Engineers (ASHRAE) has increased the requirements for outside air or filtration for new or remodeled buildings. In addition, a building or room may be changed from a classroom to a laboratory, which may require that the space receive 100 percent outside air.

Increases in outside air requirements increase the energy requirement for a space. Other factors such as additional equipment may increase the cooling requirements of a building or the entire campus. Changes in acceptable temperature or humidity of a space will also affect the campus energy requirements. The planning process should anticipate such changes as much as possible and build flexibility into the central energy system to deal with unexpected changes.

Central Plant Locations   The location of a central plant can have a large impact on the cost of operation, the plant's ability to deliver services to new buildings, and the cost of expansion. The location of the central plant should be carefully examined with an eye toward its impact on future growth of the campus. Master plans must recognize that distance, in addition to carrying a first-cost penalty, also carries an operation-cost penalty that will be paid over the life of the campus. A location that is central to loads and yet accessible is a major asset to a university. An elevated central plant location on a hilly campus can have a major impact on some equipment and some potential solutions.

Impact on Academic Functions   The location of the central plant must be integrated into the growth plans of the campus. Logical campus development and academic access to the buildings should come first. Next, the visual impact on the campus should be considered. The central plant should be located where it can serve the campus and campus expansion without interfering with access to the academic buildings and while fitting into the campus architecture.

Many details must be considered, such as smoke, cooling tower plume, and prevailing wind relationship to building air intakes. Noise and effects of vibration on sensitive areas or equipment (e.g., electron microscopes) are considerations.

Impact on Facilities Organization Functions   The location of the central energy plant can have a large impact on the efficiency with which the plant performs its services. Some of the more important considerations are as follows:

- Proximity of plant to the loads served
- Required service access to plant
- Location of the plant with respect to serving outside utilities
- Suitability of the plant to meet campus expansion needs
- Impact of plant location on maintenance and operation labor cost

Each of these points deserves careful attention. For instance, the University of Arizona has found that establishment of a new central energy plant between two campuses that were growing together appears to work well with respect to each of the above items except proximity to loads presently served. On the other hand, as expansion takes place, the proximity issue will become very positive. The problem of the impact of location on maintenance and operation labor cost will be addressed by remote operation of a chillers-only plant at the new location until the entire central plant is moved sometime in the future.

39.5 MAJOR VARIABLES AFFECTING MASTER PLANNING

When planning for a central energy system, there are several major variables that have a large impact on the system. Several are discussed in this section. During the planning process on a specific campus, there will be other factors unique to that campus that will have a major influence on the plan. The planner must keep a watchful eye for these.

Energy Cost and System Efficiency   In some cases a highly efficient system can use a more expensive energy source and still be more cost-effective. In other cases the cost of operation is not the key issue because of other factors. In some instances the disposal of infectious or hazardous garbage is the real reason for operation of waste heat recovery incinerators, and energy is a secondary issue. At other times cogeneration is installed to increase plant reliability and performance in emergency conditions, and this is the justification for increased first cost.

Energy cost and efficiency must be considered for present and projected conditions. The sensitivity of planned central plants to energy costs should be examined, and the ability of the system to maintain its efficiency should be evaluated. Some systems lose efficiency over time or with poor maintenance.

Labor Cost and Equipment Maintenance Requirements   Maintenance costs for existing and proposed energy systems must be carefully considered during master planning. Some equipment requires specialized maintenance, some requires more maintenance than an alternative, and in some cases the cost of replacement parts is high. The true life cycle cost of an energy system must take into consideration the labor and other maintenance costs associated with each system. As an example, high-pressure boiler plants have a high cost in terms of required attendance, regardless of fuel cost issues. Sometimes solutions that are less desirable for other reasons are advisable to eliminate this need.

Building Systems and Interface Requirements   The entire cost of converting a central plant system may not stop with costs at the central plant and for the distribution system. For example, if a campus is converting from steam or high-temperature heating water to low-temperature heating water, it may be necessary to change piping and coils within the buildings. In such cases it is common to find that some buildings require little or no conversion because the coils were oversized initially. Other buildings, however, may have steam or water coils that are too small. In either case the coil must be changed to use the lower temperature heating water. Note that with thicker heating coils, the air-side pressure drop may also increase enough to cause the air system to be unable to deliver the necessary energy to the space. This requires speeding up or changing the fan.

A common problem at the building interface is the way the building connects to the campus main piping. In some cases this is with bypass check valves or three-way control valves that cause bypassing of chilled water. This reduces the temperature change of energy effectiveness of heating or chilled water of the system through dilution and causes short-circuiting. Short-circuiting at buildings near the plant does not allow the necessary flow to reach buildings farther from the central plant.

Existing Systems Size and Capacity   A thorough knowledge of the size and capacity of each existing system is a mandatory starting point for the planning process. This information may indicate, for example, that certain points in a distribution system are critical, yet most of the system has excess capacity that can be used to serve campus expansion. Often the true capacity of the delivery system can be determined only by extensive computer modeling or by "stress testing" the system under extreme conditions.

Campus Diversity and Load Profile   Each major energy system on a campus has a diversity factor. This means that the peak campus load is almost always less than the total of all the building peak loads. As an example, even though the sum of the peak electrical loads on campus equals 5 megawatts (MW), the maximum electrical demand may never exceed 3.5 MW. One MW can provide normal power requirements of 500 homes. This is because not all of the loads are ever at maximum at the same time. The same concept applies to heating and cooling energy. The diversity factor allows the systems to be sized slightly smaller than the sum of the calculated peak loads.

Calculation of the diversity factor is sometimes difficult. A good way to determine the diversity factor if calculations are available is to compare the sum of calculated peak loads for existing buildings against measured peak consumption. If future expansion will involve a similar mix of buildings, the diversity factor calculated in this way should be reasonably accurate. An alternative method of calculating diversity is to use a computer model of the entire campus. This is an excellent approach but is seldom done. Typically, engineers use experience factors such as assuming that the campus cooling diversity is 20 percent, and from that assumption reducing the central plant size. These assumptions are usually conservative, which leads to their continued use.

The load profile is the measured load as it varies throughout a day, a week, a month, or a year. This information is necessary to properly predict the overall performance of an energy system. Boilers, for instance, are less efficient at part load than at full load. This is also the case with most chillers. By determining a load profile, an engineer can estimate the number of units that will be operating and their load at any given time. Load profile prediction allows calculation of an overall average efficiency, which is more meaningful than a peak efficiency value under "test stand" conditions.

Temperature Difference and Pressures Used in Design   Water systems are designed with a difference between the supply temperature and the return temperature. The greater the difference, the more capacity that can be delivered for a volume of water. Currently good designers attempt to develop high ΔT to reduce pumping energy and the necessary pipe size. Good systems do not circulate any more water than is needed to meet campus loads. These variable-flow systems provide a reasonably constant ΔT.

Steam pressure is usually designed using only a gross approximation of the steam pressure actually required. The higher the steam pressure, the greater the heat delivery per pound of steam and the greater the distance heat can be conveyed. Typically there is little correlation among design, operation, and need. Usually steam systems are either ≤15 psi or 100–150 psi. These higher pressure systems are usually attended (i.e., they require the presence of an plant operator), and the pressure is reduced at buildings. Design and operation of steam systems (or high-pressure water systems) at temperatures greater than are needed results in significant energy waste and often increased labor requirement. A good utility master plan attempts to determine what is actually required and the extent of the requirement. Operating a central boiler plant at high pressure in the summer to serve an isolated steam still or sterilizer is not a good solution. In some cases it is economical to operate the boilers at high pressure and reduce the steam pressure through a small turbine to generate electrical energy using only the energy difference between the pressure of the steam generated and the actual steam pressure required for service to the buildings.

Observation of the operation of water delivery systems is an excellent clue to campus systems. Many campuses use what is thought to be a constant-flow system. For these, typically the difference (ΔT) between supply water temperature and return water temperature indicates the amount of useful cooling or heating that is being accomplished. A low ΔT indicates either a low cooling load or a cooling water bypass. In either of these two cases, little cooling is being accomplished for the water circulation. If there is little load, this wastes distribution energy, but if there is a large load and bypassing is taking place, then heating or cooling capacity is being wasted. At the same time, service may not be provided to other buildings.

Information on heating and cooling ΔTs is necessary to evaluate the effectiveness of an existing system and the possibility of increasing its capacity. Low ΔTs also indicate where remedial measures are needed. Flow rates are also necessary to give the entire picture.

Pressure problems in water heating or cooling (hydronic) systems can be the cause of low ΔT problems. Excessive pressure difference between supply and return water can cause control valves to be forced open. This can create both control problems and low ΔTs. If pressure differences are high, the first approach is to determine whether such differences are necessary. If they are, pressure controllers will probably be required at nearby or low-elevation buildings. Good campus systems use variable-flow pumps that are controlled to maintain the ideal pressure difference in the campus piping.

Probable Developments in Energy Sources   A projection of availability and price is necessary for every energy source that is in contention for use on a campus. This information is incorporated into long-range planning. Energy sources with questionable future availability should be avoided. Where pricing is uncertain, it is wise to consider designing flexibility into the energy plans for the campus.

39.6   SOLVING THE ECONOMIC DILEMMA

Campus administrators and facilities managers are continually faced with the economic dilemma of low first costs or low operating costs. A method of evaluating the relative financial merits is available; it is called *life cycle cost comparison.* Life cycle costs consider all the costs of owning rather than just first cost. These costs include first cost, system life interest cost, energy cost, maintenance cost, replacement cost, and salvage value.

Higher First Cost Versus Higher Operation and Maintenance Costs   Central plant systems tend to have higher first costs. Central plants are designed for long life and centralized maintenance, and the cost of hookup of new systems is usually low.

Local site solutions, such as unitary or roof-top equipment, usually have lower first cost but higher operation cost.

39.7   STAYING THE COURSE

Any plan, to be useful, must be followed. Former President Ronald Reagan used the phrase "staying the course" to indicate that a plan, once begun, must be followed to determine whether it is successful. A good master plan must be followed to ultimately succeed. Considerable effort, thought, and expense go into a campus utility or utility master plan. That kind of thought is not possible with each new building or potential option. Managers should not throw out all of that work for what may seem to be a better idea during the heat of discussion in a meeting. Even more important, they should refer to the plan often and use it to prevent others from causing a change in course. Such changes in course are likely to be costly in the long run. When a truly good opportunity does come along, managers should carefully consider it and revise the master plan as discussed below rather than abandon it.

Resisting the Temptation of Low First Cost   The most common attempt to deviate from the utility master plan usually consists of pressure to accept systems with lower first cost. Budgeting is always tight, and it is easy for building users to be more interested in getting space and program equipment than in reducing life cycle operating costs. After all, they consider it someone else's problem. Managers should use the utility master plan to show the advantage of the lower life cycle cost approach.

Evaluation of Deviations from the Adopted Master Plan   No plan can anticipate every possible new requirement or opportunity. Each deviation from the adopted master plan must be subjected to careful, complete evaluation. A procedure for evaluation of deviations should be adopted and enforced.

39.8   KEEPING THE PLAN UP TO DATE

A good master plan must be a dynamic document that keeps current with campus growth, conditions, and other factors that affect the plan. The plan should be updated every three to five years, depending on the rate of growth of the campus. In addition, certain events should trigger plan update or review. Some of the events are discussed here.

New Information on Future Campus Building Needs   Changes in campus expansion plans should be reflected in the utility master plan as an update. If the changes are major (e.g., a change in the direction of expansion, or major renovations rather than new construction), a complete revision of the utility master plan may be warranted.

The effects of new buildings should be analyzed by individual computer models integrated into a master campus model. This will give the best estimate of the impact of a new building on the central plant. The energy-related costs of the new building can also be estimated with good accuracy.

Tracking Actual Utility Consumption and Operation Costs   Utility consumption, utility costs, and operational costs for utility systems should be tracked monthly. The costs and trends should be compared with the projections from the utility master plan. This information will point out potential problems if the energy use deviates markedly from the plan. Sharp changes will be definite indicators of either potential problems or expected changes because of the addition of a new building or a new system.

The energy and cost records will also form an excellent basis for upgrading the campus utility master plan. There is nothing like experience and real data to help increase the accuracy of predictions (with the exception of energy cost projections when there is an oil embargo!).

Changes in Equipment or in Energy Cost or Availability Major changes in the use or cost of energy should trigger review of the utility master plan. New boilers, new chillers, or new distribution systems should trigger examination of the utility master plan to determine whether their impact will change some of the recommendations in the master plan. If the changes are a result of recommendations in the master plan, then changes in the master plan should not be necessary. Any major change in the energy system, however, should be cause to review the plan, if only to ensure that everything is on track.

Energy costs fluctuated with various developments, such as the worldwide political situation, weather, and factors affecting competition. It seems inevitable that energy costs will increase again at some time in the future. The utility master plan should allow for this possibility; however, future changes may take unexpected or drastic turns. If this is the case, the utility master plan should be modified to respond to the challenge.

39.9 OUTLINE OF A UTILITY MASTER PLAN

In this section we present an outline of a utility master plan. This outline will not cover the needs of every master plan, nor can every institution adhere to the organization suggested. Nevertheless, this outline can serve as a starting point and as a checklist to see that the plan incorporates the needed sections.

Introductory Elements The following introductory elements should be incorporated into the utility master plan:

- Cover letter
- Table of contents
- List of figures
- List of tables

Chapter 1: Executive Summary This chapter summarizes the master plan. It is typically a few pages long and is intended to present the findings of the study for administrators who lack the time for a detailed reading of the master plan. The executive summary should also provide information on the specific chapters where more detailed information on the findings can be examined. Often tables are used to summarize key information.

Chapter 2: Background of the Master Plan   This chapter presents information on the institution, the conditions at the time of the study, and the intentions and scope of the master plan effort. Typically, credit is given to those who have participated in the master plan effort. This chapter should also cite the other documents that were used in the preparation of the master plan (e.g., previous reports, studies, and the academic and/or facilities master plan) and should be dated with the month, day, and year the plan was finalized.

Chapter 3: Description of Existing Systems   This chapter presents information on the existing utility systems, including when the systems were built, the system capacity, the condition of the systems, and the loads currently served. Plans should be included to show general routing and the capacity of systems in a graphic way.

Typically this section also includes information on utility use and costs. Examples include the kilowatt demand, kilowatt-hour use, and cost of electrical energy by month. Similar records for gas, oil, and/or other fuels; water; and sewerage are typically included.

It is useful to develop a campus grid map with the amount of loads in each grid identified. This approach is helpful in quickly identifying where the major loads served are located.

This chapter should also include the known factors that affect the expected life of the systems. Systems that need replacement or repairs to meet code or changing conditions (e.g., the chlorofluorocarbon phaseout, new air quality requirements, or new air emissions requirements) should be identified.

Chapter 4: Growth and Expansion Needs   This chapter presents information on the expected growth of the institution and the impact of that growth on the utility systems. As an example, the chapter may have tables listing expected new buildings, expected square footage, the amount of load expected to be added with the buildings, and the year the new buildings are expected. When a grid of the campus loads is developed, the location of the expected expansion should be shown on the grid and the developed loads identified. Tables that show the expected total capacity needs along with the capacity available on a year-to-year basis help establish the needed utility expansion and the time when such expansion is needed.

Chapter 5: Alternatives   This chapter looks at alternatives considered in meeting the continued needs of the institution. This includes needs involving services to the existing institution, in addition to expansion needs. As an example, a deteriorated campus electrical supply may be repaired, replaced, or sold to the utility. Another alternative may be to purchase the delivery system or perhaps the primary service transformers from the utility. Other alternatives may include total energy approaches, in which the institution provides all of its electrical service. This chapter identifies the alternatives examined, presents the advantages and disadvantages of each, and delineates the costs for competing solutions. Typically, sketches are included to explain the alternative locations where utilities are to be installed.

Chapter 6: Recommend Solutions In this chapter, solutions are recommended from the competing solutions presented in Chapter 4. Typically, this is the solution with the best life cycle cost, but there may be other factors such that the solution with the best life cycle cost is not recommended. Chapter 6 develops a list of recommendations, cost estimates for all of the recommendations, and timetables for implementation.

Appendix The appendix to the report should include information such as utility use records, utility rates, costs estimates, life cycle cost calculations, and the other information used as a basis of the master plan. Tables of takeoff information and a summary of system capacities that were determined during the process of master planning should be included. Where appropriate, manufacturer information used in preparing the study is included (e.g., pipe information or chiller or boiler cut sheets). Where quotations from vendors are key to the master plan, the actual quotation should be included as appendix material. In short, whatever information is needed to form a solid background that allows others to accurately evaluate the master plan and its recommendations should be included.

CHAPTER 40

Energy Management and Conservation

Dr. Reza Karkia, CCP
California State University, Dominguez Hills

40.1 INTRODUCTION

Of the total energy used in the United States, approximately 36 percent is consumed by the building sector. Within the commercial building sector, typically 42 percent of the energy is used in the form of electricity for lighting, heating, cooling, and miscellaneous applications. On a nationwide basis, lighting represents approximately 17 percent; cooling, approximately 14 percent; and heating, approximately 41 percent of the source energy used. Although the actual mix of energy varies widely depending on geographical location and type of occupancy (office building, hospital, school, etc.), lighting, heating, and air conditioning generally represent the largest of the energy-intensive operations in commercial and institutional buildings.

Since the mid-1980s, and particularly since 1990, certain types of energy conservation and demand-side management projects have become quite popular for reducing the utility costs of buildings. Lighting retrofits involving electronic ballasts, reflectors, occupancy sensors, and other forms of lighting controls have gained immense popularity partly because they can be implemented with minimal or no engineering effort and have a high rate of return. Similarly, in the heating, ventilation, and air conditioning (HVAC) area, variable-frequency drives, economizer controls, energy-efficient motors for large HVAC equipment, thermal energy storage (TES), high-efficiency chillers, and direct digital controls (DDC) have been extensively used to enhance the part-load efficiency and control of HVAC equipment. In all likelihood, the drive for reducing utility costs and achieving high energy efficiency will continue unabated through the balance of this century and beyond.

40.2   POTENTIAL SAVINGS THROUGH ENERGY CONSERVATION

For the purposes of illustration, we will consider a hypothetical "average" commercial facility. For simplicity, let us consider the simplest and surest type of energy conservation projects. We will assume a 1 million sq.-ft., 15- to 20-year-old commercial or institutional facility. We will consider three simple conservation projects that appear to be quite popular in the electricity conservation field: 1) lighting energy conservation through the use of T8 lamps and electronic ballasts, 2) lighting energy conservation through use of occupancy sensors, and 3) HVAC energy conservation through the use of variable-speed drives.

Typically, an average commercial facility would use approximately 14 kWh/gross square foot (gr. sq. ft.)/year. At a lighting power density of 2.2 W/gr. sq. ft. and a lighting duration of 3,200 hours/year, lighting energy use in the facility will be approximately 45 percent of the overall electricity use. Likewise, with 400 gr. sq. ft./ton of air conditioning and 1 kW/ton of air conditioning equipment, the air conditioning electricity use will be approximately 8 percent. Large fans and pumps, which typically use up to 1.5 hp/gr. sq. ft., would use approximately 22 percent. Then there are the process loads, office equipment, small fans, and small pumps, which use the remaining balance of 25 percent. Thus, the lighting and large fan areas typically use 67 percent of the overall electricity use.

Next we will look at the type of lighting retrofit potential that is typically found in such a facility. If we assume a mix of one-lamp, two-lamp, and four-lamp fluorescent lighting fixtures in a ratio of 1 percent, 25 percent, and 74 percent, respectively, in terms of connected load, it can be shown that the overall number of fixtures will be approximately 17,000 to yield a 2.2 W/gr. sq. ft. T8 lamps and electronic ballasts can save approximately 9 W, 22 W, and 42 W in typical one-lamp, two-lamp, and four-lamp fixtures, respectively, using magnetic ballasts. Putting these together, it can be shown that the lighting electricity use in the hypothetical facility can be cut by at least 30 percent[1] using T8 lamps and electronic ballasts alone.

Implementation will require various material, labor, and processing resources. In the above example, under current pricing for lamp disposal, ballast disposal, new T8 lamps, and new electronic ballasts, retrofitting 17,000 old fluorescent fixtures will cost approximately $100,000 for lamp and ballast disposal,[2] $140,000 for new T8 lamps, $400,000 for new ballasts, and $180,000 for installation labor. The overall project will therefore cost $820,000. Assuming an average electricity rate of $0.08/kWh, such a project typically has a simple payback period of five to six years.

Let us now consider the second sample project—namely, installation of occupancy sensors. Generally, occupancy sensors can be economically applied to a typical space that has at least 500 W of lighting load. If we assume conservatively that only 20 percent of the facility can utilize this form of control, approximately 280 kW[3] of lighting load could be potentially connected to the sensors. Turning off this load for as few as two hours/day, five days/week, could save approximately 150,000 kWh/year for the entire facility. In terms of material and labor resources, a typical project of this type would cost $25,000[4] in materials and $15,000 in labor costs. The overall project will have a simple payback of three to four years.

Finally, let us consider the third sample conservation project—namely, installation of variable-speed drives on the large fans. Because each facility is unique in terms of its HVAC systems, the potential for this type of project can vary significantly from site to site. However, for the purposes of illustration, let us assume conservatively that only 30 percent of the existing fan horsepower can be controlled through variable-speed drives. Modulating the speed of twenty large fans at an average fan size of 20 hp can yield an energy savings of approximately 360,000 kWh/year.[4] On a facility-wide basis, such a project will cost approximately $100,000 for materials and equipment and another $40,000 for labor. The overall project would have a simple payback of five to six years.

Figure 40-1 presents a summary of the sample projects described above. As shown, the hypothetical facility offers the potential for a minimum of approximately $1 million worth of projects, which could save approximately 2.33 million kWh/year and approximately $186,000/year in utility costs. In terms of unit numbers, the potential may be summarized as follows:

Figure 40-1
Hypothetical Million-Square-Foot Facility
Sample Project Potential

Item	Lighting Retrofit	Occupancy Sensor Control	Application of Variable-Frequency Drives	Total	Per Gross Square Foot
Project cost	$819,938	$40,744	$140,000	$999,982	$1.00
kWh savings	1,816,100	146,897	362,556	2,325,553	2.33
Cost savings	$145,288	$11,752	$29,004	$186,044	$0.19
Simple payback (years)	5.6	3.5	4.8	5.4	

- Capital cost of energy conservation projects: $1.00/gr. sq. ft.
- Energy savings: 2.3 kWh/gr. sq. ft.
- Utility cost savings: $0.19/gr. sq. ft./year

While the actual numbers could vary considerably up or down depending on a variety of factors, including age of the facility, geographical location, type of occupancy, etc., it is not unreasonable to consider the above as a conservative estimate of "typical" conditions for facilities that are more than 15 to 20 years old and have not been retrofitted with energy-conserving measures.

40.3   APPLICATION TO UNIVERSITIES

A great number of colleges and universities have found that improving energy efficiency on a large scale serves as a means for controlling both energy use and energy costs. They are also finding that well-organized energy management and conservation (EMC) programs can be implemented without disrupting facilities operations and, therefore, academic programs are not negatively affected.

EMC programs can provide a comfortable working and learning environment as well as a mechanism for substantially lowering institutional costs. To achieve these outcomes, the program must be integrated, flexible, and results oriented. This section provides a systematic approach for formulating and implementing a successful EMC program in a campus setting without inflicting or imposing risks to the campus academic mission or well-being of its residents.

This section will review the various necessary ingredients in a successful energy management program, including the following:

- Elements of success
- Strategic planning
- Administrative steps
- Technical steps

Elements for Success

EMC projects are not generally limited by energy technology but can be limited by the resources available to support that technology's implementation. Developers of an EMC program can seek support from four basic elements:

1. *Management.* Managers typically plan, organize, lead, and control the work of others. Efficiency is derived when input (money, people, and equipment) remains static and output increases, when input is reduced and output remains static, or when input is reduced and output is increased.

2. *Productivity.* Employee productivity is involved in planning and design, interaction with and education of consultants, implementation of programs, follow-through, and monitoring of the results.
3. *Energy.* The focus here is nonhuman energy—that is, energy derived as a result of the use of electricity, natural gas, oil, or coal. Nonhuman energy is as abundant as human energy when approached with rational and technically feasible solutions. Human energy can take two forms: physical and intellectual. Physical power is the amount of energy provided by a human to perform manual work (e.g., moving a mass from point A to point B). Intellectual energy is the ability to investigate, understand, quantify, predict, and stimulate. Physical power is necessary to achieve economic survival, and intellectual power is necessary for organizational survived.
4. *Information Systems.* The information system is a resource that cannot be overlooked in the effective maintenance of any management program. Computers can assist in the storage, organization, analysis, and retrieval of information, thereby freeing managers from redundant tasks so that they can pay more attention to innovative solutions.

Strategic Planning

Just as for any other organizational program, strategic planning for a successful EMC program targets every step of the management process, up to but excluding program implementation. Strategic planning provides the following benefits:

- A clear understanding of the likely future impact of a current decision
- Better anticipation of future developments
- Better information exchange within the organization
- Smoother and more efficient implementation of future decisions
- Reduction in parochialism and increased understanding of constructive conflict
- Emphasis on ongoing planning

The strategic planning process includes recognizing and providing for the following components:

- *Organization subsystems.* This is the organizational climate. Effective ways of enhancing the climate for innovative planning include 1) encouraging widespread participation in planning at all levels; 2) stressing that change is normal and is to be expected as the organization faces a changing environment; and 3) permeating the organization with planning, demonstrating that it works, and making use of it. For an EMC program, the organization should create a staff office, decentralize the profit centers within the campus, create a project team or task force, or set up a special organization.

- *Information subsystems.* This is information collection, organization, analysis, and dissemination. Planning information must be current, focused on the environmental and competitive goals of the organization, and easy to access in the form in which it is most useful. In the absence of an information system, decisions are made without relevant information. Strategic databases may include, but are not limited to, legal, political, economic, technical, competitor (i.e., other universities), and internal databases and information databases about the future.

- *Decision subsystems.* This system allows choices to be made in a systematic fashion during the entire planning process. The final plan represents a great number of choices that were made and eventually coordinated into the final set of choices.

- *System of plans.* The final outcome of the strategic planning process is a system of plans—individual plans that are integrated to guide the organizational system. Operational (short-term) plans guide an organization for approximately one year; developmental (intermediate) plans provide guidance for one to five years; and strategic (long-term) plans provide guidance for more than five years.

- *Planning management subsystems.* This process facilitates planning and consists of five phases: 1) establishing general goals (e.g., defining the organization's purpose), 2) collecting information and forecasting, 3) making assumptions, 4) establishing specific objectives, and 5) developing plans.

Administration Steps

Administration steps include convincing top management, securing personnel resources, setting policy and goals, and managing the program.

Convincing Top Management   It is essential to the EMC program's success that top management become enthusiastically involved to the program. Several steps can be taken to foster this support. First, illustrate the historical rise in energy costs and usage as well as the increasingly limited supply of energy, both nationally and regionally. Then examine potential curtailments in power supplies, using historical data and regularly issued reports.

Second, share with top management what other institutions are doing, and expand on the success stories. Data may also be gathered from organizations in a similar field. Generally, successful organizations will prepare periodic reports in addition to a complete publication detailing the history, organization, collective and individual achievements, funding successes, and planning strategies of their EMC programs. Detailed descriptions of other cost-effective energy conservation projects that may be feasible for the institution to implement should be presented to top management.

Finally, illustrate the potential impact of various local, state, and federal regulations.

Securing Personnel Resources   Securing personnel resources and determining functional placement of personnel within the organization is one of the most important steps toward a successful EMC program. The support of a continued interaction with the chief executive officer, the budget director, the planning and resource management officer, and construction/trades superintendents will aid in coordination of the budgeting, operating, planning, and constructing of energy management projects.

It must be determined whether the energy management program requires one or more full-time management positions, whether the individuals will play a staff or line role, and to whom the individuals will report in the organizational structure. In addition, a determination regarding the need for support staff is necessary. In making these determinations, educational and technical background should be considered.

Setting Policy and Goals   Using the institution's mission statement as a guideline, energy management policy as well as energy goals must be established. Management of an EMC program includes uninterrupted delivery of energy (and handling of emergency interruption); implementation of results-oriented energy conservation measures; and incorporation of the energy program into the everyday life of students, faculty, staff, and visitors.

Managing the Program   Managing an EMC program is no different from managing any other program; it includes five major management functions:

1. *Planning.* This generally includes defining the goals of the program and how to achieve them and developing a series of small plans to integrate and coordinate the activities.
2. *Organizing.* This includes what specifically is to be done, who is to do it, to whom that individual reports, and where decisions are to be made.
3. *Motivating.* Motivating personnel is one of the most important management functions, as it moves employees to exert high levels of effort to reach organizational goals while satisfying individual needs.
4. *Directing.* Directing includes overseeing the activities of others, selecting appropriate communication channels, and resolving conflicts.
5. *Controlling.* This involves monitoring the performance of the program and ensuring that it is proceeding as planned, correcting it if necessary.

Technical Steps

Approximately 14 percent of the costs of a building with an expected 40-year life span is in the building's design and construction; the remaining 86 percent of costs is in operations and maintenance. Most of the existing 50 billion sq. ft. of commercial and industrial space in the United States today is energy-obsolete. Therefore, it can be assumed that the facilities for which facilities managers are responsible are not nearly as energy efficient as they could be. To establish specific objectives to overcome identified deficiencies, a calculated and well-defined plan of action must be developed. The plan suggested in this section may serve as a guideline.

Energy/Technical Audit   Perform an energy/technical audit, and collect the resulting data. This includes calculating energy costs and determining which buildings have a higher than normal or higher than desired energy consumption. This step also includes identifying no-cost or low-cost energy conservation opportunities, such as repairing broken windows and cleaning dirty air handling units.

Priority List   Identify feasible energy conservation measures, and develop a priority list, based on life-cycle cost calculations, under the following categories:

- *Quick-fix projects* are those that can be handled by changes in operating practices and procedures. These include simple adjustments of thermostats, delamping and relamping with energy-efficient fluorescent lamps, and equipment shutdowns as appropriate.
- *Retrofit projects* are those requiring equipment and system modifications for peak energy efficiency. Retrofit items typically require funding support in the same manner as minor capital projects.
- *Major capital outlay energy projects* include a variety of capital-intensive energy conservation measures. Such projects may include computerized energy management systems for scheduling, optimized starts/stops, duty cycling, load rolling and demand control of building HVAC systems, or installation of cogeneration plants.

Setting Goals   Develop an annual consumption goal that is attainable and measurable. The goal may be to conserve energy, money, or a particular resource.

Guidelines   Prepare ongoing guidelines and procedures on scheduling, operations, maintenance, and training. As the process proceeds, continually assess major products, services, and markets; the external environment, including government actions, social mores, politics, and international affairs;

the internal environment, including strengths and weaknesses in marketing, finance information systems, and strategic planning; and competitive environments, including research and development, new product design, automation systems, and instrumentation.

Identifying Retrofits   The method used for identifying retrofits in the EMC program must be similar to that used in a full-scale engineering survey. However, checklists, reference tables, and simple calculations based on the experience of others are recommended as substitutes for the more complex analysis and measurements entailed in a full-scale engineering effort.

The purpose of the survey is to identify sound retrofit projects and provide an approximate measure of their relative merits for budgetary planning, not to develop engineering and detailed life cycle costs. Therefore, the survey method must be simplified so that a minimum of time and resources is invested.

There are four major steps in a building retrofit identification survey:

- *Step 1: Collect energy use data.* This step provides the fuel cost data necessary to calculate cost savings later in the process, as well as an overall sense of priority for retrofit projects. The fuel types accounting for the largest part of the total fuel bill should receive the greatest emphasis in planning retrofit projects.
- *Step 2: Categorize the buildings.* In this step, all of the buildings at a facility should be ranked in terms of size and thus in terms of their probable proportion of energy use. Buildings should also be categorized into type based on climate zone.
- *Step 3: Identify retrofit options.* In this step, reference checklists link the appropriate candidate retrofit option with specific energy systems as a function of building type and climate zone. In addition, retrofit projects already planned can be incorporated easily.
- *Step 4: Evaluate and rank retrofit projects.* The energy and cost savings of individual retrofit projects are calculated, along with their associated investment costs. The option are then ranked according to the time it would take for them to pay back their investment cost.

Major Energy Conservation Measures   During the survey, certain specific areas must be evaluated. These areas can be categorized into fifty-two energy conservation opportunities (ECOs) commonly found in existing buildings. These fifty-two ECOs, as identified in Appendix A, provide the framework necessary for an in-depth analysis of the ECOs tentatively selected for implementation.

The seven different ECO groups may be arranged in order of investigation and potential implementation. These groups are prioritized according to operational reductions and primary equipment load reductions.

This method of prioritization also applies to the individual ECOs with·n each group. The ECO groups to be considered are listed in Appendix A.

Energy-Saving Calculation Methodology The methodology utilized by engineers complies with universally accepted engineering practices and procedures. Project evaluations are to be determined by the cumulative effect of performing numerous energy-saving options. In addition, to further improve the accuracy of the calculations, the cumulative effect must be estimated by determining the option that provides the shortest payback period, reducing the total Btu usage by its effect, applying the next option to the adjusted Btu usage total, and continuing this process through the remaining energy-saving options. This method of calculation provides the most conservative estimate of energy savings.

Utilities Master Planning The utility master plan should consider and recommend adequate improvements to all campus utility systems. The systems that should be addressed are electricity, heating, cooling water, sewer, natural gas, telephone, computers, and instructional television.

The master plan should also address the issues encountered with the campus-wide utilities distribution to meet the needs for years to come. In addition, a sound master plan should simultaneously improve performance and safety while reducing energy use. The utilities master plan provides a road map for the future development of the campus infrastructure. Utilities projects can be phased to ensure that services are available in advance of the construction of new buildings.

40.4 SUMMARY

The most important single element in the success of an EMC program is the people who manage it. The consumption of energy is as much a business as the production of energy, and it must be treated and managed in a business-like way. In addition to traditional management skills, the manager in charge of an EMC program must take on a number of specific tasks related to the program. These tasks are listed in Appendix B. Properly structured, an EMC can be extremely effective. Many universities have saved substantial sums of money as a result of EMC programs.

Taking an Active Role In relatively recent years, the nation's utilities have taken an active role in promoting energy conservation and management and have provided numerous forms of technical assistance and financial incentives. The U.S. Department of Energy and the Environmental Protection Agency have also taken an active role promoting energy and environmental consciousness nationwide. However, more participation may be necessary at the highest levels within both industry and government to accelerate the pace at which these projects can be developed. Such additional efforts must have one simple goal: to develop a strategy by which the nation can fully tap into the economic potential offered by the energy conservation industry and use it in time to give the needed economic boost across the country.

From a facilities officer's viewpoint, these types of conservation projects can offer benefits in a variety of ways. First and foremost, if there is a sudden need to reduce costs in the operating budget, the manager can utilize private financing to implement the projects and save utility costs. If there is a management directive to trim operating staff, the manager can justify use of such staff to start a conservation program and thereby minimize the extent of staff cuts. It is conceivable that many air quality management districts may offer a "pollution credit" for the savings produced by conservation projects. Managers should use the opportunity to get such credits, which can be either resold at a price or banked to accommodate potential facility expansion at a later date.

Whether one looks at it from a microscopic standpoint (i.e., at a single facility) or from a global or national standpoint, conservation programs can offer multiple payoffs, including making the so-called weakening job base more solid throughout the country.

NOTES

1. Energy Information Administration. *Lighting in Commercial Buildings.* Publication No. DOE/EIA-0555(92)1. Washington, D.C.: U.S. Department of Energy, March 1992.
2. Energy Information Administration. *Annual Energy Outlook, with Projections to 2010.* Publication No. DOE/EIA-0383(92). Washington, D.C.: U.S. Department of Energy, January 1992.
3. Hines, Virginia. "EPA's Green Lights Program Promotes Environmental Protection, Energy Savings and Profits." *Strategic Planning for Energy and the Environment,* Winter 1990–1991.
4. Karkia, M. Reza. "Energy Conservation Projects and their Positive Impact on the Economy." *Facilities Manager,* Vol. 10, No. 1, 1994, pp. 18–23.

Appendix 40-A

Energy Conservation Opportunity Group

Group A: Operational
ECO 1.   Reduce system operating hours.
ECO 2.   Reduce space loads owing to ventilation.
ECO 3.   Control space temperature and humidity.
ECO 4.   Reduce flow and temperature of hot water.
ECO 5.   Isolate off-line boilers.
ECO 6.   Use low-temperature condenser water.
ECO 7.   Reduce operating time of elevators.

Group B: Lighting System
ECO 8.   Reduce illumination levels.
ECO 9.   Use only necessary illumination.
ECO 10. Utilize natural light.
ECO 11. Improve effectiveness of existing fixtures.
ECO 12. Use more efficient lenses.
ECO 13. Install more efficient lamps.
ECO 14. Install more efficient fixtures.
ECO 15. Install more efficient, high power factor ballasts.

Group C: Building Envelope
ECO 16. Reduce transmission of heat through walls and ceilings.
ECO 17. Reduce transmission of heat through windows and sky-lights.
ECO 18. Reduce transmission of heat through roof.
ECO 19. Reduce transmission of heat through floors.
ECO 20. Reduce space load owing to infiltration.

Group D: Distribution Systems
ECO 21. Reduce energy consumption for fans by reducing air-flow rates and resistance to airflow.
ECO 22. Reduce pump energy by reducing resistance and flow rates.
ECO 23. Insulate ducts.
ECO 24. Insulate piping.
ECO 25. Replace steam traps.

Group E: HVAC Equipment
ECO 26. Improve control and utilization of outside air.

ECO 27. Recirculate exhaust air using activated carbon filters.
ECO 28. Use separate makeup air for exhaust hoods.
ECO 29. Employ evaporative cooling of outdoor air.
ECO 30. Employ desiccant dehumidification.
ECO 31. Reduce energy consumed by reheat systems.
ECO 32. Adjust fuel-to-air ratios of firing systems.
ECO 33. Install flue gas analyzer.
ECO 34. Replace existing boilers with modular boilers.
ECO 35. Preheat combustion air and heavy fuel oil to increase boiler efficiency.
ECO 36. Maintain fuel burning equipment and heat transfer surfaces.
ECO 37. Replace steam atomizing burners with atomizing burners.
ECO 38. Reduce blowdown losses.
ECO 39. Increase evaporator and/or decrease condenser water temperatures and modify controls.
ECO 40. Isolate off-line chillers and cooling towers.
ECO 41. Replace air-cooled condensers with cooling towers.
ECO 42. Use a piggyback absorption system.
ECO 43. Utilize heat reclamation systems.

Group F: Domestic Hot Water System
ECO 44. Insulate hot water storage tank piping.
ECO 45. Use heat recovery systems.
ECO 46. Replace central system with local heating units and/or separate summer generation of hot water.

Group G: Power Systems
ECO 47. Reduce energy consumption of equipment and machines.
ECO 48. Reduce peak loads.
ECO 49. Utilize efficient transformers.
ECO 50. Replace oversized motors.
ECO 51. Correct the power factor.
ECO 52. Utilize a central power control system.

Appendix 40-B

Initial Assignments for the Campus Energy Manager

1. Collect, review, and consolidate all energy and utility consumption-related data in the campus.
2. Identify all energy consumption centers on campus, devoting particular attention to bulk consumption centers such as the central steam station.
3. Set up annual targets for reducing energy use in electricity, gas, liquid fuel, and water on the campus consistent with the system-wide policies and programs of the campus.
4. Identify the opportunities for optimizing energy use on the campus.
5. Prepare an action plan to reach the annual targets.
6. Establish an energy management team composed of representatives from facilities planning, plant operations, administration, faculty, and the student body.
7. Review with the team the annual targets and the plan for reduction in energy use, and jointly agree to an overall strategy.
8. Identify the energy reduction opportunities in the three categories: quick-fix, retrofit, and major capital items.
9. Identify those energy reduction opportunities that need to be reviewed by an outside consultant, and prepare funding justification for those items.
10. Estimate the cost of those items in item 8 that would help reach the annual campus energy reduction targets with no or low costs, moderate costs (less than $100,000), or major capital outlay.
11. Prepare a summary of the annual plan with proper identification of the anticipated reduction in energy use, tying it to funding needed to make those reductions possible.
12. With the energy management team, prepare project justifications and proposals for funding, and review these with the office of the chancellor.
13. Monitor the enforcement of the building and equipment energy standards and implementation of the steps under the no-cost/low-cost category in the annual plan.
14. Identify the bottlenecks and operational problems in the implementation of the annual program plan steps.
15. Conduct a public relations campaign to promote the program on campus. If necessary, request help from the student body, and publicize the plan's achievements.

16. Prepare responses to federal and state opportunities for funding for energy conservation projects. If necessary, request assistance from members of the faculty to prepare those responses.
17. Conduct seminars or review programs for the campus maintenance staff on preventive and energy-conscious maintenance.
18. Review the programs of the campus energy conservation program every six months.
19. Prepare an annual report on the energy conservation plan, activities, and performance of the office of the chancellor.
20. Disseminate pertinent national and local energy-related news to the campus community.
21. Prepare a monthly energy consumption report.

CHAPTER 41

Central Monitoring and Control Systems

Carl Ruther
University of Cincinnati

41.1 INTRODUCTION

This chapter will discuss central monitoring systems and direct digital control (CMCS/DDC) for college and university facilities. If properly installed, operated, and maintained, CMCS/DDC systems can greatly improve and maintain levels of comfort and greatly reduce overall building energy consumption and waste. In addition, these systems can reduce time spent in routine inspections and troubleshooting, speed the accuracy of the service response, and greatly improve the overall operation of campus buildings.

CMCS/DDC systems cover a considerable range of technical and managerial issues. They bring high demands for quality design, installation, operation, and repair. CMCS/DDC systems have become the primary tool for operating many campus building systems. Managing them has become one of the most challenging tasks in any facilities management department. College and university facilities generally have larger and more complex HVAC and building support systems than average institutional or commercial buildings. These systems are used by people who are technologically sophisticated, who have very high standards, and who are quite vocal about their needs and expectations. Because of this, campuses can be tough environments for facilities managers who are inexperienced or mechanics who are poorly trained. In addition, as building systems advance in sophistication and complexity, there are more chances for error. Systems currently are sized and built to computer precision and therefore are less tolerant of misapplication, operating ignorance, and neglect. In addition, these systems now serve a customer who has grown to expect more quality especially at the workplace. Facilities managers know how easily even a brief mechanical or electrical problem (e.g., an air handler loss on a warm day, a blown fuse in a laboratory or to a computer) can swiftly wipe out any memory of the many days of trouble-free operation that preceded the failure.

With complexity of the current building technology and the growing intolerance of building and equipment malfunctions, it is imperative that the quality of design, installation, and training for the operation and maintenance of all building systems be more rigorous than ever before. None, however, is as critical as the CMCS/DDC.

Fortunately, despite their increased sophistication, steady improvements in CMCS/DDCs have made them much more reliable and easier to use in many ways. Many provide improved equipment condition monitoring features such as equipment diagnostics, trend graphing, performance reporting in third-party software such as Microsoft Excel, and so forth. Many systems provide considerable levels of self diagnostics for troubleshooting the CMCS/DDC itself such as controller hardware, software, and CMCS/DDC communications networks.

As an example of improvements in recent years, most new CMCS installations now provide temperatures and air volumes from a digital controller located in almost every room served by the HVAC system. Comfort and room occupancy can be easily monitored directly from a computer added design (CAD) based floor plan showing these values in real time. This information gives console operators and system technicians and mechanics total system monitoring and troubleshooting down to the individual room terminal devices (for example, reheat and radiation values and VAV box dampers). If necessary, features can be enabled and changes can be made to current thermostat set points, occupant adjustment ranges, occupant override, and time schedules from the central operator's console or from the room itself. Advanced systems are being installed that sense occupancy and turn on lights as well as the room's terminal unit and the necessary central equipment. Sometimes occupancy sensors restart equipment only outside of prescheduled equipment run times.

With total DDC networks to the room terminal controller level, sensor-actuator level, advanced programming also can be installed to optimize the entire HVAC system like never before. By optimally readjusting system-wide set points for supplying air temperature, fan and duct static pressure, and volume to the exact requirements of all of the rooms, a new level of efficiency in HVAC can be achieved.

Most new CMCS/DDC systems come with built-in self calibration-loop tuning and continuous self-diagnostics. In addition, most new systems can integrate building access and security control, fire and smoke management, laboratory environmental pressurization, and fume hood controls.

Advanced systems such as these take careful planning, excellent design, and considerable attention to detail during installation and acceptance if they are to work reliably and provide the comfort and efficiencies described. This chapter will serve as a guide through the development of a new CMCS system by providing explanations and advice in planning, developing purchase justification if necessary, writing requests for information and proposals, and preparing for the new system.

41.2 CMCS/DDC DEVELOPMENT

Preparing the CMCS/DDC System Program

The first step in the procurement of a new or expanded CMCS/DDC system is to determine the return on investment (ROI) that is possible from the new system. In many instances this step is unnecessary, as CMCS/DDC systems are considered fundamental in most renovation or new construction projects. However, there are still situations where a system must be financially justified before funding will be considered or approved. The following information should help managers define their objectives in a detailed and professional manner.

There are three important elements for developing any CMCS/DDC system investment program:

1. An energy audit and analysis of potential savings and the intangible benefits gained
2. CMCS/DDC energy conservation programs and control routines that must be implemented
3. Program financing

Accurate analysis and attractive packaging of CMCS/DDC proposals are crucial to the approval and success of most college and university energy management programs. An accurate savings analysis is essential to see through biases and to identify how the CMCS/DDC proposal compares with all other energy or financial investment opportunities of the college or university. Good packaging and a quality presentation of the proposal are essential to make its benefits obvious.

The goal of the proposal is to identify how the CMCS/DDC system represents a good energy-saving investment and guarantees the most efficient use of limited college or university funds. If the CMCS/DDC proposal is strictly an energy conservation proposal, then it must make good economic or financial sense. It must have a payback that is as good as or better than that of any other investments available.

Many colleges use energy management ROI programs to reduce comfort complaints; to improve student, faculty, and staff satisfaction with facilities; to improve reliability; and to eliminate labor investment in worn-out, obsolete temperature controls and HVAC equipment. These kinds of benefits and cost savings are hard to quantify, but they are important considerations that should be mentioned briefly in the executive summary. When a CMCS/DDC system ROI proposal is developed, three levels of information should be presented to those who must review the proposal and approve it:

1. Develop an executive summary, and keep it simple. The summary should be limited to a brief description of the project: cost = x, savings = y, payback = z.
2. Give background information that presents all alternatives and reveals the assumptions underlying the analysis. This information should enable the final decision maker to easily make a decision.
3. Present detailed calculations, including sources of information, savings methodology, and CMCS/DDC system product specifications. These will ultimately be reviewed by those who are asked to review the proposal if a second opinion is requested.

Many colleges and universities have internal funds available and can develop their own ROI programs for financing campus efficiency improvements. Because funds can be borrowed from reserves at a much lower cost than going outside or requesting capital funding, this method eliminates the wait and dangers of complicated long-term contracts found in energy guarantees and shared savings agreements. Unfortunately, because facilities management projects are sometimes viewed as maintenance, financial investments such as these are hard to sell in the organization, and funds for utilities continue to be sent to the local utility.

CMCS/DDC Energy Savings Analysis

There are simple methods by which college and university facilities and engineering staffs can calculate the energy savings that come from CMCS/DDC control system installations. Many control companies will supply forms that contain guides for entering information for the most common HVAC, chiller, boiler, and lighting savings strategies. Energy calculations are usually included for the most common CMCS/DDC energy management software applications.

Most vendor forms also include cash flow analysis for estimating negative and positive cash flows for each year over a five-year period or more. Most of these forms use simple payback and an ROI analysis based on internal rate of return. These provide a quick and concise but limited technical analysis of the savings potentials of a building. These simple calculations cannot measure improvements in efficiency that come from more accurate proportional-integral-derivative (PID) control, from global or hierarchical set point readjustment optimization, or from occupancy sensor-driven DDC room control of lighting and HVAC. (For examples of typical CMCS/DDC energy management and control savings calculations, see the section entitled Digital Controller Software Applications.)

Preparing Requests for Proposals for CMCS/DDC Systems

Before writing formal specifications for a large CMCS/DDC system, many colleges and universities write requests for proposals (RFPs). Requests for proposals are a quick and professional way to collect and quickly learn about current CMCS/DDC vendor systems. In addition to enabling the staff to obtain documentation and brochures, requests for proposals allow the staff to view professionally developed presentations and talk directly with the manufacturer's most qualified personnel.

Many requests for proposals are written as loose specifications or brief outlines. Writing requests for proposals this way takes a little more work, but vendors will usually respond with more useful, realistic, and exacting proposals. Preparing specification-like RFPs also helps the department's project staff think through all aspects of the project early on. The effort also prepares them for the review of each proposal and ultimately will speed up the writing of the final specification.

Good requests for proposals clearly state the objectives of the system and the performance wanted from the end product. This includes the cost savings and the ROI required, the start date and the time allotted for implementation, the commissioning requirement, and the warranty. The request for proposal can be used to ask for demonstration systems and visits to view vendor-installed systems.

Specifying Campus CMCS/DDC Systems

Many colleges and universities write their own CMCS/DDC specifications, and some develop a shortened guide specification for architects and consulting engineers. Guide specifications ensure consistency in the way CMCS/DDC equipment is applied, describe the kinds of points wanted, and describe the way control sequences and energy management software are written. Consistency is important when a system is intended to grow for several years and to be installed in many buildings.

Contract specifications for new systems are centered around the administrative aspects of the project, or the *general conditions*. General conditions include a project description, scope of work, submittals, approval requirements, technical documentation, qualifications of vendors and contractors, project management, and so forth. A second area describes the actual system hardware and material products to be used, and a third describes the functional aspects of the system, points of control sequences, reports, energy management functions, and commissioning and training requirements.

If specifications are to be written by in house personnel, there are many sources for help. Many colleges and universities share their own specifications, and many vendors willingly provide copies of their system specifications. Both of these sources should be carefully studied and compared. Vendors' specifications will emphasize their own unique features and contain many proprietary aspects. If a particular vendor's CMCS/DDC system has all the necessary features, it should be the basis of design and their proprietary specification should be used. Other vendors bidding on the project should be allowed to take exception wherever necessary. Facilities managers who write completely generic specifications will have to carefully evaluate each vendor's proposal to determine whether vendors intend to provide all the specified features and functional requirements.

The following is a summary of the most important items that CMCS/DDC systems specifications should contain.

System Description. A brief overview of the system to be installed and the overall design and performance requirements.

Scope of Work. A short description of what is to be provided in terms of engineering, supervision, documentation, writing, equipment hardware, software, check-out, guarantee, training, and so forth.

Work by Others. Work to be done by other contractors for use by the CMCS/DDC system such as motor control circuit wiring, external equipment interlocks (for example, smoke detectors, hands-off auto selector switches, power circuits for control panels), and so forth.

Related Work. Work in other specification divisions that affect CMCS/DDC installation such as general, mechanical, and electrical.

Project Management. Person who coordinates CMCS/DDC work, the point of contact, person who makes field decisions, and so forth.

Startup and Commissioning. Initial system startup procedures, verification of completeness, tests to be performed, sequence checking, adjusting, and the content of the final CMCS/DDC system commissioning report.

Submittals. Information that must be supplied by the temperature control contractor for approval before work starts. Submittals should include name, make, model, and description of the system to be installed; a point input/output summary sheet; shop drawings; riser diagrams; panel hookup diagrams; proposed field controller; network and operators console hardware cut sheets; preliminary application software with comments and flow charts; terminal unit; and valve and damper schedules. Submittals should also include detailed product specifications and installation instructions for each device such as digital controller components, sensors, output modules, transducers, actuators, air and water flow meters, network gateways, trunk interfaces, modems, terminals, and personal computers.

Warranty. Description of how the system is guaranteed against defects in materials and workmanship, length of warranty, and how to use it.

Acceptable Manufacturers. The basis of system design, the acceptable manufacturers; and their qualifications.

Documentation. What information is to be provided at the completion of system installation such as built diagrams, layouts, all system software listings, and functional descriptions.

Control Contractors Remote Monitoring. Description of remote monitoring connection for troubleshooting and software upgrade of the CMCS/DDC during construction and warranty periods by the contractor.

Technical Support. The level of technical support, business hours in which calls can be made, the response time required, and description of how emergency calls are made.

Training. Description of new system training to be provided to the owner's staff, length of training, who is to give training, and the content of each training session.

Spare Parts. Recommended spare parts that will be needed to maintain the system once it is installed, including suggested number and types of sensors, transducers, spare controller printed circuit boards, input/output modules, and so forth. Some college and universities use this section to include a requirement for a long-term guaranteed price for all CMCS/DDC system software up grades for all system hardware after signing a CMCS/DDC purchase agreement.

Portable Operators Terminal. Description of hardware (dumb terminal or laptop computer) and software to be used by the building operator or technician to adjust thermostats and to connect to various digital controllers in the project.

Personal Computer Based Operators Console Hardware. Description of hardware components and size, speed, and quality of the personal computer or workstation to be provided for the project.

Personal Computer Based Operators Console Software. Specification of the functionality software and menus for selecting and viewing of system points, displaying graphics, scheduling equipment, adding trend points, creating a point database definition; editing; field controller control programs; creating and editing alarm limits and messages; and utilities for system management such as up and down loading of software, making backups, monitoring system status, doing diagnostics, and so forth.

Dynamic Color Graphic Displays. Description of the manufacturer, model, and picture quality of computer monitors supplied as the system–user interface. This section should include the type of computer graphics programs to be supplied for creating building floor plans, HVAC system diagrams, dynamic point information to be included on displays, graphic navigation methods, and so forth.

System Configuration & Definition. Description of site configuration and system setup for management level and controller networks, operators consoles, point and controller database maintenance, system security/user access and privileges, networkwide control strategies.

Direct Digital Controllers. Description of the DDC controller software operating system and its features (such as multi-tasking, real-time, on-line editing, compiling of programs), memory type and size, applications software, components, input types, output types and transducers, manual override switches, user interface, modems, status indicators, self-diagnostics, communication diagnostics, network terminations, power supply, backup battery, electrical interference isolation, and so forth.

Point Schedule Input/Output Schedule. All input/output points to be installed on each air handling unit and other building system, point types such as digital and analog input/output, application and energy management programs to be applied, alarms and messages required, notes, and so forth.

Wiring. Specification of the types, sizes, wiring to be used for sensing and control, type and fill of conduits and locations of each class and type of wire, how terminations are to be made, labeling of wires, power sources for panels and so forth; sealing of conduits and wall openings, National Electric Code (NEC) and National Fire Protection Association (NFPA) code requirements. This section also defines the quality of workmanship in the wiring of the CMCS/DDC system.

Sensors and Output Transducers. Description of field devices used to sense temperature, pressure, relative humidity, dew point, steam and chilled water flow, voltage, current, KWH, KWD, CO_2, and so forth. It provides detailed requirements for sensor range, accuracy, linerity, repeatability and noise rejection, and installation details. It also includes transducer types (such as I/P (current to pressure) or E/P (voltage to pressure) output various type of control signals to such things as valves, dampers and variable frequency drives, relays, contractors, totalizers, and so forth.

Network Communications. Description of the type of communication media to be used (e.g., Ethernet or Archnet), the network architecture, and the protocol standard to be used for all communication networks. This section should include ability to share data, stand alone and peer to peer capabilities, maximum time allowances for alarms, logs response. It also includes required transmission speed, error recovery techniques, network diagnostics to be provided. This section sometimes also describes the physical network, remote dial out modems, the trunk cable to be used, trunk interfacing gateways, routers, protection devices, and installation and number of devices that can be connected to the network.

Digital Controller Resident Software. Operating system and general application software that are to be provided as part of the controller usually as it comes from the manufacturer. Examples of this software include logical programming functions: AND, OR, NOT, XOR, math functions: AVG, EXP, MIN, MAX, SQRT. Resident software includes basic point alarm functions, point and trend logging, run time logging, and so forth. Software algorithms to be provided in the controller operating system software such as two-position, proportional, integral and derivative control (PID), and other software statements needed to run user developed programs that are preinstalled in the firmware of the controller. This category includes resident HVAC control applications such as proportional integral and derivative control, real-time clock function, daylight savings time switch-over, time base start stop programs, enthalpy control, optimum start stop, holiday scheduling, night setback, power demand limiting, duty cycling, lighting control, and fire and smoke control.

Digital Controller Application Software/Site Specific Customizing Software. Text or graphic-based program editing features needed to allow the user or owner of the control system to make changes to application software. This software specifies what utilities are built into the controller or central console to allow new control programs to be written, edited, compiled, and error-checked and describes how the user can modify existing program code or graphic programs to affect changes in HVAC units or other building equipment.

Sequence of Operation. Brief descriptions of how each control loop (for example, mixed air, cooling coil, fan start/stop) is to be controlled, much like the comments provided with ATC automatic control contractors sequences shown on drawings or application program listings.

System Reports. Listing of the various reports to be made available from each computer console, operator's terminal, and printer attached to the system including point logs, alarm logs, trend point definition reports, and trend logs, points disabled, operator override logs, console setup or configuration reports, controller and network diagnostics, controller status reports, equipment and lighting time schedule reports, temporary time schedule overrides, and so forth.

Alarm Software. Description of how system alarms are to be directed to operator devices, how they are to be displayed and printed. This section specifies how the digital controller of field panel is to analyze and filter alarms before sending it to the operator's console, how alarms are to be prioritized according to how critical the point is, and how alarms are to be inhibited while equipment is shut down and reactivated after equipment restart.

Optimum Start Stop Programs. Specification of resident or custom software to be provided in CMCS/DDC controller or field panel that calculates exactly when an air handling unit is to start to satisfy requirements for space temperature at time of building occupancy. Include reference to using space temperatures, outside air temperature, history of recovery time, using time and occupancy schedules for air handling units.

Enthalpy Program. Specification of resident or custom software and sensor hardware to be provided that calculates outside and return air enthalpy and selects the air stream that requires the least mechanical cooling while the system is in a cooling mode.

Demand Limiting Program. Specification of how the CMCS/DDC system measures electrical or across a single or multiple campuses and then controls connected electrical loads (such as motors, lights, chillers, and so forth) to reduce peak demands.

Metering. Description of exactly what type meter, steam, condensate, chilled water, natural gas, domestic water meters, is to be installed as well as the temperature, flow, and pressure ranges the meter is expected to encounter. Accuracy and repeatability of the meter is extremely important in applying utility metering to CMCS/DDC systems because only a small error over a period of time such as a month can lead to large undercharges or overcharges if external recharges are to be made. Exact specifications for location, up and down stream pipe lengths, and meter isolation for maintenance must be provided.

Utility Usage Reports. Reports specified for the building or system energy consumption provided by the CMCS/DDC vendor. Sometimes these are available as "canned reports" preinstalled by the CMCS/DDC manufacturer. The vendor is only required to fill in the blanks on a form and set a time for printing. The system does the rest. Some vendors use third-party reports that use external reports such as Microsoft Excel, or database report writers, that allow the user to create highly customized reports on almost any combination of point information archived in the system.

Terminal Controllers. Specification of a smaller self-contained DDC controller that many times are application specific such as for heat pumps, variable air volume terminals, fan coil units, and so forth. Although they are small, they usually require a detailed specification. Features such as night set points, day to night setback, occupant override, duct size, CFM minimum and maximums, and heating to cooling mode changeover must be specified here.

Pneumatic Control Devices. Description of any required pneumatic control devices, such as electric pressure (E/P) used for minimum outside air damper interlock, copper and polypneumatic tubing to be installed, any pneumatic controls such as room thermostats, humidity high-limit sensors, and so forth.

See Figure 41-1 for an example of a CMCS/DDC sequence of operation and a point input/output schedule usually included in a new system specification.

CMCS/DDC System Purchases

An important step that must always be done before awarding a CMCS/DDC contract is a thorough evaluation of all bidders' proposals. Many colleges and universities develop written bid evaluation criteria and include them as part of both the request for proposal and project specification. This way all vendors have a clear idea early on of how they will be judged. This eliminates confusion and arguments later and sometimes prevents lawsuits over the awarding of bids. This practice is especially useful if bid price can be outweighed by other evaluation factors.

Good evaluation forms follow contract specifications exactly but turn specification requirements into a list of short, probing questions. The form should be divided into sections that follow the specification, and a place should be provided to enter a score and a short comment if necessary. A weighing factor should be used for all system items and features that are

Figure 41-1

Typical Generic DDC Sequence of Operation Guide Specifications

SECTION 15985—SEQUENCE OF OPERATION

1.01   SUBMITTALS

A. Written sequence of operation to be submitted with shop drawing submittal of Section 15970

Part 2—PRODUCTS

2.01   GENERAL

A. The HVAC with controls shall be installed and programmed to perform as described in this section, and as applicable to the specific project.

PART 3—EXECUTION

3.01   SEQUENCE OF OPERATION

A. Start/Stop (S/S) AHU
   1. With the H-O-A switch on the starter in the "H" position, the pneumatic system shall be energized and the system safety devices shall protect the circuit.
   2. With the H-O-A switch on the starter in the "H" position, the unit shall start.
   3. With the H-O-A switch on the starter in the "A" position, the unit will operate in response to DDC control and system safety circuits.
   4. Programs
      a. Time of Day Schedule
   5. Control Points

	AI	AO	DI	IO
a. Start/Stop				X
b. Status			X	

K. Supply Air Temperature (SAT) Control, AHU.

   1. SAT setpoint established by DDC controller.
   1. SAT reset based on requirements of individual terminal box with the most cooling requirement (that is, zone temperature with the most deviation to high side of setpoint).
//OR//
   1. SAT is reset down until all zone temperatures are satisfied. Conversely SAT is reset up as zone setpoints all deviate to the low side.

2. DDC controller shall reset the mixed air temp (MAT) control loop setpoint (economizer control) and the heating coil leaving air temp (LAT) control loop setpoint, to correlate to SAT setpoint.
3. SAT shall modulate the cooling coil valve to maintain SAT setpoint.
4. MAT control loop shall modulate the economizer dampers to maintain MAT setpoint.
5. Heating coil LAT shall modulate the heating coil valve to maintain HC/LAT setpoint.

//FACE AND BYPASS DAMPER CONTROL, AHU//

6. DDC controller shall modulate face and bypass air dampers and hot water coil valve in concert, to achieve coil LAT setpoint.

//OR//

6. DDC controller shall open the face dampers to full open to the coil, and modulate the heating valve (steam or hot water) to maintain coil LAT.
7. When the outside air temperature falls below 40°F (adjustable), DDC controller shall open the heating valve (steam or hot water) to full open to the coil, and modulate the face and bypass dampers to achieve SAT setpoint.
8. Programs
   a. DDC-PID Setpoint Control
   b. DDC calculation of:
   —Time between reset adjustments
   —Reset adjustment
   —Rate of temperature change limit

9. Control points

	AI	AO	DI	DO
a. SAT	X			
b. MAT	X			
c. HC/LAT			X	
d. Economizer dampers		X		
e. Hot water (or steam) control valve		X		
f. Chilled water control valve		X		

important to the success of the system. If the specification includes energy savings and other system performance criteria, these should be included in the evaluation. Columns should be added to allow each vendor to be scored for all questions, and a place for writing in their total score should be included.

Before signing a CMCS contract, it is important to check the long-term financial stability and experience of the prospective contractor. This is especially important if the institution will be dealing with unknown distributors and manufacturers' representatives. Many construction and facilities management departments use the university's legal counsel to obtain copies of financial statements and to check into other legal, financial, or other contract disputes that might affect a vendor's performance on the project. It is not uncommon for distributors to lose a franchise or drop a CMCS/DDC product line in the middle of a project. The best way to know a vendor is to check his or her track record. Call several of the vendor's customers, not only the references provided by a vendor. When calling a vendor's customer, talk to the workers who use and maintain the system and to the financial executive who approved or obtained financing for the project. Does the system work as specified? Is it saving as much money as the vendor said it would?

Purchase of single-vendor proprietary CMCS/DDC systems will become harder to defend as campus-wide systems integration becomes the accepted norm, as they have in the computer industry. Because CMCS/DDC systems on college and university campuses form large proprietary networks, many state architects have allowed colleges and universities to write proprietary specifications to expand their existing systems. On some projects, project architects and engineers write specifications that require alternative vendors to totally integrate their systems into existing CMCS/DDC systems. As a result, most vendors decline to bid on these projects. This is changing rapidly, however, because many vendors have successfully built multiprotocol drivers for their operator consoles, allowing their systems to communicate with several vendors' field panels.

An important role for consultants is to try to eliminate unqualified vendors or distributors from bidding on projects. This is usually done by writing tight technical and performance specifications. Some require vendors to have at least 10 years of experience; others require that a vendor or distributor have 50 percent of their work to be within a 100-mile radius of the job site. Many consultants write specifications that require contractors to be wholly owned branches of a CMCS/DDC system manufacturer, rather than distributors.

CMCS/DDC Installation

One of the most exciting projects in the facilities management department is the installation of a new energy management/DDC system. This is especially true for new campus-wide systems. With the new equipment come new people from the architectural and engineering firms, control company, electricians, and field technicians all asking questions. Facilities operation and maintenance on college and university campuses is really interesting! Nowhere else does the size of the facilities organization produce the continuous level of renovation or the new buildings to visit and to learn about.

New CMCS/DDC systems bring new challenges for learning about, operating, and maintaining buildings and equipment. Frequently much is learned after adding a new DDC, sensors, and controllers to an existing piece of equipment. Operating characteristics and a new set of problems may be uncovered. Adding a software-based digital controller to a valve or damper or monitoring a coil or refrigeration unit can take on new meaning. Trying to control a worn-out damper or a leaking valve and recording detailed point information showing the problem in black and white brings new light to the subject of preventive and corrective maintenance. The installation of a CMCS/DDC system is usually a powerful catalyst for repairing and fine tuning neglected or malfunctioning buildings and equipment.

Installing a new system takes common sense and an understanding of heating and air conditioning principles and practices. Installing sensors requires that the installer understand the problems of air stratification and practical thermodynamics. Choosing the correct sensor and the right sensor location is important in obtaining accuracy and a true representative temperature. Sensors should be placed as far away from the HVAC system coils as possible and out of stratified air streams. Sampling of the coil discharge should always be done, if possible, before installation to find the most representative condition. Averaging sensors should always be used where outside and return air are mixed, for face and bypass dampers on coils, and as far away from the mixing point as possible. Sensors in piping should be installed inside thermowells and also as far away from mixing locations, but not far enough for feedback delays or tuning problems to be introduced. Flow meter locations should be carefully shown on piping drawings and designed in strict adherence to the meter manufacturers recommendations as to required up-stream and down-stream pipe diameters. Obstructions such as thermometers, sensors, and other sources of turbulence must also be kept away from meter flow sensors. Air flow pick-up sensors for VAV terminals are a particular problem. Sufficient up-stream diameters of straight duct must be provided if they are to work properly and few do. Digital inputs such as auxiliary contacts in motor starters, alarm limit switches, and on pressure switches must be carefully selected for the low voltage and current levels in CMCS/DDC circuits and so that dirt and vibration from equipment does not interfere with their operation. Pressure switches and settings for fan or pump status indication and alarms must be carefully selected and replaced if necessary to meet the actual mid-range of operation encountered.

Digital control panels should be installed in locations near the equipment they serve, in well-lit, vibration-free, clean, and as cool and dry an environment as possible. Controller cabinets and accessory panels should be accessible but in protected locations. Terminal equipment controllers should be located on or near the terminal unit, but must be accessible through drop panels or adequately sized access panels in plastered ceilings. Service personnel must have adequate room around ducts, piping, other structural components if cabinets or panels are to be properly serviced and replaced.

41.3 CMCS/DDC SYSTEMS AND SOFTWARE

CMCS/DDC Controller Hardware

Digital controllers come in many shapes and sizes and a wide variety of internal configurations. Some are designed to handle many pieces of equipment—sometimes entire equipment rooms—whereas other handle only a single, application-specific piece of equipment (e.g. one air handler or a heat pump). Older controllers tend to be more centralized, whereas newer ones have become what is called *distributed*. Distributed systems move controller hardware and software closer to the point of sensing and control, and therefore, the wiring costs and large-scale failures associated with the larger, cabinet-sized DDC controllers are reduced. However, because distributed systems are more dependent on their networks, they are more communications intensive, require higher speed, and must be carefully designed and protected from electrical interface (Figure 41-2).

DDC controllers all contain some sort of printed circuit board containing a microprocessor, random access memory (RAM), some type of nonvolatile read-write memory, and various support circuitry. Most controllers are designed to be either general purpose or application specific. General purpose controllers allow different I/O point combinations and custom control applications. Currently nearly all general purpose controllers use universal inputs and outputs. These I/Os are usually software programmable to dry contact, thermistor, or various current or voltage input levels. Most general purpose controllers contain ample input and output (I/O) points; some vendors offer controller I/Os with different point counts. Most controllers are also designed with connectors or sub-LANs that act as an expansion bus for adding many additional points.

Application-specific controllers are typically designed for the type of equipment they control. They are most often single-board controls mounted directly in or on the equipment. Their control sequences and I/O point counts are often appropriate for only one application. However, some application-specific controllers are either partly or fully programmable, which greatly improves their adaptability in unique situations.

CMCS/DDC Controller Software & Development

All CMCS/DDC systems allow for some method of developing, testing, and downloading control programs to field controllers. Most systems also allow for the creation and compiling of controller applications programs

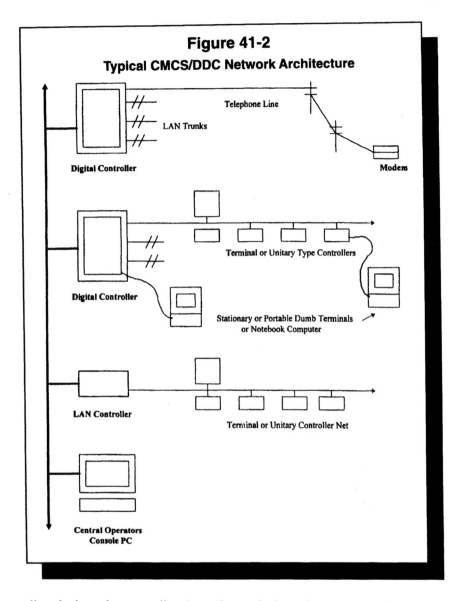

Figure 41-2

Typical CMCS/DDC Network Architecture

directly into the controller through terminals or laptop personal computers in the field.

Controller application software is usually site specific because it is designed to handle the functional requirements of each air handler, chiller, and so forth. The software contains the unique sensor and output point names, set points, logic, control statements, and routines.

Many application programs are constructed by selecting from libraries of rewritten subroutines designed for typical HVAC system functions.

Some systems use a text editor for creating line programs, and some use fill-in-the-blank forms or templates for configuring proportional, integral, and derivative control loops. Line programming uses a library of statements and arrays of Boolean, mathematical, and logical operations that can be strung together to construct powerful custom-built programs. Some application programs use graphical programming techniques that incorporate diagrammatic schematic logic to build executable program code. All of these techniques can be used for the control of all types of air handlers, terminal units, boilers, pumps, chillers, cooling towers, etc., directly from logic stored and executed in the field controller's microprocessor.

Application languages are designed to perform the majority of standard HVAC functions very efficiently. These include control functions such as dry bulb and enthalpy control of mixed air, preheat, chilled water, hot deck, cold deck, reheat, coil control, supply air static pressure, supply and return fan tracking, and humidity control. Procedural languages using line programming usually take a BASIC language-like approach.

Digital Controller Software Programming   Programming direct digital controls can be a fascinating but challenging process. The best control systems software is developed by people who have hands-on experience and field knowledge of building systems (e.g., heating, ventilating, air conditioning, and refrigeration), as well as knowledge and skill in a particular controller's programming language. This combination is hard to come by. Unfortunately the tendency is for people to be strong in one or the other. Those who have gone to a technical or four-year college and have had formal software training usually have not had time or the inclination to operate and rebuild building mechanical equipment. Finding people with the combined talents or developing such talents is a real challenge for college and university facilities managers. Training programs that combine both theory and application of mechanical, electrical, and software programming are badly needed. Typical facilities departments, even in larger institutions, usually have only a few key people who really understand their CMCS/digital control system software. Certainly this is a hindrance to operations that requires many well-rounded, informed, and educated workers to operate and maintain high-quality facilities.

Control system programming requires knowledge of HVAC system, physometric theory, and the intended sequence of operation. With regard to functionality and performance, programmers must share an understanding of what the design engineer has in mind for each sensing and control point specified in the I/O listing. This can be obtained only by insisting that consulting or in-house engineers write performance specifications that include detailed control sequences keyed to point I/O schedules. In cases where older control systems are being retrofitted with DDC, then an understanding of the operational characteristics of the HVAC units, the original control sequences, and any improvements made to the system is needed. Control programs should not be written while sitting on an old paste bucket in front of the controller. Many automatic control contractors do this, and the results are usually not very good. They should be structured and standardized to a design standard.

Program Development and Documentation   Many colleges and universities can improve their operations by taking the time to develop procedures for software development and clear documentation requirements for CMCS/DDC programs for both new construction and in-house control system installations and revision. The vast majority of DDC installations have been, and continue to be, delivered without accurate software documentation.

Development of DDC applications is made easier by using certain programming techniques. Most programs used by a large number of people and maintained over a long period of time must be developed and modified using strict access, design, and documentation rules.

The first step is to insist on program development procedures that use structured programming methods. Structured programming stresses the importance of using consistent methods and clearly defined rules when writing programs. Structure helps to eliminate the ambiguity that individuals invariably write into their programs. It stresses the importance of logical program flow, modularity, and the development process. Logical program flow follows the sequence in which program decisions are usually made. Modularity is the characteristic of structured programming that divides the program into logical or modular parts. This modularity provides independence to each part of the program and improves the efficiency of writing, testing, and maintaining a program.

Structured programs allow a program to be tested "from the top down." Many DDC systems using the common forms of line programs have features that assist the programmer in top-down analysis of their programs. Top-down testing verifies that the individual modules fit and work together as a total functional program. Many vendors include a simple diagnostic feature to their program editors that adds what are called *trace bits*. These indicators point out to the programmer which lines of a program are executing under certain conditions. Clearing trace bits and forcing execution of a program can show the programmer or technician exactly where programs are hanging up or sequences are being skipped over.

Proper documentation of program code is extremely important in the development and long-term maintenance of digital control software. Typical documentation includes flow charting, block diagrams, and decision tables, but the most common method is the embedding of comments near each functional block of program code (Figure 41-3).

Figure 41-3

Typical CMCS/DDC Application Program: PPCL

Program Report   Cabinet 83 All Lines   16:34 24-Jul-1996

```
ET  1240  OIP (COM83," MIXED AIR CONTROL")
ET  1250  OIP (COM83," ---------------- ")
ET  1260  OIP (COM83," C ")
ET  1270  SAMPLE (1) IF (D03MT1 .LE. 32767) THEN D03MT1 = D03MT1 + 1
ET  1280  IF (D03SF .NE. PRFON ) THEN $LOC1 = 0.0 ELSE $LOC1 = D03MIG
ET  1290  TABLE (D03MT1,$LOC6 ,0,200,180,80,300,79,420,D03MSP)
ET  1300  LOOP (0,D03MT,D03MLO,$LOC6 ,D03MPG,$LOC1 ,0,1,4.0,3.0,15.0,0)
ET  1310  DBSWIT (1,DOAT,68.0,70.0,D03EC)
ET  1320  IF (D03SF .NE. PRFON .OR. D03EC .EQ. OFF ) THEN GOTO 1350
ET  1330  D03MD = D03MLO
ET  1340  GOTO 1360
ET  1350  SET (2.0,D03MT1,D03MD)
ET  1360  ON ($LOC1 )
ET  1370  OIP (COM83," C ")
ET  1380  OIP (COM83," ---------------- ")
ET  1390  OIP (COM83," PREHEAT CONTROL")
ET  1400  OIP (COM83," ---------------- ")
ET  1410  OIP (COM83," C ")
ET  1420  IF (D03SF .NE. PRFON ) THEN $LOC1 = 0.0 ELSE $LOC1 = D03PIG
ET  1430  LOOP (0,D03PT,D03PLO,D03PSP,D03PPG,$LOC1 ,0,1,5.0,2.0,12.0,0)
ET  1440  IF (D03SF .NE. PRFON ) THEN GOTO 1490
ET  1450  DBSWIT (1,DOAT,32.0,34.0,D03WIN)
ET  1460  IF (D03WIN .EQ. ON ) THEN D03PHV = 2.0 ELSE TABLE (D03PLO,D03PHV,0
          ,2,10,11)
ET  1470  IF (D03WIN .EQ. ON ) THEN TABLE (D03PLO,D03PD,0,3,10,15) ELSE D03P
          D = 2.0
ET  1480  GOTO 1500
ET  1490  SET (2.0,D03PD,D03PHV)
ET  1500  ON ($LOC1 )
ET  1510  OIP (COM83," C ")
ET  1520  OIP (COM83," ---------------- ")
ET  1530  OIP (COM83," COOLING COIL CONTROL")
ET  1540  OIP (COM83," ---------------- ")
ET  1550  OIP (COM83," C ")
ET  1560  IF (D03SF .NE. PRFON ) THEN $LOC1 = 0.0 ELSE $LOC1 = D03DIG
ET  1570  LOOP (0,D03DT,D03DLO,D03DSP,D03DPG,$LOC1 ,0,1,10.0,2.0,15.0,0)
ET  1575  DBSWIT (0,D03DCV,12.0,14.0,D03CVF)
ET  1580  IF (D03SF .NE. PRFON ) THEN GOTO 1620
ET  1590  DBSWIT (0,DOAT,48.0,50.0,D03SUM)
ET  1600  IF (D03SUM .EQ. ON ) THEN D03DCV = D03DLO ELSE D03DCV = 2.0
ET  1610  GOTO 1630
ET  1620  SET (2.0,D03DCV)
```

Courtesy of Landis and Gyr.

Graphic Programming   There are significant advantages to graphic programming. Most graphic programming languages somewhat resemble pneumatic control schematics still in use in many campus buildings. Graphic programming languages provide basic logical functions and simple math functions, Boolean logic, relay-and-switch logic, conversion, proportional-integral-derivative (PID) control loops, and time clock functions. The graphic format allows the programmer to construct a diagrammatic representation of HVAC objects that have distinct functional attributes understood by both the programmer and users.

Graphic programming has the distinct advantage of combining control program development and point databases with built-in documentation capabilities. The ability to color code functional blocks and connecting lines, to label blocks and lines, and to build up layers of related graphics makes the graphic program easy to read and to follow.

In addition, the graphic format allows for a powerful simulation process to test the program off line. Programs can be simulated by entering test values or conditions as inputs or calculations. Time can also be simulated from slow to fast forward. Like the program trace bits used in line programming, through color changes in lines connecting function blocks, flaws in the site-specific application software in graphic programming can be found quickly and corrected prior to connecting the system to real building systems.

Digital Controller Software Applications

Tuning DDC Controllers   Anyone who has experience with direct digital controls knows that the tuning and calibration of DDC control loops is one of the most important tasks an HVAC control technician can perform. The basic DDC control loop consists of a sensor, a control program, and a control signal of some type. DDC control loops are analogous to the entire receiver controller in pneumatic systems. Most of the typical CMCS/DDC system is made up of these loops. They are the foundation of the DDC system, and they must be properly tuned if optimal control and operating efficiency are to be obtained.

Well-maintained DDC systems require that an experienced technician perform manual or automatic loop tuning on a periodic basis. If improperly tuned, temperatures or pressures will sometimes oscillate widely above and below the desired set point. Sometimes loops will cycle several times a minute, causing excessive wear on valves and dampers. In addition, systems will waste tremendous amounts of energy when heating and cooling coils cycle on and off in front of each other, which is a frequent occurrence in many systems. Poor loop tuning is perhaps the most common cause of frozen coils.

To eliminate these types of conditions, the technician must calculate and then manually enter various PID values into the controller and observe system responses. In most systems this is done by trial and error. Good loop tuning can take from a few minutes to several hours or more. Loop tuning takes experience, skill, patience, and time.

Self-tuning digital controllers have been developed that eliminate most of the effort and time required for manual tuning. These newer controllers contain loop tuning software either in firmware or in software applied externally to automatically bump loop output and measure system response. After measuring the response, the control calculates the proper PID gains for the loop. The new gains are then either displayed for the technician to enter manually or they are automatically entered into the control program.

Self-tuning controllers can increase the accuracy and stability of a control loop to the point where a coil discharge temperature can be controlled within less than 1° for a period of several months or more in some cases. Although this is rarely needed in most HVAC systems, the ability to automatically adjust set points for optimal efficiency and to be assured that the system will in fact go to and hold the new setting is very important.

Set Point Optimization   Many older pneumatic control systems operated with set points set in the same place for the life of the system. Set points were typically chosen by the design engineer to meet maximum design conditions, which occur only a few days per year. Because of their limited communications capabilities, pneumatic controllers had little knowledge of what the other controllers were doing. It was impossible to set up global control strategies or to really optimize set points throughout an air handler, much less a building.

Unfortunately, many potentially powerful DDC systems are still being designed and operated in much the same way as these older systems with fixed settings or adjusted based on one isolated variable (e.g., outside air temperature). DDC systems with improved communication and flexible software capabilities should be used to optimize overall system efficiency. Managers should insist that more powerful DDC software be developed that takes advantage of all of the information to minimize the use of steam and hot and chilled water.

Time-of-Day Start/Stop Scheduling   The most basic and the most effective energy savings comes from turning off energy-consuming systems when they are not needed. All CMCS/DDC systems have applications for scheduling the start-up and shutdown of building equipment. Modern time-of-day scheduling programs allow operators to create numerous time schedules based on weekly, monthly, and 365-day calendars. Many systems include an actual annual calendar showing the months for several years, onto which control points can be assigned. Many have features that allow groups of commonly controlled equipment to be assembled as one schedule to simplify rescheduling, if necessary.

An important feature is the temporary override feature. This allows the system operator or a worker at a field panel to enter the override to an existing schedule for a piece of equipment. Overrides can usually be entered anytime prior to an existing schedule for a piece of equipment. Overrides can usually be entered anytime prior to an event and will erase after the event has occurred. For example, say an air handling unit for an auditorium is scheduled to go off automatically at 10:00 pm Monday through Friday. However, next Tuesday a lecture is being held that will last until 11:00 pm. A temporary override is entered to keep the unit on until 11:30 pm on that night. Afterward the system will go back to the regular Tuesday schedule.

Most systems allow operators to change time-of-day programs both at operators' consoles and at field controllers. Scheduling from both these locations requires some coordination and good communication. Programs created at the console must be downloaded to controllers where the control points reside, and schedule changes made at the field controller must be saved to the operator's console hard disk if system schedules are to be accurately maintained. Because it is easy to forget changes, even hours after they are made, many systems have automatic upload capability or at least allow the console operator to review any changes made at the equipment room level.

Optimum Start-Stop Control   One of the most common digital controller energy savings applications is called *optimum start/stop*. In its simplest form this program uses outside and inside air temperature sensors and a predictive algorithm to calculate the start lead time necessary to bring a building space to its normal operating set point before scheduled occupancy.

There are several variations, including having the operator or technician help the system by entering "constants" that are adjusted until the HVAC system starts, with enough lead time to adequately heat or cool the space. Here the constant represents the thermal inertia of building mass, a factor that has been historically difficult for most controllers to learn on their own. More advanced systems use an adaptive program to calculate the rate of heat-up or cool-down and a prediction based on curve-fitting techniques. It then adjusts its start-and-stop multipliers as it learns the thermal response. Some vendors take a more simplified approach and build look-up tables that relate various outside air and interior temperatures collected over the preceding several days or weeks (Figure 41-4).

Because these programs are complex and prone to errors, they must be carefully tested prior to final acceptance. The best way to do this is to set up a multipoint trend log that records space temperature, fan start time, outside temperature, and before and after occupancy time. These logs must be run until the manager is satisfied that the optimum start programs for each HVAC unit work properly. Once a program works, then only during preventive maintenance inspections HVAC technicians should be required to review optimum start trend logs and verify proper operation of these programs.

Air Handling Unit Enthalpy Control   Another DDC application program commonly applied to air handling units is the *enthalpy economizer cycle*.

Figure 41-4

Typical Fan Start/Stop Schedule

```
05-JUN-96
17:14                       Zone/Schedule Report
Sections Reported:  Point Member List/ Occupancy Schedule/ Control Schedule?
Days    Reported: Mon/ Tue/ Wed/ Thu/ Fri/ Sat/ Sun/ Hol/ Spe/
-----------------------------------------------------------------------------


Zone: CAB0009              LANGSAM  AHU 4-1

  Section: Point Member List
                     <commands enabled>    <recommand>    <warmstart delay>
    L41PRI               Yes               Yes         5
    L41PRS               Yes               Yes         5

  Section: Occupancy Schedule

  Section: Control Schedule

  Monday:
    0600              ON             L41PRI
    2359              OFF            L41PRI

  Tuesday:
    0600              ON                 L41PRI
    2359              OFF        L41PRI

  Wednesday:
    0600              ON             L41PRI
    2359              OFF            L41PRI

  Thursday:
    0600              ON             L41 PRI
    2359              OFF            L41PRI

  Friday:
    0600              ON             L41PRI
    2359              OFF            L41PRI

  Saturday:
    0600              ON             L41PRI
    2359              OFF            L41PRI

  Sunday:
    0600              ON             L41PRI
    2359              OFF            L41PRI
```

This program is designed to measure the total heat content of both the return air and outside air temperature entering the air handling unit. To reduce the mechanical cooling requirements of a system, the DDC controller must determine which airstream is the coolest in terms of total enthalpy (latent and sensible heat content of the air). If the outside enthalpy is lower than that of the return, then the controller opens the maximum outside air damper, and the cooler source of air is used.

Care should be taken when calculating enthalpy savings. Bin-type charts are available from the National Weather Service showing the average outside air temperatures and relative humidity and number of hours per year they occur. These make evaluating the potential savings much easier. Because many locations experience only limited conditions in which both the temperature and the humidity are useful and because obtaining accurate measurements sometimes is difficult to accomplish, caution and great care should be taken when specifying and installing this application.

Like the other digital control applications, each enthalpy control program should be thoroughly tested and evaluated. Trend logs should record outside and return air temperatures, humidity, and the outside and return air dampers control points for each air handling unit. During HVAC system preventive maintenance, mechanics and technicians should be trained to review these logs (especially during the spring and fall months) to verify correct operation. Because of the narrow band of BTUs per pound that occurs between outside and return air enthalpy, and the inherent accuracy problems sometimes seen with humidity sensors, problems can easily occur in these applications. Many technicians have observed dampers operating completely in reverse, bringing in 100 percent of the hottest, most humid air possible. Enthalpy programs can be worthwhile, but managers cannot be too careful when applying or maintaining these widespread control applications.

Lighting Control   Lighting is the single largest user of electric power in most campus buildings. Depending on the building, this represents 50 to 75 percent of all electric usage. Lighting also contributes a significant heat load for air conditioning. If applied and then managed correctly, CMCS/DDC lighting control can save 20 to 30 percent of this power. On many campuses, the addition of just a few extra points on the digital controller has proven to be an excellent way of reducing electrical and air conditioning costs.

Lighting controls can be integrated into CMCS/DDC systems in several ways. Some vendors manufacture and install special lighting control panels specifically designed for this. These panels are simply added to the building's control system network along with other HVAC application controllers. DDC lighting panel can be located next to the lighting panel board. Power is then routed from breakers to the DDC lighting controller. Alternatively, room lighting can be switched at the room in conjunction with the light switch and an occupancy sensor as described below.

Lighting system override switches are important to the success of a CMCS/DDC lighting management system. Many colleges use a hands-off automatic switch or a keyed switch in a convenient location on each floor for this purpose.

Room DDC Control   The trend toward digital control at the room level has been steadily gaining momentum and has almost eliminated the use of the pneumatic room thermostats in new construction. Room DDC controls add a new dimension to building operational information and control.

With room DDC HVAC control, a small microprocessor-based controller is located at the room terminal device (VAV box, fan coil unit ventilator, and so forth). Sensors are installed to measure room temperature and coil temperature. Analog and digital outputs are provided to control damper actuators, heating and cooling control valves, relays for electric heat, fans, and so forth. Heat pump and single zone air handling unit controllers also are available.

Because terminal units use common applications and their control sequences tend to be identical from room to room, many unitary or terminal equipment controllers use firmware for their programming. Control sequences usually are stored in some type of memory device (for example, FlashROM, EPROM, EEPROM) and only setpoints, PID gains, and various options can be customized by the user. This type of programming tends to increase operational reliability and to reduce controller hardware and installation costs. However, when specifications call for special sequences, fixed program type controllers are a real disadvantage. Some vendors provide controllers that allow a mixture of fixed and custom programming, and some offer totally user-programmed units. Controller customization is important where global system optimization is required, or where special control sequences or features are needed.

To make the terminal controllers an integral part of the CMCS/DDC system, controllers are usually connected together to form their own local area networks (LANs), sometimes called *subLANs*, which are connected to larger centralized digital controllers at the air handling unit level. Building mechanics and console operators can view and adjust room temperatures and other point information.

Many system design engineers specify that all the rooms served by an air handling unit be connected to the air handling unit controller. This way, the rooms and the HVAC unit become a totally integrated control system. Air handling unit setpoints can be optimally set to the needs of the rooms served.

Room DDC/Occupancy Control   Controlling room heating, ventilation, and air conditioning on the basis of actual room usage can generate considerable additional savings over traditional air handling unit scheduling. Using a standard occupancy sensor as people enter or leave a room, the terminal unit controller automatically switches from the night to the day mode. Night mode setpoints lower or raise room temperature to unoccupied setpoints. When a person enters the space, the occupancy sensor immediately signals the controller to return the system to the day mode setting, and the room quickly returns to occupancy temperature and ventilation rates. As rooms become vacant, the occupancy sensor will switch off the ventilation, heating or cooling, and room lighting. When occupancy schedules are known in advance, traditional time-of-day schedules can direct the terminal controllers so that air conditioning can be turned on in advance to bring the room to its normal temperature before occupancy.

Studies of occupancy diversity show that occupancy temperature and ventilation control at the room level can save significant additional energy over simple air handling unit start/stop control. Compared with time-based control, a demand-based system can reduce average annual energy consumption by 30 to 50 percent.

Equipment Scheduling   On many college and university campuses, air conditioning and lighting CMCS/DDC control schedules for campus buildings are based on the earliest building occupancy and the end of the last class or the evening cleaning schedule. Developing and adjusting these schedules, the campus academic calendar, and the many special events held throughout the campus facilities. This is no easy task because it requires considerable coordination of many individuals throughout the campus community (for example, mailing of schedules, telephone calls, and memos passed around). After all the information is gathered, then the CMCS/DDC system start/stop schedules must be permanently or temporarily changed. Rescheduling frequently does not occur. For example, a new faculty or staff member does not know or forgets the proper procedure and fails to reserve a room, or classes are moved. As a result, the air conditioning and lighting are turned off and the lecture hall or classroom is hot and stuffy. Frequently, facilities management gets the blame, whether they deserve it or not. As a result, eventually the evening or weekend shutdown scheduling falls by the wayside, and many systems are left running to prevent dissatisfaction by the administration, faculty, and staff.

A major problem found in trying to optimally schedule HVAC systems in large campus buildings is the way HVAC systems are arranged and how room and event scheduling is done. Because the campus room scheduling department does not know anything about the building systems that must be run or their operating costs, they schedule simply by room availability and seating capacity. Frequently only a small portion of an HVAC system is really needed, and many empty offices; conference rooms; and classrooms are ventilated, heated, or cooled merely for the couple of rooms on the system being used. Sometimes major portions of buildings have to run late into the evening for one room. Systems can be better laid out and zoned for common use, or smaller systems can be installed.

Occupancy Control of Room Temperature and Ventilation   Most college and university air conditioning and lighting systems schedules are based on the earliest building occupancy and the last class or cleaning schedule in the evening. To prevent discomfort, CMCS/DDC equipment scheduling requires careful use of quarterly or semester class and academic calendars, constant review of campus events, and frequent use of the telephone and the fax machine.

Despite earnest efforts to optimally schedule HVAC equipment one of the inherent energy-wasting problems in large institutional buildings is the number of empty classrooms, offices, and conference rooms that have to be ventilated, heated, or cooled merely to operate a couple of scheduled rooms. Fortunately, reliable technology and modifications to air handlers and terminal boxes can help resolve this problem.

With fan systems, VAV terminals, and total room DDC control, coupled with occupancy sensors, as people enter or leave a room, the room terminal can automatically start up or shut down ventilation, heating, and cooling systems. For unoccupied rooms, the quantity of ventilation is automatically reduced, and thus the demand on the heating and cooling coils, humidifier, and fan motor is also reduced.

Controlling ventilation and air conditioning systems on the basis of actual demand can save colleges and universities considerable money. In demand-based control, the volume of air is based on actual requirements. Whenever there is a significant fluctuation in the number of individuals occupying a space, the air supply is adjusted. Compared with time-based control, a demand-based system can reduce average annual energy consumption by 50 percent.

Specifying room DDC along with occupancy sensing also allows for a level of air handler optimization never before possible with only DDC air handlers or pneumatic room thermostats. Formerly air handlers operated without direct feedback from all of the spaces served, and the best discharge temperature and optimum coil temperatures, static pressures, and air volumes were, at best, educated guesses. With total room control, air handler optimization is truly possible (Figure 41-5).

Balancing and Commissioning Aid   A side benefit of total room DDC is the information it gives to the air balancer. Installing DDC at the VAV terminal box allows the balancer to read the air volumes delivered to each room. With this information and point data on the air handling unit, the balancer can quickly evaluate and test an entire HVAC system. In the past, balancers had to rely on manual terminal-by-terminal measurement and adjustment methods and had to make repeated readjustments to balance a system. Now, with proper training in the use of the digital control system, balancers can test entire systems as a whole. They can check fan capacity against design requirements and measure real system diversity by adjusting room setpoints or terminal unit volumes.

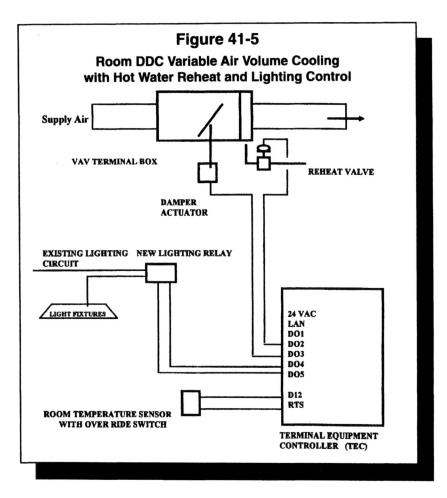

Figure 41-5

Room DDC Variable Air Volume Cooling with Hot Water Reheat and Lighting Control

Supply Air

VAV TERMINAL BOX

REHEAT VALVE

DAMPER
ACTUATOR

EXISTING LIGHTING   NEW LIGHTING RELAY
CIRCUIT

LIGHT FIXTURES

24 VAC
LAN
DO1
DO2
DO3
DO4
DO5

DI2
RTS

ROOM TEMPERATURE SENSOR
WITH OVER RIDE SWITCH

TERMINAL EQUIPMENT
CONTROLLER (TEC)

Many DDC manufacturers have designed their terminal controls interface to aid the balancer by providing convenient reports and the specific points required for balancing a terminal unit. Advanced terminal controllers request user input at the appropriate stages and perform all calculations to improve the efficiency of balancing various types of equipment. These controllers allow the balancer to check such setup parameters as actuator rotation and linkage; adjustment of rotation; flow calibration constants; fan speed; reheat minimum flow; parallel fan set point; and automatic logging of important balancing values such as minimum and maximum CFM, reheat, and control loop calibration values.

Air balancers must be capable of understanding and using the DDC control system to successfully balance an air handling unit with its room VAV terminals. They must be able to take readings with standard calibrated balancing tools such as hoods, pitot tubes, and velometers and compare them to readings obtained from a DDC system terminal. When corrections to the volume readings from the controller are necessary, balancers must be able to enter in correction factors, so that the DDC system can be made accurate and a trusted source of information.

Chiller Optimization   Most colleges and universities have combinations of centralized chiller plants and packaged chillers or absorbers scattered throughout their campuses. On many campuses with large chilled water distribution systems, a CMCS/DDC control system is used to control both the central refrigeration equipment and the building chilled water systems. Because campus-wide chilled water distribution systems can be so thermally and hydraulically complex, only a campus-wide CMCS/DDC system is capable of globally controlling and optimizing such a system. With a properly designed and programmed CMCS/DDC system, all of a building's flow rate, air handling chilled coil temperatures, and valve positions can be used by the central refrigeration plant controls to optimize chilled water supply temperature and select the correct number of chillers and pumps needed for any given condition. In addition, building information should be used to anticipate cooling demands and to allow operators to stay ahead of the cooling needs of a campus. On some campuses the global CMCS/DDC information is used to directly start (or signal the operators to manually start) central refrigeration plant chilled water pumps and chillers, thus saving hundreds of hours of unnecessary operation and considerable energy expense.

In buildings where there are two or more independent chillers, the CMCS/DDC control program can decide when the cooling load is great enough to start a second chiller. Some systems also make the decision as to which chiller best meets the particular load. Many systems optimize chilled and condenser water temperatures for compressor head pressure reductions. CMCS/DDC systems can compare the additional cooling tower fan energy costs in relation to compressor motor load costs and then make the necessary set point adjustments to minimize energy usage.

Limiting Electrical Demand   Utilities base their charges to large customers on a combination of total electricity consumption (kilowatt hours) and the maximum demand (kilowatt demand) or rate of electricity usage in a certain billing period. The utility determines a user's electric demand by continually measuring and then averaging electricity load in kilowatts or megawatts for a selected demand interval (e.g., 15 or 30 minutes) or by a sliding window method, in which the highest average load in a sliding window any time during the day's demand time period is used. The interval that is the largest then becomes the basis for demand charges for the succeeding periods, which can be as long as 11 months. Demand charges are now a substantial part of any campus utility budget, and in some campuses they are as much as fifty percent of the monthly electricity bill.

An CMCS/DDC system can be programmed to limit demand to help avoid unnecessary high-demand charges. Most systems can monitor electricity demand and consumption from a group of meters. With this information, the electrical demand programs resident in central computers or DDC field controllers forecast or predict the peak demands for each meter interval and calculate electrical loads to shed that will keep the demands below the preset kilowatt demand limits. On many campuses where there may be only one or a few main meters that are used for calculation of demand, demand control, or peak shaving, is difficult, if not impossible. Campuses quite frequently have demand profiles that resemble smooth bell curves. Reshaping this kind of demand usually requires that a couple of large chillers or many types of equipment responsible for smaller electrical loads be turned off for long periods of time, but of course, this is impossible. Where smaller areas; single, large buildings; or in-branch campuses are metered for demand by utility companies, demand control should certainly be investigated. Where CMCS/DDC systems control demand, they must be programmed to keep detailed records of demand intervals and load-shedding activities for program review and analysis. Sometimes these are used to verify the accuracy of utility billing, even when there is no demand control. In many localities CMCS/DDC demand control installations are eligible for demand-side management (DSM) programs and rebates.

Utility Metering   Many campuses use CMCS/DDC systems to measure purchased energy, utility plant production, and building consumption.

Chilled Water Metering. Most of chilled water metering consists of a primary flow sensing device and two accurate temperature sensors located in the chilled water supply and the return chilled water lines entering and leaving the building. Commonly, the primary flow sensor is a paddle-wheel type device, or an orifice plate. Paddle wheels are inexpensive and, if installed correctly and maintained, can be relatively accurate at moderate to high flow rates (>30 fps). To measure chilled water flow a small plastic wheel designed with a series of "paddles" sticking out from a central hub, much like a paddle-wheel boat, is mounted on a stainless steel axle that spins around as water flows past it. A small magnet mounted in the wheel is sensed each time it comes around by a transducer mounted in the body of the insertion device. Electrical pulses from the magnet travel to a frequency to milliamp or voltage transducer, where the frequency is amplified and converted to a signal compatible with the input needed by the DDC controller pulse accumulator or totalizer type input point. Orifice plates with differential pressure transmitters also are frequently used to measure chilled water flow. However, they exhibit inaccuracy at low and high flow rates and must be accurately sized to the flow they are expected to measure.

Condensate Metering. Many campuses use low-cost positive displacement water meters as a means of measuring the volume of condensate being generated in a building. These types of meters are usually selected for the highest operating temperature available from a manufacturer (+250° to 300°). Their accuracy is usually in the 1 to 5 percent range, but there is a possible loss of condensate upstream of the meter through condensate lost into the air in HVAC humidification, some cooking applications, or from leaking condensate pump seals, or opened drain valves. These problems can make these installations highly inaccurate at times. However, despite this possibility their low cost and simplicity make this method of steam metering attractive. CMCS/DDC inputs from these meters are typically by a low voltage auxiliary contact device added to the meter dial indicator at the top of the meter.

Steam Metering. Many varieties of steam meters can be used in conjunction with CMCS/DDC systems.

Electric Metering. Building electric meters can be initially ordered and retrofitted with a pulse contact that closes after a specified number of meter revolutions. This is a simple way to remotely read electric meters. For modern electronic meters, auxiliary outputs or higher level communications such as RS232, or RS485 signals can be ordered. These require the use of gateway products between the CMCS/DDC field panel and the meter. They are available from most major DDC manufacturers.

DDC Meter Software. When using the generic DDC controller to integrate several sensors and compute instantaneous demand and totalized consumption over a specified time period, the digital controller software must be carefully written and then rigorously tested to assure total meter end to end accuracy.

Condensate Meters. These types of meters should be installed with a bypass line sized minimum to meter size. Isolation valves on both ends should be installed to allow meter removal. A good quality strainer and a blowdown valve should be installed upstream of the condensate meter with a check valve installed downstream of the meter.

41.4   CMCS/DDC SYSTEM MANAGEMENT

Day-to-Day Operation of CMCS/DDC Systems

On many campuses a centralized communication or work controls center serves as the 24-hour monitoring site for the CMCS/DDC system. Other colleges and universities place an operator's console or an alarm printer in the central utilities plant, where operating engineers monitor the system for important alarms.

No matter where they are located, CMCS/DDC system operators' consoles or alarm printers must be understood and used if they are to be of value to the institution. If the CMCS/DDC system is located in a central dispatch or telephone operations center, then several well-trained individuals must be available to operate the system and the center's staff must have constant access to the maintenance staff to interpret alarms.

Many communications centers simply dispatch all of the alarms and messages coming into the system and leave the technical details and responsibilities to a CMCS/DDC technician or maintenance supervisor. This makes sense because it is very difficult to find staff personnel who have experience in telephone and customer relations, dispatching, work control, and CMCS/DDC systems.

Console Operators When a dedicated CMCS/DDC console exists in the maintenance and operations area of a facilities department, it is important that the individual(s) responsible be well trained in all of the aspects of campus, buildings, and utility operations. These individuals ensure that system operations and building performance information, alarms, and system failures are interpreted correctly and communicated to the maintenance and operations staff.

Good console operators start the diagnostic process when the CMCS/DDC detects abnormal conditions. Console operators must learn all they can about a building or HVAC system condition before dispatching a worker on a service call. Because the console operator has a tool with which to see a broader view of the campus operation, he or she can sometimes play a unique role in in-service operations: He or she can help the service personnel and perhaps utility plant operators work together to resolve problems more quickly and intelligently.

The successful CMCS/DDC system should have at the helm a facilities management operator who pushes the system to its limits to maximize comfort while minimizing energy use. Finding the right individual to accomplish this is probably the most important factor in a successful system installation. The console operator must really love his or her job, be fascinated by the idea of improving the operation of the HVAC systems and controls, and have some comfort and interest in computers.

Computer experts are certainly less valuable than are experienced HVAC personnel for operating or managing a CMCS/DDC system, as the focus here is on building systems people, and their comfort, not computer hardware and software technology.

Field Interface Terminals In addition to well-managed CMCS/DDC consoles, effective CMCS/DDC systems must be designed and made available to building operating mechanics and HVAC personnel in locations that are convenient and easy for them to use. Operators' terminals should be selected based heavily on the field mechanic's responses to questions on the ease of use of these devices. Consoles should display only the information needed to do the job. This can be a text display showing all point values or a simple graphic showing real point values inside a clearly recognizable HVAC diagram. Complex color graphic operators' consoles will scare away some of the best mechanics, and the system will then be largely ignored. Many colleges and universities place dumb terminals in all major equipment rooms so that mechanics have ready access to information on building operation.

Day-to-Day Operating Improvements   Excellence in building maintenance and operations takes discipline, persistence, and hard work. Significant operating improvements and energy cost reduction are still possible in many campus buildings well after most CMCS/DDC systems are installed. This can be accomplished by studying the systems; observing trends; and looking at the relationships between points for a long time after CMCS/DDC system software programs have been implemented, and over several seasons of the year. The goal is to gain tighter control and to correct the sometimes small operating problems and inefficiencies that can occur in most HVAC systems. To ensure the elimination of these problems, program debugging and refinement must go on for quite some time. Some colleges and universities specify blocks of additional days when the control system installer works with the maintenance staff to debug, refine, and improve a new building's DDC software programs during a six-month period.

Alarm Management   One of the most useful benefits of the CMCS/DDC system is its ability to inform facilities personnel about abnormal conditions. Early warning can be quite helpful and facilities personnel can sometimes resolve problems before the building occupants become aware of them. Alarms have saved many a frozen coil, chiller, or other equipment before serious damage occurred and expensive repairs had to be made.

Policies and procedures for dealing with alarms, writing work orders, and dispatching staff personnel to investigate alarms are important aspects of managing the day-to-day operations of a CMCS/DDC system. Many colleges and universities require console operators to dispatch and initial log all alarms and log their responses to each alarm that occurs during their shift.

Because they are usually quite large, some with thousands of sensing and control points, college and university CMCS/DDC systems sometimes have to manage large numbers of alarms. Because of high transmission speeds, only a couple of malfunctioning or poorly placed alarm limits can totally disrupt a system. Prompt investigation and correction of alarms is important to preserve trust in any alarm system. Those responsible for CMCS/DDC system management must develop clear objectives and procedures for this aspect of CMCS/DDC maintenance.

Alarm Logs   Alarm logs usually provide some kind of color-coded display and a printed list showing all current and past acknowledged alarm points active on the CMCS/DDC system. These logs are usually the most frequently observed information in any system and are used for dispatching service personnel and for making adjustments to the system.

Point Logs   Point logs allow viewing and printing the current status or value of any selected CMCS/DDC point information. Users usually can choose the building, floor, system or group, or an individual system point. Points can be also selected by categories such as alarm, disabled, priority, failed, and so forth.

Trend Logs   Trend logs are typically used to troubleshoot HVAC and other building systems. They can consist of one or more columns of point data showing changes occurring on selected points over an operator-selected time interval or on a fixed change of sensor value or status.

A trend log often is the only way to detect certain types of problems occurring in an air handler, chiller, heating, or cooling system. Because they show performance information in a linear, time-related fashion, the interactions that exist between valve positions, coil temperatures, set points, and so forth can be easily observed. A multi-point trend log allows the user to view several points side by side so that relationships between set points and actual controlled values for example can be compared more easily. Some systems also provide convenient summaries of trend data so that the user can quickly see the high, low, and average values in the logs.

Trends are invaluable for commissioning, troubleshooting, and fine tuning building systems. For example, an air handler trips out on high static pressure cutout, starter, or VFD overload because of a poorly tuned supply duct static control, which is causing the inlet vanes or a variable frequency drive to overreact. The trend log shows the valves of supply fan discharge and duct static pressures as well as the output signal to the drive. Usually after reviewing the trend log, the problem is easily identified and can be corrected quickly.

In older CMCS/DDC systems, there was a limitation for the number of trend points and the number of samples that could be stored in the memory of the controller because of limited amounts of RAM memory available to the user after point data and control programs were installed in the controller. With current control systems, with large memory capacities of a megabyte or more, or with field panels fitted with hard drives, this limitation is no longer a problem. Most newer systems also automatically upload trend data to the operator's console hard drive when the maximum allowable number of trend samples is detected.

CMCS/DDC systems allow both console operators and mechanics to add trend points to the field panel from the central operator's console or at a field controller using an operators's terminal or PC. The user selects the point name to be added to the trend and enters whether the trend is to be by time or change of value, whether it is a time-based log, the time interval between samples, and the total number of samples to be collected. The user then starts the log. After entry, the system automatically collects the required data as time intervals elapse or as changes of values occur on system sensors. Trends often are set up to run on a continuous basis. These logs may contain several days' values on a building's systems that are most important to the operator or mechanic. These allow the operators and mechanics to review an HVAC system's performance quickly and easily on a daily basis.

Team Effort   Building team effort in the day-to-day operation of a campus is extremely important for the success of facilities management service departments. Because many CMCS/DDC consoles are located in the work control center or other areas, a close working relationship must be cultivated and maintained between those in the buildings and console operators. One way to build team effort is to schedule frequent but short meetings between console and building mechanics where they can exchange views, discuss problems, and agree on ways to improve building and CMCS/DDC operations.

Many organizations develop "cookbooks" full of detailed information to assist console operators and mechanics in the operation and repair of their buildings. This book identifies equipment locations, service areas, and operation sequences. Log books can help track recurring problems, record actions, and communicate between shifts and other staff.

CMCS/DDC Training

CMCS/DDC systems are not at all tolerant of mistakes made by poorly trained maintenance workers. Small errors in a system controller (e.g., a single typing mistake) can produce highly erratic system operation, occupant discomfort, damage, and energy waste. It is extremely important that CMCS/DDC systems be operated and maintained by well-trained, knowledgeable people. Several methods for training are available.

Many control companies provide professional educational services at their home offices, at regional centers, and in local branch offices. The courses offered are specifically designed to help customers learn how to install, properly use, and maintain the company's products.

Trips away from the work site with others who have similar responsibilities and experiences is an excellent way to provide personnel with the training they need. Participation in a class at a remote training center also allows the student to get away from the day-to-day interruptions of the workplace and to concentrate on learning the new system. Because current CMCS/DDC systems provide many features, several trips will be necessary to cover all of the material.

Many vendors also offer their standard training center courses and custom-designed courses at the institution's location. These courses can be designed to meet the particular needs of the institution's workers and can be tailored to the institution's site-specific controller programs, field panel maintenance requirements, and systems operation. On-site courses are typically 2 to 10 days and are priced according to preparation time. These courses can be designed by local branch personnel after meeting with the facilities manager to determine the institution's training requirements.

Self-instructional materials such as workbooks, textbooks, and videotapes are also a good way to provide ongoing CMCS/DDC training. Many DDC system suppliers have self-instructional training products and programmed learning texts available for the asking. Many colleges and universities have found that the investment in training for installing, operating, and maintaining their CMCS/DDC systems provides a wide range of benefits. CMCS/DDC system can be a catalyst for improving the entire HVAC plant, because no other building system has such an influence on as many pieces of equipment. Workers who learn about installing these systems will find renewed interest in making sure all of the valves, dampers, and other components work properly.

CMCS/DDC System Service and Maintenance

Most colleges and universities maintain their own CMCS/DDC systems because they have very capable staff, want cost savings, and sometimes need better system maintenance than can be obtained from contractors. The extent to which the institution performs in-house maintenance depends on the critical nature of the installation; the size of the institution's staff; the speed of response that the institution can tolerate; and, of course, the budget.

In the past, many proprietary minicomputer-based CMCS systems required that colleges and universities enter into service contracts for maintenance and troubleshooting. This was true for at least the host computer, old mass storage units, and software. Many campuses with older CMCS systems still have full-service contracts for these systems.

A major reason for signing service contracts was the high cost of updating software. Some vendors imposed very high software upgrade costs for those without a contract. Currently, however, vendors provide alternatives to full contracts for college and university customers who have strong in-house capabilities. These limited contracts cover small portions of the system but allow the customer to receive service at the lower rate usually reserved for full-contract customers.

Preventive maintenance is critical to the reliable operation of any CMCS/DDC system. Despite the fact that these systems are nearly all solid state, they require sensor accuracy checks. Actuator, controller, and network diagnostic tests are important.

CMCS/DDC preventive maintenance programs can be designed like any other preventive maintenance program and added to the preventive maintenance work order and scheduling system. Many colleges and universities find it a good idea to schedule CMCS/DDC preventive maintenance along with regular HVAC preventive maintenance. This way systems are inspected and tested as a whole. Problems with components such as valves, dampers, and actuators are tested under more normal conditions that simulate real operating conditions. Even if separate staff are responsible for different parts of the system, much can be learned if mechanics and CMCS/DDC system technicians work together.

Many colleges and universities write good preventive maintenance instructions as part of their preventive maintenance programs. Preventive maintenance instructions must be included for CMCS/DDC field controllers, sensors, and other components. Many simple tests and inspections can be performed by the HVAC mechanic while doing routine preventive maintenance on a system. If preventive maintenance instructions are written by someone who thoroughly understands both the HVAC system and its controls, they can be excellent guides to testing control loop response, checking sensors and transducer input/output signals, and recording the results. These reports can then be passed on to the controls technician for further testing and repair (Figure 41-6). Trend logs are an excellent preventive maintenance tool for verifying HVAC or refrigeration system performance. Trend logs, if collected and printed regularly, can be used to measure quality and efficiency in building operations.

Every CMCS/DDC system maintenance program must include looking at the system as a whole. This involves running network and controller diagnostics, checking communication framing and time-out errors, controller cold and warm starts, checksum errors, changes to or hang-ups in programs, and point failures.

In addition, someone must be responsible for routinely backing up all controller databases and control programs, console graphics, alarm messages, time schedules, and configuration files. This can become very important in the event of unexpected hard drive or other system failures.

CMCS/DDC System Service Contracts

When entering into CMCS/DDC service contracts, it is important for managers to "stay in the driver's seat." If the contractor's standard contract

Figure 41-6
Digital Control Preventive Maintenance Instructions

Bookstore Digital Control System
Preventive Maintenance Instructions

Equip. No 0100HVAC1
Equipment........ HVAC Unit No. 1
Building ....Bookstore
Service Area.....1st, 2nd Floors North Side
Manufacturer ..Landis & Gyr
Model No...........SCU 45 Rev. 4.0
Trade ....HVAC

Work Order No. 38838/
Room No. 224
Issued Date 06/12/
PM Priority ....A
Print w/WO? ....Yes
Revision Date 12/21/

Tests and Inspections Steps:

1. Check sensor accuracy by comparing field readings with value displayed on the DDC terminal.
2. Check all digital to pneumatic valves by comparing the DPV gauge or pressure indicator with the DDC terminal displayed readings.
3. Test analog out put pneumatic transducer operation by commanding output from 3 to 18 psig. (Remember to put points back to priority "none" when tests are completed.)
4. Check trend logs for all AHU points to verify control accuracy against set point.
5. Tune control loops that are inaccurate or show excessive "cycling or hunting".

Sensor Point Name:		Output Setpoint/	Current Reading	OK	Incomplete	Needs Followup
B1MAT	Mixed Air Temperature	___	___	___	___	___
B1HCT	Heating Coil Temperature	___	___	___	___	___
BCWCNL	Chilled Water Coil Control	___	___	___	___	___
Pneumatic Output Points:						
B1MAD	Mixed Air Dampers	___	___	___	___	___
B1VLVS	Heating Valve	___	___	___	___	___
B1CWV	Chilled Water Valv	___	___	___	___	___

Notes and Commer

Workers Name: Completion Date: Labor Hours:

language is not acceptable, the manager should have it rewritten by the contractor or by facilities personnel. The service contractor should respond to the institution's terms, and not the other way around.

The contract should describe exactly what is wanted: what is to be tested, control loops to be tuned, and the performance level that is expected from the system. Monthly calendars showing when tasks are to be performed can be included. It is also worth the effort to include detailed descriptions of what should be done (e.g., test all start/stop points, verify status changes, test all alarms, print all controllers and network diagnostic logs, do backups, or refine software). If the institution's staff is doing part of the day-to-day system maintenance, everyone should know his or her responsibility.

The manager should request pre-approval for any replacement parts, if the contract is for labor only. Procedures that should be followed by the service technicians while on site must be clearly written; these should include arrival notification requirements, keys and access to buildings and rooms, coordination with staff, and any service report information desired by the manager.

For DDC systems, it is highly recommended that the contractor provide some kind of performance report that shows how well the building is operating. These reports can be in the form of trend logs, spreadsheets, or other types of system reports. If the system contains utility metering points, the report should also include a comparison of current energy consumption with base year consumption or number of BTUs expended per square foot.

Before the institution enters into a contract, the contractor should provide in writing the kinds of software upgrades the institution will be entitled to. Will the institution get all new features and enhancements, or only repairs of bugs in the current revision? Also, will the controller hardware be repaired with new or reconditioned boards?

Because CMCS/DDC control networks can be large, complex, and dynamic, service contracts require a clear understanding of expectations and good communication on the part of both parties. It is important to assign one person to coordinate and manage the CMCS/DDC contract and to evaluate the results.

41.5 CMCS/DDC NETWORKING AND INTELLIGENT BUILDINGS

This information is presented to help college and university facilities management and planning and construction staff understand some of the major changes that are occurring in the building systems integrated arena.

Intelligent Buildings

Although the term *intelligent building* has been used for more than a decade, there is still little consensus as to what really makes a building "intelligent." It appears that the intelligent building represents an evolving concept used principally among facilities managers and the architectural, engineering, and construction (A/E/C) industries. It includes a wide range of electronic and microcomputer based systems, products, and technologies that are designed to meet a wide variety of building and building user requirements. Truly intelligent buildings, for example, would eliminate much of the redundancy in typical building infrastructure, their management systems, and building information (for example, separate conduits, cabling, and wiring for DDC data, telephone, audio, fire, security, and so forth). The primary concept is that systems integration lowers first time costs, reduces the number of different user interfaces, and then over their lifetimes, reduces separate service/support staffs needed to maintain each of them.

Conceivably, with buildings that are truly intelligently designed, an opportunity for real improvement in the effectiveness of all systems and their management can be obtained by sharing common components, wire, computer user interfaces, and data and graphic formats. For instance, during building design and construction, and then during the building's operation and maintenance, a common format for "submittals," "shop and as-built," CAD using a common building base layer for all systems could be used. Each contractor would then supply their own drawing layers, drawing blocks with extensions to their non-graphical information for product cut-sheets, door, valve, and damper schedules, all in a common electronic format. These same information would then be used by the commissioning agent, the facilities management, and the maintenance staff. Why install five or more similar wiring systems, each of which has its own conduit, cabling and connectors, along with all of the separate sizes and styles of drawings and service information?

Historically, what were first called intelligent buildings began to appear in the mid-1980s when real estate developers and building owners and managers tried to develop a broader line of building services that would attract new tenants and keep existing ones. The general idea was that users of a multitenant building could rent services for computing, cabling, telephones, and office machines and environmental and lighting control rather than buy and maintain their own systems themselves. Unfortunately, the promoters of the concept were overly optimistic about the projection for and interest in these shared services. Few corporations wanted to risk putting their important business data or private telephone calls on shared systems managed by the building owner. Security was primitive or nonexistent, and computing, networking, and building systems were totally closed and strictly proprietary.

Currently, however, information systems, technologies, and services have evolved on their own and to the point where the shared resources concept has reappeared with a vengeance. The intelligent building concept of the 1980s in many ways has become a reality. Businesses, corporations, colleges, and universities are now freely sharing common resources, and these resources go beyond the boundaries of the single building or campus (for example, the Internet). Because of the maturing of networked computer systems, improvements in security, the merging of data, telephone, development of client servers, and distributed databases, corporations, colleges and universities are all beginning to build intelligent buildings whether they realize it or not.

Currently there is widespread interest in finding ways to integrate all of an enterprise's business operations, including CMCS/DDC, CAD, computer aided facilities management, and maintenance, all using common network hardware and cabling, distributed open databases, and user interfaces built on integrated software applications that allow sharing between all of these information resources.

CMCS/DDC System Integration with Other Building Equipment

To meet customer demands for improved integration of building systems and their information, most CMCS/DDC vendors are busy developing products for connecting third-party equipment to their own systems. Third-party integration allows incompatible equipment to look as if it is part of the vendor's own system. To accomplish integration, CMCS/DDC system manufacturers develop a family of gateway products. These gateway products are designed to accept and then translate information from another vendor's equipment or field digital controller into a format that can be accessed, read, and understood by the building's main CMCS/DDC system. Many industrial programmable logic controllers (PLCs) and other building equipment products that once operated alone can now be connected to CMCS/DDC systems.

This early form of multivendor system integration has become an important step toward promoting the single unified control system paradigm. Unfortunately this paradigm is developing without the use of a commonly accepted communication standard or protocol (Figure 41-7).

CMCS/DDC Systems Integration into Office LANs and Business Systems

There is an increasing need and requirement for building owners and operators to have direct access to building information from their business LANs. Many CMCS/DDC vendors currently make it possible to integrate digital control, life safety, and security system information on personal computers running various office software such as spreadsheets, databases, and graphical representation programs.

Vendors are finally providing system communication software that is less proprietary and uses well-known network protocols that allow the CMCS/DDC system and office LANs to be joined. As a result, many kinds of building comfort, utility, and cost reports can be obtained in spreadsheet and database program formats. There are a growing number of client computer applications for viewing CMCS/DDC system information from department LANs using third-party software. This growth requires communication protocols for sharing information.

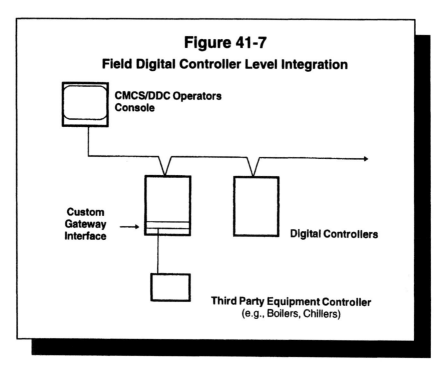

Figure 41-7

Field Digital Controller Level Integration

CMCS/DDC Operators Console

Custom Gateway Interface

Digital Controllers

Third Party Equipment Controller
(e.g., Boilers, Chillers)

Open systems integration technologies are currently emerging in the CMCS/DDC industry centered around communications protocols known as *dynamic data exchange* (DDE), *object linking and embedding* (OLE), and *open database connectivity* (ODBC). The Microsoft Windows operating system supports DDE/OLE, which enables various software applications to automatically share information with each other. Many leading Windows-based business applications (for example, Excel, Word, FoxPro) support DDE. OLE allows an object (for example, a graphic image) to be inserted in a document.

Systems integration products are available from many vendors; examples include Johnson Controls Metalink, Metsys Network Port, and Novell Netware Connection. Metalink provides the capability of using Microsoft Windows DDE to link Metasys building information to DDE and OLE applications such as Microsoft Excel, Word Access, FoxPro, or Paradox, to name a few. The Novell Netware Connection allows information packets from the Metasys ARCNET LAN to be passed through a router and understood by a Novell Netware operating system. The Metasys Network Port provides the building network with host computer connectivity through a variety of protocols. Other third-party user interface development systems such as Wonderware, Intilution, and LabView allow the user to develop a custom interface for viewing and manipulating DDC data.

DDE and OLE allow the CMCS/DDC system to automatically distribute CMCS/DDC information (such as utility meter data, building system performance logs) from the CMCS/DDC operator's console over LANs to whomever may need it. Sensor and status point information directly imported into spreadsheets and databases. Spreadsheets for air handlers, chillers, and other types of equipment automate the processing of data. These applications give the CMCS/DDC system a set of additional tools for analysis and reporting that improve the quality of information coming from the CMCS/DDC system (Figure 41-8).

BACnet: ASHRAE's Building Automation and Control Network Standard

College and university facilities and construction management departments have long wished for CMCS/DDC building management components that would allow them to connect various DDC controllers, networks, and operators' consoles together, regardless of the vendor.

The American Society of Heating, Refrigeration, and Air Conditioning Engineers' (ASHRAE's) SP-135 committee, formed to create a building automation and control network standard for building control systems communications, has approved a standard for multivendor control system integration. The SP-135 committee's building control system protocol attempts to define the types and content of information communicated among

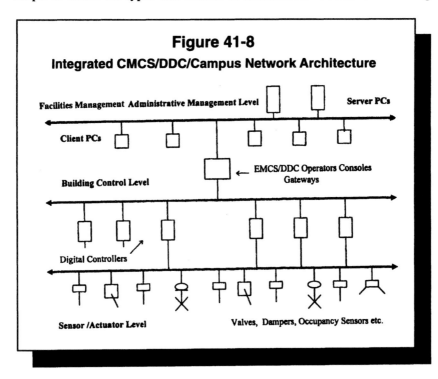

Figure 41-8

Integrated CMCS/DDC/Campus Network Architecture

Facilities Management Administrative Management Level   Server PCs

Client PCs

EMCS/DDC Operators Consoles Gateways

Building Control Level

Digital Controllers

Sensor /Actuator Level   Valves, Dampers, Occupancy Sensors etc.

various types of equipment, thereby facilitating the application and use of digital control technology in buildings.

The current standards has the potential to make interoperability between multiple vendors' equipment a reality. Only time will tell if the owners of existing systems or those purchasing new systems will see an advantage in direct competitive bidding for components and risk purchasing controls or operators' consoles from different vendors.

BACnet presents a challenge to the current proprietary CMCS/DDC construction specifications being used in many colleges and universities. These specifications name a single vendor, although sometimes other vendors are allowed to bid, providing they connect their field panels to existing campus control system networks. Many times, however, this has been technically or financially impossible. Proprietary specifications will be challenged like never before. No longer will colleges and universities be able to use the excuse of vendor incompatibility as the sole reason for developing campus-wide CMCS/DDC systems.

With BACnet, there will very likely be a "leveling of the playing field." Vendors will finally be compared with regard to price and performance. Colleges and universities will undoubtedly be one of the chief beneficiaries of the standard because of their need to competitively bid construction projects and their ability to handle the more complex technical and management aspects of multivendor systems.

The real merits of mixing various vendors' control equipment into a homogeneous multivendor network will need to be carefully studied. What will BACnet control products do to system functionality and reliability? What will be the real cost advantages? How easily can new operators' consoles and field controllers be added to existing systems? Finally, and most importantly, how will complex maintenance and service issues arising out of multivendor systems be resolved?

The protocol provides a comprehensive set of messages for conveying encoded binary, analog, and alpha-numeric data between control system devices, including, but not limited to, the following:

- Hardware binary input and output values
- Hardware analog input and output values
- Software binary and analog values
- Text string values
- Schedule information
- Alarm and event information
- Control logic

This protocol models each building automation and control computer as a collection of data structures known as *objects*, the properties of which represent various aspects of the hardware, software, and operation of the device. These objects provide a means of identifying and accessing information without requiring knowledge of the details of the device's internal design or configuration.

The BACnet objects define the devices and functions that are needed to have various vendors' products behave consistently in their interactions. Vendors are free to support all or some of the objects and to create their own. The sophistication of a device, in terms of its ability to carry out a particular service request or to understand the nature of a particular object type, is reflected in the device's conformance class. BACnet defines six conformance classes for devices connected to the network. Each class has a set of requirements that a device must be able to perform.

BACnet uses the OSI seven-layer protocol model for its foundation. Use of an international standard such as OSI allows the relatively small building equipment and building control industry to take advantage of the much larger body of computer and networking knowledge and investment. Advances that come from research and product development in these industries allow lower costs and permit more useful and reliable products to be incorporated into building management and control systems.

Because the OSI protocol was designed for high-end computer and networking environments where data can travel long distances and over many different networks, the protocol was designed to handle multiple requirements such as complex routing, error recovery, and synchronization. With typical building management and control systems, a much less demanding environment exists, except where CMCS/DDC systems use a college or university network that also links branch campuses over a wide area.

On large campuses, CMCS/DDC control networks can connect to quite a large number of field cabinets and operators' consoles. However, in most of these systems, the controller-to-controller or console-to-controller data flow occurs over fairly limited periods and usually for very brief durations. Such systems need only limited networking bandwidth and network service requirements to function satisfactorily. For this reason the BACnet SP-135 committee has chosen to use only four of the seven layers of the OSI protocol. This reduces network communication software overhead and costs associated with implementing the full OSI model in building control system products.

The data link layer organizes the DDC controller and console data into information packets, controls when the controller and console can access the network and gives them the address where the data is to be sent, controls how transmission errors are handled, and controls how two devices talk back and forth on the network.

The purpose of the BACnet network layer is to provide a means by which messages can be relayed from one BACnet network to another, regardless of the data link technology used on the network. The network layer allows messages to be sent to a single remote device (i.e., a device on another network), to be broadcast to all devices on a remote network, or to be broadcast to all devices on all networks. To do this the network layer provides translation services between what are called *global addresses* and local *addresses* and performs message sequencing and flow control, error handling, and what is called *multiplexing* (or *broadcasting*). This layer is used when a building or campus has different combinations of networks such as Ethernet, fiber distributed data (FDDI), and ARCHNET joined together through various routes. BACnet allows networks to be chosen from one of the four most well-known types of networks found in most CMCS/DDC systems:

- *Ethernet protocol (ISO 8802-3)*. This is the most common high-speed, wide-bandwidth LAN found on college and university campuses. Ethernet is used to connect many vendors' operators' consoles and high-end controllers together. It is a low-cost, simple network for both campus network engineering staff and facilities management CMCS/DDC technical staff to design, install, and maintain. Using Ethernet for CMCS/DDC systems is advantageous, because many campuses and their buildings already have Ethernet cabling installed using coaxial and 10-base-T and 100-base-T wiring systems.
- *ARCHNET protocol (ISO 8802-2)*. ARCHNET is also a high-speed, high-bandwidth protocol, but has a somewhat lower capacity than Ethernet. ARCHNET is well known in the control industry (i.e., it is used by Johnson Controls) and is low in cost.
- *Master-Slave/Token-Passing (MS/TP)*. This protocol was selected and designed by BACnet specifically for low-cost building automation and control networks. The MS/TP protocol will provide an interface to the network layer and access to the network physical media layer known as *RS-485*. This option uses shielded twisted-pair cable and is a well-known standard used by many equipment and instrument manufacturers.
- *Dial-Up Networks*. Dial-up serial communication trunks allow for communication with existing CMCS/DDC systems that use RS-485. Dial-up networks use what is called *point-to-point* communications, in which two devices establish a connection through a dial-up telephone modem link using the RS-232-D standard. This BACnet standard specifies a protocol that allows two BACnet network devices to establish a BACnet dial-up connection, exchange data, and terminate the connection in an orderly fashion.

Many facilities departments on large campuses want to use their transaction control protocol/internet protocol TCP/IP, Novell Internet Package Exchange IPX, and IP protocols with BACnet. Because these protocols are not designed to understand any other protocol, the BACnet standard was written to allow the BACnet message packet to be incorporated into these protocols.

CMCS/DDC and the LonWorks Network Protocol

One of the most important, and some say the only, de facto CMCS/DDC network standard that is currently emerging is the Local Open Network (LON) protocol. LON network and control technology is showing up in all kinds of systems and products from many CMCS/DDC building management and equipment manufacturers. College and university personnel will do well to become acquainted with this technology.

The Echelon Corporation of Palo Alto, California, has defined and developed a highly distributed control system that includes a network protocol that can be applied to nearly any piece of equipment containing switches, sensors, and actuators. The system, which is known as *LonWorks,* is built around a custom integrated circuit called the *Neuron C chip.* The chip contains three internal processors that allow it to drive sensor and control functions while simultaneously managing communications. In addition, the chip carries in its firmware the LonTalk communication protocol, which is the basis for defining the ways in which information is passed in the system (i.e., the sensor values, control signals, and other information passed between the various parts of a network).

Echelon has licensed the manufacture and sale of the chip to Motorola and Toshiba. LonWorks is not designed for a particular application and aims to establish itself as the de facto standard for all forms of control systems, from washing machines to automated buildings and factories. Several major control manufacturers have adopted LonWorks and made it an integral part of their system. For those who want a complete LonWorks system, Echelon supplies the hardware, network protocol, and the development tools needed to implement for nearly any application.

LonWorks certainly appears to have the potential to integrate the different vendor subsystems in a typical facility into one common building management and control system. Like any product trying to achieve de facto status, such status will be achieved only when enough vendors choose to adopt this protocol as part of their products. As is common with de facto standards, the marketplace will decide. Currently several of the major temperature control companies include LonWorks products as additions to their own CMCS/DDC building control systems.

The idea that inspired LonWorks is the fact that control systems manufacturers have had to handle a wide range of technology and skills to develop and market their systems. This has resulted in sometimes limited and superficial solutions to many customers' control needs. What LonWorks tries to do is to off-load the networking, microprocessing, and communications protocol development burdens of control system manufacture so that manufacturers can concentrate on improving the overall quality of products and services to their customers. Echelon sponsors an interoperability testing and conformance program called *LonMark*. Vendors products that meet the standard are given a LonMark logo.

What is unique about LonWorks is that it is implemented at the sensor, actuator, or system component level. LonWorks distributes intelligence and control to the lowest level of the system, where most of the control interaction takes place. Small LONs can be placed inside original-equipment-manufacturer packaged products such as chillers, generators, pumping stations, and air handlers. Larger LONs can connect groups of devices, such as would be found in a custom-built elevator. The approach completely eliminates the field panel and its discrete wiring to individual sensors and actuators; thus, considerable conduit and wiring are saved. The network is designed as one continuous wire or bus connecting all devices. It is designed to be expanded simply by extension on either end. LonWorks also uses radio frequency transceivers or power line carrier transceivers for use on a facilities power wiring system.

With the LonWorks system, users supply only the application code (which can also be purchased through third parties), the input and output electronics of their choice, a power supply, and their choice of several types of communications transceiver. For most building control applications, sensor and control nodes are available off the shelf for twisted-pair networks; for a linked power transceiver that uses a common wire for both communication and power to the transceiver; and for a power line carrier module, for communication over a building's existing alternating current, direct current, or unpowered telephone wiring systems.

A high-level development system called *LonBuilder Developer's Workbench* is sold to those who have the background, skills, and desire to develop their own application programs. The Workbench includes a development system, a network manager, and a protocol analyzer. Each language (a derivative of the C programming language). The Workbench also includes software tools for debugging, project management, and object database and program editing. Training classes and technical support for learning to design and install a LonWorks system are available in several cities. The company offers unlimited telephone, fax, and e-mail support.

⌐ Appendix 41-A ─────────────────────────

A Sample University Return on Investment Program

The university will provide ($___) in start-up funds to be used by facilities management to form return on investment (ROI) energy management projects. These projects are designed to decrease energy consumption at the university by upgrading facilities systems, resulting in utility cost savings. The utility cost savings will initially be used to pay back the cost of the project (ROI concept). Savings will be set aside for use by facilities management to fund future ROI projects. The remaining utility savings will be returned to fund undesignated fund reserves. The procedures required to monitor this program are outlined below.

ROI Agreement　Facilities management will provide a project agreement to the financial budget and analysis office for each ROI project. The agreement will provide the following information:
- Project description/identifier
- Building affected
- Estimated project cost
- Loan amount required
- Project start date and completion date
- Estimated annual utility savings
- Utility savings verification method (metering, math model)
- Loan repayment schedule
- Facilities management approval signature(s)

Loan Repayment　Projects funded with a loan from the start-up money are required to use any utility savings to pay back the loan to the designated fund. The repayment period begins at project completion. Utility savings resulting from the project will be computed beginning at project completion. Any incremental savings occurring prior to project completion will not be considered.

A loan repayment schedule based on estimated project cost and estimated utility savings is included in the ROI agreement. At project completion facilities management will recalculate the repayment schedule based on actual cost and savings data and forward a copy of the revised schedule to the financial budget and analysis office. The loan payment will be made by transferring one-year funds from the utility budget to the designated fund on an annual basis.

Savings Calculation   At project completion, facilities management will calculate the annual savings from each ROI project. This fixed savings amount will be used for all future years; it will not be recalculated annually. Any savings resulting from an ROI project will be used to initially pay back the project loan amount. Once the project has paid for itself, any savings from the project will be split as follows:

- Twenty-five percent of the utility savings amount will be transferred from the utility budget account to a plant fund account. This account will be used by facilities management to fund other ROI and utility upgrade projects. Any other use of the funds in this account will require university board of trustees approval.
- Seventy-five percent of the utility savings amount will be transferred from the utility budget to an undesignated budgeted reserve account to be reallocated by the university board of trustees.

Accounting Procedures   To account for the ROI projects, the following transactions or procedures must be performed:

- Upon receipt of an approved ROI agreement, budget and accounting will establish a project account. Facilities management must process and transfer funds from the plant fund control account to the project account using the ROI agreement as supporting documentation.
- Facilities management will develop a report to monitor ROI projects. This report should include each ROI, project status, loan payback schedules, and annual savings. The report should also include a summary section showing the total annual amount of loan paybacks and utility savings. This report will provide supporting documentation to transfer monies for the utility account. A copy of this report will be sent to the financial budget and analysis office.
- Annually, facilities management must estimate the amount of any utility savings expected from the completion of ROI projects. Facilities management will transfer monies from the utility account. The transfer entry will be processed to show this estimated amount as an expenditure against the utility account, so that an analysis of the utility account will show the expected effects of the transfer. At year end, facilities management will provide actual utility cost savings, and the transfer entry will be adjusted to actual savings as part of the annual closing process.

CHAPTER 42

Primary Fuel Management

Cheryl L. Gomez
University of Virginia

Warren W. Weeks
San Jose Convention Center

42.1 INTRODUCTION

Until the 1960s, fuels used for heating, cooling, and electricity were readily available and relatively inexpensive. A local regulated utility company provided electricity, the same or a separate regulated utility company supplied natural gas, and regional fuel suppliers provided coal and fuel oil. The role of the facilities manager in fuels management consisted primarily of ensuring that contracts were in place with the various fuel suppliers for the provision of energy on demand. The energy suppliers were responsible for the procurement and transportation or transmission of energy and the storage of local fuel reserves and for ensuring that energy was available on demand.

The Arab oil embargo in the 1970s restricted the world supply of petroleum products and forced facilities managers to assume a greater role in managing the cost and availability of fuel to the institution. Natural gas supplies were curtailed, local fuel oil and coal suppliers were not able to deliver on demand, the production of electricity was placed at risk, and the cost of energy skyrocketed. This problem persisted long after the oil embargo was lifted and world market prices for oil had stabilized. This continuation of fuel shortages and inflated costs was caused by actions taken by large electrical utilities to secure fuel supplies by agreeing to long-term purchase agreements at inflated prices. The electrical utilities were less concerned with fuel prices than availability, as they were able to simply pass on the higher fuel costs to customers.

Most institutions reacted to the fuel crises by appointing a full-time energy manager whose primary responsibility was to control the cost, reduce the use, and ensure the continuous availability of energy. Under the stewardship of energy managers, many institutions reactivated long dormant coal-fired equipment, invested in central plant systems, and constructed large oil or coal storage facilities. In addition, most took advantage of projected energy savings and the Institutional Conservation Program sponsored by the U.S. Department of Energy to finance building energy management systems and energy conservation projects.

The Public Utilities Regulatory Policy Act (PURPA) and the Natural Gas Policy Act (NGPA), both of 1978, provided energy managers with more options for managing energy costs and availability. PURPA allowed electrical consumers to generate part or all of their electrical requirements and obligated the local electric utility to furnish standby capacity and to purchase any excess electricity produced. NGPA established the ground rules for the deregulation of the gas industry.

By the second half of the 1980s, deregulation of the natural gas industry had become a reality. Deregulation, combined with an abundant supply of natural gas and a drop in the cost of all fossil fuels, provided the energy manager access to low-cost gas supplies from producers and brokers, in addition to gas supplied by the traditional local gas utility.

The first half of the 1990s was marked by the passage of the landmark Energy Policy Act (EPAct) of 1992 and a reinvigoration of energy conservation initiatives as many institutions took advantage of rebate programs offered by local utilities. Lighting systems were converted to high-efficiency fixtures, motors were replaced with high-efficiency types, constant-volume motors were converted to variable-frequency drives, and building control systems were replaced with building automation and energy management systems. Regional heating and cooling plants were expanded, thermal energy storage systems were constructed, ground source heat pumps were installed, standby generation was implemented, and controls were placed on emergency generators to permit peak demand management.

One of the challenges for the energy manager in the second half of the 1990s and beyond will be to thoroughly understand electricity deregulation. Experience indicates that unavoidable disruptions and confusion will occur with electricity deregulation, probably more so than with natural gas deregulation because of the inability to store electrical energy. Ensuring inexpensive and consistent power on demand, especially to critical facilities, will be an important and potentially time-consuming task for the energy manager.

The energy manager has and will continue to have many opportunities to minimize costs through the comprehensive management of fuels purchasing, use, and storage. Implicit in the opportunity to reduce costs is the risk of incurring significant financial penalties or having inadequate fuel supplies if this function is not carried out in an informed and carefully managed manner.

42.2 HYDROCARBON FUELS

Ensuring adequate supplies of hydrocarbon fuels in the form of natural gas, fuel oil, coal, and other solid fuels is currently relatively easy to manage, as most are readily available and reasonably inexpensive and can be stored to accommodate changes in demand. The primary issues associated with hydrocarbon fuels are cost, storage requirements, availability, criticality of fuel supplies, environmental requirements, and the development of good purchasing contracts that address each of these areas.

Issues to be considered when evaluating fuel costs include the seasonal impact on market prices for the various fuels, cost comparisons of the various fuels on an equivalent performance basis, short-term and long-term cost projections for the fuels, and accounting for any cost penalties associated with environmental compliance requirements.

The geographical location of facilities, particularly their proximity to fuel supplies, affects the availability of a particular fuel to an area, especially for natural gas distribution pipelines and coal rail service. The availability of fuels to serve critical facilities such as hospitals and the possibility of strikes or another oil embargo are extremely important issues to consider when making a decision to commit to a specific fuel.

Cost, fuel availability, and aesthetic considerations all factor into determining storage needs. Large storage capacity results in a lower risk of inadequate fuel supplies to serve facilities, especially critical areas. An added benefit of large storage capacity is the flexibility to purchase fuels during off-peak periods when the fuels typically cost less. However, large storage facilities cost more to construct, can tie up money in inventory, and can often raise significant aesthetic issues. Outsourcing for storage typically entails higher purchasing costs for the fuels and also ties up money in inventory.

Environmental regulations have resulted in greater controls on air emissions, waste water discharge, storm water discharge, and the construction of underground and aboveground storage tanks. Nonattainment areas often are precluded from using certain fuels. Compliance almost always entails the construction of costly pollution control and monitoring equipment.

Gaseous Fuels

Natural gas, a by-product of petroleum exploration, is a mixture of methane (55 to 98 percent), higher hydrocarbons (primarily ethane), and noncombustible gases. The composition of natural gas varies depending in large part on the surrounding underground conditions and the proximity of the gas deposit to oil deposits. Wet natural gas is found near oil deposits and, as such, has absorbed heavy hydrocarbons. Dry natural gas has no contact with oil deposits and, as such, contains no heavy hydrocarbons. The nitrogen content in natural gas can range from 0 to 87.69 percent by volume. The composition of sulfur in natural gas in the form of hydrogen sulfide ranges from 0 to 7 percent by volume.

Liquefied petroleum gases (LPG), a by-product of oil refinery operations or natural gas stripping, are commercially available as butane, propane, or a mixture of the two. Although some institutions use LPGs as a backup fuel, most rely on natural gas, which is more readily available and less expensive.

Assessments indicate that the original quantity of natural gas was an energy equivalent of 2.576 trillion barrels of oil, including 463 billion barrels of propane, butane, and natural gasoline. Of the original amount, 14 percent has been consumed, 55 percent has been discovered, and 84 percent of the remaining 31 percent is located in the Eastern Hemisphere.

The focus of this section is on natural gas and the regulatory, procurement, and management issues associated with its use.

Regulatory Development

Most of the original natural gas pipelines were constructed by holding company offshoots of major petroleum producers. These pipelines crossed state boundaries and therefore were not regulated by states. This resulted in a considerable monopoly of power being exercised by the petroleum companies. In at attempt to regulate the gas industry, Congress enacted the Natural Gas Act (NGA) in 1938. The NGA actually protected pipelines from competition and resulted in self-dealing among affiliated producers of gas. However, it was the NGA that later gave the Federal Energy Regulatory Commission (FERC) the authority to regulate the construction of pipeline facilities and the transportation of natural gas in interstate commerce. In 1955 the U.S. Supreme Court decided that purchases from all producers should be regulated by the FERC. This action led to administrative difficulties, price distortions, and eventually an acute gas shortage in the 1970s.

In 1978 Congress enacted the Natural Gas Policy Act (NGPA), which attempted staged regulatory reform and resulted in some components of the industry being deregulated while others were still subject to price controls. This resulted in a supply "bubble" of natural gas and "take-or-pay" contracts in which pipelines were contractually liable for paying for billions of dollars worth of gas that they were then unable to sell at a commensurate price.

Orders 436 (1985), 500 (1988), and 636 (1992) provided several regulatory changes that addressed the "take-or-pay" crises, articulated an "open access" policy that enabled utilities and industrial customers to purchase gas directly from pipelines or upstream suppliers and resulted in pipelines becoming common carriers, with the gas supply business being separated from the pipeline subsidiaries.

Management

The energy manager has essentially two mechanisms for purchasing natural gas. Natural gas can be procured through the local distribution company (LDC), which has established rate structures for firm or interruptible service. Various levels of interruptible service can be negotiated, depending on how much risk the purchaser is willing to share with the LDC. Risks include shortages in local availability of fuel, severe weather, and volatile market prices. The second gas procurement option is the direct purchase of gas. The following is a discussion of application issues and the advantages and disadvantages of each of these options.

Procurement Using an LDC   Most small users of natural gas contract directly with the LDC for the provision of gas. The LDC can be a municipality or a local regulated utility company that accepts gas at the "city gate" (i.e., the point at which the transportation pipelines end and the LDC pipelines begin) and distributes gas to customers to meet their energy needs. If the facility has a backup source of fuel, the energy manager can opt to purchase gas from the LDC on an interruptible basis. If the facility has no backup fuel, the energy manager is required in most states to purchase the gas at a firm rate. Most LDCs require a minimum annual consumption of gas to qualify for interruptible service.

The rates and other terms of service are based on the LDC's cost of service and are usually approved or set by the state public utility commission. When the LDC is a municipality, the rates often include a component for local social programs such as police and fire protection, low-income energy assistance, energy conservation, and other similar programs. Typically, both the firm and interruptible gas rates are charged in incremental steps in which the rate decreases with increasing quantities of gas consumed. Most LDCs set fixed rates for a given year for firm and interruptible service, although some allow their rates to rise and fall depending on seasonal market conditions. Both firm and interruptible customers are charged a minimum monthly fee for gas service; this fee is usually higher for the interruptible rate.

The advantage of contracting for interruptible service is lower rates. Obviously, the disadvantage of interruptible service is the likelihood of service interruptions that force the use of an alternative fuel such as oil, coal, or electricity. This may result in higher operating and maintenance costs or place the institution at risk of not having an alternative energy source during the period of gas interruption. The latter is a major concern for those institutions with critical areas that cannot sustain even a short interruption in service.

Procurement Using Direct Purchasing   Large users of natural gas can still opt to purchase firm or interruptible gas from the LDC. However, most large users have been able to achieve savings of up to 25 percent of the cost of gas furnished by the LDC by directly purchasing their gas. To purchase gas directly, the energy manager enters into a transportation agreement with the LDC. Most LDCs charge a monthly transportation fee and offer transportation rates for firm to various levels of interruptible service. In addition to the transportation fee and rates, the LDC is allowed under regulatory procedures to charge a purchase gas adjustment (PGA) for changes in supply costs as an automatic pass-through to ratepayers. PGAs show up as a varying cost on each monthly gas bill. LDCs are also allowed to deduct for shrinkage, which assumes that some of the gas purchased by the customer is lost in transportation. Shrinkage essentially reduces the quantity of gas purchased by the customer by 1 to 3 percent of the total quantity of gas nominated.

The direct-purchase gas contract, which can be negotiated using the request-for-proposals (RFPs) process or contracted using the invitation-for-bids (IFBs) process, should include the following minimum provisions:

- *Price.* The cost of the gas purchase can be established as a fixed price: a spot market-priced, open-ended contract that reflects market prices at the time of purchase; or a negotiated base price that is adjusted based on specified criteria such as the indexed cost of oil. The cost of gas may be slightly higher if the contract requires a guaranteed supply of gas to ensure certainty of supply. The latter arrangement also benefits gas producers and suppliers, who are guaranteed a market for their gas. In this case, the purchaser should include a price reopener clause in the contract, exercisable at specified periods in the contract, to enable flexibility in renegotiating the purchase price of the contract to reflect prevailing market conditions.
- *Purchasing options.* The purchaser can negotiate 1) gas production costs, 2) transportation rates, 3) transportation line losses, 4) penalties for over- and undernominations, penalties or credits for take-or-pay, and 5) contract management costs as separate contracts or as one overall contract. Contracting separately provides greater opportunities for cost savings but can result in substantial losses if the purchaser is not thoroughly familiar with each of these issues or is unable to devote adequate time to managing the contracts.
- *Time of contract.* Although the term of the agreement can be as short as 30 days, most contracts are established on a one-year basis with an

option for annual renewal of up to three years. Shorter term contracts can be the most advantageous, as they provide the purchaser the most flexibility in negotiating prices. However, they are the most vulnerable to seasonal fluctuations in price and provide no protection against long-term price increases. Most purchasers opt for longer term agreements that contain a base price agreement with provisions for market-based adjustments included. All contracts must contain a term of agreement and should have provisions for contract cancellation.

- *Quantity*. Most contracts specify maximum annual gas consumption and indicate daily, weekly, or monthly use. The purchaser is responsible for correctly nominating gas quantities for a specific pipeline pressure at the point of consumption. The latter is extremely important, as pipeline pressure directly affects the amount of gas that must be nominated.

Many energy managers choose to use a full-service gas supply broker for managing their gas purchasing needs. The broker secures gas supplies, arranges for transportation to the "city gate" or "burner tip," and assumes all responsibility for reconciling the quantity of gas purchased with the quantity of gas delivered. Full-service brokers usually require the institution to report meter readings daily or weekly and at the first of the month; these are used to nominate gas quantities. The responsibility for payment of any penalties for overnominations that result in storage costs by the LDC should be negotiated as part of the contract with the broker. Undernomination of gas usually results in the institution obtaining gas from the LDC at the nontransportation rate, which is usually at the high end of the rate scale because of the small quantity of gas involved.

The gas purchase contract can be awarded to one or two brokers. In the latter case, shares of the contract are split between the brokers and set up to reward the best performing broker with the majority of the contract. In addition to directly purchasing all gas for the institution, it is possible for the institution to use the full-service gas broker to furnish gas only to a central heating plant or a cogeneration facility and to continue to contract with the LDC to furnish gas to individually metered buildings that utilize small quantities of gas. This reduces record keeping and frequency of meter readings, which require more staff time with little or no added benefit in savings.

The energy manager can further reduce costs by serving as his or her own gas broker. He or she can procure gas directly from a producer, contract with a transportation company for national or regional delivery of the purchased gas to the LDC, and contract with the LDC for local transportation to the burner tip. As the brokering agent, the energy manager is responsible for timely and accurate nomination of gas and for reconciling nominated quantities with the quantities delivered and consumed. The reconciliation of gas quantities nominated with the quanitities delivered and consumed is often a daily task and must be accomplished for each of the gas production, transportation, and delivery contracts. As with the full-service broker, if the nominated quantities differ from the delivered amounts, the institution may be required to purchase gas from the LDC at a premium price (in the case of undernomination) or pay for storage (in the case of overnomination). To avoid these situations, the energy manager must establish procedures for ensuring that accurate forecasting is used in the nomination process. The financial risks are high with this method, which makes it attractive only to large consumers, who can anticipate at least a 10 percent savings using this method over the use of a full-service broker. It is recommended that even large consumers of natural gas initially contract for gas management from a full-service broker and simulate the same process with in-house staff to identify areas of risk or vulnerability. This provides in-house staff training, which needs to be accomplished regardless of the final management process.

Liquid Fuels

Fuel oil is available in several grades, including No. 1 (light distillate), No. 2 (distillate), No. 4 (light residual or heavy distillate), No. 5L (light residual, heavier than No. 4), No. 5H (heavy residual), and No. 6 (heavy residual, also known as Bunker C). Each of these fuel oils has a distinct fuel composition, ignition temperature, flash point, pour point, viscosity, specific gravity, and heating value. Preheating of No. 5L may be necessary for burning and handling in colder climates. Preheating of No. 5H is usually necessary for burning and handling. Preheating of No. 6 oil in the storage tank is required to enable pumping, and additional preheating at the burner is typically required to enable atomizing. Figure 42-1 lists the ranges of heating values; weights; sulfur levels; and pour, pump, and atomizing points of some fuel oils.

Assessments indicate that the original quantity of light and medium oils was 2.39 trillion barrels of oil, of which 30 percent has been consumed, 23 percent has yet to be discovered, and 78 percent of the remaining 47 percent is located in the Eastern Hemisphere. For heavy oils, the original quantity was estimated to be 467.5 billion barrels, of which 14 percent has been consumed, 20 percent is undiscovered, and 52 percent of the remaining 66 percent is located in the Western Hemisphere.

Low-sulfur residual oils are available in many areas to permit users to meet sulfur dioxide emission regulations. Low-sulfur fuel oils are produced

Figure 42-1

Heating Values; Weights; Sulfur Levels; and Pour, Pump, and Atomizing Points of Fuel Oils

Grade No.	Sulfur Content (% by Weight)	Weight (lbm/gallon)	Heating Value Range (Btu/gallon)	Pour Point (°F)	Pump Point (°F)	Atomizing Point (°F)
1	0.002 – 0.38	6.675 – 6.950	132,000 – 137,000	<0	Atmospheric	Atmospheric
2	0.03 – 0.64	6.960 – 7.296	137,000 – 141,000	<0	Atmospheric	Atmospheric
4	0.46 – 1.44	7.396 – 7.787	143,100 – 148,000	10	15 min	25 min
5L	0.90 – 3.50	7.686 – 7.940	146,800 – 150,000	30 min	35 min	130
5H	0.57 – 2.92	7.890 – 8.080	149,400 – 152,000			
6	0.32 – 4.00	8.053 – 8.488	151,300 – 155,900	65 min	100 min	300

Note: Min = minimum temperature at which this can occur.

1) by refinery processes that remove sulfur from the oil, 2) by blending high-sulfur residual oils with low-sulfur distillate oils, or 3) by a combination of these two methods.

Diesel oil is available as No. 1, No. 2, and No. 4 grades and has the same property specifications as fuel oil except that it can be specified by a cetane number, which is the measure of the ignition quality of the fuel. The cetane number requirements depend on engine design, size, speed, and load variations. Use of a diesel oil with a cetane number higher than that indicated for the specific engine is not recommended, as it does not greatly enhance engine performance and is typically more costly and difficult to obtain.

Regulatory Development

The Interstate Commerce Act (ICA) and the EPAct are the two primary pieces of legislation used to regulate the rates and practices of oil pipeline companies engaged in interstate transportation. The 1970 Clean Air Act (CAA) and the 1977 and 1990 amendments to this act placed restrictions on emissions that limit the sulfur content of the fuel oil used in most plants and prohibit the use of fuel oil in many urban areas except as a backup fuel or for testing.

Management

The selection of a fuel oil grade for a specific application is usually based on fuel availability and economic factors such as fuel cost, clean air requirements, preheating and handling costs, and equipment costs.

Contracts   The fuel oil contract usually specifies a minimum annual use for each type of fuel. Terms and conditions of the contract typically include indemnification clauses, transportation responsibilities, auditing procedures, and provisions for cancellation of the contract. The contract must include provisions to enable compliance with air pollution control requirements such as limitations on sulfur content. Lower sulfur content in the oil provides a secondary benefit of reducing overall corrosiveness in the flue gas. Finally, it may be desirable to minimize ash (noncombustible material) in the oil, which causes high wear on the burner pumps.

Storage   Federal and state laws regulate the construction, installation, and use of above-ground storage tanks (AST) and underground storage tanks (UST) used for the storage of petroleum products. The goal of these regulations is to prevent the potential contamination of drinking water supplies, soil, and other resources from the release or threatened release of petroleum products. Although each state has its own AST and UST standards, most regulations include the following minimum requirements:

1. New tanks must be constructed of fiberglass-reinforced plastic, steel that has been cathodically protected by a suitable dielectric material or a field-installed cathodic protection system, a steel–fiberglass-reinforced plastic composite, or an equivalent approved construction system.
2. Piping must be constructed of steel and cathodically protected.
3. Spill and overfill prevention equipment must usually be installed.
4. Leak detection must be provided on piping and tanks, or leak testing accomplished on a periodic basis.

Specific procedures and requirements have been established that allow the continued use of existing storage tanks. These include upgrading the tanks with internal lining and periodically inspecting for soundness or periodically monitoring for releases or testing for tightness.

Although seldom a problem, oxidation or microbial growth in large No. 2 fuel oil storage facilities is occasionally encountered. Either of these might occur when fuel oil is stored for five or more years with little or no turnover in product. Oxidation and microbial growth over a long period of time can degrade the fuel oil and make it unsuitable for combustion, thereby requiring its removal and remediation. To prevent this, any fuel oil that is stored for extended periods of time with no movement of product should be tested at least annually and antioxidants or antimicrobial agents added as needed.

Solid Fuels

Solid fuels include waste products, wood, coke, and coal. Waste products from industrial, agricultural, and municipal operations in the form of raw material or as refuse-derived fuel (RDF) are used in waste-to-energy facilities (WTE) primarily for the generation of electricity or for the cogeneration of electricity and steam.

RDF is obtained when the combustible material in municipal solid waste is separated from the noncombustible portion and packaged into a form that can be fired in a boiler. High-quality RDF that is free of grit, glass, metals, and other noncombustibles is sometimes used as a supplemental fuel in existing coal-fired boilers.

Source reduction and recycling efforts in most communities are adversely affecting the availability of high-quality mass burn solid waste or RDF. The uncertainty of long-term availability of combustible materials from the solid waste stream, combined with the inconsistency of quality, makes it difficult to assess the long-term impact of relying on solid waste or RDF as a primary fuel.

The demand for wood in the building construction and furniture fabrication industries, the value of wood as an environmental and aesthetic resource, and the comparatively high cost of wood compared with other fuels usually make it a less attractive option for most energy generators as a primary fuel source. However, geographical location and local market conditions for wood can make it a less expensive fuel source than other types of fuels. Several energy generators have been able to negotiate with local paper mills, wood construction industries, municipalities, and other generators of waste wood products to obtain wood chips at no cost other than transportation to their wood burning facilities. Often the wood waste product can be used as a primary fuel when it is readily available and as a backup or peak burn fuel during other periods.

Coke is the ash- and sulfur-containing carbon residue that is produced by heating coal in the absence of oxygen. It is smokeless when burned and is used primarily in blast furnaces.

Coal is generally classified into four major categories: anthracite, bituminous, subbituminous, and lignite. Anthracite is a clean, dense, hard coal that creates little dust in handling and burns freely once ignited. Bituminous coal encompasses many types of coal that generally ignite easily, burn freely, and are strong enough to permit screening to remove fines. When improperly fired, bituminous coal produces large quantities of soot and smoke, especially at low burning rates. Subbituminous coal ignites easily and is susceptible to spontaneous ignition when piled or stored. It burns freely, breaks up easily into small pieces, and generates little smoke and soot. Lignite has a low heating value, is most susceptible to spontaneous ignition, and tends to break up in the fuel bed, which results in burning pieces falling into the ash bed. It generates little smoke and soot when burned.

Assessments indicate that the original quantity of coal was 6.9 trillion short tons, of which only 2.5 percent has been exploited. It is projected that coal will last from a few hundred to more than 1,000 years, depending on technological advances and the rate of use. Sixty percent of the coal deposits are in the United States, Russia, and China.

The heating values of coal are reported on an as-received, dry, dry and mineral matter-free, or moist and mineral matter-free basis, with the higher heating values for the various coals typically being used. Figure 42-2 lists the heating values and the nitrogen, sulfur, and ash content of the four major classes of coal on an as-received basis.

Regulatory Development

The enactment of the Clean Water Act, the Clean Air Act of 1970, and the Clean Air Amendments of 1978 and 1990 resulted in further restrictions on all boiler plants, most notably coal-fired facilities. These acts required most coal-fired plants to limit sulfur, nitrogen, and ash content in coal; to monitor particulate, sulfur dioxide, and/or nitric oxide emissions; and to limit emissions of these as well as volatile organic compounds and carbon monoxide from the plant. These limitations are typically based on boiler or facility size, types of fuels used, age of equipment, and location of the facility and are set to not exceed a certain number of pounds per hour, tons per year, or parts per thousand British thermal units per hour (MBH). Some facilities were required to install enclosed coal handling systems, coal stor-

Figure 42-2
Heating Values and Nitrogen, Sulfur, and Ash Content of Coals

Class	Heating Value BtU/lbm	Sulfur Content % by Weight	Nitrogen Contents % By Weight	Ash Content % By Weight
Anthracite	12,700–13,500	0.7–1.1	0.9–1.1	8.510.5
Bituminous	11,000–14,350	1.23.5	1.1–1.5	6.09.4
Subbituminous	8,5400–9,000	1.0	0.8–1.0	9.6–9.8
Lignite	6,900	1.0	0.7	7.3

age silos, and ash handling systems to protect against fugitive dust emissions and ground water contamination. In some cases, especially in nonattainment areas, restrictions on emissions became so rigorous that some facilities had to be converted to fire natural gas as a primary fuel.

The reader should note that above discussion of federal legislative initiatives being considered by the House and Senate was current at the time this manual went to press. Continuing discussion and updates on pending legislative initiatives will be provided in APPA's magazine, *Facilities Manager*, as the issue develops.

Management

The selection of a coal type for a specific application is usually based on fuel availability and economic factors such as fuel cost, transportation cost, clean air requirements, storage needs, handling costs, and equipment costs. Coal management issues include ensuring an adequate supply of fuel, minimizing fuel procurement and transportation costs, and meeting or exceeding air pollution control limitations.

Contracts The energy manager can opt to purchase coal and transportation as one complete package or as separate contracts. The benefit of a single contract is that it establishes a single point of responsibility for both the fuel purchase quantity and delivery. However, this approach typically results in higher unit costs for the fuel and less flexible delivery schedules. Flexibility in delivery schedules is important for ensuring that fuel deliveries and quantities meet the daily fuel burn requirements while maintaining an adequate inventory.

The use of separate contracts for fuel purchase and transportation results in a lower unit cost for the fuel and provides local control over delivery times and quantities. The separate transportation agreement also provides the energy manager with the flexibility to contract with a second coal supplier in the event of a contract default by the primary coal supplier. A default in a coal supplier contract can occur for a variety of reasons, including not providing specified quantities; not complying with limits on ash, sulfur, and nitrogen content; and providing coal that has excessive fines or low heating values or that is contaminated with debris. The transportation agreement is usually with a national railroad company and rarely goes into default. The disadvantage of separate contracts is that the energy manager becomes responsible for coordination of the two contracts and risks supply disruptions or monetary penalties known as *demurrage charges* caused by not being able to process coal sitting in rail cars or trucks. Similar to the fuel oil contract, the coal contract typically specifies minimum annual coal use and provides for indemnification, transportation responsibilities, auditing and cancellation procedures, and air pollution compliance requirements.

The award of the coal contract should be based on the energy content of the coal rather than on the cost per ton, as the heating value of coal can vary widely. The bidder typically supplies a cost per ton of coal, a cost per ton for freeze protection, and a heating value content for the coal, from which a total unit cost per MBH is calculated. The coal contract typically contains a penalty clause that specifies monetary penalties for supplying coal with a lower heating value or with higher ash or sulfur content than that that was bid. In addition to the monetary penalties, the penalty clause must indicate that the purchaser reserves the right to reject any shipments that do not meet the specifications at the coal vendor's cost. This is especially important when the ash and sulfur content of the coal shipments exceeds the limitations imposed by air pollution control requirements.

The contract should assign to the coal supplier the responsibility for testing the coal for heating value content, ash and sulfur content, and percentage of fines and should require the supplier to send a facsimile of the results to the purchaser prior to shipment. This should eliminate shipment of unsuitable coal to the plant, which is extremely important during periods of critical need. The purchaser may opt to contract with an independent testing agency for testing of coal samples as an added quality control check. However, the coal supplier is federally liable for the accurate reporting of ash and sulfur content of the coal. In addition, the coal vendor typically pulls samples from a continuous flow process, which is more representative of average coal quality than samples analyzed by an outside testing agency, which are usually obtained from the top or bottom of the rail car.

The rail transportation agreement, whether included in the purchase contract or established as a separate contract, should contain terms and conditions that are similar to those in the coal purchase contract and should identify major rail lines and local switching requirements. The energy manager may want to arrange for backup transportation of coal by truck in the event that rail service is unavailable. A separate contract should be used for truck transportation. Truck transportation is often included as a unit bid item in the coal contract and is typically priced at two or three times the cost that could be obtained through a separate contract.

Storage   On an equivalent heating value basis, delivered coal can cost up to 50 percent less than other thermal fuels. However, the capital investment in coal handling and storage equipment, pollution control equipment, and ash handling and storage equipment, as well as the maintenance costs associated with coal-fired plants, are higher than for gas- and oil-fired plants. If adequate storage capacity is not provided for at the coal-fired plant, the institution is at risk of supply shortages and may be forced to use a more costly backup fuel for generating heat or electricity. Use of a more costly fuel can quickly undermine the capital and ongoing maintenance investments in the coal-fired facility.

To protect capital and maintenance investments and to ensure availability of fuel for critical facilities, the storage facilities should provide for at least a 30-day inventory of coal at the peak burn rate. A 30-day inventory is an absolute minimum. A larger inventory is highly recommended. Several factors can quickly erode the coal inventory, including a contract default by the coal vendor, mine and transportation strikes, severe weather, low coal supplies at the mine, frozen coal that cannot be quickly unloaded, receipt of several shipments of unsuitable coal, and a variety of other factors. With the exception of strikes, most institutions have experienced some or all of these problems in the last few years.

To avoid coal fires, storage facilities must be carefully designed for the type and quantity of coal being stored. This is especially true for subbutiminous or lignite coals, which are highly susceptible to spontaneous combustion. Some states require or recommend that a fire suppression system be installed in coal storage facilities.

42.3   ELECTRICAL POWER

Electricity is usually the single most expensive line item of the energy budget. Most electrical power is supplied to retail customers by a local regulated public or private utility. Some institutions cogenerate part or all of their electrical power in an effort to control their electrical costs. This is particularly true of institutions located in the northeastern, western, and other parts of the country where the cost of electricity is much higher than average.

Most of the approximately 3,200 electric utilities operating in the United States are rural electrical cooperatives, municipal power systems, or independent power producers (IPP). About 80 percent of all generated power is produced by investor-owned utilities (IOUs), which make up less than 9 percent of the total number of electrical utilities. These IOUs usually function as the energy producer, the transmission company, the primary distribution company, and often as the secondary distribution company and bundle the cost of these various service components into their electrical rates.

Electric transmission lines cross state boundaries and are the mechanism by which electrical power is transmitted from the power plant to regional high-voltage substations. From the regional substations, electrical power is distributed via primary distribution lines directly to facilities or to a local substation. The local substation can be owned and operated by the utility company or the institution and is used for secondary distribution to a cluster of buildings. Secondary distribution to several buildings usually reduces the peak demand component of the electrical service because of the diversity of electrical use in the buildings.

The peak demand component of the electrical bill is typically the most expensive item of the rate. The implementation of demand-side management initiatives, such as the construction of local substations for secondary power distribution, the use of emergency generators and capacity banks to manage peak demand and the power factor, and the installation of thermal storage systems, can result in significant savings without any reduction in electrical use. In the case of thermal storage, electrical use actually increases while cost decreases as a result of shifting the time of use to an off-peak period. A thorough discussion of the impact of varying electrical loads and the different components of the electrical rates is provided in Chapter 39.

Most utility companies offer a variety of service agreements to fit different customer needs, including large general service, small general service, cogeneration service, standby generation service, demand-side management service, thermal storage service, and similar agreements.

Regulatory Development

EPAct required electric utilities to develop integrated resource planning (IRP) and to offer funding and planning support for demand-side management, thermal storage, innovative technologies, and other energy conservation incentives. The intent of the EPAct was to encourage investments in energy improvements, efficiency, and conservation through new rate standards; to support research into innovative technologies for alternative and renewable energy sources and improved quality and reliability of energy generation and delivery; and to keep energy purchase costs to a minimum.

The Federal Power Act (FPA) of 1935, PURPA, and EPAct provided legal authority to the Federal Energy Regulatory Commission (FERC) to oversee wholesale electric rates, service standards, and the transmission of electricity in interstate commerce. State public utility commissions (PUCs) retained the legal authority to oversee retail transactions and intrastate transmission and distribution.

On March 29, 1995, the FERC issued the "Notice of Proposed Rulemaking and Supplemental Notice of Proposed Rulemaking" (Docket numbers RM95-8-000 and R94-7-001), commonly called "Mega-NOPR", which provides for open access to the power transmission grid. The intent of the rule is to reduce or eliminate the current monopolistic control of the electrical industry by enabling retail wheeling. Retail wheeling entails the unbundling of power generation, transmission, and distribution and the introduction of competition in each of these areas. Permitting open access to transmission lines provides power generator access to customers outside the immediate region and gives customers options in choosing power suppliers.

Prior to the proposed new rule, retail customers were required to purchase electricity only from the local utility company, who in turn was obligated to serve all customers within its service territory. Only wholesale customers had access to the interstate transmission grid. Mega-NOPR provides the framework for deregulation of the interstate transmission of power, thereby allowing retail customers access to wholesale markets. The authority to effect changes for retail customers has been left up to the states, which will decide individually if, how, and when they wish to implement deregulation of retail power.

Included in the number of issues that need to be considered during the implementation of retail wheeling are the following:

1. *Interstate transmission costs (governed by the FERC).* The terms and conditions for how the costs of construction, operation, and maintenance of interstate transmission lines are to be distributed must be defined. These costs may be charged by the competing suppliers or provided for in the costs borne by the purchasing customer.
2. *Intrastate transmission and distribution tariffs (governed by PUCs).* How the embedded costs of intrastate transmission and distribution are to be supported and what, if any, liabilities are to be assumed for failure by competing suppliers to furnish the contracted quantities must be defined.
3. *Stranded cost recoveries.* Prior to deregulation, utility companies were required to provide power on demand to their retail customers, which resulted in significant long-term investments on the part of the utility companies. Deregulation allows utilities to recover these stranded costs only if the investments were legitimate, verifiable, and prudent, and the utility had reasonable expectation of recovery. However, it does not define how these stranded costs are to be recovered, nor does it provide protection for a utility that has noneconomic assets or investments. Utility companies can now assign stranded costs to retail customers but have not yet established a mechanism for assigning them to transmission customers.
4. *Demand-side management/standby generation.* Local regulated electric companies provided financial incentives to customers for the implementation of standby generation and demand-side management programs to reduce the need for the companies to obtain or build additional power generation capability. With the advent of deregulation, many utility companies have reassessed their need for these programs and have reduced or eliminated the number of programs that they support.
5. *Public good/benefit charges.* Utility companies currently provide social benefits, which include research and development in the power industry, low-income assistance, energy conservation programs, demand-side management programs, rebate programs, and renewable energy research. Deregulation provides for the lawful and appropriate setting of a public good/benefit charge by states to distribution customers for the continuation of these programs.
6. *Municipal rates.* Municipal utility companies often charge electrical retail customers for local social programs such as police protection, fire protection, park maintenance, sidewalk and street construction and

maintenance, lighting, recycling, trash collection, and other locally beneficial programs.

7. *Exit fees.* When a large utility customer opts to cogenerate its own electricity, it is often required to pay exit fees to the utility company to offset any undue burden to the remaining customers of the utility company. States must determine when, under what conditions, and how exit fees are to be assigned under deregulation.

8. *Re-entry fees.* A customer who opts to directly purchase electricity and bypass the local utility company may wish to reinstate a purchasing agreement with the local utility company. The local utility company may charge a fee for the reinstatement.

9. *Reliability and quality.* Prior to deregulation, the retail customer purchased power from a single utility company, which was responsible for responding to the customer's demand for a specified level of reliability and quality of service. With deregulation, the retail customer will be able to purchase electricity from the interstate transmission grid supplied by several power generators. As such, there may be less control over the reliability and quality of power provided by several sources compared with the power supplied by a single source.

10. *Future load growth planning.* Local utility companies are currently required to estimate and plan for future growth in their service areas by negotiating long-term contracts with other power generators for the purchase of their excess capacity or by constructing their own new power generation plants. The FERC and PUCs must determine who will be responsible for future load growth planning.

11. *Uneconomic customers.* Currently, local regulated utility customers are required to provide electricity to all customers in their service area. Some such service is uneconomical because of the difficulty accessing these customers, the remoteness of their location, or poor load profiles. Provision of power to customers based on market-driven incentives places these customers in jeopardy of not having access to power. States must identify how customers for whom service is uneconomical can continue to be served.

12. *Competitive inequities.* Deregulation provisions related to power generators apply only to investor-owned utilities. Investor-owned utilities are not allowed to compete for customers located in service areas served by municipalities and rural electric cooperatives. However, municipalities and rural electric cooperatives can compete for customers served by investor-owned utilities. In addition, municipalities and rural electric cooperatives often receive government subsidies or tax exemption status, which contributes to the inequity.

Both the House and the Senate are currently considering various federal legislative initiatives to promote competition through electricity deregulation. The proposed Electric Power Competition Act of 1996 (H.R.

2929) would establish overall federal standards for competition that could be met by either divesting generation from transmission and distribution assets or by permitting power generation competition on an open and nondiscriminatory basis. It would establish minimum certification requirements designed to protect retail consumers from discriminatory pricing and to encourage energy conservation and renewable energy programs. Those states that meet the competition standards and minimum certification requirements of the bill would no longer be required to meet PURPA's federal power purchase mandate. The bill had one hearing before the House Commerce Subcommittee on Energy and Power. No action is expected this session.

The Electricity Competition Act of 1996 (S. 1526), a bill that is being considered by the Senate, calls for the repeal of the Public Utility Holding Company Act (PUHCA) and includes six principal provisions: 1) retail access for all electricity consumers by the year 2010, 2) assured stranded cost recovery, 3) shared federal and state responsibility to track current jurisdictional responsibilities, 4) a clear timetable for the transition to a competitive market, 5) reform of PURPA and PUHCA, and 6) assured recovery of costs to decommission nuclear power plants. The bill had a hearing in March with no mark-up scheduled for the last mark-up session of Congress.

The Forrestal Marshall Institutes proposal would establish two institutes aimed at facilitating the use of private investment to upgrade federal energy facilities. The House Budget Committee included the Institutes in its budget resolution, but the Office of Management and Budget is against the creation of a nongovernment corporation.

Management

Several states, particularly those whose utility companies charge the highest electrical rates, are aggressively pursuing the deregulation of electricity. The successful implementation of regional or statewide power pooling by independent wholesale power producers—as in Florida, where savings of more than $1 billion have been achieved since 1980—exemplifies the opportunities for cost savings that can potentially be achieved through deregulation.

At this time there is considerable speculation concerning the final form of deregulation; its implementation; and its impact on national, regional, and local electrical costs. Many believe that it will take several years for retail customers to see any economic benefit from deregulation. Many also believe that the long-term impact of deregulation will be a leveling of rates across the nation. It is anticipated that customers who currently enjoy low electrical rates will see a general increase in their rates, whereas those who experience high electrical costs will experience a reduction in their rates.

The uncertain outcome of deregulation makes it extremely difficult to assess the long-term economics of the industry. The inability to project long-term electrical costs make it difficult to evaluate the economic attractiveness of projects oriented toward local control of electrical costs such as cogeneration. Institutions that currently have difficulty justifying cogeneration because of the low cost of electricity may find cogeneration an attractive option if their electrical rates increase. Those institutions whose financing of cogeneration facilities were based on a rapid payback on investment may find their payback period extending as the cost to purchase electricity decreases. Increasing restrictions on environmental emissions, the requirement to install new emission control technologies, the fines imposed on emission quantities, local aesthetic concerns, maintenance costs, and fluctuations in fuel purchase costs all should be considered when evaluating the economic attractiveness of cogeneration.

The focus of electric deregulation has been on increasing competition and reducing cost. However, many energy managers are just as concerned with power quality and consistency. Much of the equipment used in patient care and clinical and academic research is extremely sensitive to power quality and reacts to even minor fluctuations in power. The direct purchase of electricity from the wholesale pool may reduce the local control the energy manager has over power quality and consistency.

42.4 SUMMARY

The field of fuels management offers many opportunities and challenges. Continuing deregulation of energy production, transportation or transmission, and distribution provides many opportunities for saving on the purchase cost of fuels and electricity. Therefore, it is extremely important for the energy manager to keep abreast of state and federal regulatory changes and to be familiar with the successes and failures of deregulation to be able to capitalize on opportunities to reduce purchased energy costs. Equally important is the need to ensure consistent and reliable fuel supplies, especially to critical facilities and equipment.

The energy manager must continuously evaluate mechanisms for reducing energy purchase costs and use at the institution. Any demand-side management programs, ice or chilled water storage systems, cogeneration facilities, energy conservation measures, building automation and control systems, fuels storage systems, and other mechanisms for controlling energy use and cost should be evaluated at least annually to ensure that they continue to operate cost-effectively and are the most efficient management of resources.

The proper management of fuel availability, consistency, quality, and price is a time-consuming function. It requires dedicated and highly qualified managers who are experts at energy management, knowledgeable of state and federal regulatory issues, and technically proficient and who understand basic business principles. Significant savings can be achieved and programmatic requirements met with the proper management of fuels.

ADDITIONAL RESOURCES

American Society of Heating, Refrigerating, and Air-Conditioning Engineers. *1993 ASHRAE Handbook, Fundamentals,* I-P edition. Atlanta: ASHRAE, 1993.

U.S. Federal Energy Regulatory Commission. Notice of Proposed Rulemaking and Supplemental Notice of Proposed Rulemaking. Docket No. RM95-8-000: Promoting Wholesale Competition Through Open Access Non-discriminatory Transmission Services by Public Utilities. Docket No. RM94-7-001: Recovery of Stranded Costs by Public Utilities and Transmitting Utilities. Washington, D.C.: U.S. Federal Energy Regulatory Commission, March 29, 1995.

CHAPTER 43

Regulatory Issues for Utility Plants

Mohammad H. Qayoumi
University of Missouri-Rolla

43.1 INTRODUCTION

Humankind's ability to harness various form of energy has played a key role in our becoming the dominant species on the planet. The extensive use of fossil fuel provides the means of sustaining rapid growth of world's population and improved standard of living. Currently the world is consuming about 346 quad (quadrillion British thermal units) of energy per year, and this is expected to increase at the rate of 1.6 percent at least for the next two decades. This means that world energy consumption could increase to between 450 and 500 quads by the year 2020. Currently, the burning of fossil fuel adds approximately 5.5 billion tons of carbon, principally in the form of carbon dioxide, to the atmosphere.

The intensive burning of fossil fuel is irrevocably changing the earth's climate in fundamental way. Scientists believe that the increase in the concentration of carbon dioxide will lead to global warming, which will increase the earth's temperature. If the current accumulation rate continues, with the carbon dioxide concentration increasing from its present level of 340 ppm to 600 ppm, the average earth crest temperature will increase between 1.5°C and 4.5°C, which may have a cataclysmic impact in some parts of the world. For instance, a number of small island countries could disappear because they are at sea level, and low-lying nations such as Egypt or Bangladesh could lose a significant part of their land. Global warming would cause the polar ice caps to melt, thus increasing the water level in all of the oceans. Another gas that has a had a significant contribution to the global warming is chlorofluorocarbon, the principal refrigerant for mechanical cooling. Although the concentration of these compounds is markedly smaller than that of carbon dioxide, their impact on global warming is more than an order of magnitude higher.

In addition to global warming, the other environmental impacts of burning fossil fuel include the release of large quantities of sulfur dioxide, nitrogen oxides, and particulate. Sulfur dioxide produced by fossil plants has contributed to the formation of acid rain, which has polluted many lakes and destroyed hundreds of thousands of acres of land. For instance, the major source of acid rain in New England and eastern Canada is attributed to sulfur emissions from coal-fired plants in the Midwest. Particulate emissions from many coal-fired plants have resulted in high ambient airborne particulate levels in many areas. Similarity, nitrogen oxide is the primary source of smog in many major metropolitan areas in the nation.

The environmental impacts of burning fossil fuel have been grave. For instance, about 30 percent of Americans live in an area where at least one of the federal pollutant levels is exceeded. Responding to this and other similar concerns, the U.S. Congress has enacted legislation to improve the overall environment of the nation. This legislation has greatly affected the installation and operation of new energy sources.

In this chapter some of the major legislation in this area is examined. The legislation that has had the most significant impact is the Clean Air Act. The second area examined is indoor air quality issues. Although no final legislation has been enacted, American Society of Heating, Refrigerating, and Air-Conditioning Engineers (ASHRAE) guidelines have increased outside air requirements by almost a factor of 4. This has resulted in major load increases in both cooling and heating requirements from central utility plants. The last legislation examined is the Energy Policy Act of 1992, which involved the deregulation of electricity.

43.2 THE CLEAN AIR ACT

The first Clean Air Act (CAA) was signed into law by President Lyndon B. Johnson in 1963. The first major amendment to the act, in 1975, established primary standards that set limits to protect the health and safety of humans, as well as secondary standards to safeguard animals and plant life. The act differentiated regions of the country based on national ambient air quality standards. Regions that met the standards were considered *attainment areas,* and those that did not, *nonattainment areas.* For attainment areas, the air quality guidelines were supposed to safeguard and prevent any significant deterioration (PSD). For nonattainment areas, limitations were placed on the addition of new pollution sources to the areas.

The latest amendments to the Clean Air Act were proposed in 1989 and were signed into law by President George Bush in 1991. These amendments primarily addressed national environmental issues such toxic air emissions, phaseout of ozone-depleting substances, acid rain, and urban air pollution. There are eight titles in the amendments, which are outlined as follows:

- *Title I:* Maintenance of national ambient air quality standards.
- *Title II:* Mobile sources.
- *Title III:* Toxic air emissions and establishment of maximum available control technology (MACT).
- *Title IV:* Control of acid disposition.
- *Title V:* Permitting procedures.
- *Title VI:* Stratospheric and global climate protection.
- *Title VII:* Enforcement issues concerning the amendments.
- *Title VIII:* Miscellaneous items related to offshore oil and gas drilling, training opportunities, and impacts of the amendments.

As can be seen, the provisions that primarily relate to utilities and energy systems are titles I, V, and VI. The highlights of these, specifically as they affect utility systems, are discussed in the following sections.

Title I

This provision addresses the pollution problem relating to common ambient air and to what extent a particular area must be in compliance with the national ambient air quality standards (NAAQS). Specifically, it deals with pollution resulting from carbon monoxide, ozone, particulate matter, sulfur oxides, lead, and nitrogen dioxide. Based on NAAQS, a region that meets the standards is referred to as an attainment area. As mentioned earlier, for these areas the act safeguards against any major deterioration under the PSD guidelines. Regions where pollution exceeds one or more of the NAAQS levels are called nonattainment areas. For nonattainment areas, based on the severity of nonattainment, three different solutions are proposed. For moderate nonattainment levels, reasonably available control technology measures (RACMs) are prescribed. If the nonattainment level is higher than moderate levels, best available control technology (BACT) is prescribed. If the nonattainment level is considered serious, the only way a new source of pollution can be added is through the achievement of negative offsets somewhere in the system. For instance, if an institution is in a severe nonattainment area and is planning to install a new boiler that will emit X tons of nitrogen dioxide, it can obtain a permit only by one of the following ways:

1. The institution has other operating boilers that currently emit X or more tons to the environment and decides to decommission these units.
2. The institution can make retrofits to existing operating boilers that result in a net reduction of X or more tons of nitrogen dioxide.
3. The institution agrees to make retrofits to the boilers in another institution in the region that result in a reduction of X or more tons of nitrogen dioxide.

4. The institution finds a third party that is decommissioning a unit in the region that had an emission equal to or greater than X tons of nitrogen dioxide and that is willing to trade or sell the rights to this unit to the institution.

Thus, one can clearly see that adding new sources of pollution in nonattainment areas brings up a new set of challenges for the utility plant manager. The issue of negative offset creates a market for the trade of emission rights, especially for plants that are being closed.

No specific technologies have been prescribed by the act concerning RACM and BACT, and there is room for broad interpretation by local offices of the Environmental Protection Agency (EPA). This ambiguity makes the job of cost estimation very difficult. Therefore, in most cases the actual cost of projects will be higher than originally estimated owing to a lack of specificity regarding environmental pollution control devices.

Depending on the particular nonattainment substance, the choice of primary fuel may be greatly influenced. For instance, if particulate emission is the problem, then adding sources that burn solid fuels such as coal, wood chips, or solid waste will be very difficult, and shifting to liquid or gaseous fuels may be the only feasible option. If acid rain caused by higher sulfur emissions is a concern, then burning medium- or high-sulfur coal will be problematic. In this situation low-sulfur coal (coal with less than 1 percent sulfur), liquid fuels, or gaseous fuels may be the most feasible choices. If the nitrogen oxide level is the problem, the choice of fuels does not need to be altered. Formation of nitrogen oxide can be minimized by reducing the combustion temperature; the most common method is by reinjecting a water spray. Thus, it is clear to see that the choice of fuel may be dictated by the local ambient air quality, which in turn can have an impact on the type and complexity of equipment needed, as well as the cost of producing thermal energy.

Title V

This provision deals specifically with permitting procedures. All states were required to submit a state implementation plan (SIP) when the bill went into effect. The motivation behind this was to give stronger enforcement powers in the area of national ambient air quality. According to this provision, a permit can be given by a state agency for a maximum period of five years. If any state fails to satisfactorily submit an SIP that is acceptable to the EPA, two possible sanctions can be imposed: the EPA can remove federal highway improvement funds, and it can impose its own federal implementation plan (FIP). Therefore, this provision gave states a strong incentive to impose state rules that are more stringent than federal guidelines in an effort to satisfy the EPA. However, this translates into more barriers to getting permits for new sources and to getting renewal permits for some sources that are deemed to be big contributors to air pollution problems for local areas. For facilities managers, this means a longer and more costly permitting process.

Title VI

This provision deals with stratospheric ozone and global climate protection. The principal motivation behind it was to bring U.S. laws in line with the Montreal Protocol.

Before discussing the impact of this legislation, let us look at some background information. The earth is engulfed by a layer of ozone at the stratosphere that acts as a shield against the ultraviolet radiation from the sun. Based on data obtained from the National Aeronautics and Space Administration (NASA), the concentration of ozone in the stratosphere has been reduced since the 1960s so that at some parts of the year there is an "ozone hole" over the South Pole. Any reduction in the ozone layer translates into an increase in the number of skin cancer cases. For instance, the number of the skin cancer cases in the United States is about 400,000 annually. Based on studies by the EPA, a 1 percent decrease in the ozone layer results in a 2 percent increase in skin cancer cases, or an additional 8,000 cases annually.

Scientists have shown that the principal cause of ozone depletion is the release of chlorine-based halogenated substances. The primary substance responsible for this problem is chlorofluorocarbon (CFC).

Because of the global public health implications of CFCs, in 1987 the United Nations Environmental Programme (UNEP) established the Montreal Protocol on ozone-depleting substances, which called for capping production levels and gradual reductions in the manufacturing of these substances until they were phased out. However, by 1990 it was realized that the problem was more serious than originally understood. As a result, the phaseout of ozone-depleting substances was accelerated; the production of CFC-containing substances was banned effective January 1, 1996, and a more accelerated phaseout schedule was adopted for hydrochlorofluorocarbons (HCFCs).

Because 80 percent of mechanical refrigeration equipment uses CFC-containing refrigerants, this particular ruling significantly affected cooling and air conditioning processes. The primary effects are as follows:

- It required mandatory and certification training for those who handle refrigerants.
- It required record keeping relative to the amount of refrigerant a site has. Also, the amount of annual losses in a machine must be kept below 5 percent. This necessitated the installation of high-efficiency purge equipment on all existing units.

- ASHRAE developed standards relating to refrigeration safety; these require the installation of a leak detection system as well as the use of a self-contained breathing apparatus.

The manufacturing phaseout of CFCs has caused manufacturers to look into new refrigerants that are not chlorine based. These non-CFC refrigerants are used exclusively in new chillers and as replacement refrigerants in existing units. Replacing the refrigerant in an existing chiller results in some loss of efficiency as well as a 5 to 15 percent reduction in capacity, although in more recent years manufacturers have been able to minimize the efficiency and capacity deterioration to only a few percent. A more important effect of this legislation was faster replacement of chillers that would otherwise have operated for many years. Chillers that are more than 15 years old have an efficiency of about 1.1 kW per ton, whereas new chillers have an efficiency of about 0.55 kW per ton, which made replacement the most attractive option. This in turn resulted in a need for more capital for chiller replacement.

43.3 INDOOR AIR QUALITY

Since the 1980s, concern has been expressed regarding indoor air quality for nonindustrial buildings. Such problems have occurred in buildings of all types, structures, and ages, from newly constructed buildings to renovated facilities or old buildings. Currently most commercial and institutional buildings are mechanically ventilated, with virtually no natural ventilation from the outside. Moreover, because of rising energy costs, designers, owners, and operators have tried to minimize unwanted air infiltration. This, coupled with various chemicals present in building materials and furniture, is the root cause of "tight building syndrome." Therefore, in addition to other physical factors in the workspace, such as noise, lack of operable windows, temperature variations, and poor ergonomic design, tight building syndrome needs to be addressed. Poor indoor air quality is viewed as another source of employee complaints, although it is difficult to assess with specificity.

Indoor air quality problems are generally classified as sick building syndrome (SBS) or building-related illness (BRI). Symptoms of SBS or BRI include irritation of the eyes, nose, and throat; fatigue; headache; respiratory infection and cough; nausea; and dizziness. This list is not all-inclusive. Based on studies conducted in Denmark, Britain, and the United States, it is hypothesized that about 20 percent of office workers are exposed to indoor conditions that manifest as SBS. Also, according to a 1987 national survey of 600 U.S. office workers, 28 percent of women and 15 percent of men perceived that their performance was adversely affected by poor indoor air quality.

SBS symptoms can be divided into two categories: symptoms attributable to chemical exposures (fatigue; headache; dry, irritated eyes, nose, and throat; nausea; and dizziness) and symptoms attributable to microbial exposures (itchy, congested, runny nose or eyes; wheezing, light chest; or flu-like symptoms).

BRI consists of sensory irritations, respiratory allergies, hypersensitivity, and legionnaires' disease. Susceptibility is influenced by immune system status; for instance, individuals with pulmonary diseases such as asthma are more susceptible than others. Currently the list of known indoor air contaminants is long; contaminants of concern include volatile organic compounds (VOCs) in solvents, which are generally used in the formulation or manufacturing of consumer products; formaldehyde; compounds from plywood, carpets, paneling, and insulation; combustion gases; compounds from man-made fibers; ozone; vehicle exhaust; tobacco smoke; pesticides; and chemicals used in cleaning. These substances, separately or in synergy, can cause a variety of health effects. Thus, a plethora of building materials, interior furnishings and appliances, office equipment, and supplies can potentially be the root cause of BRI. Microbial contamination in the form of algae, bacteria, and fungi can occur if the relative humidity is above 60 percent.

To address the indoor air quality problem, ASHRAE revised its guidelines for minimum outside air ventilation quantities. The latest American National Standards Institute (ANSI)/ASHRAE Standard 62-1989, Ventilation for Acceptable Indoor Air Quality, increased outside air quality several-fold compared with old guidelines.

Since the 1980s, litigation involving indoor air quality problems has been on the rise. The plaintiffs have alleged many claims, ranging from neurological damage to pulmonary diseases and newly acquired allergies, for which they have sought compensating as well as punitive damages. In many cases the plaintiffs have sued their employers, but the list of potential defendants can include building owners, developers, and managers; design architects and engineers; contractors; building product manufacturers; and leasing agents. This has naturally made many facilities managers and owners nervous.

43.4 ENERGY POLICY ACT

In 1992 President Bush signed the Energy Policy Act (EPAct) into law. There are a number of provisions in this law that directly or indirectly affect utilities management. Two areas, lighting and deregulation of electricity, are briefly discussed as follows:

- *Lighting efficiency:* EPAct imposed two provisions for lighting: efficiency labeling and efficiency standards. The purpose of efficiency labeling is to enable consumers to select the most energy-efficient lamps. Efficiency standards were established to improve the overall

lighting efficiency for all types of lamps (e.g., incandescent, fluorescent, and low- and high-pressure lamps). This provision is discussed in more detail in Chapter 26.
* *Deregulation of electricity:* EPAct also provided the framework for state public utilities commissions to deregulate the generation of electricity. In other words, the act created the opportunity to break the monopoly enjoyed by investor-owned utilities so that a facility has the choice of purchasing power from an alternate energy source and paying a transmission fee to the local electric company. This concept is discussed in more detail in Chapter 42. The major impact of this is two-fold. First, it creates an avenue for more competition, which will tend to decrease the cost of electricity. Second, the process of procuring electricity for most plant managers will become far more complicated. In other words, greater expertise will be required to decipher various power procurement options and to project power demands for the facility with a high level of accuracy.

In addition to the above, there are a number of other regulatory provisions that have affected the operation of utility plants, such as deregulation of natural gas and the Public Utilities Regulatory Policy Act (PURPA). The deregulation of natural gas resulted in lower gas prices, which, coupled with environmental regulation, increased the proliferation of natural gas boilers. The deregulation of natural gas is discussed in more detail in Chapter 42. Similarly, PURPA encouraged the proliferation of cogeneration units, which many campuses installed during the 1980s. PURPA is discussed in more detail in Chapter 46. However, it is sufficient to mention that PURPA not only provided new opportunities for facilities to lower the overall energy costs, it increased the operational complexity of utility plants. This is because operating a cogeneration unit requires more expertise than running boilers or chillers.

In conclusion, since the late 1970s, much legislation has affected the operation of central plants directly or indirectly, with the primary effect being to increase the complexity of operating utility plants.

ADDITIONAL RESOURCES

Dingman, Robert. *Regulatory Compliance for Facilities Managers.* Alexandria, Virginia: APPA, 1989.

Hines, Virginia. "EPA's Green Light Program Promotes Environmental Protection, Energy Savings, and Profit." *Strategic Planning for Energy and the Environment,* Winter 1990–1991.

Qayoumi, Mohammad. "Negawatt or Megawatt." *Northern California Executive Review,* Vol. 8, No. 1, 1994, pp. 9–12, 18.

Williams, Dan, and Larry Good. *Guide to the Energy Policy Act of 1992.* Lilburn, Georgia: The Fairmont Press, 1994.

SECTION III-B

DISTRICT ENERGY SYSTEMS

Editor:
Alan R. Warden
University of Missouri/Columbia

INTRODUCTION

District Energy Systems

The mission of facilities operations is to provide a suitable environment for the activities of universities and colleges. There are several objectives involved in this mission. One important objective is to ensure that the temperature and humidity are at the appropriate level to permit students, faculty, and staff to work productively. Another objective is to provide electrical and other energy sources for university or college activities.

When an institution grows beyond a few buildings on a single campus, central energy systems begin to make sense. At some point, having one boiler or heating plant as well as a cooling plant to serve multiple buildings becomes a logical economic choice. There are several advantages of central plants:

1. Centralized equipment requires less overall space.
2. Economies of scale provide both capital and operating efficiencies.
3. A central plant allows operating staff to be deployed most efficiently.

Chapter 44 deals with central heating facilities, whereas Chapter 45 covers central cooling facilities. These two chapters provide a good introduction for those who are new to these concepts.

Cogeneration, defined as the production or generation of two forms of energy in the same process, has been practiced for more than 100 years. Traditionally, cogeneration involved producing heating steam and electricity from the same stream process with coal as the primary fuel. Currently, natural gas or oil may be used as primary fuel in a combustion turbine with steam produced in a waste heat boiler. More combinations are available and are described in Chapter 46.

The primary advantage of cogeneration is operational efficiency. Because cogeneration uses energy that is otherwise wasted, it can result in significant savings. Sometimes cogeneration is included in central cooling plants using innovative combinations. Many of these combinations are introduced and discussed in Chapter 46.

Institutions with several buildings and a central plant require distribution systems. These systems may include steam, hot water, chilled water, electricity, and so forth. Each utility has unique characteristics and technology that are involved in its distribution. As much as 75 percent of the energy distribution to campus buildings may be in the form of steam or hot water. The remaining 25 percent will be in the form of electricity. Chapters 47 and 48 discuss the concepts and methods most widely used on modern campuses.

The authors of these chapters have provided a basic introduction to their respective fields. Some authors have included considerable detail in describing a process or technology, but none have given sufficient detail to permit the novice to design systems or a plant. Another excellent source of competent help is a sister university or college already employing the concept or technology. Their experience, as well as the information contained in these chapters, could be invaluable. However, those interested in implementing these concepts should seek the advice of qualified experts or consultants.

—Alan Warden

CHAPTER 44

Central Heating Plants

David J. Miller, P.E.
Iowa State University

44.1 INTRODUCTION

Today's facilities manager must evaluate many alternatives to meet energy demands and must make sound decisions regarding large capital expenditures for plant additions and alterations. An understanding of basic heating and power plant cycles and equipment is essential.

This chapter discusses the fuels, processes, and equipment of central heating and power plants. The discussion of fuels, fuel firing, boiler control, and emission control applies generally to all sizes and types of boilers.

Boilers are the basic building blocks of any plant system for the generation of hot water or steam. Whether fueled by gas, oil, coal, or refuse, boilers are used by virtually every college and university. They may be located in a central plant or distributed among various campus buildings as package boilers. The energy derived from these boilers is generally in the form of steam. This steam is used to 1) generate electricity through turbine generators, 2) heat buildings with direct steam or hot water, 3) cool buildings with steam-driven centrifugal or absorption chilled water systems, and 4) provide steam for processes. To increase plant efficiency, a variety of auxiliary equipment is available, including economizers, air preheaters, feedwater heaters, superheaters, and various heat exchangers, to maximize the use of the heat generated in the burning of fuels. In addition, other equipment, such as mechanical collectors, dust collectors, electrostatic precipitators, baghouses, scrubbers, and waste water treatment systems, is often required to satisfy emission standards.

Reliable performance of the plant system is critical to institutional operations. Efficient delivery of energy services to control operating costs is equally important. It is not uncommon for utility operating expenses to approach one-half of the facilities budget. For these reasons, the responsible facilities manager must devote considerable time to ensure reliable utility service at the least possible cost. This chapter will cover the fundamental operation and maintenance procedures that the facilities manager can use to maximize the inherent advantages of a central plant system and achieve cost-effective and reliable service.

44.2   CENTRAL SYSTEMS

The basic power plant cycle and configuration for steam or hot water distribution are shown in Figures 44-1, 44-2, and 44-3. A central plant system has several economic and operational advantages.

Advantages

The advantages of a central plant system are as follows:

- Less capital is required for equipment in a central location than in many individual buildings. Total system load will be lower because all connected buildings will not peak simultaneously. This relationship between the sum of the peak loads for individual buildings and the actual aggregate central system peak load is known as *diversity factor.*
- The installation of standby equipment is economically feasible.
- Net assignable square footage for buildings is increased owing to the reduction of in-building machinery space requirements.
- Twenty-four-hour supervision by skilled operators is economically feasible.
- Aesthetically undesirable cooling tower plumes, drift loss, and noise are concentrated in a single location instead of at each building.
- Operating and maintenance staffing costs are minimized because of the centralized equipment location.
- Increased efficiencies are possible with large heating and cooling equipment, which reduces operating cost per unit of energy output.
- Part-load performance efficiencies are substantially improved by the ability to meet the system load with the most efficient equipment.
- A single point of delivery for purchased utilities allows for favorable rates as a large-volume customer.
- Multiple fuel sources are a practical alternative.

The advantages allow the facilities manager of an existing system to minimize operating cost, but they can also assist the manager of a distributed system to evaluate the potential savings that might be realized by replacing individual building heating and cooling equipment with a central energy system.

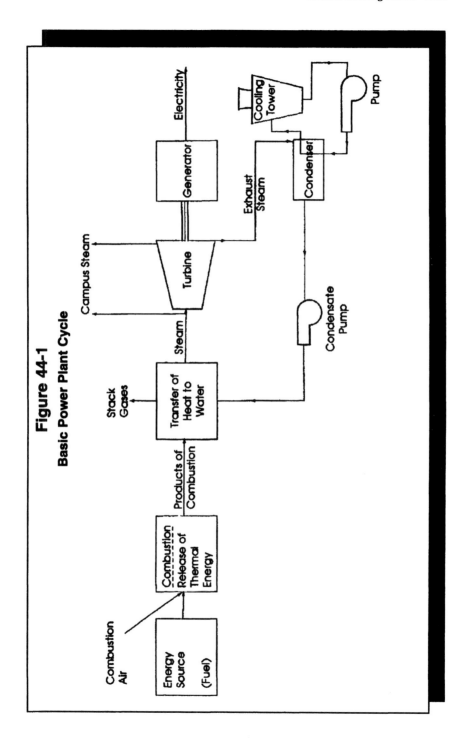

Figure 44-1
Basic Power Plant Cycle

Figure 44-2

Basic Arrangement for Steam Heating System

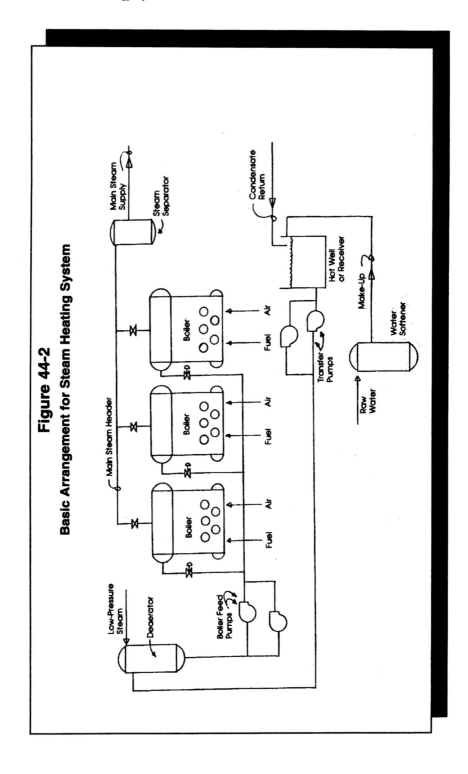

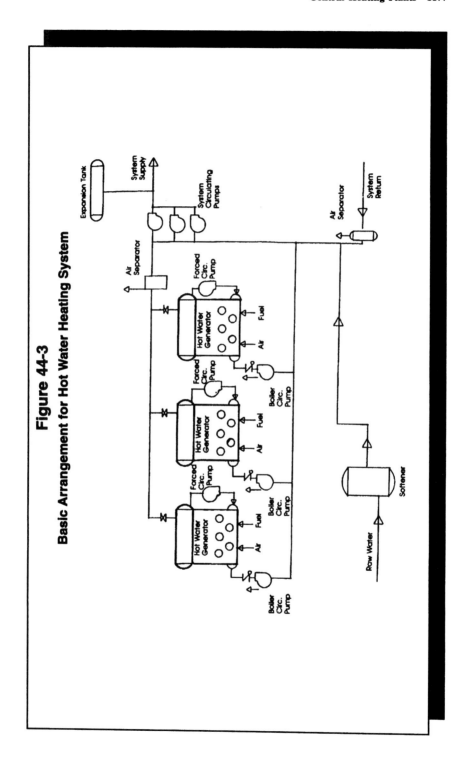

Figure 44-3

Basic Arrangement for Hot Water Heating System

Disadvantages

The disadvantages of a central plant system are as follows:

- Initial construction cost requires a large capital investment.
- Thermal and hydraulic losses occur in a large distribution network rather than in a distributed system where thermal utility services are generated at the point of use.
- Large systems may require compliance with more stringent environmental regulations.

44.3 FUELS

A wide variety of fuels are used in central plant boilers. Primary fuels such as natural gas, fuel oil, and coal can be augmented with alternate fuels such as refuse-derived fuel (RDF), tire-derived fuel (TDF), bark or other wood products, petroleum coke, anthracite culm, and various manufacturing by-products.

Each fuel must be evaluated on the basis of its availability and price as delivered to the point of use. Transportation charges at times can exceed the actual cost of the raw fuel. In evaluating fuels, consideration must be given to impurities in the fuel that may affect combustion performance or environmental emissions, as well as the variability in the higher heating value (HHV) of the fuel measured in Btus per pound. The HHV of the fuels varies from 23,500 Btu/lb. for natural gas to 4,000 Btu/lb. for anthracite culm. Ash and moisture content also must be monitored. In fluidized bed combustion, a limestone source must be secured that has adequate reactivity to remove sulfur from the flue gas efficiently.

The normal range of heating values for various fossil fuels is given in Figure 44-4.

44.4 PRINCIPLES OF COMBUSTION

Combustion of all fuels consists of combining oxygen with carbon and hydrogen (oxidation) to release heat, carbon dioxide, and water. If there is a lack of oxygen, some of the carbon will not be completely oxidized, and carbon monoxide will be formed. Carbon monoxide is itself a fuel with a heating value of about 4,300 Btu/lb. Formation of carbon monoxide indicates incomplete combustion of the fuel. The products of combustion may also include nitrogen and sulfur oxides, which are regulated pollutants that can cause chemical fouling and corrosion of boiler equipment (Figure 44-5).

Three conditions must be met for combustion to occur:

1. The fuel must be gasified.
2. The oxygen-fuel mixture must be within the flammable range.
3. The mixture must be above its ignition temperature.

Figure 44-4

Normal Range of Heating Values for Various Fossil Fuels

Natural gas	20,000—23,500 Btu/lb.
	(1,000 Btu/cu. ft.)*
No. 1 fuel oil	19,670–19,860 Btu/lb.
No. 2 fuel oil	19,170–19,750 Btu/lb.
No. 4 fuel oil	18,280–19,400 Btu/lb.
No. 5 fuel oil	18,100–19,020 Btu/lb.
No. 6 fuel oil	17,410–18,990 Btu/lb.
Bituminous coal	10,500–14,500 Btu/lb.
Subbituminous coal	8,500–11,500 Btu/lb.
Lignite	6,300–8,300 Btu/lb.
Anthracite culm	4,000–5,000 Btu/lb.

* A Btu is equal to the amount of energy required to raise the temperature of 1 lb. of water 1°F.

Once the combustion process is started, the quality of combustion is determined by time, temperature, and turbulence. Good combustion is rapid, has a high flame temperature, and is turbulent. Turbulence is the key factor in boiler furnace combustion. If turbulence is high, mixing of the oxygen and fuel will be good, and combustion will be rapid and result in high temperatures.

The specific amount of air required to complete combustion is known as *theoretical air*. In actual combustion, excess air is required, because the mixing of fuel and air is never perfect. The amount of excess air depends on the boiler type, fuel properties, and burner or stoker characteristics. Because excess air is supplied to the combustion process, all the available oxygen in the air will not be used. Excess air is a primary indicator of system performance.

To determine the amount of excess air, first measure the oxygen or carbon dioxide present in the flue gas. Measuring oxygen is generally preferred to measuring carbon dioxide; the instrumentation is simpler and cheaper, and the oxygen-to-excess-air relationship is less variable than the carbon-dioxide-to-air relationship. An oxygen analyzer is used to measure the percentage of excess oxygen in combustion products. The excess air can be determined from the measured excess oxygen and known chemical composition of the fuel. Excess air requirements are stated as a percentage, as is the excess oxygen in the flue gas. Typical ranges for excess air are given in Figure 44-6.

Figure 44-5
Basic Combustion Equation

$$+ \quad O_2 \; + \; N_2 \; + \; S \qquad CO_2 \; + \; N_2 \; + \; SO_x \; + \; HEAT$$

$$\underbrace{\qquad\qquad\qquad}_{\text{Air}} \quad \underbrace{\quad}_{\substack{\text{Impurity} \\ \text{(Sulfur)}}} \qquad \underbrace{\qquad\qquad\qquad\qquad}_{\text{Products of Combustion}}$$

Figure 44-6
Typical Ranges for Excess Air

Fuel	Combustion Type	Excess Air (%)
Coal	Pulverized coal	15–20
	Spreader stoker	30–60
	Chain grate	15–50
Fuel oil	Register-type burners	5–10
	Multiflame burners	10–20
Natural gas		5–10
Wood		25–50

44.5   BOILER TYPES

There are two basic boiler types: fire tube and water tube. Boilers may be further classified as either package or field-erected units, based on the manufacturing method and installation. A package unit is built, tested before shipment, and delivered as a one-piece unit requiring little field erection other than connection of auxiliaries. Field-erected units require field assembly of the various boiler components.

Fire Tube Boilers   Fire tube boilers have a shell that holds the water and tubes running the length of the unit. Flames and hot gases from the burner pass through the tubes, thereby heating the water. The boilers are manufactured in ratings that allow as much as 20,000 lb. of steam to flow from the boiler in one hour at a maximum practical operating pressure of around 250 psi. The rating of these boilers is often given in terms of boiler horsepower, such as 600 boiler horsepower for a 20,000 lb./hour unit.

Fire tube boilers feature simple, rugged construction and have a relatively low initial cost. Their large water capacity makes them relatively sluggish in operation and slow to achieve operating pressure from a cold start. Several operational configurations can be used depending on the number of times the hot gases are routed through the shell. Two-pass, three-pass, and four-pass designs are available. Additional passes increase the initial cost as well as the unit efficiency. Forced draft is normally used with multiple passes of the combustion gases (Figure 44-7).

Water Tube Boilers   A wide variety of water tube boilers are available. Identifying these boilers is complicated by the numerous methods of classification: straight tube or bent tube; horizontal, vertical, or inclined tube; longitudinal or cross-drum; and so on. However, their distinguishing characteristic is that the water is contained in tubes located in the combustion chamber. The tubes are connected to a larger pipe or header leading to a steam drum. As heat is transferred to the water in the tubes, steam is generated and flows to the steam drum.

The initial cost of a water tube boiler is higher than that of an equivalent fire tube boiler, but efficiency is significantly higher, and performance is much more responsive to load changes. Package-type water tube boilers are available in sizes up to 100,000 lb. of steam per hour. Above the 100,000 lb./hour rating, the units are generally field erected.

44.6   COMBUSTION EQUIPMENT

Natural Gas   Natural gas contains about 25 percent hydrogen and 75 percent carbon by weight. It is the cleanest burning and easiest to handle of all fuels. Products of combustion include water, carbon dioxide, hydrogen, oxygen, and nitrogen oxides. Many designs of gas burners exist, dif-

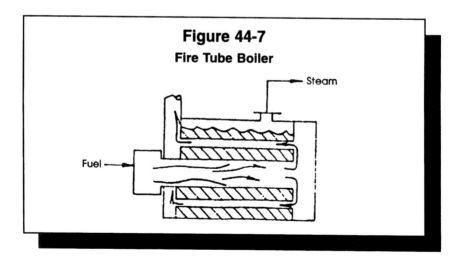

Figure 44-7
Fire Tube Boiler

fering primarily in the orientation of burner orifices and their location in the burner housing.

Oils The use of oil is more complicated than the use of natural gas because of the preparation required. Solid foreign matter must be removed by straining. The oil is heated by tank and/or flow line heaters for lower viscosity and must be atomized before mixing with combustion air. A gun introduces the oil into a burner in a fine spray. Products of combustion include water, carbon dioxide, nitrogen, oxygen, nitrogen oxides, sulfur, and particulate matter. The particulate matter sticks to tubes and boiler surfaces and leads to boiler fouling if these surfaces are not cleaned regularly. Sulfur oxides combine with water to form sulfuric acid, which can cause boiler corrosion (Figure 44-8).

Coal In a coal-burning system using stoker/grate firing, air is supplied to the combustion process in two stages. Primary air is introduced under the fuel bed, and overfire air, or secondary air, is introduced above the bed. The oxygen content of the primary air rising through the fuel bed is consumed, forming carbon dioxide. A portion of the carbon dioxide rising through the fuel bed is converted to carbon monoxide by reacting with the carbon content of the fuel. This combustible gas passes into the combustion space above the bed where overfire air is admitted. Here the combustion process is completed. As a general guide, about half the air by

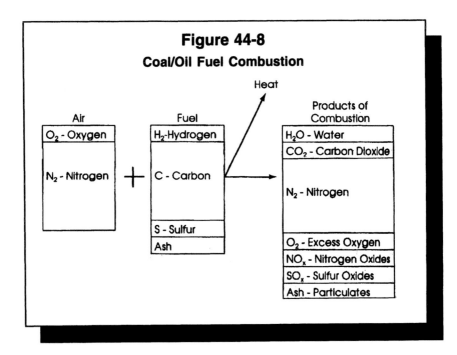

Figure 44-8
Coal/Oil Fuel Combustion

weight is supplied below the bed and half above the bed. The rate of burning is controlled by the primary air, and the completeness of combustion is controlled by the overfire air. The products of combustion vary with the grade of coal but include carbon, hydrogen, nitrogen, oxygen, sulfur, moisture, incombustible materials, and nitric and sulfur oxides.

With a coal-burning system using pulverized coal, the primary air transports the pulverized coal into the furnace. Secondary air is added in the combustion zone to provide more oxygen for combustion and stabilize the flame. Tertiary air may be introduced at some point remote from the main combustion zone to complete the combustion process. The principal advantages of using pulverized coal over other types of coal are as follows:

- Capability of better mixing of fuel and air
- Quick response to changing requirements
- Minimization of fuel waste in starting, banking, and other steps
- Ability to maintain high rates of combustion without forced draft because of the absence of a thick fuel bed

Stokers In all types of stoker boilers, the fuel is burned on a moving mechanical grate. These grates are available in several configurations, including stationary or dump grate, chain-grate, traveling grate, vibrating grate, and spreader stoker. Each type of grate has been developed to optimize the use of specific fuels such as coal, wood products, or municipal waste. Chain-grate and spreader-stoker boilers are the most common for coal-burning units rated at 200,000 lb./hour steam flow or less. Mechanical stoker boilers can handle a wide variety of fuels. Response to load changes is moderate, as there is a large supply of fuel in the bed at any time. Overall unit efficiencies of 80 to 82 percent can be expected (Figure 44-9).

Pulverized Coal In pulverized coal boilers, grinders (pulverizers) are used to reduce the coal to a fine powder. Coal is supplied to the pulverizer in various sizes ranging up to 2 in. The pulverized coal is then dried and classified before being conveyed into the boiler by a combustion air stream. Three of the most widely used pulverizers are the ball-and-tube type, the ball-and-race type, and the roll-and-ring type.

Pulverized coal burners are similar in design to oil-fired burners, and combustion is similar to that of gas. Combustion temperatures can reach 2,000°F. At these temperatures, many coals form ash deposits and slag that can build up in steam-generating sections of the boiler. Response to load change is rapid, and overall unit efficiency is high, approaching 86 percent (Figure 44-10).

Fluidized Bed Use of fluidized bed boiler technology is growing in the United States. This method of combustion burns the fuel in a turbulent atmosphere, generated by combustion air entering at the bottom of the furnace, in the presence of limestone, which absorbs the sulfur. The fuel may be either contained in an agitated bed or completely suspended by air, depending on the unit design. Two advantages of using this method of combustion are the removal of sulfur (and, thus, compliance with environmental standards without additional equipment such as scrubbers) and the ability to use a wide range of fuels. Two primary types of fluidized bed boilers are available: bubbling bed and circulating type.

Bubbling bed boilers are considered to be the original fluidized bed boilers. They have a relatively low velocity of combustion air moving

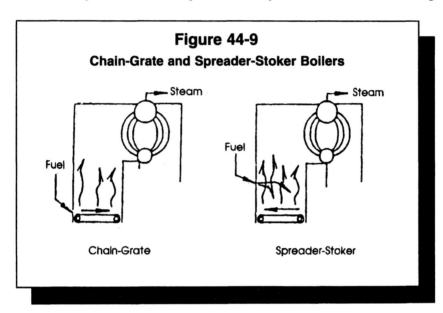

Figure 44-9

Chain-Grate and Spreader-Stoker Boilers

Chain-Grate   Spreader-Stoker

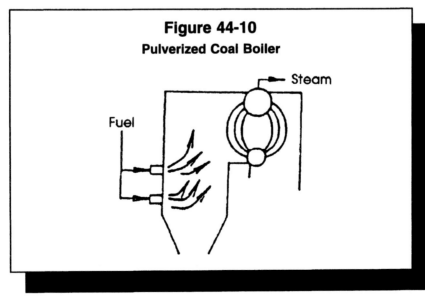

Figure 44-10

Pulverized Coal Boiler

through the bed. Most bubbling bed boilers have heat exchange tubes inside the fuel bed to absorb the heat of combustion from the fuel. An inert material, such as sand, often is added to the fuel bed with limestone to achieve the desired interaction between the fuel and inert materials. The fuel bed material is typically 4 to 6 ft. in depth in a bubbling bed design.

In the circulating-type boiler, combustion air velocities are increased such that a definable bed is not experienced. Rather, the fuel is completely suspended by air or is air entrained. As the bed is dispersed, the fuel is more evenly distributed throughout the volume of the combustion chamber. Better fuel utilization and increased heat absorption in the combustion chamber walls mean that in-bed tubes are not required. These boilers are smaller in size and have a higher combustion efficiency than bubbling bed units.

All fluidized bed boilers have the capability to handle a wide variety of fuels. They can handle feedstocks such as coal, RDF, wood waste, agriculture product waste, anthracite culm, petroleum coke, or any combination of these fuels. Response to changing load demands is rapid, approaching that of the pulverized coal boilers. Overall unit efficiencies of 86 to 87 percent can be expected (Figure 44-11).

Waste Heat Boilers   Waste heat boilers are used in many cogeneration facilities. This type of combustion uses the hot gases from another process, such as exhaust gases from a gas turbine, to transfer heat to steam generation banks. The gas stream may or may not have a fuel content. The steam-generating

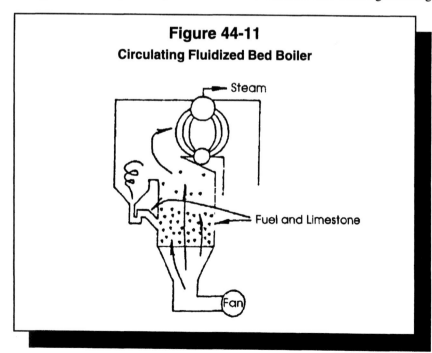

Figure 44-11
Circulating Fluidized Bed Boiler

sections of these boilers are typical of any of the boiler types previously mentioned. Usually a supplementary fuel, such as oil or gas, is required to maintain a constant furnace temperature.

Cyclone Boilers   Cyclone boilers use one or more small combustion chambers attached to a conventional furnace and steam-generating section (convection pass). These small combustion chambers are operated with a turbulent atmosphere at high temperatures. Slag is intentionally formed in the combustion chamber and drained out of the cyclone area. This boiler design results in reduced furnace size and the ability to burn a large variety of fuels owing to the turbulent combustion chamber. These boilers produce high levels of nitrogen oxides (NOXs) because of the higher combustion temperatures.

44.7   BOILER EFFICIENCIES

Three factors can inhibit heat transfer to the steam and water contained in the boiler, resulting in lost energy: combustion factors, heat transfer factors, and steam loss factors.

Combustion Factors

Losses associated with combustion fall into three categories: flue gas losses, combustible losses, and radiation losses.

Flue Gas Waste Heat

Exhaust gas waste heat exists in two forms: dry gas loss and moisture loss. Dry gas loss is the unrecovered sensible heat energy contained in the hot flue gases, excluding water vapor. Moisture loss consists of both latent and sensible heat of the water vapor resulting from the combustion of hydrogen and any moisture present in the fuel or combustion air.

Two methods are used to reduce flue gas losses. One method is to reduce excess air to a minimum. Reduction of excess air reduces the amount of air in the flue gas that can absorb heat. Flue gas velocity is lowered, and heat transfer to the water or steam is increased. Excess air can be reduced by better mixing of the fuel and air. A second method to reduce flue gas losses is to increase heat recovery from the flue gases. Care must be exercised, however, in reducing stack temperatures in boilers that have economizers, air preheaters, and other auxiliary equipment, because reduced stack temperatures may lead to condensation of water vapor. This water vapor can combine with sulfur to form a corrosive acid in the equipment or the stack.

Combustible Losses

Incomplete combustion is evidenced by solid combustibles in the ash, carbon carryover in the fly ash, the presence of carbon monoxide in the exhaust gas, and unburned fuel. Methods used to correct this condition for each fuel type follow.

Natural Gas Carbon monoxide is the only combustible product normally formed in the combustion of natural gas. Carbon monoxide results from too little or too much excess air, from insufficient fuel-air mixing, or from flame impingement on cold water walls. Care should be taken to ensure that the burner is operating in the acceptable excess air range, that diffusers and other mixing equipment are operating properly, and that the flame shape prevents impingement.

Fuel Oil Carbon monoxide is formed during the combustion of fuel oil, as it is for natural gas, and the corrections are the same. In addition, the formation of carbon monoxide may result from improper oil viscosity and inadequate atomization. These conditions can be corrected by checking and adjusting the oil temperature and the operation of the diffuser and atomizer.

Pulverized Coal Carbon monoxide and carbon carryover may be formed by the same factors that affect combustible formation in natural gas and can be corrected in the same way. Incomplete combustion can result from variations in coal sizing. Generally the coal must be pulverized so that 70 percent will pass through a 200-mesh screen.

Stoker-Fired Coal Without careful monitoring, carbon monoxide and smoke may be formed by too much or too little excess air or during low load periods. Correcting the supply of excess air, increasing overfire air velocity, and shifting loads from other boilers may overcome the problem. With stoker-fired coal, solid combustibles are always present in the fly ash, but the amount of unburned material can be reduced by reducing the excess air. Carbon carryover can also be diminished by fly ash reinjection, but reinjection will normally increase the particulate loading at the stack. Carbon monoxide, carbon carryover, and clinkering (solidified slag) may also result from too many fines (undersized coal), wet fines, insufficient bed thickness, improper undergrate air distribution, or improper feeder adjustments on spreader stokers. Plant engineers should check for proper combustion conditions.

Radiation Losses

Radiation loss results from heat that escapes through the boiler shell. This loss constitutes a higher percentage loss in low-load conditions and with smaller boilers because of the increased surface-to-volume ratio. Radiation losses can be cut by ensuring that both the boiler jacket and ductwork are in good condition.

Heat Transfer Factors   Deposits inside and outside the heat transfer tubes act as insulators that impede heat transfer. When deposits accumulate, less heat is able to be absorbed by the water or steam. Deposits can be detected by monitoring flue gas temperatures: rising temperatures indicate that less heat is being transferred in the boiler and more is being lost to the stack. Improper combustion can speed soot deposits on boiler tube surfaces. Several steps must be taken to counteract buildup. For example, water tube boilers should be subjected to frequent soot blowing, sometimes as often as three times a day. Water side deposits can be controlled by effective water treatment and by mechanical or chemical cleaning.

Steam Loss Factors   Steam losses can result from faulty steam traps, leaks to the environment from drains and vents, and inadequate insulation of steam lines. Of the three, malfunctioning steam traps are probably most significant. A variety of tools exists for detecting faulty traps such as temperature-indicating crayon, temperature-actuated color-changing tape, surface temperature gauges, and ultrasonic detectors. Pipe insulation is determined when steam lines are installed, based on cost-effectiveness. However, increases in energy costs change the incremental cost-versus-benefit relationship, and at some point it may be cost-effective to add insulation. Figure 44-12 identifies a variety of boiler problems and their common causes.

44.8   POWER PLANT AUXILIARY EQUIPMENT

A variety of auxiliary equipment may be added to the basic boiler system to recover heat and increase overall unit efficiencies. The most common auxiliary equipment, heat exchangers, increase the temperature of either the water or air supplied to the boiler. An explanation of various heat exchangers and other types of auxiliary equipment follows (Figure 44-13).

Because each installation is unique, no attempt has been made to quantify the potential savings realized by increased efficiencies when auxiliary equipment is added. Any analysis of potential savings must take into account equipment configuration, steam characteristics (pressure and temperature), purchased power costs, and fuel costs. A study must be made of each power plant by qualified engineers to determine efficiency improvements through the addition of auxiliaries.

Economizers   The most commonly used auxiliary to increase unit efficiency is the economizer. The economizer transfers heat from the flue gases to the boiler feedwater. Flue gases are passed through a heat exchanger (economizer) as they leave the steam-generating section of the boiler. Most economizers operate at a relatively low temperature, thus requiring a large

Figure 44-12
Boiler Performance Trouble-Shooting

System	Problem	Possible Cause
Heat Transfer Related	High Exit Gas Temperature	1. Buildup of gas- or water-side deposits 2. Improper water treatment procedures 3. Improper sootblower operation
Combustion Related	High Excess Air	1. Improper control system operation 2. Low fuel supply pressure 3. Change in fuel heating value 4. Change in oil fuel viscosity
	Low Excess Air	1. Improper control system operation 2. Fan limitations 3. Increased ambient air temperature
	High CO and Combustible Emissions	1. Plugged gas burners 2. Unbalanced fuel/air distribution in multiburner furnace 3. Improper air register settings 4. Deterioration burner throat refractor 5. Stoker-grate condition 6. Stoker-fuel distrubtion orientation 7. Improper overfire air systems 8. Low fineness on pulverized systems

Figure 44-13

Boiler Efficiency Improvement Equipment

Air Preheaters	Transfer energy from stack gases to incoming combustion air	2.5% for each 100°F decrease in stack gas temperature
Economizers	Transfer energy from stack gases to incoming feedwater	2.5% for each 100°F decrease in stack gas temperature, 1% for each 10°F increase in feedwater temperature
Firetube turbulators	Increase turbulence in the secondary passes of firetube units	2.5% for each 100°F decrease in stack gas temperature
Combustion control systems	Regulate quantity of fuel and airflow	0.25% for each 1% decrease in O_2
Sootblowers	Remove boiler tube deposits that restrict heat transfer	Dependent on gas temperature
Blowdown system	Transfer energy from expelled blowdown liquids to incoming feedwater	1 to 3% depending on blowdown quantities and operating pressures

amount of surface area. Economizers must be operated above the gas dew point to avoid condensation of flue gas on the economizer tubes and to prevent external corrosion. To prevent internal corrosion caused by dissolved oxygen, water to economizers generally is deaerated.

Air Heaters   Air heaters recover heat from the flue gas by warming combustion air before it enters the boiler. Air heaters can be either recuperative (tube type) or regenerative (rotary type). In older plants without air heaters, a chimney of sufficient height will produce enough draft to maintain negative pressure in the furnace. When air heaters are added to these structures, an induced draft fan must be used to overcome the airflow restriction introduced by the air heater. Air heaters typically are placed after the economizers in the flue gas flow. An ideal air heater design would reduce the gas temperature to near but not below its dew point (i.e., the temperature at which moisture begins to condense out of the gas). Operation below the dew point will cause excessive corrosion from acids formed from sulfur products in the flue gas.

Feedwater Heaters   The water supplied to the boiler is termed the *feedwater.* Feedwater heaters may be used with boiler systems that supply extraction-type turbines to increase the overall plant cycle efficiency. Feedwater heaters are heat exchangers that heat the feedwater with steam extracted from the turbine or with the turbine exhaust. The two basic types of feedwater heaters include the closed feedwater heater, in which the heat is transferred by means of a shell and tube-type exchanger, and the open feedwater heater, in which the water and steam are mixed to accomplish feedwater heating. Deaerators are most commonly the open type. Typically, a rise of 10°F in feedwater temperature will result in approximately a 1 percent savings in fuel consumption.

Superheaters and Desuperheaters   Boilers used for heating systems can operate at or near the saturation temperature of the steam (i.e., the temperature at which the water is vaporized and the water and vapor are in equilibrium). However, steam supplied to turbines must be well above the vaporization temperature to maximize efficiency and prevent damage to the turbine blading from condensation. The temperature of the steam is raised above its saturation point in a method called *superheating.* Superheat sections in the boiler raise the temperature of steam taken from the drum to the desired superheat temperature.

Superheat temperature will vary according to load, and the characteristics of radiant versus convection superheaters are distinctly different. Radiant superheaters absorb heat by direct radiation from the flame but exhibit a drop in steam temperature as load increases. Convection superheaters outside of the radiant portion of the boiler will experience a steam temperature rise as load increases owing to the increased mass flow of gases within the boiler. To control these temperatures and deliver consistent steam quality to the turbines, desuperheaters must be applied. Desuperheating is accomplished by spraying pure water into the steam so that the steam temperature is lowered to the desired point. Proper application of a desuperheater can control the overall steam temperature and quality. Desuperheaters may be applied at the exit of the boiler or between boiler superheater sections.

Blowdown Heat Recovery   The concentration of impurities in the boiler increases with operation because of system leakages and impurities in the boiler makeup water. To keep impurities at an acceptable level, it is necessary to remove water concentrated with impurities from the boiler, a process called *blowing down* the boiler. This blowdown is accomplished by a combination of periodic and/or continuous removal of water from the boiler system. Removal is typically done from the steam drum or drums and the downcomer areas of the boiler. The amount of heat lost during blowdown tends to be high, so a blowdown heat recovery system is often used and easily justified. Heat from boiler blowdown water is recovered by routing to a heat exchanger through which feedwater is flowing. In addition, low-pressure steam from the flash tank may be used to supplement extraction steam and other steam requirements of the plant.

Ash Reinjection   Complete, or 100 percent, combustion is not possible. There will be a certain amount of unburned carbon in the fly ash entrained in the flue gas exiting the boilers. Carbon content of the fly ash varies from 1 to 20 percent. This carbon loss can dramatically affect the overall efficiency of the boiler system. Ash reinjection involves capture of this fly ash and the corresponding unburned carbon for reintroduction into the combustion zone. Two common points of ash collection for reinjection are at the bottom of the economizer section and at the discharge of the mechanical collector.

Combustion Additives   Previous discussions have centered on auxiliary equipment that may be added to the basic boiler system to increase overall system efficiencies. A fireside approach also may be used to increase efficiency, particularly when fuel oil and coal are used. Because these fuels are not homogeneous in nature, variations in combustion characteristics can be anticipated because of impurities and physical characteristics. Combustion additives help oxygen react with the combustible elements of carbon and hydrogen in the fuel. Combustion catalysts increase the reaction rate between the carbon and oxygen and lower the reaction temperature; thus, more carbon is burned at a given excess air level. This increased carbon utilization directly increases overall boiler efficiency. When fuel oil is burned, oil additives may be used to dissolve and disperse complex hydrocarbons that can interfere with the combustion process. An additional benefit of combustion additives is that particulate emissions may actually be reduced, since unburned carbons often make up a significant portion of the particulate emission from a unit. In particular, stoker-fired boilers often experience decreased particulate emissions with the use of combustion additives.

44.9   POLLUTION CONTROL EQUIPMENT

An expanding variety of federal, state, and local environmental regulations and restrictions govern power plant emissions. Jurisdictions vary from state to state, but any major plant addition or modification is likely to require oversight and approval from any or all of the regulating agencies.

Mechanical Collectors   Mechanical collectors are used to control particulate emissions. These collectors change the velocity and direction of the gas stream sufficiently to allow the heavier particulates to fall into a hopper below. Mechanical collectors can be used to collect large amounts of particulate matter, often in series with other pollution control devices. Many mechanical collectors use a tube design whereby each tube is an individual centrifugal dust collector. Particulate matter is collected through cyclonic action created by turning vanes on one end of the tube. Collector tubes range in diameter from 6 to 24 in. Mechanical collectors have no moving parts and are characterized by a low drop in pressure across the unit. They do, however, require maintenance, because they must be kept clean to operate correctly. Their collection efficiency depends on the size and weight of the particles; they are more efficient in removing heavier particles. Mechanical collectors can remove up to 90 percent of all particulates.

Electrostatic Precipitators   Electrostatic precipitators often are used when collection efficiencies of 99 percent or less are needed. Electrostatic precipitators give an electrical charge to the particles in the gas stream and then attract those charged particles to a collecting electrode. The electrostatic precipitator's electrical field operates at a high DC voltage level (typically 50,000 to 75,000 V) imparted to a framework of weighted wires. The charged particles are collected on electrically grounded suspended plates. These plates are rapped or vibrated mechanically to remove the fly ash to a storage hopper. Performance is a function of the chemical constituents of the coal and the electrical characteristics of the fly ash. Efficiencies will be notably higher when burning higher sulfur coals. A properly designed precipitator requires full definition of the fuels to be burned.

Baghouses   One of the most efficient methods of particulate removal is the baghouse. Baghouses can remove more than 99 percent of all particulate matter and are smaller and less expensive than a comparable precipitator. A baghouse removes the fly ash from the boiler exit gases by passing the exhaust through fabric filters. Collection is allowed to continue until the pressure drop across the baghouse reaches a predetermined level, at which time the bags are cleaned. The ash cake formed on the fabric also acts as a filter, so that maximum collection efficiency occurs immediately prior to cleaning the fabric filters.

There are two basic designs with different methods for cleaning bags. A *reverse air baghouse* collects the fly ash on the inside of the bags and cleans them by reversing the airflow through the bags. A *pulse-jet baghouse* collects the fly ash on the outside of the bags, and the bags are cleaned by pulsing with a jet of compressed air. A variety of bag materials, weights, and mesh designs are available to meet collection needs. Bag design depends on the characteristics of the flue gas, not on the fuel's sulfur content or the fuel type. Because of their construction, the use of baghouses may be limited by high temperature or humidity conditions.

Scrubbers   Federal, state, and local environmental regulations require most new boilers to have gaseous emissions limitations. Gaseous pollutants are more difficult to manage than particulate matter. The most common restrictions apply to sulfur and nitrogen emissions, but many installations are also regulated for trace elements, heavy metals, organic compounds, and other toxic emissions. The most prevalent pollutant is sulfur dioxide. The sulfur oxides can be controlled by removing sulfur prior to or during combustion, as with fluidized bed combustion. The primary method of removing sulfur from the boiler exit gases is with scrubbers.

Wet Scrubbers.   A wet scrubber system removes sulfur dioxide from the flue gas by introducing a limestone slurry into the flue gas stream in a spray-type chamber. The atmosphere within a wet scrubber is much like that in a wet cooling tower. A wet scrubber system is characterized by large water usage, large quantities of waste materials, and high operating costs. If sulfur recovery is desired, a magnesia solution is substituted for the limestone slurry to recover a sulfur product. Nearly 90 percent of all sulfur oxides can be removed with wet scrubbers.

Dry Scrubbers.   One type of dry scrubbing, the spray dryer system, uses lime reagent that is atomized and mixed with the incoming flue gas. The lime droplets react with the sulfur dioxides in the flue gas and are simultaneously dried. The spent solids are collected in the bottom of the absorption chamber. The dry scrubber system is advantageous because water usage is minimized, waste drying is unnecessary, and a dry fly ash conveying system can be used to handle wastes generated. Another type of dry scrubber removes sulfur dioxide from the flue gas stream by passing the flue gas through a fixed absorbent bed material such as char. The absorbent bed material is regenerated once the material becomes saturated.

Compliance Equipment   To demonstrate compliance with state, federal, and local emission restrictions, it may be necessary to add gas analyzing equipment to the boiler. The complexity of the equipment and the reporting requirements will vary depending on the regulating agency. Equipment costs range from $25,000 to $200,000 per boiler installation.

Opacity Monitors   Opacity monitors measure particulate emissions from a specified source. Although the boiler exit gas would certainly be one source, other equipment, such as coal-handling dust collectors, ash blower exhausts, or any other dust-laden particle stream may require monitoring to ensure compliance.

Continuous Emission Monitors   The regulating agency often requires continuous emission monitors (CEMs) after any significant plant modification or addition. These monitors provide extensive analysis of the flue gas stream for sulfur dioxide, nitrogen oxide, dilutive gases, or other regulated gaseous emissions. A typical CEM system consists of a gas sample point, gas analyzers, and data reduction computers with output devices. The three basic types of continuous emission monitors are in situ, extractive, and dilutive extractive. The in situ device is mounted at the point of collection on the gas ductwork or at the chimney. The analyzers are mounted at the sample point and the data reduction hardware at some remote location. The extractive system extracts a flue gas sample and transports it to a remotely located analyzer cabinet, where the data reduction equipment is also located. The dilutive extractive system suctions the flue gas through a metered orifice to provide a diluted gas sample to the gas analyzers and data reduction equipment.

Ambient Dust Monitors   Where fugitive dust emissions are a concern, ambient dust monitors are beginning to be required by the regulating agencies. These monitors are placed at the edge of an institution's property to measure fugitive dust in the sub–10-micron range that may escape the site.

44.10 TURBINES

Steam turbines receive high-pressure, high-temperature steam from the boiler and convert the thermal energy to mechanical (shaft) energy, which can then drive a generator or a chiller. The steam passes through nozzles, giving it a high velocity, then impinges on the turbine blading to rotate the turbine shaft. The conversion process involves pressure and temperature reductions as thermal energy is converted to mechanical energy. The steam expansion process can be in several turbine sections connected to a common shaft.

Turbine Efficiency

Heat engine efficiency relates to temperature, which in turn relates to pressure. The basic formula for heat engine efficiency is as follows:

$$\text{Efficiency} = 100(T_1 - T_2)/T_1$$

where T_1 = inlet temperature and T_2 = outlet temperature (temperatures in absolute [degrees F + 460]).

The larger the change in temperature $(T_1 - T_2)$, the more efficient the engine.

The change in temperature can be increased in two ways: by increasing the inlet temperature and pressure and by lowering the exhaust temperature and pressure. Raising the inlet temperature and pressure requires alloy steels to withstand the higher temperatures and pressures and more elaborate piping arrangements, insulation, pump capacities, and feedwater heating to avoid boiler stresses. Lowering the exhaust temperature and pressure is generally more feasible. However, steam should not be allowed to condense in the turbine.

For example, by reducing the turbine exhaust pressure from atmospheric (approximately 15 psi.) to 5 psi., efficiency would be improved by almost 6 percent. This is the principle involved in a condensing turbine discussed below.

Types of Turbines

Back-Pressure Turbine   Technically, a back-pressure turbine exhausts at or above atmospheric pressure. The inlet temperature and pressure are relatively high, although they operate over a wide range of conditions. A typical use is in cogeneration, where the turbines exhaust into a steam distribution system that supplies the campus thermal requirements.

Condensing Turbine In a condensing turbine, the exhaust is condensed, lowering the pressure to 2 to 5 psi. The treated feedwater is retained, collected in a hot-well, and pumped back to the boiler. Configurations where steam is extracted after one of the turbine stages to meet campus thermal loads are termed *controlled extraction units*. If all steam is condensed in the condenser, the unit is termed a *straight condensing unit*.

Gas Turbines Combustion turbines are popular as prime movers of electrical generators. They have the benefit of short lead times and low capital cost. Gas turbines come on-line quickly (less than 10 minutes) and can offer an excellent solution to backup power requirements or for peak shaving to limit electrical demand charges. Natural gas and fuel oil are typical turbine fuels. Gas turbines range in size from several hundred kilowatts to several hundred megawatts.

The basic gas turbine has three main sections: compressor, combustor, and turbine. The compressor draws air in from the atmosphere, pressurizes it, and introduces it to the combustor. Fuel is added and burned in the combustor, and the hot gases are allowed to expand through the turbine section. Increased efficiency can be developed by adding a regeneration (air heater) section, an intercooler (split compressor and cooler) section, or a reheat (split turbine and second combustor) section. Another method to improve gas turbine system efficiency is the combined cycle plant. The combined cycle plant routes the hot turbine exhaust gases to a boiler section to extract additional thermal energy and generate steam. Typically, an auxiliary fuel is used in the boiler to promote complete combustion and to control steam temperature.

The only pollutant of concern with gas turbines is NOX. Gas turbines can be high NOX generators, and some method of control usually is required. Control methods include water or steam injection into the combustor to keep flame temperature low and the use of selective catalytic reduction (SCR). Steam injection also will increase power from the turbine by boosting the mass flow through the turbine. Selective catalytic reduction consists of ammonia injection into the exhaust stream.

Condensers

Condensers are heat exchangers that transfer heat from the turbine exhaust directly to the atmosphere or to a cooling water, from which it is released to the atmosphere. They generally handle large quantities of heat and differ in how they transmit heat to the atmosphere. The six major types are as follows:

1. *Once-through cooling.* The water is pumped from a source such as a lake or river, through the heat exchanger, and back to the source. The discharge must be sufficiently removed from the source to avoid heating it.

2. *Cooling pond.* Water from the condenser is discharged into a pond from which heat is transferred to the atmosphere by evaporation, convection, and radiation.

3. *Spray pond.* In a spray pond, the water is sprayed 5 to 10 ft. in the air. They require only about 5 percent of the area of a cooling pond for the same heat transmission. Spray ponds sometimes are used to supplement cooling ponds during hot weather.

4. *Natural draft evaporative cooling.* This method employs a cooling tower with water sprayed counter to the airflow. Natural draft cooling requires large structures and therefore carries high construction costs.

5. *Mechanical draft evaporative cooling tower.* These can be either forced draft or induced draft towers. They have a lower construction cost than natural draft cooling towers but require large quantities of water, which causes high operating costs.

6. *Dry cooling towers.* These can be either direct, in which the steam from the turbine condenses in finned tubes in the cooling tower, or indirect, in which the heat from the turbine exhaust is transferred to a second fluid that is then pumped to the cooling tower.

44.11 CHEMICAL TREATMENT

A sound chemical treatment program is essential to protect the large capital investment associated with a centralized heating plant. Boiler water must be treated to lessen scale formation, corrosion of metal, and carryover of solids. Scale will lower the thermal efficiency of the unit, and corrosion will decrease its life while increasing outages caused by tube failures. In addition, solids carryover will damage equipment, particularly steam turbines, when the contaminated steam enters the turbine blading. The cooling water must be treated to protect against scale, corrosion, microbiological contamination, and fouling and to avoid increased maintenance costs, reduced heat transfer efficiency, and production cutbacks or shutdowns.

Boiler Water Treatment Pure water is an active solvent that will pick up or dissolve part of everything with which it comes in contact. The average level of impurities in midwestern U.S. water is about 500 parts per million (ppm) or about one-half pound of residue for every 1,000 lb. of water which has been evaporated. These impurities can cause scale, corrosion, and carry-over within the boiler itself. In the past, most boiler feedwater was treated with phosphates until the development of chelate and polymer-type chemicals. These chemicals condition the calcium and magnesium in the feedwater so

that these impurities will remain in suspension to prevent scale formation on boiler surfaces. Most boiler feedwater systems also contain a
deaerating feedwater heater which removes oxygen and dissolves gases
from the feedwater. If additional oxygen scavenging is desired, chemicals such as sodium sulfite and hydrazine are added. A good boiler internal treatment program includes the addition of hardness-controlling
and degassing chemicals with a blowdown system to discharge concentrated solids from the boiler's lower regions.

Cooling Water Treatment   Cooling water systems provide an environment
where corrosion, scale, and microbiological contamination and fouling can
become problems. Corrosion is an electrochemical phenomenon that must
be controlled by adding corrosion inhibitors to the cooling water. Corrosion
inhibitors establish a protective film on either the anode or cathode elements
of the cooling water system. Chemicals such as chromates, nitrites, ortho-
phosphates, bicarbonates, and polyphosphates typically are used. The primary protection in scale prevention is control of phosphate levels (or pH) in
the cooling water and system blowdown to eliminate impurities. Typically,
pH is controlled by an acid feed system, and microbiological contamination
is controlled by adding biocides to the cooling water. The most common
chemical used as a biocide in cooling water systems is chlorine.

44.12   WATER TREATMENT

Centralized heating and cooling plants with associated boiler supply water, condenser cooling water, and chilled water systems consume large
amounts of water. Many municipal water systems cannot cope with this
large water demand, so heating plants must operate their own water treatment plant. A water plant provides a source of potable water for use in the
boiler, cooling tower, chilled water system, and other uses. Depending on
the raw water source, a wide variety of equipment and systems may be
used to develop potable water. This potable water is used directly in chilled
water and cooling tower systems, but additional processing equipment such
as condensate polishers, zeolite softeners, or demineralizers are needed to
further purify the water for use in the boiler.

Water Plants   A variety of equipment is used to produce a potable water
supply from raw water sources such as wells, lakes, and rivers. Although
the system equipment and configurations may vary dramatically, the principles of operation are the same. The primary processes are clarification
and sterilization.
    Clarification is the removal of suspended matter and color from the
water supply. The suspended particles may be removed with settling basins, filters, or coagulating chemicals. Many systems involve several or all
of these. Water plant design is dependent on the raw water source, the

desired potable water quality, the design and emergency flow rates, and the available equipment space. Water treatment plants may include such equipment as aerators, flash mixers, flock tanks, settling basins, clarifiers, lamella filters, gravity filters, pressure filters, and a variety of chlorinators and chemical feed equipment.

Sterilization is the process of controlling the level of microorganisms in the potable water to a point lower than the local regulatory standards. Sterilization is generally accomplished with chlorine. Both maximum and minimum chlorine residual levels will apply to most potable water systems.

Condensate Polisher Large power generation plants often use condensate polishers to further remove impurities from the condensate flow from the turbine generators. University systems employing steam export systems must cope with the return of condensate from remote building systems and significant lengths of distribution piping, all of which add impurities to the returning condensate. For these systems, condensate polishers are generally used to clean the campus condensate return water before the reintroduction of this flow into the boiler. Most condensate polisher systems incorporate a mixed bed design with ion-exchanging cationic and anionic resins in a deep bed configuration. Bed depths vary from 2 to 6 ft. Condensate polishers can effectively control contaminants such as iron, copper, sodium, chloride, silica, calcium, and magnesium to significantly improve water quality in the heating plant cycle.

Zeolite Softener Potable water does not provide satisfactory water for use in the boiler itself because of the solids dissolved in the water. Zeolite softeners may be used to soften the water source by removing scale-forming solids. A sodium zeolite system softens hard water by exchanging the calcium and magnesium salts for various soluble sodium salts. This softener consists of a vessel containing a bed of zeolite resin that attracts the hardness from the water as the water percolates downward. When the electrolytic charge is exhausted in the bed, the bed is regenerated. This is accomplished by rinsing the resin bed with a solution of ordinary salt, which is rinsed out, rendering the softener ready for another cycle of operation. This system of softening is relatively simple and economical to operate, since ordinary salt is used as the regenerate material. One drawback is that this method produces water with a high alkaline content that must be corrected chemically.

Demineralizer Demineralizers also may be used to soften water for the boiler. In the demineralizing process, the water is passed through both cation and anion exchange resins to remove the scale-forming impurities. These positive- and negative-charged ion beds trap the impurities and allow only pure water to leave the system. When regeneration of the resin bed is required, the cationic resin is washed with an acid solution, and the anionic resin is washed with a caustic solution. Demineralizers are available in two configurations: mixed bed and dual train. In the mixed bed system, the anion and cation exchange resins are contained in one unit. In the dual train system, separate beds exist for the anion and cation resins. The main advantage of demineralization is its ability to produce better quality water than can be obtained by any other method. The initial capital cost is significantly higher than for other methods.

Reverse Osmosis   Reverse osmosis is another method available to pretreat boiler water and remove impurities. This process utilizes a membrane that is selectively semipermeable (i.e., open to the passage of fluids). This membrane allows only the desired ions to pass between two chambers. High internal operating pressures of 300 to 900 psi. overcome osmotic pressure and concentrate dissolved solids on one side of the membrane, thus filtering out impurities. This type of system generally is more costly to operate and install than a comparable demineralizer. However, chemicals are not required, and fewer waste products are generated.

44.13   CONTROL SYSTEMS

Combustion controls have two purposes: to adjust the fuel supply in order to maintain the required steam flow or pressure under varying loads and to maintain the optimum ratio of combustion air to fuel. There are three basic control systems: on-off, positioning, and metering.

On-Off Control System   On-off control is regulated by a steam pressure-actuated switch. When the pressure drops to a preset level, fuel flow is increased, and operation continues at a constant firing rate until the pressure rises to a preset level. This type of control generally is used only for fire tube and very small water tube boilers.

Positioning System   Positioning controls also respond to steam pressure. In this system, however, the controller responds to changes in the steam drum or header pressure by positioning fuel supply valves and forced draft dampers. This type of control is used on single-burner boilers and is restricted to systems that burn one fuel at a time. There are three types of positioning controls:

1. *Fixed positioning.* A single actuator moves both the fuel and air controls to preset positions through mechanical linkages. This system cannot compensate for changes in fuel or air density or fuel supply pressure, so controls are normally set for high excess air to guard against dropping below the minimum excess air requirements.

2. *Parallel positioning with operator trim.* Pneumatic or electronic positioning of fuel and air supply controls are actuated by a single pressure controller. A combustion guide is required to enable the operator to

position the excess airflow. This is the most widely used type of combustion control for units rated at below 100,000 lb./hour.

3. *Pressure ratio.* A parallel pneumatic or electronic system is used with the windbox-to-furnace pressure ratio to trim the fuel flow and airflow. Manual controls to change both the ratio of pressure and excess airflow are normally provided with a combustion guide.

Metering System In a metering system, the fuel flow and airflow are metered, and the fuel supply and air supply controls are modulated in accordance with measured flows. This kind of combustion control is restricted to fuels that can be accurately metered. A refinement of this system is cross-limited metering, which limits the change in fuel flow through control logic to available airflow at all items. The airflow also is tied to fuel flow. The system can be further refined by using a continuously monitored flue gas analysis and by trimming the fuel-to-air ratio based on the oxygen content. This compensates for variations in fuel heating values and combustion air conditions.

Currently most boilers are controlled by microprocessors. Software-based systems offer controls that are flexible, responsive, dynamic, and easily tuned to match system requirements. However, there is a tendency to incorporate more complex control strategies requiring more highly skilled personnel on site for design and maintenance of the systems. The rewards often are realized in higher system efficiencies and fewer forced outages. An older boiler often can be made 1 or 2 percent more efficient by retrofitting a microprocessor control system for the pneumatic or analog-type controls already in place. Cost recovery can occur quickly when fuel budgets range in the millions of dollars per year.

44.14 MONITORING AND CONTROLLING PERFORMANCE

Prior to the start of each heating season, all steam and hot water generators should be performance tested after the completion of an annual water side, fire side, and control system maintenance and inspection. This performance test will provide the operator with a basis for assessing future operating efficiencies during the high fuel consumption heating season.

With the performance test as a base, the operator can best monitor central heating system performance through regular review of fuel-to-steam conversion efficiencies. If this efficiency begins to deteriorate, the operator should investigate further to determine the reason for the lost efficiency. Attention should be given to stack gas analysis to determine if excess air levels are being maintained within the desired limits. System water makeup quantities should be evaluated to determine whether system losses are excessive. Stack gas temperatures should be reviewed to determine whether soot blowing intervals are adequate and to whether the water treatment program is maintaining adequate water side cleanliness.

Operating personnel must be provided with adequate instrumentation to continuously and accurately monitor plant operating efficiencies. Operators must be furnished with concise written operating instructions that indicate control limits for various plant operating parameters. Hourly rounds should be made to record plant machine status, operating temperatures, operating procedures, and all meter readings where flow rates are available. If continuous indication of stack gas oxygen content and boiler water condition is not provided, stack gas and boiler water should be manually analyzed and recorded at least twice each shift.

It is important that plant supervisors continually reinforce the necessity of routine and accurate recording of plant operating parameters. These records will serve a vital role in assisting the facilities manager to identify the cause of any loss in plant performance efficiencies.

Plant auxiliary equipment should also be subjected to annual performance testing. Pump and drive efficiencies should be tested and compared to manufacturer's data. Deaerating feedwater heaters should be tested to ensure complete oxygen removal. (If an oxygen scavenger is fed prior to the unit, feed must be discontinued before testing.) All operating instrumentation and controls should be calibrated and adjusted to original specifications. Steam trap function should be verified and valve packing replaced. Valves should be checked to validate their shutoff capability and overhauled when necessary. Makeup water softeners should be tested to determine whether mineral removal meets original specifications and whether resin is cleaned or replaced when needed. Auxiliary heat exchangers such as boiler feedwater heaters, vent condensers, and boiler blowdown heat exchangers should be cleaned and inspected. Stack gas cleanup systems such as mechanical collectors, electrostatic precipitators, baghouses, and sulfur dioxide removal equipment should be serviced in accordance with the manufacturer's recommendations.

44.15   SYSTEM RETROFIT POSSIBILITIES

A wide variety of field retrofit opportunities exist that can substantially improve efficiencies and reduce operating costs. Some of the available options are as follows:

- Retrofit economizers are available that are compact and designed to replace a section of boiler exhaust ductwork. Care should be exercised in specifying economizers to ensure that stack gas temperatures will not be too low during light load operation, which could cause condensation and corrosion.
- Gas and oil burners are available that will operate at excess air levels as low as 3 percent and have good turndown. Some burners

are available as packages complete with burner management systems and forced draft fans. This packaging simplifies the installation in existing facilities and can substantially reduce costs.

- Boiler blowdown heat recovery can be accomplished with the installation of a small heat exchanger to transfer heat from boiler blowdown to boiler water makeup. Another method employs a pressurized flash tank connected to the plant exhaust steam system. In this system, boiler blowdown is directed to the receiver, where it flashes to steam; thus, a portion of the waste heat is recovered as low-pressure steam. Automatic blowdown controllers are also available that monitor boiler water conductivity and automatically adjust boiler blowdown; thus, energy loss is minimized.
- Microprocessor-based controllers are available that will substantially outperform older control systems. They can also include economic dispatch that causes the system to automatically adjust loading on combustion equipment to maximize efficiency for any given load where multiple boilers are in service. Oxygen trim control and multi-element boiler water level control are also available. If oxygen trim control is installed on boilers that operate with negative furnace pressures, care must be taken to ensure that carbon monoxide is not present in the flue gases at low oxygen levels. This is necessary because boiler casing leaks will introduce air into the furnace downstream of the combustion process. This air will be detected by the flue gas oxygen sensor and cause the controls to reduce airflow. Incomplete combustion will result.
- The addition of insulation to piping may also improve efficiency.
- In large distribution systems with low summer loads, the addition of small local steam or hot water boilers may allow complete shutdown of the central heating system and result in substantial savings. These shutdowns will also allow for comprehensive maintenance to be performed on the entire system in an orderly fashion.

With stable fuel prices, many or all of the above retrofits may not be economically feasible. However, the facilities manager should thoroughly investigate all retrofit options so that a timely response can be made should energy prices surge as they did in the mid-1970s.

44.16   MAINTENANCE

Central heating plant equipment maintenance intervals can be scheduled and tracked through a larger facilities preventive maintenance system or through a smaller system that serves only the central plant. Regardless of the maintenance scheduling system used, a detailed history should be maintained for all major equipment. This history should contain the original equipment specifications, parts ordering information, year installed, when service was performed, details on repairs, and parts replaced. This information will be useful in determining service interval requirements and in deciding whether a piece of equipment should be repaired or replaced after a major breakdown.

Major pieces of equipment such as boilers, turbines, chillers, and heat exchangers should be inspected thoroughly on an annual basis. Checklists should be developed for each overhaul to coordinate activities and to ensure that items are not overlooked. Major overhauls should be scheduled based on unit condition, operating hours, idle hours, and startup-shutdown cycles. Major overhauls can be anticipated every 3 to 5 years for solid fuel boilers, every 7 to 10 years for gas-fired boilers, every 5 to 6 years for turbines, every 5 to 7 years for chillers, and every 10 years for cooling towers. Depending on service conditions, large pumps may need rebuilding every 7 to 10 years and large fans every 10 to 15 years, depending on air or gas conditions. Other auxiliary equipment should be reconditioned based on the operating and maintenance history experienced at the individual plant.

Many plants find that they do not have the staff or equipment to perform all of the maintenance activities required for a central plant. Many plant managers rely on outside contractors to perform specialized or nonroutine tasks. Some of the tasks that plants contract include vibration analysis, code-type pressure vessel welding, application of specialized coating systems, refractory repair, instrument calibration, protective relay calibration, stack lighting system repair, stack gas monitoring equipment repair and calibration, water treatment, major equipment overhauls, seasonal maintenance, metal fabrication, and machining.

The maintenance requirements of any plant necessitate a wide variety of skills and specialty equipment. Maintaining a proper mix of in-house equipment, skills, and personnel supported by specialized outside contractors is difficult. When inside and outside skills are combined effectively, the university will be rewarded with lower costs for utility services and higher reliability for all utility customers.

44.17   STAFFING

The operational staffing requirements of a central steam or hot water production facility are driven by a number of factors. A major consideration is the complexity of the system and the physical layout of the production facility. In complex systems that encompass central cooling and electrical production as well as central heating, larger operating staffs will be required than for a central-heating-only facility. In facilities that burn solid fuel, staffing requirements will increase owing to the operation of fuel and ash handing systems. Figure 44-14 shows the staffing and organization for a modest central heating facility and should be considered the minimum base in determining staffing requirements. Figure 44-15 shows the staffing

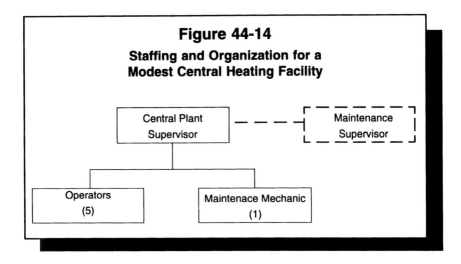

Figure 44-14

**Staffing and Organization for a
Modest Central Heating Facility**

and organization for a large facility and should be considered the most comprehensive staffing arrangement.

Regardless of staffing level or plant complexity, the facilities manager must arrange the working schedules of operating personnel to ensure continuous coverage with a minimum of overtime work. An effective way to achieve continuous coverage is with the rotating shift schedule shown in Figure 44-16. Not only will this schedule limit each operator's work week to 40 hours, it will also provide a relief operator. The relief operator can be used to fill shift vacancies, provide plant cleanup services, or support maintenance activities. If fixed shifts are used, one variation would be to rotate each operator sequentially into the relief position, with the charge arranged so that the relief operator moves into the schedule at the beginning of swing shift duty. This variation will allow all operating personnel to share equally in the burden of the relief role.

Maintenance staffing will also be driven by system complexity and the scope of central services provided. However, the facilities manager has considerable flexibility in determining how these services are provided. At one extreme, all central plant maintenance and repair services can be furnished from central shops not organizationally under central plant management. At the other extreme, all central plant and distribution maintenance and repair can be performed by dedicated staff under the line management function within the central plant organization. The facilities manager can best determine which maintenance functions should reside in the central plant organization and which should be provided from central maintenance shops by carefully examining workhour and craft requirements to perform annual maintenance tasks.

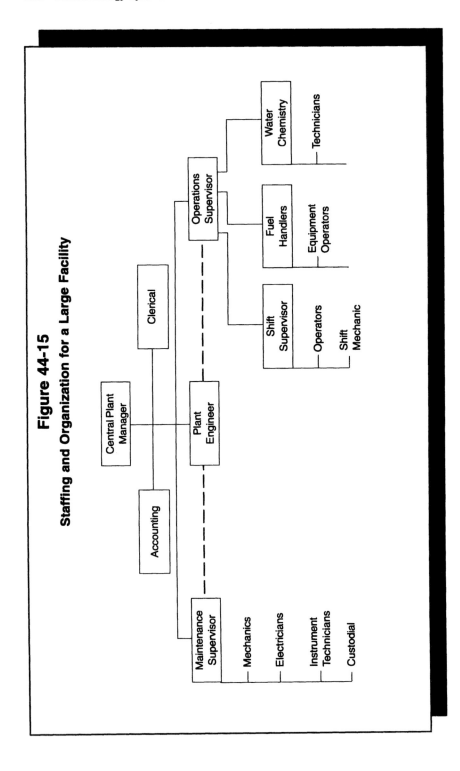

Figure 44-15

Staffing and Organization for a Large Facility

Figure 44-16
Rotating Shift Schedule

APRIL	SAT. 1	SUN. 2	MON. 3	TUE. 4	WED. 5	THU. 6	FRI. 7	SAT. 8	SUN. 9	MON. 10	TUE. 11	WED. 12	THU. 13	FRI. 14	SAT. 15	SUN. 16	MON. 17	TUE. 18	WED. 19	THU. 20	FRI. 21	SAT. 22	SUN. 23	MON. 24	TUE. 25	WED. 26	THU. 27	FRI. 28
6 – 2	5	4	3	5	5	5	5	5	4	3	5	5	5	5	5	4	3	5	5	5	5	5	4	3	5	5	5	5
2 – 10	2	2	2	3	3	2	2	2	2	2	3	3	2	2	2	2	2	3	3	2	2	2	2	2	3	3	2	2
10 – 6	1	1	1	1	1	3	3	1	1	1	1	1	3	3	1	1	1	1	1	3	3	1	1	1	1	1	3	3
7–3:30				4	4	4	4				4	4	4	4				4	4	4	4				4	4	4	4

APR/MAY	SAT. 29	SUN. 30	MON. 1	TUE. 2	WED. 3	THU. 4	FRI. 5	SAT. 6	SUN. 7	MON. 8	TUE. 9	WED. 10	THU. 11	FRI. 12	SAT. 13	SUN. 14	MON. 15	TUE. 16	WED. 17	THU. 18	FRI. 19	SAT. 20	SUN. 21	MON. 22	TUE. 23	WED. 24	THU. 25	FRI. 26
6 – 2	4	3	2	4	4	4	4	4	3	2	4	4	4	4	4	3	2	4	4	4	4	4	3	2	4	4	4	4
2 – 10	1	1	1	2	2	1	1	1	1	1	2	2	1	1	1	1	1	2	2	1	1	1	1	1	2	2	1	1
10 – 6	5	5	5	5	5	2	2	5	5	5	5	5	2	2	5	5	5	5	5	2	2	5	5	5	5	5	2	2
7–3:30				3	3	3	3				3	3	3	3				3	3	3	3				3	3	3	3

(1) Shearer, Mesenbrink, Coffman, Johnson, Farrell
(2) Young, Kimsey, White, Oberender, Shirley
(3) Garland, Foley, Garcia, Smith, Doran
(4) Hiles, Pervier, Eichorn, Bornholt, Gift
(5) Staebler, Wisecup, Terrones, Ball, Mayfield
   Break and Lunch at Duty Station
Relief Boiler Operator 7:00 am to 3:30 pm – Epstein
Clean-up & Relief Shift 7:00 am to 3:30 pm
   Break: 9:00 am to 9:15 am
   Lunch: 12:00 pm to 12:45 pm
6:00 am to 4:30 pm – Water Systems Operators
Sun. through Wed. – Toman/Wed. through Sat. – Kalsem
   Break: 9:00 am to 9:15 am
   Lunch: 12:00 pm to 12:30 pm

44.18   TRAINING

The facilities manager must put in place and maintain an in-house training program to achieve two important objectives. The first is to maintain and improve the skills of existing operating staff. This skills maintenance and improvement program should include regular review of operating procedures, actual exercises in operating the plant in various configurations that would be necessary in the event of equipment failure, changing over to an alternative fuel, review of chemical handling and spill containment, and precise instruction on newly instituted plant operating procedures (Figure 44-17).

The second objective is to train entry-level employees in the operation of the central plant to ensure a ready resource of replacement operators in the event of staff variances. A similar program should also be implemented to cover the maintenance functions performed by in-house staff. Some maintenance training can be provided by representatives from equipment manufacturers of various plant equipment and can be held on site to reduce costs.

Regardless of plant size, an effective, regular training program is a cost-effective approach to furnishing reliable and efficient central heating services (Figure 44-18).

Figure 44-17
Training and Safety Program
Division of Responsibilities

Managers

Identify work unit training needs
Generate and implement training
  plans
Generate new programs
Adapt programs for the work unit
Assume responsibility for employee
  training
Maintain employee training records
Review existing programs annually
Develop work procedures
Pre-plan non-routine tasks
Provide jobsite monitoring
Identify safety equipment needs
Help with monthly workplace
  inspections

Program Coordinator

Identify applicable regulations
Communicate regulatory changes
Generate new programs
Locate training resources
Assist managers in their roles
Perform periodic workplace audits
Facilitate a monthly training meeting with
  manager
Coordinate safety consultant activities
Coordinate with local agencies
Schedule and conduct respirator fit
  testing
Coordinate purchase of safety equipment
Maintain safety equipment records

Employees

Follow established procedures
Report unusual conditions
Request procedural changes
Request needed training

Safety Committee

Meet monthly
Perform monthly workplace inspections
Review "Safety Recommendations"
Review injury reports
Communicate activities to all personnel
Recommend procedural changes

Figure 44-18

OSHA Required Employee Safety Training (Utilities Division of Facilities Planning and Management—ISU)

Training/Instruction	Initial Training (Required for New Employees)	Refresher Training Frequency (months)	Heating Plant Operators	Water Plant Operators	Heating Plant Coal Crew	Heating Plant Laborer	Heating Plant Mechanical Maintenance	Heating Plant Electrical Maintenance	Heating Plant Insulators	Electrical Distribution	Mechanical Distribution	Support Staff
Chemical Risks Right-To-Know	Y	Audit Based	x	x	x	x	x	x	x	x	x	x
Industrial Chemical Spills	Y	Audit Based	some	x			some					some
Fire Prevention	Y	Audit Based	x	x	x	x	x	x	x	x	x	x
Equipment Lockout	Y	Audit Based	x	x	x	x	x	x	x	x	x	some
Confined Space Entry	Y	Audit Based	x	x	x		x	x	x	x	x	some
Emergency Procedures	Y	Audit Based	x	x	x	x	x	x	x	x	x	x
First Aid	Y	36	some				x	x		x	x	
CPR	Y	12	some				x	x		x	x	
Fire Extinguishers	Y	12(OSHA)	x	x	x	x	x	x	x	x	x	some
Blood Borne Pathogens	Y	12 (OSHA)				x					x	
Personal Protective Equipment	Y	Audit Based	x	x	x	x	x	x	x	x	x	some
Respirator Training/Fit Testing (asbestos abatement)	Y	6 (OSHA)							x			some
Respirator Training/Fit Testing	Y	12 (OSHA)	x	x	x		x	x		x	x	some
Noise/Hearing Conservation	Y	12 (OSHA)	x	x	x	x	x	x	x	x	x	some
Electrical Safety	Y	Audit Based	x	x	x	x	x	x	x	x	x	some
Hand/Power Tool Safety	Y	Audit Based	x	x	x	x	x	x	x	x	x	some
Welding/Cutting Safety	Y	Audit Based					x	x	x	x	x	
Hoist and Sling Safety	Y	Audit Based					x	x	x	x	x	
Ladder and Scaffold Safety	Y	Audit Based	x	x	x	x	x	x	x	x	x	some
Forklift Safety	Y	12 (OSHA)		x			x					
Aerial Lift Truck Safety	Y	Audit Based					x	x		x	x	
Vehicle and Mobile Equipment Safety	Y	Audit Based	x	x	x	x	x	x		x	x	some
Work Site Barricading	Y	Audit Based								x	x	some
Excavation/Trenching Safety	Y	Audit Based								x	x	some
Asbestos Abatement	Y	12 (OSHA)							x			some

ADDITIONAL RESOURCES

Bender, Rene J. "Steam Generation: A *Power* Special Report." *Power,* June 1964 (entire issue).

Combustion: Fossil Power Systems, third edition, edited by Joseph G. Singer. Windsor, Connecticut: Combustion Engineering, 1981.

NALCO Chemical Company. *The NALCO Water Handbook.* New York: McGraw-Hill, 1979.

Steam: Its Generation and Use, 38th edition. New York: Babcock & Wilcox, 1972.

CHAPTER 45

Central Cooling Systems

Clark Thompson
Iowa State University

45.1 INTRODUCTION

District cooling is an attractive method for cooling individual buildings by connecting them onto a cooling loop. District cooling can displace several small localized chillers with central systems that have options that are not feasible at individual sites.

Facilities managers should consider a number of factors when evaluating the merits of district cooling. These factors include the environmental issues associated with the phaseout of some refrigerants, increasing restrictions on the use of groundwater, the age and condition of the existing system, and availability of capital.

Advantages of Central Cooling Systems

Central chiller plants offer several advantages over individual building air conditioning systems. Central chiller plants can take advantage of the diversity factor in the sizing of equipment and operation of the plant, as all connected loads will not peak at the same time. Less capital is required for central cooling equipment than for equipment in many individual buildings. Operating and maintenance staffing costs are minimized owing to the centralized equipment location. Increased efficiencies are possible with large heating and cooling equipment, which reduces operating cost per unit of energy output. Part-load performance efficiencies are substantially improved by the ability to meet the system load with the most efficient equipment. Continuous and accurate monitoring of operating efficiencies is practical when the equipment is centralized. Single-point delivery of purchased utilities allows for favorable rates to a large-volume customer. Multiple fuel sources are a practical alternative.

Disadvantages of Central Cooling Systems

Central systems present some disadvantages over cooling equipment distributed in individual buildings. Thermal and hydraulic losses occur in large-distribution networks. These losses must be evaluated against the increased generating efficiencies of a central plant. The initial construction cost requires a large capital investment. Therefore, the most cost-effective options may have to be deferred if capital cannot be secured.

45.2 COMPONENT DESIGN CONSIDERATIONS

Major equipment such as chillers, pumps, and cooling towers should not be purchased without a set of detailed specifications on the items being purchased. These specifications establish the minimum quality and the maximum energy consumption that will be acceptable for each item. The equipment should not be accepted until it is tested to prove compliance for capacity and performance.

Chillers

Many chiller types are available to match the specific needs of a given chiller plant. Factors affecting chiller selection include energy sources, prime movers, physical size, load requirements, and refrigerant selections. Energy sources, prime movers, and refrigerants are discussed separately later in this chapter.

There is no assurance that selections made today will be the most economical selections in the future as energy prices change. The costs of electricity and fossil fuel, along with the need to balance electrical and thermal loads, are the most important factors in selecting a chiller.

Types

The three types of chillers most commonly used in central chiller plants are centrifugal, reciprocating, and absorption. A wide variety of chiller combinations can occur, especially in plants that have undergone multiple phases of expansion.

Reciprocating Chillers Reciprocating chillers have been used in some central chiller plants, but they are normally too small to be practical for most installations. They are available in sizes ranging from 10 to 200 tons, so several units must be used together to meet large cooling loads. Reciprocating chillers are generally lower in cost per ton capacity than other types of chillers, but they have a shorter life expectancy and higher maintenance costs. Because of the nature of their design, they tend to vibrate and are noisy.

Rotary Screw Type Chillers Rotary screw compressors normally operate at speeds around 3,600 rpm. They can also be designed to operate at variable speeds that range from 1,800 to 3,600 rpm to meet partial load requirements. These compressors can be coupled to slower operating prime movers by using speed increasers

Centrifugal Chillers Centrifugal chillers are by far the most popular chiller type in central cooling systems. They are available in sizes ranging from 90 to 10,000 tons. They are simple to operate, reliable, compact, and relatively quiet; have low vibration; and are designed for long life with low maintenance.

Centrifugal chillers can be selected for hermetic or open-type drives. Hermetic units use a hermetic compressor with an electric motor that is totally enclosed in a refrigerant atmosphere. The hermetic motor can be smaller and less expensive than motors used in open configurations. However, hermetic units consume slightly more power than identical-capacity open drive units, and in the event of a motor failure, the repairs are considerably higher. Open-type centrifugal chillers use a compressor driven by a steam turbine, a reciprocating engine, or an electric motor.

Chillers can be operated at constant speed by using the inlet guide vanes and hot gas bypass at part-load conditions, both of which waste energy. A compressor with a variable speed drive can be operated at its optimum speed for various part-load conditions. Steam turbines can be operated at variable speed by adjusting the governor and the hand wheels on the nozzles. Electric motors can provide variable speed outputs if equipped with variable frequency drives.

Centrifugal compressors that are designed to accept speed control as part of load control will usually accept only a 20 percent reduction in speed and still remain safely outside of surging conditions. The speed control will allow chilled water load reductions to approximately 50 percent of the compressor rating. Further chiller load reductions are accomplished by compressor downloading, which can allow the chiller to operate down to 10 percent of the rated load.

Absorption Chillers: Steam-Driven and Gas-Fired Absorption chillers are used in many central plant applications. They are available in sizes ranging from 100 to 1,500 tons and are usually operated by low-pressure steam or hot water or are directly fired with natural gas. The higher operating and maintenance costs associated with these chillers, compared with those of compressor-type units, usually make them uneconomical to use except where electric power is expensive, where fuel costs are low, or when balancing electrical and thermal loads in cogeneration facilities.

Absorption machines can provide a non-chlorofluorocarbon (CFC) solution to meet Environmental Protection Agency (EPA)–mandated reduction of CFC and hydrochlorofluorocarbon (HCFC) refrigerants that may be present in other types of existing chillers within the chiller plant. Absorption chillers use fossil fuel as their energy source rather than electricity.

These chillers can be operated in conjunction with electrical chillers. To reduce the overall utility cost, loading of the chillers can be shifted from electric chillers to absorption chillers based on electrical rates and demand charges.

Absorption machines can be a viable replacement of existing chillers. This solution can be especially attractive if existing cooling towers and pumps can be utilized. Because of the increased heat rejection compared with other chiller designs, replacement chillers may have to be downsized owing to the capacity limitation of the cooling towers. If existing chillers are oversized compared to the required load, the capacity reduction requirement may not present any detriment to the overall system. Two of the most common energy sources for absorption chillers are steam and direct-fired natural gas.

Direct-fired absorption chillers can produce hot water in addition to chilled water. This can be desirable if the chiller is located near a central heating plant. Recovered rejected heat from the chiller can be utilized to heat water and thereby supplement the hot water generated from another energy source. If the hot water needs are seasonal, the economics of utilizing the hot water by-product potential or even operating the direct-fired chiller may also be seasonal.

Steam-driven absorbers can be single-effect type, which use about 18 pounds of steam per ton-hour, or they may be double-effect type, which use about 12 pounds of steam per ton-hour.

Absorption chillers operate more efficiently and generate more cooling as the entering chilled water increases in temperature. Chiller capacity can increase as much as 1 to 2 percent for every 1°F rise in entering chilled water temperature.

Vibration

Practically every machine with rotating parts is susceptible to vibration. An unbalanced rotor is the most common cause of vibration and can result in noise, gear and bearing wear, mechanical fatigue, power loss, and possibly machine failure. Vibration can be a cause of trouble, the result of trouble, a symptom of trouble, or any combination of the three. Monitoring the vibration levels helps determine the proper time to overhaul a machine. This allows for scheduling the repairs into the regular maintenance program.

One problem with vibration monitoring is selecting the parameter to use for the vibration measurements: displacement, velocity, or acceleration. Vibration can be measured in terms of any one of these three, but each has a unique feature and application. Displacement measurements can be used on low-speed equipment such as cooling tower fans but is inadequate for a variable-speed gas turbine. Acceleration may be the best choice for monitoring antifriction bearings but would not be satisfactory for a heavy-cased compressor with sleeve bearings. The selection of the proper analytical equipment requires technical expertise. It is important to realize the equipment's potential and include it in the preventive maintenance program.

Refrigerants

The Montreal Protocol, followed by mandates issued by the EPA, has established limits on the use and availability of CFCs and HCFC refrigerants. Owners of chilling equipment containing CFC and HCFC refrigerants must establish a plan to retrofit, replace, or retain existing equipment. Time during which these mandates must be implemented is relatively limited.

One of the first refrigerants used in early-generation refrigerant systems was ammonia (R-717). Its most important characteristic was that it made the overall efficiency of the refrigeration cycle very high. This refrigerant was replaced with freon products as a result of the inherent dangers of ammonia exposure. Safety concerns and the corresponding capital expenditure for the installation and operation of ammonia-containing chillers made them unattractive. Recently added code requirements associated with replacement CFC and HCFC refrigerants have caused installation and handling procedures to be somewhat comparable to those for ammonia. Therefore, some chiller manufacturers have reviewed the feasibility of using ammonia in central cooling system chillers and currently provide this equipment. As a result, there has been a resurgence of ammonia chillers into the marketplace. If the exposure potential to the public is low, central chiller plant locations that are relatively remote may evaluate ammonia as the preferred refrigerant.

Refrigerant storage tanks are usually furnished by the chiller manufacturer as part of the chiller package. A large plant usually has one pump-out and storage unit system to serve all chillers that have the same refrigerant. The storage tank is sized for 200 or 300 percent of the capacity of the largest chiller. This provides the necessary volume to keep some backup refrigerant on hand yet allows space to put a charge in when it is necessary to remove the refrigerant from the chiller. The tank has an additional space to accommodate expansion of the stored refrigerant.

Prime Movers

Several different types of prime movers are used to drive chillers. Electric motors and steam turbines are the most common, but reciprocating engines and gas turbines have also been used, with varying degrees of success. Commercial cooling places the highest summertime demand on the electrical systems and the second highest annualized energy consumption on electrical utilities. Growth in cooling is expected to significantly increase in upcoming years, and electrical utilities will have difficulty meeting these demands if the chilling equipment is driven primarily by electric sources. That is why the utility companies have provided, and will continue to provide, incentives to encourage their customers to look at fossil fuel energy sources and district cooling alternatives.

Torsion vibration elimination between any prime mover and any driven equipment is a necessity. All variable- and constant-speed systems should be provided with a soft or fluid-type coupling to ensure that critical torsional vibrations do not exist in the system. Manufacturers should supply torsional analysis throughout the entire operating speed and load. This analysis applies to all components that make up the drive train.

Steam Turbines   The steam turbine drive is excellent for larger capacity chillers, because it is a smoothly rotating power source, is available in all horsepower ranges, and can usually match the compressor's design speed without using a speed-increasing gear. Steam turbine drives are sometimes selected to make use of existing boilers in a central heating plant. Using the existing boilers saves on the capital cost, improves the year-round load factor on the steam-generating equipment, and takes advantage of possible reductions in off-season fuel rates.

Electric Motors   Electric motors are the most common drives on centrifugal chillers, especially with hermetics. However, hermetics are available in sizes only up to about 1,850 tons, so conventional-type motors are used on open drive centrifugal chillers in the larger sizes. Electric motor drives offer several advantages but also have limitations. Synchronous electric motors run at exact speeds: 3,600 rpm, 1,800 rpm, 1,200 rpm, 900 rpm, and so on. Induction-type motors run at slightly less than synchronous speeds, depending on the slip. However, centrifugal compressors operate most efficiently at speeds much higher than the available motor speeds, so it is necessary to provide a speed-increasing gear between the motor and the compressor. The speed-increasing gear imposes additional frictional losses and additional equipment that must be maintained. Gear losses may amount to 1 to 2 percent of the required compressor horsepower. It is sometimes possible to eliminate the speed-increasing gear by selecting a two-stage compressor that operates at 3,600 rpm. This speed may be less than optimum for the compressor but will not result in as much loss as a gear. Also, 3,600-rpm motors in 2,000+ horsepower sizes are not off-the-shelf items; each is custom designed and manufactured to meet the requirements of the application.

Motors in the large horsepower sizes can be manufactured to operate at practically any voltage. However, economics will be a key factor in the selection of the voltage. The voltage is usually related to the horsepower: the higher the horsepower, the higher the voltage. Normal voltage ranges are as follows:

Horsepower Range	Voltage
100–500	480–2,400
500–5,000	2,400–5,000
5,000–10,000	5,000–12,000

Existing electrical service must be considered when selecting the voltage for a new large-capacity chiller. It may be necessary to bring in a new feeder or to change transformers. In many cases the central chiller plant will be the largest electrical load on campus, and the plant may become the focal point for the incoming utilities.

Natural Gas Engine–Driven Chillers   The use of internal combustion reciprocating engines to drive refrigeration equipment was popular in the 1960s. Many installations fell short of desired outcome as a result of inadequate design and construction, and redesigns were necessary to correct some of the deficiencies. Every aspect of the design must be evaluated. This type of experience underscores the necessity of having an experienced engineering team design all aspects of the system.

In the 1960s the most common fuel source was natural gas provided by a local utility company. As electrical generation plants continued to expand, the availability of electrical power at an economical price rate increased. The economics became unattractive for natural gas-driven chillers, and electric motor-driven chillers became the selection of choice. This trend was not so predominant with central district heating and cooling facilities. Currently electricity is not available at a reasonable cost in many locations.

Natural gas engine-driven chillers can be operated without penalty of electricity demand charges. These units can be used as the basic loading machines or as seasonal machines to serve as a tool for electricity demand side management. Internal combustion reciprocating engine drives are once again becoming a viable consideration where high electrical rates exist and where natural gas can be economically purchased during the cooling season. Engine-driven chillers are available in sizes ranging from 50 to 6,000 tons.

New engine technology, along with current component designs, allows engine-driven chillers to be offered in many configurations. Current systems are much more reliable, efficient, quiet, and environmentally friendly than systems that were installed in the late 1980s.

With proper control, engine-driven chillers can operate efficiently over a large range of loads. Payback may be quick as a result of the price differential that may exist between an electric motor-driven machine versus a gas motor-driven machine. Overall operating costs can be enhanced in favor of natural gas-driven engines if the waste heat from these chillers can be recovered and utilized for process heating needs; such a system is especially compatible with district heating systems.

Automatic control should normally be provided by the engine supplier. Current microprocessor technology should be used in lieu of mechanical or relay-type technology. The controls should start, operate, control, supervise, and stop the system with signals from the engine of the compressor. It is critical to equip the engine with governor control that can accurately respond to varying engine speeds and load on the compressor. Caution should be exercised when considering systems that have separate controls for the engine and the compressor.

Location

It is common for the central chiller plant to be located in or adjacent to the central heating plant. A central heating plant can meet campus heating requirements with relatively low temperature/low pressure steam or hot water. Higher temperatures and pressures are required for steam turbines for the chilling units, but lower temperature and pressure may be suitable if single-stage absorption chillers are used. Double-effect absorption chillers require steam pressures of 45 psig. minimum. Steam turbines can be condensing or noncondensing types and can be selected to operate on saturated steam at a few hundred pounds of pressure or on superheated steam at several thousand pounds of pressure. Many factors must be evaluated to determine the best combination of temperature and pressure for a given installation.

The electrical system should be designed in accordance with an electrical utility master plan that makes provisions for future expansion of the distribution system as well as the central plant. The central plant will require a considerable amount of space for the electrical switchgear because of the number and size of motors served. Transformers will also be required at the plant to serve the lower voltage equipment. Owing to the amount of electrical equipment normally associated with the central cooling plant, this may be the logical place to locate the incoming feeders, substations, buses, and switchgear to serve the entire campus. Having the primary electrical switchgear in or near the central plant can be even more advantageous if cogeneration equipment is installed.

Thermal Storage

One feature that may be included in the chiller plant is thermal storage. Several types have been developed. The most popular arrangement consists of chilled water that is stored in tanks, which are generally constructed of carbon steel with epoxy liners. Warm water is stored in the top of the tank, with cooler water at the bottom. When thermoclines (temperature gradients) occur within the tank, the tank is referred to as *stratified*. Minimum disturbance to the tank is a requirement to maintain a stratified condition. This is accomplished by using low-velocity input and output distributors. Monitors should be installed to determine the thermocline magnitude and stored capacity.

Corrosion control and water quality within the thermal storage system are important issues. The expertise of a qualified chemical water treatment consultant and chemical provider should be an integral component of the design. The consultant should be included from the conceptual design stages through commissioning and operation of the system.

Thermal storage is used to reduce electrical consumption during times when demand charges are high. Typically, chilled water is generated during the evenings when the electricity demand charges are low and the chilled water system load is low. The thermal storage system is therefore charged during the evening and discharged during the day.

Thermal storage allows the chilled water plant to generate more units of chilled water without having to install more chilling equipment. The amount of capital investment can be reduced. Investment can be made in thermal storage instead of chillers, cooling towers, and ancillary equipment.

Justification of various scenarios depends on the load profile of the system, the cost of the installation, the availability of space and the severity of electricity demand charges.

System designers many times do not associate thermal storage with absorption chillers because of the low temperature limitation of the chilled water. If the chiller plant is a hybrid chiller plant with chiller types in addition to absorption, a properly designed system can function effectively.

If absorption equipment is used in an application with an on-peak (daytime) load and no off-peak (nighttime) demand, the absorption machine may be able to charge a chilled water tank during the day. Again, justification of each system depends on the load profile of the system, the cost of the installation, the availability of space, and the severity of electricity demand charges.

Chilled water storage and absorption chillers both reduce electricity demand. The absorption chiller uses nonelectrical energy sources, and the thermal storage system also offsets electricity demand by allowing an electrically driven chiller to run during off-peak times. In extreme cases of electricity demand charges, the existence of redundant capacity to meet the chilled water demand economically with a combination of electrically driven chillers, absorption chillers, and thermal storage may be justified. This situation may be encouraged by the electrical utility in the form of utility rebates or financial incentives for the chilled water plant. It is imperative that hybrid systems with the required degree of sophistication be operated with a computerized energy analysis system.

Pumps

The major pumps associated with the central chiller plant are the chilled water and condensing water pumps. Other pumps that may be required include condensate return pumps when steam turbine drives are used. Booster pumps will be required for the chilled water system if the plant domestic water pressure is below the system pressure. Chilled water pumps may be end suction, horizontal double suction, or vertical turbine pumps. The type selected will be influenced by the flow, head, efficiency, and space availability.

Variable-speed motors should be considered for the chilled water system. Pump outputs can adjusted to match required system flows without overpressurizing the system, which improves the overall operating efficiencies.

Like chilled water pumps, condensing water pumps can be end suction, horizontal double suction, or vertical turbine pumps. If horizontal double suction or end suction pumps are used, then the cooling tower basin must be at an elevation that is sufficient to provide a positive head on the suction side of the pumps. Vertical turbine pumps tend to be the preferred type for the larger tonnage cooling towers. The vertical turbine pumps allow most of the basin to be located below grade, which in turn improves accessibility to the pump motors and cooling tower screens. The sump pits associated with the vertical turbine pumps should be designed in strict accordance with the recommendations of the Hydraulic Institute. If end suction or horizontal double suction pumps are selected for the condensing water system, it will be mandatory to elevate the cooling tower basin or locate the pumps in a pit to provide sufficient head to the suction of the pumps. Because the head is critical, it is not advisable to use Y-type strainers on the suction of these pumps. It is best to use a rough screen inside the tower basin and then pump through a Y-type strainer to remove the small debris.

Pump seals are either mechanical or packing gland-type seals. Mechanical seals are adequate, provided the water is clean and the water treatment is compatible with the seal material. Replacing a mechanical seal is more difficult and time consuming than repacking a gland-type seal. The packing gland seals depend on friction between the shaft and the packing material to prevent leakage. To prevent damage to the shaft, the packing should not be too tight. It should allow one or two drops of water to leak each minute, which will provide cooling and lubrication to the shaft at this point.

Piping Systems

The major considerations in the design of piping systems are pressure and temperature within the system, velocities in the pipes, pipe material and its compatibility with the contents, expansion and contraction, supports, and insulation.

The velocity of the fluid in the pipe is directly related to the pressure loss in the system: the higher the velocity, the higher the losses. Velocity is therefore inversely proportional to the pipe size: the smaller the pipe, the higher the velocity for a given flow. Smaller pipes equate to lower first cost, but the higher losses mean higher pumping cost in perpetuity. There must be an optimum balance between the two in design.

Thermal expansion and contraction do not present much of a problem in chilled water systems because the differential temperatures are relatively low, but they cannot be ignored.

Chiller Plant Piping

The most common piping material and method of fabrication for a central chiller is standard-weight, black steel pipe with welded fittings. In addition to welding, methods used to join the pipe include the use of grooved pipe with bolted couplings. The method selected is usually based on personal preference of the owner, the engineer, or perhaps the contractor, if two methods are allowed.

Distribution Piping

A central chilling plant system requires supply and return piping to deliver chilled water to the various buildings. This is the primary distribution system, and it may be an intricate network of pipes with hydraulic loops and cross-connections serving many buildings or loads. A large network distribution system can also be served by several plants simultaneously. The piping system may be direct-buried in the earth, located in a shallow trench, or routed in a utility tunnel. The construction materials used will depend to a large degree on the environment in which the piping will be located.

The primary distribution system must be designed as carefully as any part of the chilled water system. Size and location of the pipes should be determined from a thermal utility master plan. Pipes should be sized and located to accommodate future buildings, if applicable. Pumping cost must also be considered.

Materials   Four of the most common piping materials for direct-buried chilled water distribution systems are polyvinyl chloride (PVC), polyethylene, ductile iron, and black steel pipe. Material selection depends on the initial material cost, corrosion requirements, operating pressures, joining methods, and expected life. Listed below are some of the advantages and disadvantages of each piping material.

- *Polyvinyl chloride (PVC).* Advantages: corrosion resistant, low thermal conductivity, joints are simply pushed together. Disadvantages: higher leak potential, requires thrust restraint, difficult to find with utility location equipment without a tracer wire.
- *Polyethylene (PE).* Advantages: corrosion resistant, high-quality weld joints, low thermal conductivity, can tolerate freezing of chilled water. Disadvantages: pressure is normally limited to 100 psig., requires specialized equipment and contractor, difficult to find with utility location equipment without a tracer wire.
- *Ductile iron (DI).* Advantages: joints are simply pushed together. Disadvantages: higher material cost, high thermal conductivity, higher leak potential, difficult to find with utility location equipment without a tracer wire.
- *Black iron.* Advantages: higher pressure rating, high-quality weld joints. Disadvantages: requires a protective coating for corrosion control, requires cathodic protection for corrosion control, requires electrical isolation from other systems to reduce corrosion potential, time consuming to install, high installation cost.

Terminal Components

Performance and Design

Maximizing cooling coil performance is crucial for the entire chilled water system operation. Each coil should be selected to achieve the highest possible chilled water temperature differential while meeting the air-side performance requirements. Listed below is a specification example that can provide some guidelines when specifying coils at a specific location.

- Entering water temperatures shall be 40°F.
- Coil shall perform with a minimum of a 20°F temperature rise at design conditions.
- Coil shall be drainable, with a vent at the highest location and a drain in the lowest location.
- Aluminum fins shall be 0.010 in. thick.
- Tubes shall be 0.035-in. copper with 0.049-in. walled U-bends.

- Casings shall be galvanized steel.
- Maximum air velocity shall be 550 ft./min.
- No water carryover shall occur at rated airflow.
- Minimum tube velocity at rated capacity shall be 4 ft./sec.
- Turbulators are not allowed.
- Maximum water pressure drop shall be 10 psig.
- Coils shall be Air Conditioning and Refrigerant Institute (ARI) rated, with a 0.005 fouling factor.
- Coils shall be rated for a pressure of 200 psig.
- Coils shall be sized to the stated entering air condition, airflow rate, discharge air temperature, and entering water conditions.
- Performance testing is required.

Flow Control Valves

Flow control valves are a necessity for all cooling coils. Control valves should be selected to match the cooling coil they will control. Pressure drop at the rated flow rate normally should be approximately one-half the pressure drop of the cooling coil. The control valve will modulate to maintain the desired coil discharge air temperature.

Two-way control valves should be installed rather than three-way valves. Three-way valves cause recirculation of chilled water, which increases the pumping charges and decreases the overall chilled water temperature differential.

Heat Rejection

Cooling Tower

Types Cooling towers come in many different types and configurations: packaged, field erected, counter flow, cross flow, induced draft, and forced draft. They are a part of every central chiller plant, from those with loads of a few hundred tons to those with loads of several thousand tons, except in smaller plants where air-cooled condensers are used.

Although cooling towers are available in various types and configurations, the main difference in the larger towers is the materials used for their construction (i.e., metal, wood, ceramic, fiberglass, and plastic).

Metal Towers. Metal towers are assembled at the factory and shipped to the job site, complete and ready for installation. As the name implies, all the major components, including the enclosure, basin, fill, deck, stack, and fans, are constructed of galvanized metal. This type of tower is limited to a few hundred tons because of shipping limitations.

Wood Towers. Wood towers are the most common of all towers because they are economical and easy to fabricate. Wood towers have been the choice for many years. The shortcomings of wood towers have been identified and either corrected or eliminated as much as is practical and economical. For many years redwood was the choice material for the structure, fill, decks, casing, and basin. Other pressure-treated woods have proved to be economical substitutes for structural members. PVC fill has become a durable replacement for wood. Asbestos cement siding was used for the outer casing material and the louvers on wood towers for many years, but corrugated fiberglass panels are currently used. Fiberglass stacks have become standard on most wood towers because they are durable and lightweight and can be fabricated into a smooth venturi shape. A properly designed stack can reduce the fan horsepower if it has a venturi shape and is tall enough (12 to 16 ft.). The basin of wood towers can be constructed of wood or concrete. If a tower is to be located on the roof of a building, the basin may need to be made of wood if there are weight limitations. If the tower is located on the ground, a concrete basin and sump may be the best choice, as concrete is practically maintenance free. Basin depth, and therefore the volume of water, is unlimited with a concrete basin, whereas there are practical limitations on the size and volume of a wood basin.

Ceramic Towers. In these towers ceramic is used for the fill, which is a refractory clay tile with multiple openings. The tiles are stacked several layers deep, with the openings of the tile in the vertical direction so that water can fall down through the opening and air can be drawn up. This gives good contact between the water and air, a primary objective in any cooling tower. The tile fill is supported on concrete columns and beams, and the enclosure, deck, and basin are all constructed of concrete. The stacks may be concrete or fiberglass. Except for the mechanical and electrical equipment (fans, gears, motors, and distribution nozzles), there is little that can fail or deteriorate on a ceramic cooling tower. The advantages of a ceramic cooling tower are 1) it has long life; 2) there is no loss of capacity owing to fill sagging or failure; 3) it is fireproof; and 4) it can be made aesthetically pleasing. The main disadvantage is the high initial cost.

Hybrid designs have evolved that try to take advantage of each type. One design uses ceramic tile fill in a factory-fabricated fiberglass enclosure. This greatly improves the initial cost of the ceramic-type cooling tower, but there is not enough history on these units to predict the possible maintenance costs over their lifetime. Another hybrid is a tower with a concrete basin, enclosure, and fan deck, with PVC film fill and fiberglass stacks. Compared with the wood tower, this design improves the life and the looks while decreasing the fire hazard, all at a reasonable increase in first cost. PVC will burn or melt only if it is held in contact with a flame. It does not support combustion and will extinguish itself when the flame is removed.

Cooling Tower Capacity   Deciding on the design of a cooling tower for performance is based on the amount of heat to be rejected, the flow of water, the temperature in, and the desired temperature out. The tower must be guaranteed to satisfy these requirements under the worst atmospheric conditions normally expected (i.e., the design conditions). The tower is also expected to operate satisfactorily during winter, rainstorms, temperature inversions, high winds, or other adverse conditions, including little or no maintenance. Towers are also expected to operate efficiently, without causing any problems such as drift. If the central chiller plant is to operate year round, the cooling towers must have equipment to facilitate operation at part-load conditions; such equipment should include multiple-speed fans.

Cooling Tower Piping The cooling tower piping consists of condensing water return piping that will distribute water to the hot water basins near the fan deck level (cross flow tower) or to a distribution spray header located inside the tower above the fill (counter flow tower). Balancing valves are required to adjust the distribution of the water over the fill. The condensing water supply piping starts on the suction side of the condensing water pumps and may be a pipe connection through the wall of the sump, preferably with a suction bell located near the floor of the sump. If the pump is a vertical turbine type, the suction bell will be mounted directly to the bottom of the pump. Other piping associated with the cooling tower is the water makeup line, with a float-operated valve, and the overflow pipe, which limits the maximum elevation of the water in the tower. The overflow line ties directly into the drain system, and each tower cell should have a drain valve so that each can be drained and cleaned independently of the other cells. Other lines would possibly include chemical feed lines, sample lines, and fire protection piping. Any small-diameter lines or lines with stagnant water should be protected from freezing by heat tracing or draining during winter months.

Cooling Tower Screens Cooling tower screens are required to keep paper, leaves, feathers, rags, and other debris out of the condensing water system. On a wooden basin, the screen is located over the sump, which is mounted on the bottom of the basin. Access to the screen is through a door in the tower casing. Towers with concrete basins may have dual screens located between the tower basin and the sump. Most of the debris will collect on the first screen, which is the first to pull when cleaning. The second screen remains in place to catch any debris in the water while the first screen is out. Screens with small openings require more cleaning, but they keep the water cleaner. Screens with larger openings may let too much solid matter pass into the circulating system. The opening should always be smaller than the diameter of the tubes in the chiller condenser. The overall size of the screens will determine the velocity through them. The recommendations of the Hydraulic Institute call for a velocity of 1 ft./min. or less through the screen.

Recovery

Recovery systems on reciprocating engine systems can be used to generate hot water and low-pressure steam for process use or district heating. Total recovered heat can be about 40 percent of the fuel energy value on reciprocating engines. This recovered energy can also be utilized in a piggyback arrangement to provide an energy source to operate an absorption chiller system to improve the overall system coefficient of performance.

Groundwater

Groundwater has been used in the past for heat rejection when an abundant groundwater supply is present. Relatively new regulations have restricted the quantity and use of available groundwater. Phaseout of groundwater usage in many states does not make it a very attractive option for heat rejection in the future. Strategies should be established to address other means of heat rejection for existing systems that presently use groundwater.

Plate Heat Exchangers

Plate heat exchangers can be used in many applications to isolate two separate water circuits while providing energy transfer between the two media. Applications include exchanging energy 1) between condenser water and chilled water for free cooling, 2) between chilled water storage tanks and chilled water, and 3) between primary chilled water and building systems for static heat isolation in tall buildings.

The plate heat exchanger construction consists of a series of metal plates bolted together to provide channels for counter-flow energy exchange between the two water sources. Heat transfer is highly efficient because of the turbulent flow of the fluids, which allows the approach temperature to be 1° to 2°F.

Auxiliary Equipment

Chemical Feed Systems   Chiller plants have two water systems that require conditioning and treatment. Condensing water systems have equipment to monitor the quality of the water, to add chemicals, to maintain desired levels of dissolved solids, and to add makeup water to offset evaporation, leakage, and blowdown. The chilled water system has pot feeders for adding corrosion inhibitors to the system and a coupon station for measuring the effectiveness of the inhibitor.

Sidestream Filters and Separators   A filtering system is necessary to remove solids such as dirt, rust, and debris from the chilled water. Individual strainers and filters are required on sensitive equipment that may be plugged by contaminants in the system.

Sidestream filters can be installed within the chilling plant to continually filter a small portion of the total flow, as it is generally not feasible to install a filter system with sufficient capacity to accommodate the entire chilled water flow.

Chilled Water Makeup   Chilled water makeup is needed to replace losses from leaks and maintenance activity. Makeup can occur by pumping water from a storage tank or by using a regulator and backflow preventer to take water directly from the domestic water system. Overall system pressure is regulated by this makeup. It is desirable to have the chilled water system pressure below the domestic water pressure to prevent potential contamination of the domestic water system if a cross-connection inadvertently occurs. For convenience and simplicity, the number of potential makeup locations should be kept to a minimum. Makeup can be easily measured by using a conventional water meter.

Expansion Tank   Expansion tanks are required on the chilled water system to accommodate the expansion and contraction associated with any thermal liquid system and to provide a point of constant pressure in the system. The expansion tank should be built with bladders to isolate the air from the liquid.

Automatic Air Release Vents   Air becomes trapped within the chilled water system whenever equipment or piping is restored to service after draining the chilled water from the system. Entrapped air can adversely affect the operation of the chilled water system by significantly reducing chilled water circulation and heat transfer. Difficulty due to the compressibility of air can occur when the system pressure on a particular segment of the system is relieved for maintenance activities. Automatic air release valves should be added to high points within the system where air can be trapped, including chillers, tanks, piping, and terminal equipment.

Controls and Instrumentation

Operating and safety controls are furnished as part of the chiller package. Instrumentation such as pressure gauges, thermometers, and flow measuring devices must be specified where they are required or desired. Pressure gauges should be provided on the inlet and outlet of all vessels, pumps, and strainers. Thermometers with wells should be provided at the inlet and outlet of all equipment where a change in temperature will take place.

Metering

Chilled water systems should have sufficient metering to measure the system performance as well as individual components. This metering is necessary to determine system optimization and to analyze capacity-related issues.

Flow measuring devices should be installed in chilled water, condensing water, steam, and makeup water lines to the cooling tower. The flow meters must have sufficient straight runs of pipe upstream and downstream of the meters to ensure meter accuracy. Flow-sensing elements can be of the ultrasonic, magnetic, vortex shedding, full-pipe-size positive displacement, full-pipe-size turbine, insertion turbine, insertion differential pressure, orifice plate, or venturi style.

Early chilled water meters consisted of a mechanical flow measurement device and two thermal sensing devices. Modern chilled water energy meters consist of a wide variety of flow-sensing elements, several temperature-sensing devices, and an electronic processor that receives input to calculate and totalize the energy. Programmable electronic devices can communicate to even more sophisticated centrally located computer systems.

The accuracy of chilled water meters is a function of the turndown (range of the sensing), the precision of the flow-measuring element, and the accuracy of the temperature-sensing device. Care must be taken to clearly understand the implications of the specifications on the accuracy of the energy meter. The greatest potential energy calculation inaccuracy occurs with the temperature-sensing devices. For example, a temperature-sensing device with a range of 0° to 200°F, with an accuracy of 1 percent of the full scale range, will have an output accuracy of ±2°F. In a chilled water system with a design differential of 10°F, the accuracy of the system would be ±20 percent.

For any meter to function within its accuracy range, it must be routinely calibrated and accurate records maintained on the calibration procedure.

Insulation

Thermal insulation with a vapor barrier is required on chiller evaporators, refrigerant suction lines, compressors, expansion tanks, chilled water supply and return lines in the plant, and any other equipment connected to the chilled water system that is subject to sweating. The vapor barrier should be sealed at regular intervals along the pipe so that in case of a leak or damaged vapor seal, the travel of the moisture will be limited.

Chillers, heat exchangers, and tanks should be insulated with material such as fiberglass or closed-cell foam rubber sheet insulation. Acoustic insulation may be needed to reduce the noise level on certain items in the central plant, such as chiller condensers and compressor discharge piping. Removable heads on chillers and heat exchangers should be insulated with covers that can be easily removed to allow access for inspection, cleaning, and dismantling. Insulation material that is not subject to damage by moisture is preferred.

All low-temperature insulated piping within the chiller plant, buildings, and vaults should have insulation at each hanger, support, and anchor. The insulation should also be protected with shields of galvanized metal extending not less than 4 in. on either side of the support bearing area, and it should cover at least half of the pipe circumference. Preinsulated steel pipe is a popular material and minimizes field insulation labor.

Soil temperatures at burial depths will determine the magnitude of energy loss to the soil with uninsulated direct-buried pipe as well as various insulation materials. An energy evaluation is needed at each central chilled water site to determine what, if any, insulation is needed. If it is determined that it is economical to install insulated pipe, then preinsulated pipe is available in pipe materials.

45.3 SYSTEM DESIGN CONSIDERATIONS

The central chilling system criteria are a set of requirements that provide guidelines for the design and operation of all equipment as well as the thermal systems. The central chilling plant represents only part of the overall chilled water system, and the system criteria should not be limited to this facility alone. Other equally important parts include the distribution system and building systems. A single philosophy must exist for the design and operation of the entire chilled water system if the individual parts are to function correctly and economically. Operating problems and difficulties in many central cooling systems can be traced to a single common cause: incompatibility among the chilling equipment, piping systems, and terminal units.

Prior to deciding on the choice of piping and pumping configurations, a thorough study of the proposed or existing system must be completed. The four fundamental steps are as follows:

1. A complete hydraulic analysis is a necessity to determine the system performance. Deficiencies and strengths of the system can be identified with such an analysis. Without this comprehensive evaluation, many systems have been installed with serious "ailments." Significant rework of previously installed components, with the attendant significant replacement and operating costs, has occurred in many institutions as a result of failure to perform this step. This is one of the most important steps to be completed before proceeding with any capital investment.

2. Component compatibility can be analyzed after completing the hydraulic analysis. The hydraulic analysis addresses the volumetric component of the chilled water, but it does not include the energy component of the chilled water. Therefore, an energy analysis must be completed.
3. The goal of any system analysis should take into account the installed cost along with full consideration of the operating cost over the life of the system. The temperature differential between the chilled water supply and return should be maximized, which will minimize the volume of chilled water to meet the energy capacity of the chilled water. A reduction in chilled water volume reduces the pump energy required to move the water and also reduces the pressure loss required to transport the chilled water throughout the system. Therefore, increasing the temperature differential between the chilled water supply and return has a dual effect on reducing the pumping energy by reducing the volume and pressure loss within the system. The energy capacity of a given distribution main can be increased simply by increasing the temperature differential between the supply and return main.
4. After the previously listed items have been completed, the pumping methods and piping configuration should be examined. Caution should be exercised not to attempt to correct component incompatibility by altering pumping methods or piping configuration, as this can plague the performance of the entire chilled water system for years to come. The piping and pumping configurations should result in the least complicated and most energy-efficient system. The quantity and sophistication of controls and pumps associated with the system should be kept to a minimum. If the system cannot be easily explained to and understood by a nontechnical person, then errors have probably been made in arriving at the optimal system configuration.

There are three commonly used piping and pumping systems in most chilled water systems: primary, secondary, and tertiary systems. There are numerous permutations of equipment layout within these three types.

A *primary system* involves pumping the entire chilled water system from pumps that are in a central cooling plant. These pumps circulate the chilled water through the chiller, supply distribution piping, building supply piping, terminal unit, building return piping, and return distribution piping to return the chilled water to the pump suction.

A *secondary system* has two individual piping loops. Each loop has its own pumping loop, and the two pumping loops are generally connected together with a common hydraulic decoupling bypass line. Individual loops can occur within the chiller plant, distribution, or building systems.

A *tertiary system* has three individual piping loops. It adds one additional pumping loop to the secondary system as described above.

Chillers can be connected to individually dedicated cooling towers or into a common header. This physical layout should be fully analyzed to ensure equipment compatibility. Chiller and tower equalization must be met so that capacity or efficiency is not compromised throughout the range of varying loads.

Pumping and Piping Systems

Pumping costs should be minimized to keep the overall efficiency of the chilled water system as high as possible. Therefore, flow rates to individual components and bypasses around equipment should be kept to a minimum. Delivered pressure should be only high enough to meet the circulation needs of the system. Excessive pressure causes control valves to throttle the flow, which creates an energy loss in the system. To prevent overpumping, variable-frequency-drive pumps should be installed in most situations to minimize pumping energy for the system. Pumping energy is transferred into the chilled water, which ends up adding to the cooling load of the system.

The pressure required to circulate the chilled water from the chiller through the buildings and then back to the chiller should normally be less than 40 psig. If greater pressure drops occur, the system should be analyzed to locate inappropriately sized equipment and piping.

Chiller Plant

Decisions that are made in selecting and arranging equipment will probably affect system operation for many years. Therefore, care should be taken to accurately analyze all aspects of the decision-making process. The design requires an investigation of all details and coordination of the many ideas and requirements into an optimum end product or facility. A good design will make provisions for future expansion and anticipate the flexibility needed to take advantage of new ideas, equipment, and technology. A design that considers only present needs and technologies probably will not make for a cost-effective facility in the future.

During the development of the design for a central chiller plant, the primary concern is the process, equipment layout, access for maintenance, and future expansions. A plant building should not be designed until the layout of the equipment and all support systems is well established. The building is an enclosure to protect the water chilling equipment and should be a functional part of the overall cooling facility, not the dominant factor. The process should not be changed to accommodate the size of the building or restrictions imposed by the building. The same is true of the site or location for the plant; if major equipment layout changes are required to adapt a plant to a particular location, then perhaps the site is wrong.

System reliability is a product of component quality and durability in conjunction with the preventive maintenance programs. Redundant equipment is sometimes employed for seasonal load variation and reliability, and where critical environments justify the additional capital and maintenance expenditure. Certain electricity demand rates can also justify adding particular system components to avert expensive electrical penalties if equipment downtime occurs.

The system criteria are tools for selecting equipment and developing operating procedures. The criteria must be established when the design of the central chilling plant is started and then must create a compatible design among the plant, the distribution system, and the buildings served. The requirements established by the system criteria must be considered each time the plant is expanded or a new building or facility is added. The combined characteristics of all the building air-side systems are one of the major factors in developing the system criteria. These same characteristics will be a determinant of plant economics. Air-side systems must not be operated far from their design conditions if economical, high-quality air conditioning is to be provided.

Designing and constructing a central chilling system are major undertakings. System reliability, performance, and serviceability are all critical elements in the design process. Initial decisions will have significant implications for plant size. It is obvious that an undersized plant will have detrimental end results. Oversizing a plant may not have the obvious disadvantage of undersizing, but it can cause the overall project to be burdened with excessive capital expenditures. Careful thought should be given to sizing decisions early in the design process.

Pumping arrangements for water circuits within a central chilled water plant normally fall into the following categories:

- A unitary arrangement, in which a single pump is dedicated to a specific chiller (Figure 45-1). This arrangement may be found in both primary and primary/secondary pumping systems, as well as in condenser water pumping systems.
- A primary/secondary pumping system, in which the hydraulic head requirements for the chiller and in-plant piping are furnished by pumps dedicated to specific chillers, and the distribution system hydraulic head requirements are furnished by a separate decoupled pump circuit (Figure 45-2).
- A headered arrangement for chilled water pumps, in which a number of pumps discharge into a common header serving a bank of chillers (Figure 45-3). This arrangement may be found in both primary and primary/secondary pumping systems. This type of arrangement may also be found in condenser water pumping systems.

Building Interconnection

Building connection analyses are important for the entire chilled water system. Return valves should not be installed on the return main coming from the buildings. This method artificially attempts to increase the building temperature differential and can have disastrous results. Building humidity control and system hydraulics can be hindered to the point of making the system inoperable.

Low temperature is primarily the result of improperly selected coils or coil control valves. Coils should be designed for the maximum chilled water temperature differential. This requires great attention during the coil acquisition and installation process to make sure that the coil performance can maximize the chilled water temperature differential and still meet the building cooling requirements.

Hydraulic interfaces between central systems and building systems can vary widely in control strategies but will generally be described by one of the following hydraulic arrangements:

- A straight primary interface, in which the necessary building circulating head is supplied by the central system pumps (Figure 45-4).
- A primary/secondary interface, in which central system pumps deliver water to the building and any residual central system head is

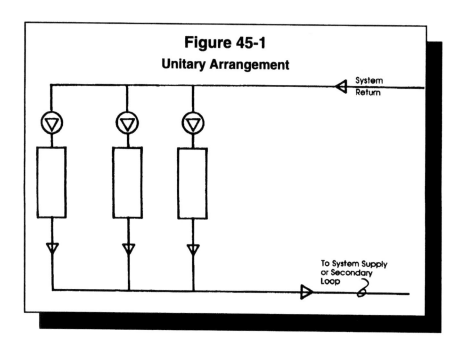

Figure 45-1
Unitary Arrangement

System Return

To System Supply or Secondary Loop

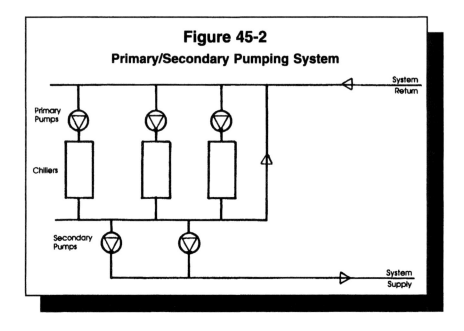

Figure 45-2

Primary/Secondary Pumping System

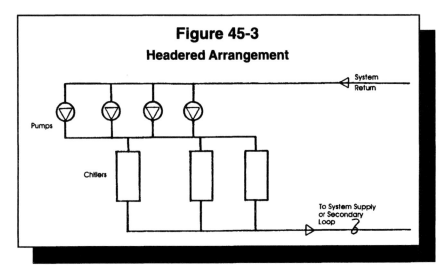

Figure 45-3

Headered Arrangement

throttled away by a control valve (Figure 45-5). Building circulation is provided by building chilled water pumps.

• A hybrid primary–primary/secondary building interface, in which central plant pumps provide building circulation when adequate head is available, and building chilled water pumps provide building circulation when central system head is not adequate to meet load requirements (Figure 45-6).

Retrofit

System retrofits should be considered if they will substantially improve the operating efficiencies of a central chilled water system and reduce operating costs. Following are eight of the available options:

1. Cooling coils can be replaced to achieve a high water temperature differential. This will reduce pumping costs and allow the system flow to become more compatible with the design operating conditions of the chillers.
2. Two-way control valves can be installed on terminal units to replace oversized two-way valves, three-way valves, or wild (uncontrolled) circuits.
3. Unnecessary pumps can be removed from the system to reduce energy consumption.
4. Undersized piping can be replaced.
5. Computer control systems are available that will allow automatic dispatch of chillers to ensure that the most efficient equipment is in service and appropriately loaded to efficiently serve the system load. These systems can also automatically optimize condensing water temperature and minimize chiller energy requirements.
6. Chilled water storage can be added to a system to reduce peak electricity demand as well as serve additional loads without the need for added chiller capacity.

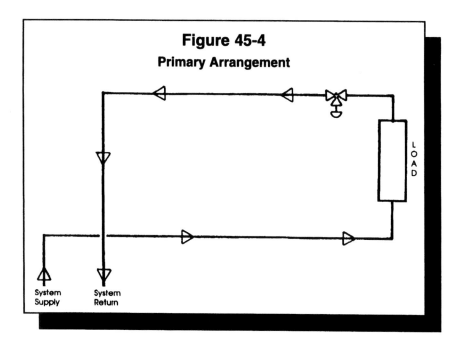

Figure 45-4

Primary Arrangement

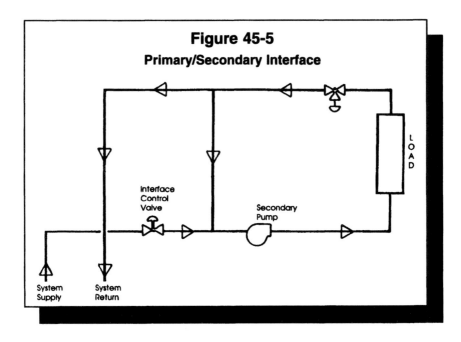

Figure 45-5
Primary/Secondary Interface

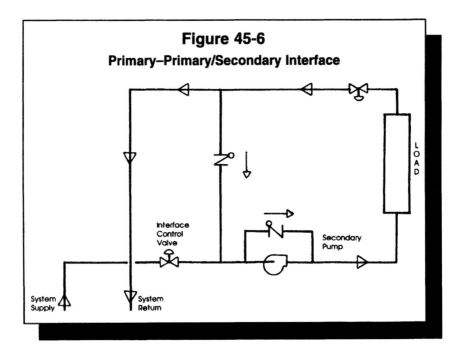

Figure 45-6
Primary–Primary/Secondary Interface

7. A computerized hydraulic model of the distribution system can be developed to determine minimum plant pumping requirements to meet any given load and also to identify needed distribution system improvements to serve planned growth.
8. Plate and frame heat exchangers can be installed to take the place of mechanical refrigeration during periods when low condensing water temperatures are possible. A typical arrangement of this method is shown in Figure 45-7.

If chilled water systems serve loads that are relatively constant throughout the year, such as computer systems or clean rooms, the installation of small stand alone chiller units may allow the central system to be shut down entirely during winter months. The free cooling season may also be extended on those systems that run 12 months a year.

System Performance

Diversity Factor Buildings connected to a central system will not necessarily experience peak load at the same time. This relationship between the sum of the peak loads for individual buildings and the actual aggregate central system peak load is known as the *diversity factor.* For example, dormitories may have reduced loads during the day and peak loads in the evening; libraries and laboratories can have substantial loads during the day that may extend into the evening hours; classrooms and administrative areas usually have peak demands during the day only, and auditoriums and athletic facilities have peak demands associated with specific activities. It is difficult to predict diversity with new systems, whereas with adequate metering, information on existing buildings that are being considered for connection onto a central system can be determined with reasonable accuracy.

Central plants can be designed for a capacity of something less than the sum of the individual buildings. The magnitude of this reduction is affected by the type and quantity of building connections. This phenomenon should not be overlooked, as this is an opportunity to save capital when installing new equipment. If a plant can be sized to operate near design conditions, overall plant efficiency will be optimized.

Load Factor The ratio of the total cooling energy produced over a year compared with the total potential generated by the installed chilling equipment is defined as the *load factor.* Load factors typically vary from 9 percent to more than 25 percent. This ratio is highly dependent on the climate and the type of loads that are connected to the system. Comparisons can be made between similar installations to arrive at some guidelines for evaluation of existing and planned systems.

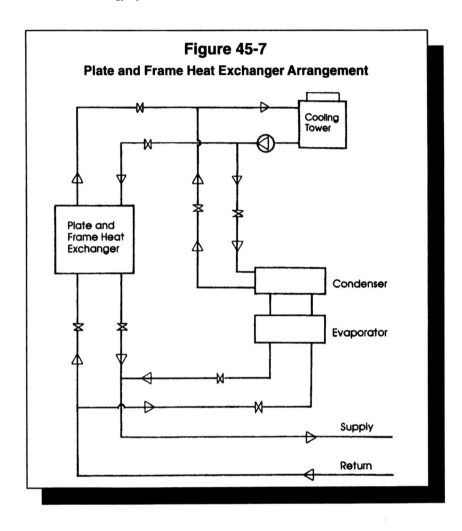

Figure 45-7

Plate and Frame Heat Exchanger Arrangement

Even with a load factor of 25 percent, it is evident that chilled water systems have the capability of delivering significantly more chilled water than is actually generated. Because most load on the systems is comfort cooling, additional comfort load cannot be added without affecting the peak demand on the system. Adding process loads that are present year round increases the load factor without substantially affecting the peak demand. These process loads take advantage of the invested capital.

Load Duration Curve Load duration curves are used to graphically show the central plant installed capacity, the load demands, and the time duration per year for the system load operated at each level. This is illustrated in Figure 45-8.

The load duration curve can be helpful in determining equipment sizing. The total cooling produced is equal to the area under the curve. The area under the horizontal line, representing the plant installed capacity, equates to the total potential capacity for the plant over a year. The ratio between these two areas is equal to the plant load factor.

Load duration curves can also show the amount of time the system operated at a specific capacity. The equivalent full-load hours can be determined by taking the area underneath the operating curve (total energy produced) and dividing it by the total installed plant capacity.

Horizontal lines can be drawn to indicate the incremental available capacity as individual chillers are operated. Machine sequencing can be illustrated to show when specific chillers will be operated. It can be seen that, as additional chillers are needed to operate, hourly utilization of these chillers begins to diminish. This will coincide with operating the chillers at their highest efficiency, as individual chillers operate at the highest efficiency when operated at rated capacity. Multiple units within a facility allow chiller generation capacity to more closely match overall system needs by sequencing the chillers to match the load profile. The downside to having multiple chillers is that the cost to purchase and install many small machines is significantly more expensive than fewer larger machines.

The magnitude of the load duration curve can exceed the plant installed capacity curve on systems that do not have the capacity to meet the peak demand on the system. This can be a temporary state caused by recent additions or a condition that is not intended to be addressed based on an economic evaluation versus the duration of peak. Options may exist to shed noncritical loads a few hours per year. Other systems may allow the entire system to uniformly shed load by allowing the chiller discharge temperature to rise after rated capacity is achieved.

Thermal storage is another element that can be included in the load duration curve. Thermal storage benefits can be illustrated to show how load requirements can be met, when exceeding the installed capacity of the chiller plant. The total generated chilled water will be the same with thermal storage as when using chiller equipment. The peak of the generation curve is removed and added back into the area under the curve.

Building Performance Determining the peak chilled water demand for specific building types can be calculated by applying industry standards for gross square footage per ton. The demand for a particular building can be calculated by multiplying the building square footage by this factor.

For central cooling systems, an industry-accepted standard ranges from 200 to 450 sq. ft. per ton. The lower range generally applies to buildings that have low air exchange rates and are well insulated. The upper range applies to buildings that have high air exchange rates (e.g., laboratories and hospitals). Individual buildings have larger performance factors if they

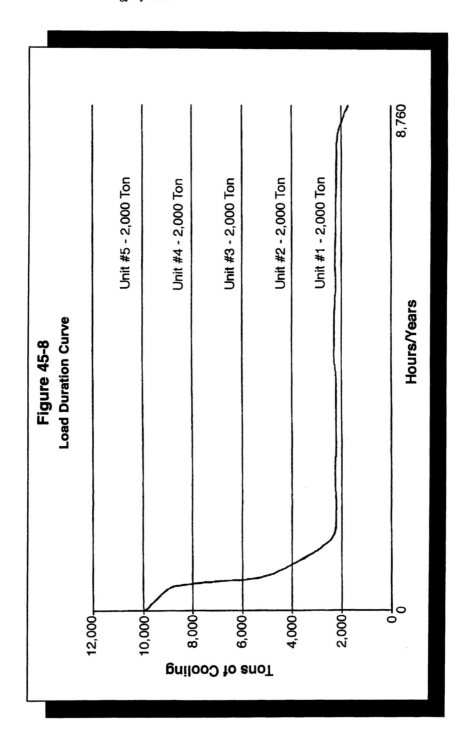

Figure 45-8
Load Duration Curve

are going to be served by localized equipment, because central cooling systems experience load diversity.

Plant Cooling and Dehumidification

Air conditioning in a central chiller plant has been largely limited to the office, the control room, and perhaps the electrical switchgear area, with the balance of the plant cooled by ventilation.

Cooling and dehumidifying of the central chiller plant should be considered for plants located in areas of high humidity or with electric motor–driven chillers. Air-conditioned plants are easy to keep clean, have better security, reduce maintenance on electrical gear, extend equipment life, and create better working conditions. Although it is generally not practical to air-condition plants that have chillers and boilers in the same space, spot cooling may be an option.

Total, Firm, and Reserve Capacity

Central chilling plants usually have multiple water chilling units, cooling towers, pumps, boilers, and associated equipment. From time to time, each item of equipment will be out of service for cleaning, maintenance, or repairs. Cleaning and maintenance usually require a scheduled outage for a relatively short period of time. Planned extended outages are normally scheduled during periods of minimum cooling loads. On the other hand, required repairs to major equipment may not be scheduled

The *total capacity* of a central plant is the sum of the capacities for all units installed. However, the firm capacity is the sum of all units installed minus the capacity of the largest unit. This assumes that all units are potentially operational and can produce their rated capacity; otherwise only the units that are actually operational at the time should be used to determine plant capacity.

The *firm capacity* is the maximum capacity that the plant can be expected to produce on a continuous basis. As buildings and new loads are added to the system, reserve capacity is used, and expansion of the plant will eventually be required. *Reserve capacity* is any plant tonnage above the maximum system demand, up to the firm capacity.

Some extra capacity can be attributed to reserve and future capacity. When multiple machines are used to achieve the needed capacity, reserve capacity is already built into the system in the event that one machine is out of service. Although it is good to design a plant with some excess capacity, extremes of excess capacity will hinder the project economics and return on investment.

45.4 OPERATION AND MAINTENANCE

A central chiller plant represents a large capital and operating cost. To determine optimal performance of a central chilled water system, the full- and part-load performance data for each chiller should be used to determine which chiller or combination of chillers will deliver cooling in the most efficient manner. Maintaining the equipment in good working order with proper controls and adjustments for optimum energy efficiency takes on great importance. In the following paragraphs, certain operations and maintenance considerations unique to central chiller plants are discussed.

Maintenance

Each chiller has a manufacturer-recommended charge of refrigerant. These recommendations are based on maximum summertime cooling. The theoretical charge for other operating conditions will be different. Operating personnel from various parts of the country have reported significant energy savings by reducing the charge during periods of low load operation.

Chiller condenser and evaporator heat exchanger cleanliness should be monitored throughout the cooling season by calculating the fouling factor to determine when equipment must be cleaned. Automatic on-line tube-cleaning systems for chiller condensers are proven energy conservation methods. These are designed to keep the inside (water-side) surface of the tubes free of any deposits that would interfere with the heat transfer process. Two types of on-line tube cleaners are available: a brush system and a sponge rubber ball system. In the first type, the flow of water through the condenser is reversed and causes a small brush to be pushed through each tube. A plastic cage at the end of each tube holds the brush until the next cleaning cycle. The second type injects sponge rubber balls into the water entering the condenser. They pass through the tubes and are then collected by a screen located in the leaving water. From the collection screen, the balls are routed to a circulating pump that reinjects them into the entering water.

Energy Audit

Equipment in the plant should be checked from time to time to be sure that it is operating efficiently. This is vitally important on the larger items of equipment, such as chillers, that use the largest portion of energy. A unit that has scaled-up heat exchangers, improper refrigerant charge, bad seals, or worn parts or is dirty will consume more energy than a similar unit that is well maintained. The energy input divided by the output (kilowatts per ton or pounds of steam per ton) is a convenient yardstick of performance. If the values begin to change, the cause should be determined and corrected. A heat balance should periodically be made on all major equipment.

The importance of keeping records on equipment is well accepted. For many years the history of equipment performance was limited to logs that were filled out by the operators, along with utility receipts. Many plants currently have computer-based data logging systems. These systems can log all data monitored at any time interval and can provide operating profiles on an hourly, daily, weekly, monthly, or yearly basis. They can monitor performance continuously and sound an alarm if allowable limits are exceeded.

Energy Conservation and Optimization

Compressor Power Reduction Compressor power consumption for a chiller increases as the compressor head (pumping energy) increases. Compressor head is reduced by increasing the chilled water temperature and/or lowering the condenser water temperature. A 1°F increase in chilled water or a 1°F decrease in condenser water will reduce the required compressor consumption by 1.5 to 2.0 percent. Temperature constraints and the economics of operating under various scenarios should be investigated to determine the optimal operating temperatures under a given service condition.

Free Cooling Many central cooling systems operate year around. During periods of cool weather, savings can be realized by using the cooling tower condenser water to cool, rather than operating chilling equipment. A heat exchange device is required to separate the condenser water from the chilled water. Operating in this mode is called *free cooling*. However the chilled water is not free, because auxiliary equipment still must be operated. Free cooling can occur when the outside ambient air conditions are cool, which is typically at times other than the normal comfort cooling season.

Discharge chilled water temperature to the chilled water system is usually dependent on the outside air conditions unless controls are installed to mix the discharge from operable chillers with the chilled water generated from free cooling. Chilled water supply temperatures therefore increase with increasing outside air temperatures and humidity. The limitation of chilled water temperature fluctuations is dependent on the type of loads that are connected to system. Process cooling requirements usually can tolerate elevated temperatures. Comfort cooling at locations where there is high internal heat gain within the occupied space typically requires much cooler water than process cooling loads. If the comfort cooling requirement outside of the normal cooling season is small in comparison to process cooling, then the installation of small localized cooling systems to meet these needs may be justified. Localized cooling systems can significantly extend the free cooling season. Capital expenditures for installation of such equipment may be justified if large chilling equipment can be turned off for extended periods of times. Chilling equipment in northern climates may be able to be shut off for as long as six months a year by utilizing free cooling.

Cooling tower freeze protection must be considered. Options should include circulating water only in the tower basin or cycling tower fans when the outside air temperatures are well below freezing. It is desirable to run the cooling tower supply water temperature as high as possible when the outside air temperatures are below freezing.

Thermal Storage   Thermal storage can be an effective means for conserving energy under the right circumstances and conditions. The equipment associated with a thermal storage system large enough to serve a central chiller plant is very expensive. Therefore, it is necessary to evaluate the economics of this option carefully. Some utility companies are participating in the funding of thermal storage projects and are offering reduced rates for night or off-peak consumption. Usually both of these are needed to make the project viable. Thermal storage systems tend to be large, especially if they are storing chilled water. An ice storage system requires less space for storage, but must have additional cooling capacity to produce the ice.

Load Shedding

System chilled water demand may exceed the available or economical capacity of the chilling equipment. Regardless of whether the installed capacity has been exceeded or electric demand charges make it desirable to limit the load on the chilled water systems, the methods to shed load will probably be the same. Loads can be selectively reduced, or the inherent characteristics of chilled water systems can be changed to allow the load shedding to occur somewhat uniformly throughout the system.

Selective load reduction can be as basic as shutting off equipment to as sophisticated as an energy management system that has control over all chilled water system components. Energy management systems can reschedule activities and change set points on individual air handlers to decrease load for a limited period of time to remove peaks on the system.

Increasing the chilled water supply temperature to the terminal units results in a uniform load reduction across the entire system. This normally will not be readily apparent to building occupants unless significant load reductions are needed or existing comfort cooling equipment has marginal capacity before the load shedding occurs. The chilled water temperature can be increased intentionally by increasing the chiller set point. Another option is to load the chillers to achieve maximum capacity, at which time any further attempts to increase load will result in a decrease in the discharge chilled water temperature.

The anticipated need should normally be recognized well in advance of the actual event. All users should have a full understanding of what to expect during a load shedding situation. Feedback should be provided by the end user so that undesirable outcomes do not result from this process.

Billing Methods: Rate Schedule

Energy consumption may be the only component that is used in calculating cooling cost or a cooling charge. This approach fails to address pumping inefficiencies that are directly associated with circulating additional water to arrive at the same energy usage that would occur with a large temperature differential between the supply and return lines. Low chilled water temperature differential can also reduce the efficiency of the chilling equipment. Therefore, energy and volume totalization should be included in the calculation to generate a bill. Energy and volume components in the rate creates an incentive for the user to maintain the highest possible chilled water temperature differential, which results in a cost reduction to produce the chilled water.

Water Treatment

An effective water treatment program is necessary for the continued efficient operation of a central chilled water plant. Water treatment reduces fouling of the chiller heat exchangers and system corrosion.

Water treatment programs for any central chiller plant should be formulated by water treatment professionals. Consulting professionals are available to oversee the treatment program and to monitor its efficiencies through laboratory analysis. Vendors can provide complete turnkey systems that address all aspects of water treatment from the control-and-feed system to corrosion monitoring and chemical supplies.

Cooling Tower   The condensing water system is an open circulating system and is subject to problems of scale, corrosion, slime, and algae. As water is evaporated in the cooling tower, the dissolved solids will be concentrated in the remaining water. If the concentration is allowed to build up, the solubility of various salts will be exceeded, and scale will form on the hotter surfaces such as condenser tubes. This can be controlled by blowdown or bleed-off in some cases, but it may be necessary to feed sulfuric acid for pH control, in addition to the blowdown, if the water is extremely hard and high in alkalinity.

Open recirculating cooling water systems provide optimum conditions for microbial growth, and these microorganisms can adversely affect the efficiencies of the operation by sheer numbers, metabolic waste products generated, or deposits created. Microbiological treatment programs use oxidizing and nonoxidizing biocides, such as chlorine, hypochlorites, organic chlorine donors, or bromine compounds. Chlorine is effective but must be used carefully, because excessive chlorine will increase corrosion and adversely affect tower wood.

Some plants have tried to reduce their expenses by cutting back or eliminating the chemical for water treatment and have caused irreversible damage to their systems. Occasionally a new nonchemical device appears on the market with claims for scale and corrosion control in cooling and boiler systems. These nonchemical devices may be based on mechanical, electrical, magnetic, electrostatic, or ultrasonic principles. If a nonchemical water conditioning device is being considered, it should be thoroughly investigated. Several successful applications on similar facilities should be inspected and evaluated.

Chilled Water   The chilled water system is contaminated to some degree each time a new building is added to the system or the distribution piping is modified. The degree of contamination depends on the condition of the new pipe installed and the thoroughness of the flushing and cleaning prior to connecting the system.

Chemical treatment of the chilled water system usually includes the addition of a corrosion inhibitor. The system should be equipped with a feeder for introducing the chemicals. The corrosion inhibitor protects the piping from rusting and pitting and prevents the general deterioration of the piping system. This conserves energy by preserving the integrity of the heat exchange surfaces and prevents an increase in pumping head owing to system deterioration.

Water Makeup Monitoring

It is important to know what quantity of chilled water makeup is required for the system. This information can be used to quantify system leaks or dumping that may be occurring. Losses should be minimized to reduce the required cost of chemical and water as well as the potential environmental problems associated with discharging this chemically treated water down the sanitary sewer or storm sewer or into the groundwater.

Communication

Communication and cooperation among the building, distribution, and generation personnel are vital components to operating a chilled water system. Information must flow freely between the three commonly defined territories of the chilled water system. Discussions should include operating problems, operating parameters, calculation of rates, anticipated growth, outages and modifications.

Training

A training program must be put in place to maintain and improve the skills of the existing operating and maintenance staff and to train entry level employees. These training programs should include equipment start-up and shutdown procedures, operating parameters, energy optimization, and routine maintenance. If major equipment overhaul or additions are implemented, staff training by factory personnel should be considered.

Staffing

The operation staffing of a central chilled water plant will be driven by the size and complexity of the system and should be integrated with the operation of other central utility services.

The staffing of the maintenance organization for a central chilled water system can take a variety of forms. The maintenance function may be restricted entirely to the central chilled water plant or may encompass the delivery and end-use systems as well. Because the total performance of the system depends not only on the efficiency of production but also on the efficiency of utilization, an organizational and staffing approach that consolidates both functions may prove to be beneficial. The scope of maintenance services provided by in-house staff is a decision that will require careful review. In large systems it may be more economical to perform annual maintenance and overhauls with in-house personnel, while smaller installations may be served through contract services. In almost all cases, specialty services such as oil sample analysis and eddy current testing can be most economically provided through contract services.

ADDITIONAL RESOURCES

American Society of Heating, Refrigerating, and Air-Conditioning Engineers. *HVAC Systems and Equipment Handbooks*. Atlanta: ASHRAE, 1992.

Leitner, Gordon F. *Some Tube Fouling Investigations and the Effect of Fouling on Chiller Performance*. Paper presented at Central Chilled Water and Heating Plant Conference, Syracuse, New York, 1979.

Lowrance, Randy M., and Billy M. Nichols. *Optimum Chiller Performance Through On-Site Power Generation and Energy Recovery*. Paper presented at Central Chilled Water and Heating Plant Conference, Syracuse, New York, 1979.

Nichols, Billy M., and Stephen M. Redding. "Conversion of chiller drives." In *Proceedings of the 67th Annual Meeting of the Association of Physical Plant Administrators of Universities and Colleges.* Washington, D.C.: APPA, 1980.

Proceedings from the 9th Annual International District Heating and Cooling Association Cooling Conference, Rochester, Minnesota, October 1994. Washington, D.C.: International District Heating and Cooling Association.

Temple, Stuart. "Testimony Before the House Appropriations Committee, February 4, 1987, on DOE Funding for DHC Research in FY 88." *District Heating and Cooling,* First Quarter 1987, pp. 10–11.

Westcott, Ralph M. *The Role of Water in Central Plant Chilled Water Systems.* Paper presented at Central Chilled Water Conference, Pasadena, California, November 1973.

CHAPTER 46

Cogeneration

Paul Hoemann
University of Missouri—Columbia

46.1 INTRODUCTION

The utility needs of a college or university, and how it meets those needs, can vary from institution to institution. The location, size, and age of the institution, as well as fuel price and availability, can determine whether it operates a large independent power plant or contracts most services from the local utility company. It is common for colleges and universities to own and operate their own central heating and cooling systems (see Chapters 44 and 45), but it is less common for them to produce their own electricity. Cogeneration, the simultaneous production of electricity and useful thermal energy, has been employed on many college campuses since World War II and continues to gain in popularity. Major changes in government regulations and escalations in fuel prices since the mid-1970s have prompted more colleges and universities to invest in cogeneration facilities.

Maximizing a campus heating plant's efficiency through cogeneration reduces the cost of utilities supplied. Cogeneration efficiency is achieved by utilizing plant steam to produce electricity in addition to sending steam to the campus for its thermal value. Because a central plant usually is cost-effective for heating and/or cooling a large campus, the economics of adding cogeneration facilities in an existing central plant can be very attractive.

This chapter describes various cogeneration options for colleges and universities and outlines the potential benefits of owning and/or operating these systems. It does not provide an exhaustive discussion of cogeneration, but rather emphasizes the integration of electric power generation with heating and cooling. The decision to employ cogeneration at a particular site will depend on a variety of factors, including thermal loads, local electric utility rates, government regulations, and other facilities needs and priorities. The type of system, fuel choice, and amount of benefit or payback from cogeneration will also be determined by these same factors.

Even though a cogeneration plant is cost-effective to operate by virtue of its thermal efficiency, this subject must be understood in the context of evolving government regulations. Facilities managers must understand current federal, state, and local regulations and keep abreast of changes to these regulations. Mastery of current regulations, along with a clear understanding of the end use of campus utilities, will provide the necessary tools for analysis of cogeneration options. It is extremely important that facilities managers also take into consideration the age and configuration of existing utility supply equipment and how new equipment can be integrated into the existing facility.

Finally, this chapter will look at how colleges and universities work and interact with their local electric utility suppliers and what type of utility contracts are available. Life cycle costing, other financial considerations, and options such as third-party ownership also will be explored.

46.2   DEFINITION OF COGENERATION

Cogeneration is the simultaneous production of two forms of useful energy, usually thermal energy and electrical or mechanical energy. Cogeneration also can be defined as achieving energy output with a minimum energy input, keeping overall energy costs as low as possible. The primary principle is that it takes less fuel to cogenerate steam and electricity than would be needed to produce the two separately.

Cogeneration is not a new concept. Colleges and universities have had cogeneration facilities since the early 1900s. It has always been and continues to be an economical way to heat and cool a college campus. Cogeneration facilities operate at two to three times the overall thermal efficiency of conventional electric generation plants. There are many possible cogeneration configurations. Figures 46-1, 46-2, and 46-3 show a typical utility plant cycle, a pure cogeneration cycle, and a combination of the two cycles.

These diagrams show that the advantage of cogeneration technology is that it puts to use what would be waste heat in a typical utility cycle. In a typical utility plant cycle, steam expended in the electric generation process simply is cooled and condensed by use of a cooling tower or water-cooled condenser. In cogeneration, steam expended in the electric generation process serves a useful purpose: it is cycled to the campus for heating and cooling. The cycle efficiency can be raised from about 33 percent in a typical utility cycle to as high as 85 percent in a pure cogeneration cycle.

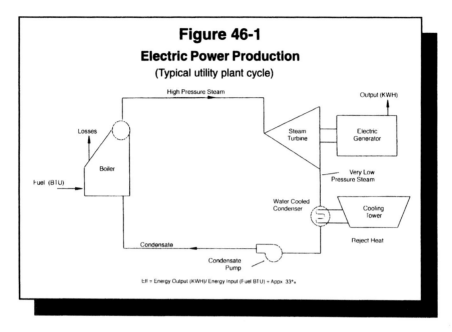

Figure 46-1

Electric Power Production

(Typical utility plant cycle)

46.3 OVERVIEW OF COGENERATION

Government Regulation

As a result of rapid price increases for fuels and threats of energy shortages in the early 1970s, the federal government began to establish regulations to promote energy efficiency. In 1978 the Public Utility Regulatory Policy Act (PURPA) was enacted, which provides incentives for cogeneration. PURPA states that a power plant that meets the criteria to be a "qualifying facility" has the right to an interconnection and parallel operation with an electric utility; the right to sell power to the utility at their marginal or avoided cost; and the right to purchase supplementary power, backup power, maintenance power, and interruptible power at nondiscriminatory rates.

Legislation implementing the National Energy Strategy provides even greater opportunities for economy power purchases. This legislation effectively opens the electric grid to cogenerators (and potentially even to retail customers) and could have an even greater impact on the electric industry than PURPA did in 1978.

If a college or university has a cogeneration plant capable of supplying all of the institution's own electric needs, it may be able to negotiate an interconnection agreement with the local electric utility to purchase economy power when the purchased cost is cheaper than the incremental cost to generate it. It is possible to bid power from electric utilities, power marketers,

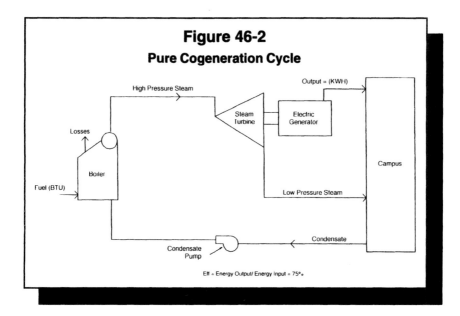

Figure 46-2
Pure Cogeneration Cycle

and nonutility generators, especially if an arrangement can be made with the city or local electric utility to transmit, or "wheel," the power over their lines. This type of bidding or request for proposal will become more common as "open transmission" becomes widespread and accepted. The emergence of an open transmission philosophy for the electric industry is similar to what has happened in the natural gas industry since the 1980s.

Cogeneration Configurations

Topping Cycles   In cogeneration, the rejected heat of one process becomes a source of energy for a subsequent process. If electricity is generated in the first process and the rejected heat becomes an energy source for a subsequent process (such as heating and cooling a campus), then it is called a *topping cycle*. Topping cycles are the most common cogeneration cycles employed on college campuses. A schematic diagram is shown in Figure 46-2.

Bottoming Cycles   If the first process produces rejected heat and the rejected heat is used to generate electricity in the second cycle, then it is called a *bottoming cycle*. A bottoming cycle usually involves a waste heat recovery boiler that produces steam to drive a turbine generator.

Steam Cycles   Steam is a convenient heat transfer medium, and steam cogeneration systems are quite popular. The most common component in a cogeneration system is a steam turbine. In general, steam turbines are reliable and durable and have a high operating efficiency. The disadvantage of a

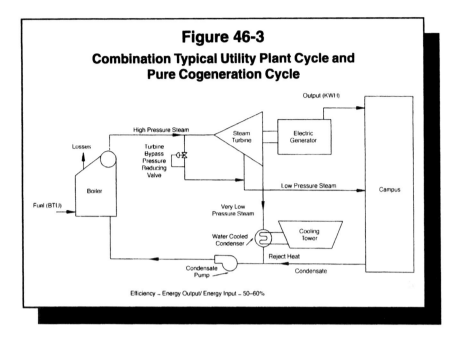

Figure 46-3

**Combination Typical Utility Plant Cycle and
Pure Cogeneration Cycle**

Efficiency – Energy Output/ Energy Input – 50–60%

steam turbine generator is that it requires a large proportion of steam energy relative to electric output.

Combustion Turbines A combustion turbine is another common component of a cogeneration system. It can be used in an open cycle or a closed cycle configuration (Figures 46-4 and 46-5). In the open cycle, which is more prevalent in the industry, air is drawn directly from the atmosphere. The air is compressed and heated in the combustion chamber, is then used to drive a turbine, and finally is exhausted back to the atmosphere. In a closed cycle, a working medium (usually air or helium) that is physically isolated from the air intake is used. The advantage of a closed cycle is that combustion products and the corrosion and erosion they produce are not present in the turbine. This increases equipment life and allows for use of a wide variety of fuels such as coal and refuse-derived fuel. An open cycle combustion turbine, on the other hand, is limited primarily to natural gas and fuel oil.

Combined Cycles A combined cycle is a combination of a topping and a bottoming cycle. In this case, electricity is produced on both ends of the cycle. A schematic diagram of a combined cycle using a gas turbine, heat recovery boiler, and extraction steam turbine is shown in Figure 46-6. Many other configurations are also possible.

In a combined cycle cogeneration system, higher electric generation efficiencies can be achieved than with a combustion turbine alone. This is

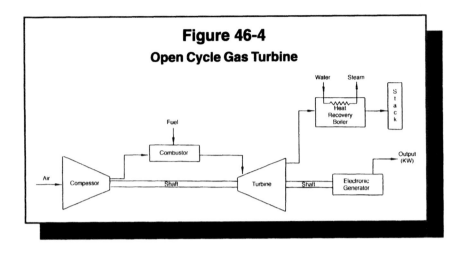

Figure 46-4
Open Cycle Gas Turbine

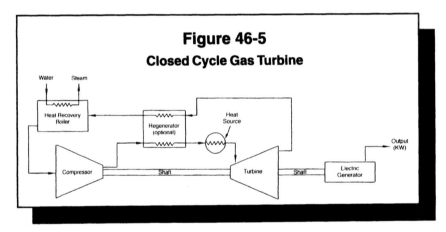

Figure 46-5
Closed Cycle Gas Turbine

because there are two interconnected energy production cycles operating simultaneously at different temperatures. Supplemental firing also is possible with combined cycle facilities to increase thermal output of a heat recovery boiler.

Diesel Engines   A diesel engine cogeneration system employs an internal combustion engine to drive an electric generator, with waste heat being recovered either in a heat recovery boiler or as hot water. Diesel engines exhibit quite high efficiencies of electric generation and have good partial-load efficiency as well. A schematic diagram is shown in Figure 46-7.

Fuel Cells   Fuel cells are gaining popularity as their technology becomes more refined. Fuel cells operate at a high temperature (up to 1,000°C) and convert

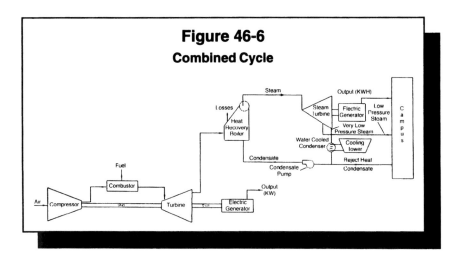

Figure 46-6
Combined Cycle

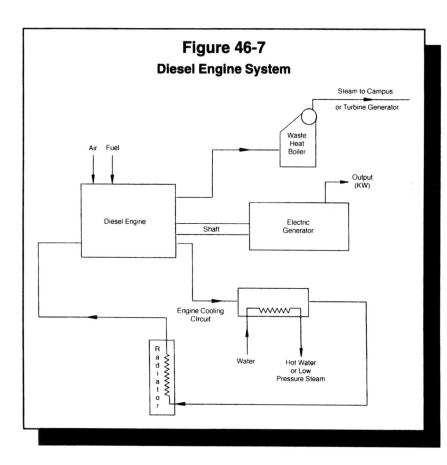

Figure 46-7
Diesel Engine System

chemical energy into electricity without a combustion process. Fuel cells eliminate many environmental problems that go along with more traditional combustion-based cogeneration systems. Fuel cells produce direct current and usually require a power conditioning system to convert direct current to alternating current. A schematic diagram is shown in Figure 46-8.

46.4 OPERATION AND MAINTENANCE OF COGENERATION PLANTS

Thermal Loads

The key to cogeneration system efficiency is a stable, consistent thermal load (also referred to as a *steam host*). A college or university campus usually is an excellent steam host, because it has many large buildings in a concentrated area that must be heated and cooled. Using steam from a central plant as an

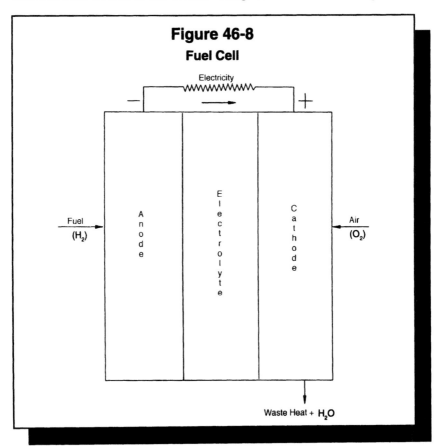

Figure 46-8

Fuel Cell

energy source for heating a campus has the added benefit that it saves space and capital expense in individual buildings. Use of absorption steam chillers or steam-turbine–driven chillers in a centralized cooling system can provide a summer steam demand that enhances cogeneration efficiency throughout the year. The benefits of the year-round system include better capacity utilization and a faster payback on cogeneration investments. However, when evaluating whether to add new thermal loads or to convert existing chillers (for example, from electric to steam), a careful life cycle cost analysis should be done, including cogeneration benefits. Depending on the size, two-stage absorption chillers can be an attractive life cycle cost alternative. Single- or two-stage absorption chillers also can be supplied with low-pressure steam from a turbine driving a centrifugal chiller or other rotating equipment (e.g., compressor or boiler feed pump).

Operational Philosophy

A cogeneration plant should be designed with as much operational flexibility as possible. Usually college and university power plants do not have a backup source of steam. Therefore, a cogeneration plant should have enough spare capacity to meet the campus thermal energy demand with its largest steam producing unit out of service. Contracts should be established to obtain electricity from the local electric utility. The electric generating capacity of the cogeneration power plant will determine the specific contract requirements.

Operational Technique

Adequate training of operators and plant personnel is essential in the operation of an effective cogeneration system. Operators not only should know the equipment, but also should understand the cogeneration concept and operational philosophy. There are many packaged training materials available to help operators understand *how* and *why* a cogeneration system works, along with *what* to do to operate it.

Keeping the system operating at maximum efficiency means being aware of the parameters that are primary indicators of efficiency. Performance tests should be run periodically to determine the current operating capacities and efficiencies of each piece of equipment.

A competent engineering staff is essential to the successful operation of a cogeneration plant. Performance testing, design of efficiency improvements, implementation of new cost-effective technologies, and long-range planning all require sound engineering judgment. Consulting engineers can provide valuable specialized design expertise, but they cannot replace engineers on staff who understand the plant equipment and needs.

Maintenance Issues

The various configurations of cogeneration systems have their own unique maintenance requirements. Environmental regulations require that many specialized maintenance functions be performed and documented on emission-monitoring equipment. Preventive and routine maintenance also must be conducted on a regular basis.

The first maintenance priority is ensuring that the boiler or steam generator is operating safely and efficiently. Boiler maintenance falls into several categories, including maintenance and monitoring of pressure parts, maintenance of combustion and auxiliary systems, maintenance of rotating machinery, cleaning, controls, and care of idle equipment.

Maintenance and Monitoring of Pressure Parts This type of maintenance work includes checking tube thickness in the furnace and superheater sections of the steam generator. Many times external visual inspection of tubes can indicate overheating or thermal stress. In addition, rebuilding and testing of safety relief valves should be done annually and are usually required by state boiler and pressure vessel regulations and insurance carriers. Internal inspections of boiler steam and mud drums also should be done at least annually to ensure that the tube internal surface remains free of scale and corrosion.

Certain maintenance checks of pressure parts can also be performed while a boiler is in operation. For example, drum level devices should be checked and cross-checked against each other to verify that the boiler is operating with the proper water levels and flow. Boiler water quality tests should be run routinely, preferably every eight hours, to ensure proper water chemistry and blowdown are being maintained.

Monitoring of differential pressures across the various sections and "passes" of a boiler can help determine cleaning needs during scheduled outages. This also indicates the effectiveness of the soot-blowing system.

During every boiler inspection, boiler steam drums should be inspected for cleanliness and evidence of excessive solids leaving the drum. All steam separation equipment and baffles should be checked for corrosion or mechanical integrity.

Maintenance of Combustion and Auxiliary Systems Most cogeneration plants either have a dedicated preventive maintenance person or a preventive maintenance weekly or daily schedule that is rotated among the maintenance staff. The following routine checks should be performed:

- Checks of burner and combustion controls and safety devices
- Lubrication checks of moving parts on fuel handling, fuel feed, and auxiliary systems
- Checks for proper operation, plugs, and leaks in material handling systems

- A general "listening" for unusual noises or changes in the way a piece of equipment is functioning

One of the best tools in a preventive maintenance program is a computer database. First, a lubrication schedule should be kept listing each piece of equipment, the type and amount of lubricant required, and the frequency with which it should be checked and changed. Second, an equipment database should be set up to track maintenance history, including all inspections, conditions, and repairs for each equipment item. Third, a spare parts inventory should be maintained, especially for parts needed in routine maintenance but known to have long delivery schedules. There are many maintenance software programs on the market that will fill many or all of these needs, or one can be customized and written in house by an experienced programmer.

Maintenance of Rotating Machinery   Special note is given here to rotating machinery because of the many technical advances made in this area. First, vibration monitoring should be done on all rotating equipment on a routine basis as part of a predictive maintenance program. Records should be kept to track patterns that could indicate potential problems or failures. Once again, there are a number of vibration monitoring hardware and software packages available on the market. The primary objective is to incorporate maintenance into a scheduled routine and to keep good records to identify and correct problems before they become serious.

Second, computer balancing and laser alignment of couplings are becoming more commonplace in cogeneration plants. Equipment has become easier to use, and training is available to make the maintenance staff proficient in its use.

Cleaning   Clean heat exchange surfaces and gas flow paths make for the highest efficiency in operation. A boiler should be inspected for cleanliness on an annual or semiannual basis depending on the type of fuel being used. Condenser or heat exchanger cleaning frequency will be dictated by the type of service or duty it receives and from experience during inspections. There are a number of methods for cleaning tube internals in condensers and heat exchangers, including high-pressure water cleaning and brushing. The method employed must be based on the needs and application of the cogeneration system.

External cleaning of boiler tube surfaces and gas passes in a coal-fired boiler can pose a challenge to any maintenance crew. Any of several cleaning methods can be used, each of which has its own cautions and advantages. If a water wash is chosen, care must be exercised in how the boiler is drained and dried. The effluent will likely be very acidic, and disposal must follow state and local regulations. To prevent corrosion, the boiler should be dried immediately after cleaning using auxiliary heaters or a low firing rate.

Another method that has been used successfully is percussion cleaning. Experts in this method strategically place explosives at various locations in the furnace and gas passes to clean surfaces with sound waves. It may seem that this technique would weaken tube joints and damage refractory, but it has been tested and used successfully since the 1960s in many industrial and utility boiler applications.

Controls   Good operation of instrumentation and controls is essential to a well-maintained and efficient cogeneration system. A regular schedule should be established for calibrating transmitters and flue gas monitors and for metering.

There are many different types of control systems available. Most cogeneration systems employ a digital distributed control system. If such a system is used, consideration must be given to extensive training of maintenance personnel versus relying on outside vendor support of these systems. Because of the rising cost of vendor-supplied control systems and operator interface control stations, some in-house computer design and support of controls systems may be justified. There are software packages available that allow a user to create an operator interface to a vendor control system using a basic personal computer.

Care of Idle Equipment   To minimize the potential for corrosion damage, boilers and turbine generators that are removed from service must be properly stored. Dry or wet storage methods can be used. Owners may consult with water treatment consultants to establish the best lay-up procedure for their particular application and situation. In dry lay-up, dry air or nitrogen is usually introduced into the steam path, and trays of lime, silica gel, or other moisture-absorbent materials are placed in the drums to draw off the trapped moisture. Wet lay-up involves adding an oxygen scavenger and other boiler water chemicals to a full boiler. Frequent checks of the water chemistry must then be made to ensure that proper chemical balance is maintained to prevent corrosion. Circulation of the water through the boiler is preferred, if possible. Many boilers do not have drainable superheaters, which may dictate the type of lay-up used.

Contracts

Well-negotiated fuel and purchased utility contracts ensure that a cogeneration facility provides maximum financial benefit to the college or university. Just as environmental regulations have been rapidly changing since the 1970s, so has the fuel and purchased utility market.

Fuel   When evaluating what fuel is best for a given cogeneration situation and configuration, facilities managers often give first consideration to cost. Coal, natural gas, fuel oil, waste products (e.g., paper, wood, tire-derived fuel, refuse-derived fuel), and coke are the primary fuels available for cogeneration plants. Each has its own advantages and disadvantages from the standpoint of cost, availability, environmental concerns, and waste disposal. Facilities managers should stay informed of new developments in these areas. Supplemental or alternative (backup) fuels also should be identified.

Contracts vary depending on the fuel, but facilities managers should take a hard look at the market. The natural gas market has changed significantly since the passage of Federal Energy Regulatory Commission (FERC) Order 636. Gas pricing and purchasing have become much more complex than calling up the local gas supplier and asking for a short-term or long-term contract. Using a blend of fuels or designing a system with the flexibility to change fuels at a later time if the market changes are also important considerations. If a college or university has an existing cogeneration plant, evaluation of switching to an alternative fuels may be justified depending on the local fuel market conditions.

Electricity The market is changing regarding purchased power contracts including contracts to operate in parallel with a local electric utility. If a college or university power plant is a qualifying facility under PURPA, there are certain legal rights that must be considered (see Section 46.3). In addition, there may be opportunities to bid purchased power if arrangements can be made to transmit or "wheel" the power through the local utility distribution system.

By operating a cogeneration plant, the option of purchasing interruptible, low-cost supplemental power may become possible. If the cogeneration plant has adequate capacity to meet the entire electric needs of the campus, the facilities manager is in a strong bargaining position to purchase power at costs lower than market rates because the local utility still wants to "make a sale." Some local utilities will offer to sell electricity at low prices if the campus is willing to accept the risk of interruption. An advance-notice provision can be negotiated to give the campus adequate time to increase electric production from the campus cogeneration plant. This arrangement gives the cogenerator the best of two worlds. First, low-cost power can be generated by means of cogeneration efficiency. Second, the purchase price of power may drop as well. If a local utility company does not want to lose the campus as an electric customer, then having a feasibility plan to install or expand a cogeneration facility may be enough to negotiate a better purchased electricity contract.

Parallel Operations When operating in parallel with a local electric utility, the following factors must be considered, both physically and contractually:

- Adequate protective devices (relays) and schemes will have to be put in place to interface with the utility. These devices must be installed at both the interconnection point (substation) and the cogeneration plant.
- Agreement will have to be reached with the local utility regarding power flow from the cogeneration facility to the utility ("inadvertent" power exchange or actual power exports or sales).
- Synchronizing schemes will have to be determined.
- Circumstances and consequences of interconnection disconnection must be spelled out.
- Safety and lock-out provisions must be addressed.

A good paralleling agreement will have the following four sections:

1. Firm power sales—rates, terms, and conditions
2. Emergency power sales—availability and pricing
3. Interruptible (nonfirm) power sales—rates, terms, and conditions
4. Surplus (economy) energy sales—wheeling rates, terms, and conditions

Environmental Issues

The regulatory environment is an ever-changing one, and keeping up to date with changes in federal and state requirements can be a real challenge. Many colleges and universities have a specialized environmental group that takes responsibility for the needs of a cogenerator. If that is not the case, it is advisable to designate one or more persons within the utility organization to keep up with monitoring, testing, and reporting requirements.

Air emission permits, requirements, and regulations for power plants have been in place for many years. Air quality regulations began with the Clean Air Act (CAA) of 1963, which gave state and local governments authority to regulate air emissions. In 1970 the CAA amendments were passed, which mandated federal air quality standards and set timetables for their implementation. Additional provisions were added in 1977 with another set of amendments.

The passage of the CAA amendments in 1990 added even more regulatory requirements for existing as well as new facilities. The Environmental Protection Agency (EPA) is still working on rules to implement many of these changes. Some of these rules and standards may take 5 to 10 years to finalize. Changes include obtaining operating permits for existing and new fuel-burning equipment. The 1990 amendments also designated 189 chemicals or compounds as hazardous air pollutants. Prior to 1990 the EPA had issued national emission standards for only seven hazardous air pollutants: sulfur dioxide, carbon monoxide, nitrogen oxide, ozone, particulate, hydrocarbons, and lead.

In addition to tracking federal legislation such as the CAA, cogeneration owners must be aware that states can add regulations for stationary sources of air pollution, provided that the state requirements are at least as stringent as federal requirements. Overall, the regulations and standards require maximum achievable control technology for limiting emissions of hazardous air pollutants.

Cogeneration facilities, however, produce fewer emissions for equivalent power production than do conventional power plants. This is because cogeneration facilities are much more efficient. As such, cogenerators provide real environmental benefits.

A college or university that is considering installation of a cogeneration facility is usually required to follow these three steps:

1. The institution prepares an environmental impact statement.
2. The institution performs ambient air quality monitoring and modeling. The goal is to meet National Ambient Air Quality Standards in the air quality control region that would be affected by the plant. The state regulatory agency also may have a state implementation plan that specifies control strategies necessary in the air quality control region.
3. The institution must undergo new source reviews conducted by the state before it will be granted the required Prevention of Significant Deterioration permit. Performance standards in the new source reviews require institutions to use best available control technology or reasonable achievable control technology to ensure that the national standards are met for a given pollutant in an air quality control region.

As can be seen from the process described above, the complexity of operating or constructing a cogeneration plant requires plenty of planning from an environmental standpoint.

These regulations govern every type of cogeneration system, from fossil-fueled boilers to gas turbines and diesel generators. The environmental regulations that govern gas turbines are complex, especially relative to the formulas that must be applied for nitrous oxide emissions. There are many knowledgeable environmental consultants who can provide advice on environmental issues in each region, and it is advisable to elicit their expertise.

46.5 FINANCIAL CONSIDERATIONS

Cost Factors

The feasibility of adding a new cogeneration system or modifying and/or expanding an existing cogeneration system is determined at most colleges or universities by economics. Several cost factors must be considered in a cogeneration analysis.

Capital Cost   The initial capital cost of the equipment required for a given configuration is probably the most important factor in determining whether a cogeneration system is economical. Therefore, it is recommended that two independent capital cost estimates be obtained.

Fuel and Purchased Utility Costs   When evaluating cogeneration and purchased utility alternatives, it is important to know the pricing and escalation rates from the local electric utility and fuel suppliers. One source of escalation rate information is the Federal Department of Energy. It is valuable to model possible scenarios and conduct sensitivity studies of pricing variations. These studies can help identify the financial risk if the assumptions prove to be inaccurate.

Operational Costs   Operational costs include labor; auxiliary plant energy use; water treatment chemicals; supplies; spare parts; lubrication; routine equipment overhauls; preventive maintenance; training; safety equipment; and environmental testing, monitoring, and reporting. These costs can be identified by contacting a similar operating facility that has maintained a cost history.

Life Cycle Costing

To accurately evaluate the economics of a cogeneration addition or modification, facilities managers should run a complete life cycle cost analysis. The first step is to collect data on the current electric and steam hourly demands for a full year, making any necessary adjustments for normal weather. A projection of the institution's construction and renovation plans is also necessary to adjust for utility needs expected in coming years. Then a complete load profile can be developed. The next step is to identify the best technologies that match the institution's needs and energy requirements.

At this point, all alternatives should be looked at, including the "do nothing" case, which may involve purchasing energy from the local electric utility at current or negotiated rates. Various cogeneration technologies and configurations may be considered. Rough cost estimates and payback calculations may be used to narrow the list of alternatives to five or less. A thorough life cycle cost analysis should be run on the most viable alternatives.

The life cycle cost analysis takes into account the time value of money, using a discount rate that reflects the current financial market. Each analysis should include the following elements:

- A yearly financial model for the life of the project. This model should identify the capital outlay, any debt repayment involved, operating expenses, and savings.

- Calculation of the net present value (NPV). A cash flow diagram that supports this calculation should be included.
- Calculation of the discounted payback
- Calculation of the annual equivalent cost
- A graph of the NPV versus the discount rate. The graph should show the sensitivity of the project economics to the discount rate assumption.

There are computer software packages available that are tailored to this type of analysis, or a common spreadsheet software package can be used.

Third-Party Ownership

Contracting for services in the college and university setting is not new, but the idea is receiving increased attention. Numerous companies are attempting to sell their services to college administrators. They claim that they are removing the burden of operating or maintaining a system or service from the institution and putting it in the hands of someone experienced in the field.

For some institutions, contracting for utility services might be an attractive alternative. If the institution has a cogeneration project that requires high capital costs and the institution cannot fund or finance the project, a third party might be able to provide the financing needed. If the existing power plant is in need of major repairs, is unreliable, or is being mismanaged or operated improperly, then contracting for the service could provide better service at lower cost.

However, there are disadvantages to contracting utility services as well. Any third-party owner/supplier of utility services will have to make a profit, usually at least 20 percent of its investment. This is a long-term added cost to an institution that could own and operate its own facility. Another disadvantage is the loss of control of the operation, which can translate to less responsive service to special needs or to unexpected changes in requirements. Most third-party contracts require guaranteed minimum purchases over the long term and also may include caps on what must be supplied.

The arguments for contracting services usually include guaranteed cost savings to an institution. Usually, however, these same cost savings are available directly to the institution along with the savings that the for-profit third party is keeping. Each situation is different, but the economics of contracting for utility services must be examined carefully using the same life cycle costing principles described earlier. The expertise touted by most third-party private utility suppliers usually can be developed in house. University-owned and operated facilities have the added benefit of loyal employees who are dedicated to the institution for which they work.

46.6 SUMMARY

Cogeneration technologies allow colleges and universities to provide low-cost utility service because of the high efficiencies they offer. The economics of implementing cogeneration for a given institution depend on the cost factors and conditions unique to its campus. A thorough evaluation of the cost, environmental impact, financing options, and operational considerations is essential in the decision-making process. Negotiating favorable contracts with fuel suppliers and local electric utility companies can have a significant impact on the economics of building or operating a cogeneration system.

The utility industry is one that has undergone rapid change since the 1970s and promises continued change in the future. It is important that facilities managers keep informed of changes in cogeneration technologies, fuel and utility purchase options, and government regulations to make the most of opportunities to lower the cost of utility supply to their colleges or universities.

ADDITIONAL RESOURCES

Ferrey, Steven. *Law of Independent Power Development/Cogeneration/Utility Regulation.* New York: Clark Boardman Company, 1989.

Spiewak, Scott A. *Cogeneration and Small Power Production Manual.* Lilburn, Georgia: The Fairmont Press, 1987.

Stultz, Steven C., and John B. Kitto (Eds.). *Steam: Its Generation and Use,* 40th edition. Baberton, Ohio: Babcock and Wilcox, 1992.

CHAPTER 47

District Heating and Cooling

Distribution Systems

Douglas L. Spellman, P.E.
University of Missouri

47.1 INTRODUCTION

Many colleges and universities use central heating and cooling systems. A central system can reduce the total size of the heating and cooling plant and its operating costs. Central systems increase the efficiency and control of a campus system and decrease the number of maintenance personnel required for system operation.

For central heating and cooling plants to work properly, a high-quality, reliable distribution system must be installed. Distribution systems link the heating and cooling source to campus buildings. Most systems are installed underground to protect them from damage, to increase their lives, and to maintain campus aesthetics.

Central cooling systems use chilled water as the distribution medium. Central heating systems use one of two types of fluid to transfer energy: steam or hot water. Installing these distribution systems requires extensive planning and coordination with other campus systems to keep installation costs down and avoid future problems.

47.2 DISTRIBUTION SYSTEMS

Chilled Water Distribution Systems

The main purpose of a central cooling plant is to utilize diversity in campus buildings to downsize the total chiller tonnage required. For the central chiller plant to work properly, a chilled water distribution system must be installed. This distribution system supplies chilled water from the chiller plant to campus buildings and returns warm water from the buildings to the chiller plant. The chiller plant can be either a central chiller plant or several chillers located in multiple buildings. When installing a new chilled water system, facilities managers should consider looping the system. Looping can provide redundancy to buildings so that they are not without chilled water during maintenance or repairs. Figure 47-1 shows a typical chilled water distribution system.

Piping can be exposed or buried below ground. Above-ground systems are only acceptable if they can be hidden from view naturally or with landscaping. In general, it is better to install pipe underground when the pipe is exterior to the buildings, as buried pipe is more aesthetically appealing. However, there are some exceptions when it may be more convenient to route pipe above ground through a building rather than underground around the building.

Piping that is routed through a building is usually constructed of steel, with either welded or grooved joints. Plastic pipe in buildings is becoming more popular but has not gained wide acceptance with maintenance personnel. The risk of damage to the pipe and the risk of leaks is greater. There are also fire codes that restrict the use of plastic pipe in buildings.

All piping in buildings must be well insulated with a properly installed vapor barrier. The vapor barrier is especially important if the pipe passes through an unconditioned space. If the vapor barrier is not properly installed and maintained, air moisture will migrate through the insulation and condense on the pipes. This condensation will saturate the insulation and ruin its insulating properties, making the condensation worse. Condensation will then drip on floors and equipment and damage university property. When running chilled water pipes through buildings that are unconditioned, facilities managers should consider using closed-cell foam insulation to limit potential condensation problems. Closed-cell insulation acts as its own vapor barrier and, if installed properly, will control the condensation better than fiberglass with a vapor barrier. It is also less susceptible to water and physical damage.

Although some pipe may be run through buildings, the majority of distribution piping is underground. Underground piping for chilled water distribution should meet the same specifications as underground piping for domestic water. This pipe can be ductile iron or plastic. There are several types of plastic pipe that can be used. One of the best underground piping systems consists of pipe made of American Water Works Association (AWWA)-grade polyvinyl chloride (PVC) pipe with push-on joints and ductile iron fittings. The fittings can be mechanical joint with restraints or mechanical joint with thrust blocks for restraint. This piping is the same type used in potable water distribution systems and fire protection systems. It must be buried below the frost line to prevent freezing. In warmer

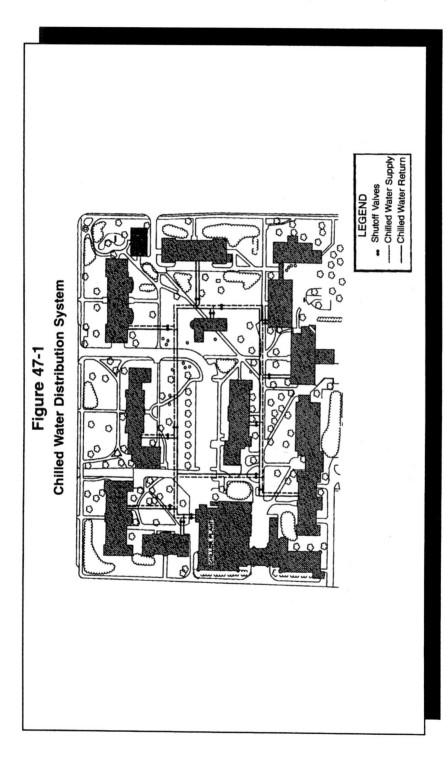

Figure 47-1

Chilled Water Distribution System

LEGEND
• Shutoff Valves
—— Chilled Water Supply
—— Chilled Water Return

climates or areas where long runs are anticipated between the chiller plant and the end users, facilities managers should consider insulation for the buried pipe. In the northern United States, the heat gain from the ground is usually insignificant if the pipe is buried below the frost line, where soil temperatures stay at a constant temperature of below 60°F. Insulation adds significant cost to an underground chilled water system.

The piping can be bedded in compacted soil or in rock that has a uniform distribution of less than $3/4$ in. Pipe embedded in rock costs more for the fill material but saves time in installation because compaction is less critical. Pipe installed under roadways and other paved surfaces must have soil below the road surface compacted to at least 95 percent Standard Proctor per American Society for Testing and Materials (ASTM) standard D-698.

Valves should be installed with valve boxes or with hand holes so that the valves can be accessed for operation. Valves also need to be exercised periodically so that they will remain free and will operate when required. All valves must meet AWWA specifications for underground water distribution systems. Each building should have shutoff valves so that it can be isolated for maintenance without affecting the operation of other buildings on the loop. It is also important to install valves periodically in the loop so that sections on the loop can be isolated without having to shut down the entire loop. This is especially important in loops that utilize multiple chiller sites. If there is a break in the pipe, it can be isolated and repaired while affecting the cooling in only a minimum number of buildings.

It is extremely important when installing a chilled water loop that facilities managers take into account system operation and maintenance. A well-thought-out plan can save many headaches later when problems arise. The use of high-grade materials will help ensure that the system operates satisfactorily over its expected life. Most systems will operate for 50 years, and if piping is selected and installed with care, little maintenance will be required on the underground portion of the system.

Steam Distribution Systems

Steam distribution systems supply steam for heating buildings and generating domestic hot water. Steam distribution systems are common on college campuses. The steam is distributed from the central plant through a distribution system of piping installed in tunnels or chases or direct-buried. Steam distribution systems should be looped so that buildings can be fed from two directions. By looping the systems, a building with a problem can be isolated from the system without affecting all of the buildings. Figure 47-2 shows a typical looped system.

Along with planning the system layout, facilities managers should carefully select the piping material. When selecting pipe materials for steam distribution, accessibility for repair or replacement work should be a major

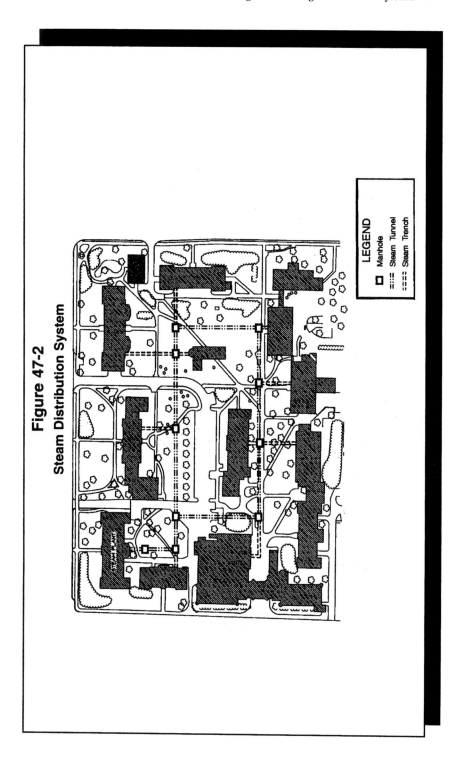

Figure 47-2
Steam Distribution System

LEGEND
□ Manhole
=::= Steam Tunnel
==== Steam Trench

consideration. The materials selected must provide for the long life of the system. Even though steel is the material used in all systems, facilities managers must choose the grade of steel and thickness of the steel pipe wall. The thicker the pipe wall, the longer the life of the pipe. For high-pressure systems, special steels may be required to extend the life of the system and to ensure it will carry the pressure and temperature.

Condensate pipe is subjected to more corrosion, both internally and externally, than steam pipe. The presence of oxygen and carbon dioxide causes the condensate to attack steel more readily. External corrosion is also greater on condensate pipe because the lower temperature—160°F to 180°F—creates favorable conditions for corrosion if water is present. This is a consideration for all types of systems, whether direct-buried pipe or pipe in chases. Generally the pipe wall thickness is increased to schedule 80 for condensate pipe because of the higher corrosion rate.

Direct-buried steam and condensate piping is the cheapest of the various systems. One type of direct-buried system is a conduit system. A conduit system consists of preinsulated piping with preinstalled waterproofed jackets (Figure 47-3). The system is welded and waterproofed as it is put in the ground. This system can be partially factory fabricated or fully field fabricated. The outer casing or conduit can enclose one pipe or multiple pipes. The direct-buried system is the cheapest of the steam distribution systems to install, but it also has the shortest useful life. If the insulation gets wet in the direct-buried system, the pipe will corrode from the outside in. This is more of a problem on condensate piping, as there is not enough heat to evaporate the water and keep it away from the pipe. The insulation also will lose much of its insulating value when it gets wet.

A second type of direct-buried system utilizes a pourable insulation (Figure 47-4). A trench is dug, and a layer of insulation is put in the bottom of the trench. The pipes are laid on the insulation, and more insulation is poured over the pipe to the proper depth. The insulation is compacted, and the trench is backfilled. These systems are relatively new, and the results have been mixed. Useful life is expected to be about the same as that for a conduit system.

A better method is to install steam and condensate piping in a concrete chase or trench (Figure 47-5). The chase is only large enough to enclose the pipe with insulation, guides, and supports. Trench internal dimensions are 2 to 3 ft. high by 4 or 5 ft. wide, depending on pipe size. Chase walls are made of concrete, and the tops are removable. The tops are waterproofed to prevent the infiltration of ground water. The trench bottom is sloped and usually has a channel installed in the bottom to channel water to the manholes. This type of system costs more than a direct-buried system but less than a full utility tunnel. Maintenance costs for a chase are lower than for a direct-buried system and higher than for a tunnel system. Life of the pipe is longer because there is less chance of water saturating the insulation.

Figure 47-3
Conduit Pipe Systems

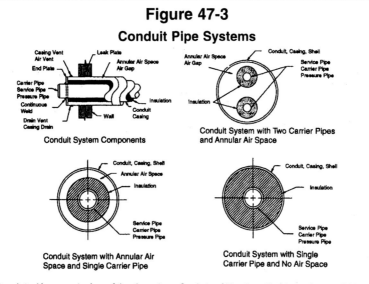

Conduit System Components

Conduit System with Two Carrier Pipes and Annular Air Space

Conduit System with Annular Air Space and Single Carrier Pipe

Conduit System with Single Carrier Pipe and No Air Space

Reprinted by permission of the American Society of Heating, Refrigerating and Air-Conditioning Engineers, Atlanta, Georgia, from the 1992 *ASHRAE Handbook—Systems and Equipment.*

Figure 47-4
Poured Envelope System

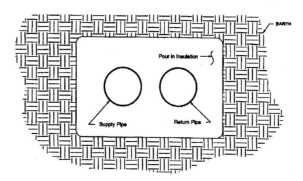

Reprinted by permission of the American Society of Heating, Refrigerating and Air-Conditioning Engineers, Atlanta, Georgia, from the 1992 *ASHRAE Handbook—Systems and Equipment.*

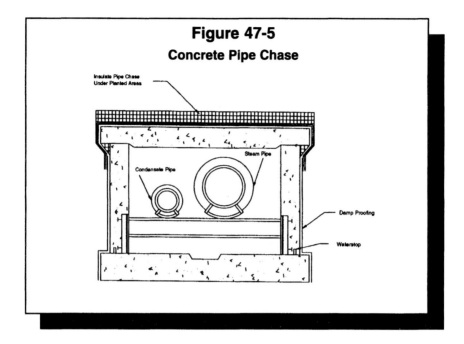

Figure 47-5

Concrete Pipe Chase

Repairs to the pipe system require the chase to be exposed so that the top can be removed. If the chase is shallow such that the top of the chase is at or slightly below grade level, removal of the tops is relatively inexpensive. If the chase is buried several feet deep, removal of the top is more expensive, especially if installed under a street or parking lot.

The best distribution method is to install steam piping in underground concrete tunnels (Figure 47-6). These tunnels are large enough to route steam pipe to the buildings and allow maintenance personnel to repair and modify the system as needed. The easy accessibility offered by tunnels can save a great deal of money over the life of the system. Tunnel systems can last more than 100 years. The tunnels generally are a minimum of 6 ft. high and 6 ft. wide. They can be installed so that the top of the tunnel is a sidewalk, thus limiting snow removal, because the heat from the tunnel will melt any snow that falls on it. This feature offers additional savings to the university.

Steam traps must be installed at low points in the system and periodically in the main to remove condensate. Location of the traps is important for controlling water hammer and for personnel safety. When a steam system is shut down, condensate forms as the line cools. If the line is not properly drained, water can accumulate in front of the shut-off valves. This water accumulation, when added to condensate formed while the line is heating up on startup, can lead to serious damage to the system and possible injury to personnel. The high velocities of steam in the pipe can carry a slug of water through the system, causing the pipe to break when the water hits a restriction or change in direction. Only experienced personnel should be allowed to start up and repair steam systems.

Valves used for steam systems must be of the highest quality and located at frequent intervals so that buildings and sections of line can be isolated. Valves in all steam and condensate lines should be made of steel. Brass and cast iron valves will not provide the long life required for a good-quality system.

Manholes are required in all systems to allow access to service valves, traps, and expansion joints. Sump pumps are installed in the manholes so that any water that enters the chase system can be pumped out. In tunnel systems, the manholes also allow access at various locations so that personnel do not have to walk the length of the tunnel with parts and equipment during repairs and routine inspections.

Hot Water Distribution Systems

Hot water distribution systems supply hot water to buildings for heating and for generation of domestic hot water. The water in the system can have a temperature as low as 180°F or as high as 350°F. Hot water systems are

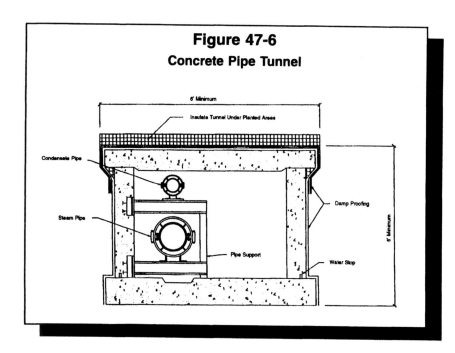

Figure 47-6
Concrete Pipe Tunnel

not as common as steam systems because the cost of transporting energy using hot water is significantly higher. Every pound of steam in a distribution system has a latent heat capacity of approximately 1,000 Btu/lbm, whereas water cooled from 350°F to 250°F has a net heat effect of 103 Btu/lbm. This difference in energy content per pound means it takes ten times the mass of hot water to transport the same amount of energy. Hot water systems require pumps to move the fluid through the system, whereas steam moves through the system as a result of pressure generated by the boilers. The additional pumps and the greater volume of fluid moved causes the hot water systems to have higher operating costs.

Even though the mass required to transport energy with steam is smaller, the volume required is much higher because of steam's lower density. This lower density requires the steam distribution system to have a larger supply pipe, but the reduced mass allows for a smaller condensate pipe than must be used in a hot water system. This difference in pipe size causes the installation costs of the two types of systems to be similar.

The piping system used for hot water is similar to the piping used for steam. The system consists of steel pipe with insulation and protection from the elements. The pipe can be direct buried or installed in chases. The system design and installation are similar to those used for steam pipe, and the same considerations must be given to expansion and contraction.

There are some cost savings in hot water systems, because manholes are not necessarily required. Expansion loops can be installed instead of expansion joints, and valves can be direct buried. This would not be the ideal type of installation for maintenance work, because the cost to repair buried valves would be high.

Expansion must be taken into account in all steam and hot water systems. Expansion can be taken up with several different methods, including expansion loops, slip joints, and ball joints. The best method of controlling expansion is expansion loops. In this method, the pipe is installed with a Z or a U in the pipe (Figure 47-7). As the pipe grows, the expansion is taken up with the elbows, and the stress on the pipe remains within acceptable levels. This method of expansion control requires considerable space because of the size of the loops. Because most campuses have limited space and because there are usually other utilities adjacent to the steam piping, the designer and owner may choose to use a different type of expansion control.

A second method of expansion control is ball joints. Ball joints are joints with a ball and socket that work like an elbow. Ball joints allow for greater flexibility and movement, yet they still permit steam to pass though the joint. By using ball joints, the size of loops can be reduced.

A third method of expansion control is slip joints or bellows. Slip joints are essentially a pipe within a pipe, sealed so that steam does not leak out. The two pipes move relative to each other. Bellows are made of corrugated

Figure 47-7
Pipe Expansion Loops

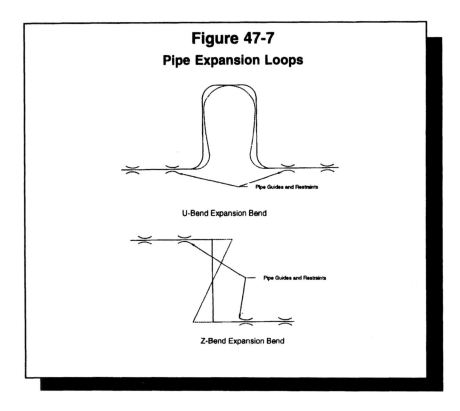

U-Bend Expansion Bend

Z-Bend Expansion Bend

metal that expands or contracts with the expansion of the system. Bellows act like metal flex joints, but the movement is along the axis of the pipe rather than perpendicular to the pipe. Both slip joints and bellows require maintenance throughout their life spans. They must be checked periodically to make sure they are not bound up or leaking. Maintenance cost is increased, but first cost is reduced, and system installation is more compact.

Manholes are required in the system to allow access to isolation valves, expansion joints, and building connections. Also, manholes provide a place to install the steam traps required to drain the steam mains. Water must not build up in the system and cause "water hammer," which can destroy the piping system. The valves installed in the manholes must be of high quality, as they are the only way the system can be isolated in the future for maintenance and repair. The use of high-quality valves will help ensure that the valves will shut off when required.

Special consideration must to be given to the sizing of all utility systems. The systems should be able to handle the current load and have the capability to expand for future loads without excessive additional costs.

47.3   PROTECTION OF DISTRIBUTION SYSTEMS

All piping must be protected from corrosion and physical damage. The most damaging thing for steel pipe is contact with water for long periods of time. For steam and condensate piping, much care must be taken to keep water away from the pipe. Tunnels and chases must be well constructed and waterproofed to limit the infiltration of water. They also should have a method for removing any water that does get into the system. The most common method for removing water is by routing the water to the manholes and using pumps to remove it. Pumps should be capable of handling some solids, because trash, dirt, and other debris will build up over time and can clog or even ruin a standard sump pump.

Also important is protection of the piping, insulation, and waterproofing systems during construction. Any damage to the waterproofing can cause the system to leak and can lead to premature failure of the piping. Protection is especially important for direct-buried systems. In these systems, loss of waterproofing will cause premature failure of the outer conduit and, ultimately, premature failure of the insulation and piping.

47.4   PROTECTION OF SURROUNDING VEGETATION

It is important to control plantings over steam and chilled water lines. Because the life of the system is more than 50 years, trees planted over the pipes and trenches will grow to be of significant size. Roots from large trees can damage water piping and waterproofing on steam tunnels. When the system finally must be dug up for repairs, any trees located over the pipes must be removed, and no one wants to destroy the beauty of a campus by removing mature trees.

A final consideration when locating steam and hot water piping is where the pipes should be placed and what the minimum depth of the chases should be. When steam chases are located below electrical ductbanks, they should be insulated to avoid overheating the power cable and reducing its current-carrying capacity. Likewise, additional insulation should be considered for steam and hot water lines below grass and other plantings, especially if the lines are shallow. The excessive heat can cause the plantings to die prematurely and leave ugly bare spots. An ideal location for these utilities is under sidewalks or streets. The cost to replace or repair them will be slightly higher, because the concrete or asphalt is more expensive to replace and repair. There can be a benefit to locating this heat-generating equipment under paved areas, as the heat can help remove snow accumulation.

47.5 UTILITY CORRIDORS

One way to control the planting of trees and other encroachments on the utilities is to establish utility corridors. Utility corridors serve the same purpose as easements established by public entities to control utility space. The utility corridors can be monitored, and rules can be established to control planting and to limit the use of the space to utilities only. When planning utility corridors, the university must consider the master plan for future building sites and establish the corridors to serve all present and future spaces without encroaching on building sites.

When the size of the corridor is being planned, it is necessary to consider the most inflexible systems first. Steam and sewer lines are the most inflexible, as they must maintain fixed slopes and routings. If these systems are planned first, the other utilities can be laid in the corridor around them.

Future maintenance and replacement must be considered when planning the utility corridor. Space must be allowed so that the pipe can be uncovered and repaired without adversely affecting the adjacent utilities. Proper planning in the present will save many dollars in the future by avoiding costly utility moves, temporary reroutes of other utilities, and costly upgrades to undersized systems.

47.6 RECORD KEEPING

Facilities managers must keep accurate records of the location, size, and depth of all utilities. Good drawings recording the utility locations can save money on future projects by avoiding delays and change orders resulting from unexpected piping encountered during construction. Unknown pipes found during construction require contractors to stop work while it is determined whether the exposed pipe is active. If it is still active, then construction is further delayed while the engineer decides how best to reroute the new piping to avoid the existing system.

47.7 SUMMARY

Underground heating and cooling systems are more complicated than laying pipes in the ground and attaching them to the building. Consideration must be given to the type of heating or cooling system, the best method to use in distributing the energy, and the best value in piping and distribution. Choices made in the present will affect the university for the ensuing 50 to 100 years. By utilizing a qualified engineer, making decisions based on life cycle cost rather than first cost, and planning for future expansion, facilities managers can save the university thousands of dollars over the life of the system.

ADDITIONAL RESOURCES

American Society of Heating, Refrigerating, and Air-Conditioning Engineers. *ASHRAE Handbook: Heating, Ventilating and Air-Conditioning Systems and Equipment.* Atlanta: ASHRAE, 1992.

American Water Works Association. *AWWA Standard for Polyvinyl Chloride (PVC) Pressure Pipe, 4 in. Through 12 in., for Water Distribution.* Denver: American Water Works Association, 1989.

Piping Design and Engineering, seventh edition. Exeter, New Hampshire: Grinnell Corporation, 1994.

Swinson, Steve, George Hoffman, and Donald R. Bahnfleth. "Campus Central Chilled Water Plant Plan: 1." *Heating/Piping/Air Conditioning,* Vol. 59, November 1987, pp. 51–55.

Swinson, Steve, George Hoffman, and Donald R. Bahnfleth. "Campus Central Chilled Water Plant Plan: 2." *Heating/Piping/Air Conditioning,* Vol. 60, January 1988, pp. 159–163.

CHAPTER 48

Electrical Distribution Systems

Mohammad H. Qayoumi
University of Missouri-Rolla

48.1 INTRODUCTION

E lectricity is a unique power source in that it must be used at the instant it is generated—it cannot be stored or stockpiled to meet future requirements. Generating capacities must be able to meet peak load requirements instantaneously. Since the first system to sell lighting to New York City was installed in 1882, this has created two problems: how to deal with the voltage drop during transmission over long distances, and how to meet widely varying voltage requirements. High-voltage alternating current (AC) and the development of transformers in the late 19th century resolved these problems and made possible efficient distribution systems that would meet wide-ranging customer requirements. They also led to the phenomenal growth of the electric industry.

The electric systems in use before the turn of the century were direct current systems. The generation systems were small, the distribution network was limited, and the voltage levels were low. Alternating current distribution systems developed rapidly, when it was recognized that interconnecting generation sites produced economic benefits. The need for higher voltages became apparent as the size of the electric networks increased in size and power-carrying capability.

Although simple in concept, current electric distribution equipment and systems are characterized by highly sophisticated technologies that continue to develop rapidly. Because electricity is invisible and its effects are not readily discernible, a mathematical approach is needed to achieve a full understanding of the design and operation of modern distribution systems. This requires highly technical training and is beyond the scope of this manual; the intent here is to describe the physical devices, their purposes, and their relationships to provide a more general understanding of the systems.

Presently transmission lines in the United States carry voltages of 345,000, 500,000, and 765,000 V. For distribution systems, utilities use 13,200, 69,000, and 138,000 V. The primary voltages for medium to large customers are 13,200, 4,160, and 2,400 V. Three main research projects dealing with higher transmission line voltages are currently being conducted:

1. 1,000-kV line, by Bonneville Power Administration
2. 1,000-kV line, by Electric Power Research Institute (EPRI) and General Electric Company
3. 2,000-kV line, by American Electric Power (AEP) and the Swedish corporation Allamanna Svenska Electriska Atievalaget (ASEA)

The introduction of high-voltage direct current (HVDC) transmission lines has opened new horizons. The advantage of HVDC over AC for long distances is its lower cost. Presently, the break-even point is 500 miles. For transmission lines longer than 500 miles, HVDC is cheaper than AC, and for lines shorter than 500 miles, AC is cheaper. When using HVDC, doubling the voltage of a cable increases the power-carrying capability of the cable by four-fold. However, as the network voltages increase, so do the costs of design, installation, and maintenance.

The electric distribution systems described here are typical of university-owned facilities at which electricity (whether generated on campus, purchased, or both) is received and further distributed to points on campus. Not covered are situations in which a municipally or commercially owned electric utility furnishes electricity in utilization voltages to individual buildings.

College and university electric distribution systems generally consist of 1) a switching station for receiving the electricity into the university system, 2) switching substations (which include transformers), 3) high-voltage conductor circuits, 4) electric power generation, and 5) system protection.

48.2   SWITCHING STATIONS

Switching stations perform a number of essential functions. They switch electric power from a larger transmitting system to the college or university system and switch the electric power that is generated on campus into the system. A switching station normally has more than one feed, or there is more than one station serving the college or university system, each with a separate feed. The station provides for switching between feeds as necessary.

For greater reliability of service, a two-feed system is recommended. During normal operation each feeder carries about half of the campus load, in which case the tie switch connecting the two feeders remains open. If a feeder is lost, the feeder switch opens, and the tie switch closes, thus minimizing power interruptions. This switching can be manual or automatic. For life-sustaining applications such as medical facilities, a triple-feed system is advisable, if economically feasible.

The switching station reduces high-voltage electricity from the incoming system to the voltage that is required by the college or university distribution system. For safety and economy in equipment costs, and because of limited transmission distance, university systems usually operate at lower voltages. The transformers in the switching station reduce incoming voltages to levels at which a university or college system is designed to operate. Normally, the incoming voltage to a university campus is 4.16, 13.2, or 138 kV, depending on the campus size. The campus distribution voltages are 13.2 kV, 4.16 kV, and 480 V.

Finally, the switching station houses fault detection and circuit interruption facilities to protect the institution's system from exterior faults and overcurrents.

48.3 SWITCHING SUBSTATIONS

Substations in the distribution system perform functions similar to those performed by switching stations. They switch the electric service of the supply mains from the switching station, usually located on the campus periphery, to feeders that supply campus areas. Substations contain sectionalized assemblies of switches, circuit breakers, and metering equipment that control and monitor electrical service to the feeders, which in turn supply individual buildings or groups of buildings. Substations may house transformers for stepping down the power to utilization voltages or to an intermediate voltage. The elements of a substation include 1) switches, fuses, and circuit breakers; 2) switchgear; and 3) transformers.

Switches, Fuses, and Circuit Breakers

Switches are circuit-interrupting devices that can make, break, or modify the connection in an electrical network, typically only under normal circuit conditions. Fuses are overcurrent protective devices that interrupt the circuit under fault (abnormal) conditions and usually are employed in combination with switches. Circuit breakers are switching devices that can make, carry, and interrupt the circuit under normal conditions and under special abnormal conditions. Therefore, switches are used only during normal operations, fuses operate only when abnormal conditions occur, and circuit breakers can perform during either condition. Switches, fuses, and circuit breakers are rated based on the system voltage, continuous current capacity, and short-circuit current interrupting capacity.

Circuit Interruption

Assume that a purely resistive load is connected to a system. The switch is closed, and the system is energized. At the time the switch begins to open and the contacts are separated, an arc is drawn between the two contacts, thus generating high temperatures. The high temperatures ionize the medium, creating a plasma between the contacts and sustaining the arc. As the current waves pass through zero, arcing ceases, and the voltage across the contacts increases. As the voltage builds up, a restrike occurs owing to the high electric field and the hot plasma still available from the initial arc. The above process continues and additional restrikes occur until the contacts have opened wide enough and the plasma has sufficiently cooled that a restrike cannot occur. At this point the circuit is interrupted.

Because in a resistive circuit no energy is stored in the system, current and voltage are in phase. If the contacts can withstand the arcing, the circuit will be eventually interrupted in a few cycles at most. However, if there are reactive elements in the system (particularly if there is a capacitor), arc quenching can be a problem.

Two parameters must be considered when opening a circuit-interrupting device: transient recovery voltage (TRV) and the rate or rise of recovery voltage (RRRV). If a device has a higher RRRV than the system, then the dielectric value between the two contacts grows faster than the system, and therefore no restrikes can occur. Similarly, if a device has a higher TRV than the system, then the dielectric value between the contacts can withstand the peak system transient voltages, and no reignition can occur. Therefore, quenching the arc and avoiding restrikes are key elements in the operation of circuit interrupting devices, and different technologies have been developed to address this problem.

Switches

Interrupter Switches   Interrupter switches employ unique techniques for extinguishing the arc by lengthening it, squeezing it, and cooling it. On opening, the switch blade separates from a set of contacts in the arcing chamber and draws an arc, which increases in length as the blade moves. Within the arcing chamber, the arc is squeezed by a mechanism that compresses it. Furthermore, the hot arc is allowed to play on the special quenching materials that line the arcing chamber and generate gases that cool the arc. Ultimately, through the processes of elongation, constriction, and cooling, the arc is extinguished. Interrupter switches typically are used on systems rated at 4.16 through 34.5 kV, with current-interrupting capabilities of up to 1,200 amperes and with the capability to withstand momentary currents of up to 61,000 amperes. Interrupter switches may also have a duty cycle fault-closingrating, permitting them to close into a fault a specified number of times while remaining operable and capable of carrying and interrupting their rated continuous current.

Fuses

Fuses are overcurrent protective devices designed to interrupt the circuit when a fault condition occurs. There are essentially two types of fuses: solid-material fuses and current-limiting fuses. Solid-material fuses employ a fusible element in air surrounded by a solid-material medium that generates deionizing gas from the heat of the arc. Fast, positive fault interruption is achieved by high-speed elongation of the arc within the fuse tube and by the efficient deionizing action of the gases liberated from the solid-material arc-extinguishing medium. The arc is lengthened by a spring-charged mechanism within the fuse that is released when the fusible element melts owing to an overcurrent, thereby separating the contacts at high speed. With power fuses, the arc extinguishes at a natural current zero.

Current-limiting fuses employ a fusible element surrounded by sand. An overcurrent melts the fusible element, and the arc formed causes the surrounding sand to vitrify, which in turn creates a glass tunnel that confines the arc. Rapid cooling and restriction of the arc increases its resistance. As a result, the current is reduced and forced to an early current zero before its natural zero. This causes high-voltage surges on the system, much like those occurring in any device that uses a vacuum as the interrupting medium.

Power fuses and current-limiting fuses have other significantly different performance characteristics that affect their suitability for circuit protection. Power fuses contain fusible elements that are indestructible and do not age. The time-current characteristics of power fuses are permanently accurate; age, vibration, and extreme heat caused by surges will not affect the characteristics of these fuses. There is no need for any safety zones or setback allowance. Because of these performance characteristics, power fuses allow fusing closer to the transformer full-load current, providing the maximum degree of protection against secondary-side faults. This attribute also facilitates coordination with upstream protective devices by allowing the use of lower ampere ratings or settings for these devices, resulting in faster response.

The construction of current-limiting fuses, on the other hand, makes them susceptible to element damage caused by in-rush currents approaching the fuse's minimum melting time-current characteristic curve. Because of this potential for damage, and because of the effects of loading and manufacturing tolerances on the time-current characteristic curve, a safety zone or setback allowance typically is required. This safety zone or setback allowance, combined with the shape of the time-current characteristic curve, results in the selection of a current-limiting fuse ampere rating that is substantially greater than the transformer full-load current. However, the use of such a high ampere rating is undesirable because the degree of transformer protection will be reduced, and thus coordination with the upstream protective device may be jeopardized. Also, because high-ampere-rated current-limiting fuses typically require the use of two or three lower ampere fuses connected in parallel, increased cost and space requirements may result.

Selection of the various types of protective devices and their ratings and settings is a complex matter. However, publications are available that provide complete, simplified procedures for selecting the optimal fuse, taking into consideration all factors associated with the application. Fuses typically are used on systems rated from 4.16 kV through 34.5 kV and are available with continuous current ratings of up to 720 amperes and with short-circuit interrupting ratings through 50,000 amperes symmetrical.

Circuit Breakers

Air Circuit Breakers   Air breakers use the simplest technique for extinguishing the arc: they lengthen it, and in this way can interrupt up to thirty times their full rated current. Air circuit breakers are of different types. A horn-gap type uses V-shaped arc-interrupting devices. As the contact is opened, the arc is drawn at the bottom of the horn. However, because of higher temperatures and electromagnetic forces, the arc moves up the horn. As the arc becomes larger, it is cooled by convection. Another style is the molded-case circuited breaker, in which the arc is cooled by forcing it to go through narrow insulated fins called *arc chutes*. Air circuit breakers are used for low-voltage systems (up to 600 V) with current-interrupting capabilities of up to 100,000 amperes.

Air-Magnetic Breakers   In an air-magnetic breaker, the magnetic field is applied on the arc, forcing it along a number of insulating fins. As the arc lengthens, it cools down and extinguishes. Two sets of contacts operate in air-magnetic breakers: main and arcing contacts. The arcing contacts carry the current when the main contacts open, so arcing contacts are first-make, last-break contacts.

The arc chute where the arc is extinguished consists of a number of insulated fins. The arcing contacts initiate the arc above the bottom of the slot, which establishes a magnetic field before the arc is drawn. The arc runner configuration moves the arc up the chute. In the meantime the air puffer blows a jet of air across the contact to help move the arc up the arc chute. Air-magnetic breakers are used for systems of up to 15kV with interrupting ratings as high as 1,000 mVA. Currently there are only a few companies that still manufacture air-magnetic switches and circuit breakers. Several manufacturers make conversion kits that use vacuum switches for existing air-magnetic switch cubicals.

Oil Circuit Breakers   In an oil breaker, the arc is drawn under oil. As the arc is established, oil around the contact is vaporized, and a large bubble surrounds the arc. Hydrogen comprises roughly two-thirds of this bubble, and because hydrogen is an unfavorable gas for ion pair production, the arc is cooled and interrupted.

Oil breakers are used outdoors for up to 345 kV. At 345 kV they are capable of interrupting currents as high as 57,000 amps. Environmental requirements for oil circuit breakers are not as stringent as those for an air-magnetic circuit breaker, but oil breakers are prone to fire and explosion.

Vacuum Circuit Breakers   A vacuum is an ideal environment in which to open switch contacts. As the contacts open in a vacuum, an arc is initiated, but because of the high dielectric value of the vacuum, the arcing plasma cannot maintain itself and is extinguished in less than 20 microseconds. The arc is interrupted at first current zero and usually does not reignite. A $1/4$-in. gap is sufficient to interrupt 100 kV. Vacuum breakers do not require a supply of gas or liquid, so they are not fire or explosion hazards. Unlike oil breakers, they can be installed in any environment. They are compact and lightweight, and switch operation is silent and requires relatively small amounts of energy. Vacuum circuit breakers can be used outdoors, in manholes, or in metal-clad switchgear for indoor operation. Vacuum switches are rapidly becoming the most popular types of switches for 4.16- and 13.2-kV systems.

Sulfur Hexafluoride Circuit Breakers   Sulfur hexafluoride (SF_6) circuit breakers have been in use since the 1960s. Here the arc-extinguishing medium is a colorless, odorless, nontoxic, noncorrosive, nonflammable, inert gas with an excellent dielectric value. These breakers are available for voltage loads ranging from 13 to 765 kV. The remarkable performance of SF_6 as an arcing medium is due to its ability to recover quickly; it is almost 100 times more effective than air in extinguishing the arc.

Sulfur hexafluoride breakers have many advantages. They are lightweight, self-quenching, and compact; present no fire hazards; and can be installed in any position. The ambient environment for SF_6 breakers is less restrictive than for other types. The disadvantage in using SF_6 breakers is their high cost. However, as technology improves, they will become more cost-competitive with oil and air-magnetic breakers.

Metal-Clad and Metal-Enclosed Switchgear

This is a particular type of electrical equipment in which the circuit breakers, disconnecting devices, relays, metering, potential transformers, and current transformers are in separate metal compartments. When the switch assembly is removable, it is called *metal-clad;* when it is not removable, it is called *metal-enclosed*. This type of switchgear normally is used for voltages between 13.2 and 34.5 kV.

Transformers

Different generation, transmission, and utilization requirements dictate different voltage and current combinations, hence the need for a component capable of changing, or transforming, voltage and current at high power levels in a reliable and effective way. This is the function of the power transformer, an extremely important link between the transmission and use of electric power. Transformers make it possible to generate energy at any suitable voltage, change it to a much higher voltage for transmission over long distances, and then deliver it to a college or university system at still another voltage.

All transformers have two basic elements: two or more windings insulated from each other and from the core, and a core that usually is made of thin, insulated, laminated sheet steel. Power transformers used for stepping down the voltages in a distribution system are classified according to type of core construction and type of cooling employed.

Two types of core construction are core and shell. In the core type, the magnetic circuit comes in the form of a single ring, with the primary and secondary windings encircling the two legs of the core. In the shell type, the relative positions of the coils and the magnetic circuit are reversed. Here the winding forms a common ring in which two or more magnetic circuits are interlocked.

Transformer Ratings

Like most other electrical equipment, transformer limitations are thermal in nature. The nameplate data indicate the permissible winding temperature when the transformer is at full load. If the windings are subjected to sustained high temperatures, insulation life will be tremendously shortened, which may result in system failure.

It is important to note that the temperature rise in a transformer, or any other electrical equipment, is a function of kilovolt-amperes and not of kilowatts. Moreover, the nameplate data are based on 40°C of ambient temperature; if the ambient temperature is higher, the nameplate rating should be reduced according to the manufacturer's relevant data.

Transformer Insulation Classes

There are currently four insulation classes with their respective National Electric Manufacturers' Association (NEMA) specification and temperature limits. In Class A transformers, provided they are operated at a maximum ambient temperature of 40°C, the temperature rise on the winding will not exceed 55°C. Class B transformers use a higher-temperature insulating material, so at an ambient temperature of 40°C or lower, the temperature rise on the winding will not exceed 80°C. For Class F transformers, at an ambient temperature of up to 40°C, the winding temperature rise will not exceed 115°C. Class H transformers use insulation that can withstand high temperatures and are the most compact transformers. At an ambient temperature of up to 40°C, the winding temperature rise will not exceed 115°C.

Transformers in Parallel

When the load increases so much that one transformer cannot meet the power demand, an additional transformer can be connected in parallel. If two transformers are connected for parallel operation, the turns ratio and the impedance of both units must be examined to ensure proper load sharing between the two, with little or no circulating current. Otherwise one transformer might be overloaded while the other is lightly loaded, or the circulation current between the two units may be such that one unit will be overloaded with a relatively small load. This situation will result in high energy losses without utilizing the full capacity of both units.

When two transformers are installed in parallel, the units must be a matched set. This means that in addition to primary and secondary voltages, the line frequency, transformer connection, turns ratios, and impedances are such that they will share the load based on their relative kilovolt-ampere ratings. If both transformers have the same ratio, then the turns ratios and impedances are almost identical. For two transformers with identical 3 percent impedances (which is typical of most distribution transformers), a 1 percent difference in turns ratio can result in a 15 to 20 percent circulating current. In addition to creating higher losses, circulating currents reduce the total capacity of the transformers.

Transformer Types

There are three common types of transformers: dry, mineral oil, and polychlorinated biphenyl (PCB).

Dry Transformers   Dry transformers use air as coolant. Air circulation is achieved either by natural convection or by a forced-air system. Dry transformers usually are larger than oil or PCB transformers of equivalent rating. They are explosion free, self-extinguishing, and less expensive and usually are used for relatively small loads. The ambient condition is important for dry transformers, as a source of clean, filtered air is needed.

Oil Transformers   Oil transformers are the workhorses of power distribution systems. They can be self-cooled, using natural circulation of the oil, or air-cooled with blowers. The transformer's core and winding are surrounded by insulated mineral oil, which protects the insulation and provides cooling and dielectric strength to the transformer. Because the oil must be able to withstand voltage surges and thermal and mechanical stresses, as well as act as a good coolant during the entire useful life of the transformer, the oil should be supplied or approved by the transformer manufacturer, and adequate care should be exercised to guard against its deterioration.

The major causes of oil deterioration are water and oxidation. Moisture contamination can result from condensation, especially when the transformer is down; such contamination drastically reduces the oil's dielectric strength. An increase in water of 10 to 50 ppm reduces the dielectric strength by half. Oxidation causes oil deterioration, which results in sludging. Oil transformers are used both outdoors and indoors. Because they are fire hazards, when used indoors, they must be installed in a vault to conform to fire codes.

PCB Transformers   PCB is a dielectric fluid that has been used in transformers and power capacitors since about 1960. It is a stable compound that has good fire resistance. Manufacturers of transformers have preferred PCB over mineral oil, because PCB transformers do not require a vault. PCB liquid is known primarily under the brand name of Askeral. Other common trade names in the United States are Aroclor, Asbestal, Chlorextol, No-Flamol, Pyronal, Elemex, Dykanol, and Interteen.

In 1976 Congress enacted the Toxic Substance Control Act, which required the Environmental Protection Agency to establish rules governing the disposal and marketing of PCBs. From that point on, these PCB-filled devices were regulated. Since that time, practically all but a small number of PCB transformers have been either replaced or retrofilled. Currently any PCB spills that contain more than 5 ppm are subject to hazardous waste regulations with regard to treatment and disposal.

48.4   HIGH-VOLTAGE CONDUCTORS AND CIRCUITS

There are two basic circuit systems for feeding from the substations to building systems: the radial system and the network system. In the radial system, separate feeders radiate out from the substation, each supplying an area. From these feeders, subfeeders or branches split off to transformers serving individual buildings or a cluster of buildings. The radial circuits are equipped with tie switches so that in the event of a fault, the circuit can be supplied by another feeder. Radial feeders with loop or throwover switching are most commonly employed.

In the network system, the secondaries of two or more transformers are tied together. Adjacent transformers may be supplied from the same or different feeders. Distribution, therefore, is normally at utilization voltages.

Three principal factors determine the distribution voltages: 1) energy loss in transmission versus cost of equipment, 2) strength of the conductor, and 3) overhead vs. underground installation. There is a trade-off between the cost of energy loss in transmission and the cost of transmitting equipment. For a given percentage energy loss in transmission, the cross sectional area and, consequently, the weight of the conductor required to transmit a block of power varies inversely as the square of the voltage.

The strength of conductors also must be considered. Overhead transmission lines must be strong enough to carry any load that may be reasonably expected. The most severe loads are experienced during winter ice and wind. Underground conductors must be able to withstand allowable stress to which the cable is subjected during installation. The need for adequate physical strength of a cable will help determine its electrical conductive capacity.

When comparing costs on overhead or underground transmission lines, it should be noted that the cost of underground construction is much higher. Overhead lines, however, are unsightly and detract from the educational environment. They also create problems of routing to building transformer vaults, as these often are located in basements. As a consequence, underground transmission lines are most commonly used in new installations.

The power cables are critical elements of the high-voltage network, because they are the arteries of the system. Traditionally, they are the system component that receives the least attention, perhaps because "out of sight is out of mind." Cables usually are located in duct banks, and insulation that weakens prior to failure cannot be seen, which often results in inadequate maintenance. It is important to realize that the reliability of the electrical network can be greatly improved and costly downtime avoided simply with a little attention to the cables.

Cable Insulation

Paper-impregnated lead cable (PILC) and varnished cloth (VC) have been the insulation workhorses of the industry since 1910. PILC has compound migration problems if used on vertical risers, and termination and splicing also are more difficult. VC cables are relatively more expensive for the quality of the dielectric but do not have the compound migration problems. The combination of VC cable for vertical risers and PILC for horizontal runs has been used successfully.

Since the 1970s the petrochemical industry has introduced a variety of polyethylene compounds as insulation materials, all of which have good insulating characteristics, such as high moisture resistance, low temperature characteristics, high ozone resistance, and greater abrasion resistance. These cables are lighter in weight compared to PILC, and terminations and splicing are relatively easier.

Termination and Splicing

There are different splicing kits available, and manufacturers have a wide variety of techniques for splicing. Therefore, it is important to first make sure that the proper size and type of splice are used for every situation, the manufacturer's recommendations are followed, and the work is performed by skilled personnel. Cable splices and terminations are usually the weakest points in a cable system, so adequate attention must be devoted during installation and subsequent maintenance.

Cable Maintenance

Insulation Resistance Test   This test determines the insulation resistance between the conductor and ground. A megohmmeter is used to measure the resistance. It is basically a high-voltage ohmmeter consisting of a small DC generator and a milliampere meter. The generator is hand cranked or driven by an electric motor, the latter being preferred for consistency of rotor speed. Megohmmeters generally have ranges from 100 V to 5,000 V.

Good insulation is indicated by an initial dip of the milliampere meter pointer toward zero, followed by a steady rise; the initial dip is due to the capacitive effect of the cable. If the pointer makes slight twitches down scale, however, this implies current leakage along the surface of dirty insulation. To compare the insulation with the historical record, a spot test is performed. The megohmmeter is applied for 60 seconds, and the reading is recorded at the end of this time.

Dielectric Absorption Test   This test provides better information than the spot test but takes considerably longer than the insulation resistance test. Because the current is inversely related to time, insulation resistance will rise gradually if the cable is good and flatten rapidly if the insulation is faulty. The insulation resistance is plotted against time.

High Potential Test   The above two tests cannot determine the dielectric strength of cable insulation under high-voltage stress. A high potential test, or hypot test, applies stress beyond what a cable encounters under normal use. It is the only way to obtain positive proof that the cable insulation has the strength to withstand overvoltages caused by normal system surges. There are two types of hypot tests, AC and DC. The AC hypot test is used almost exclusively for insulation breakdown. If applied properly, the DC hypot test is a nondestructive test, so it is commonly used for maintenance.

Surge Arrestors

Surge arrestors protect electrical apparatus against overvoltages from lightning, switching surges, and other disturbances. Without arrestors, flashover and equipment damage can result. During normal system voltages, arrestors are dormant. When a high-voltage impulse is imposed on the system, regardless of source, the arrestor will ground it, thus preventing it from going through the equipment. There are three classes of surge arrestors:

1. *Station class arrestors.* This is the best type of arrestor, as it is capable of discharging the most energy.
2. *Intermediate arrestors.* These have lower energy discharge capability than station class arresters.
3. *Distribution arrestors.* These have the lowest energy discharge capability and the least desirable protection level.

48.5 ELECTRIC POWER GENERATION

Generators

Generators are electromechanical devices that convert mechanical energy into electrical energy. Generator operation is based on Faraday's law, which states that a voltage will be induced on a conductor if the conductor moves through a magnetic field. The voltage induced is directly proportional to the number of turns in the conductor, the strength of the magnetic field, and the speed at which the conductor moves through the field. In addition, the closer the magnetic field is crossed at 90°, the higher the voltage. The types of generators include AC synchronous, asynchronous, emergency, and DC. Most of the generators currently used in industry are synchronous.

AC Synchronous Generators   A synchronous generator is structurally identical to a synchronous motor. The magnetic field is produced by a direct current in the rotor circuit. The rotor, also called the *exciter,* is powered by brushes and slip rings. The armature circuit located in the stator produces the electricity. There are a number of different ways to power the exciter field. One is to supply it from a separate DC generator, but in most cases the exciter is fed from the armature through a diode and a silicone-controlled rectifier (SCR). The diode converts the AC power to pulsating DC, and the SCR provides voltage regulation. Here the generator is initially excited by residual magnetism.

A third way to power the exciter field is to have two rotors—one main, one auxiliary—on the same shaft. The small auxiliary winding is excited initially by residual magnetism. The AC voltage generated in the winding goes through a set of diodes and supplies the main rotor. In addition, a stationary exciter field regulates the voltage output of the generator. Because the entire exciter circuit is on one shaft, there is no need for brushes and slip rings. These units are called *brushless generators* and require less maintenance than other generators.

Asynchronous Generators   If an induction motor is driven faster than synchronous speed by a prime mover, it will become a generator. Because the generator speed is different from synchronous speed, the generator is called an *asynchronous generator.* The generated power frequency varies but is always more than 60 Hz. Asynchronous generators are simpler in construction and cost less than synchronous generators. This is why most small cogeneration units use asynchronous units. Also, if the prime mover energy is not controllable, such as in wind-powered generators, asynchronous units are the most appropriate. The power output of an asynchronous generator usually is not used directly; instead it passes through a rectifier bridge to convert it to pulsating DC power. The DC power feeds an inverter, which converts the power to constant 60-Hz AC power before it supplies the load. Harmonics can be a problem in these units, so their size is limited to less than 150 kW.

Emergency Generators   In using emergency generators, both the normal power source and the emergency generator are connected to a transfer switch. If the normal power source fails, the emergency generator is started. In about six seconds the generator attains its rated voltage and frequency, and a transfer switch sends the load over to the emergency generator. When the normal power source is restored, there is usually a 6- to 10-minute delay before the load is transferred back to normal power. This transfer can be done manually as well as automatically, depending on the configuration of the transfer switch.

When the normal power goes out and then is restored, the power to the load is interrupted twice, presenting a potential problem for computers, digital private branch exchange (PBXs), and life-sustaining equipment. In such applications, an uninterruptible power supply (UPS) is used. In a UPS, AC power is obtained by connecting battery power with the use of inverters. The transfer switch and the generator are connected to the battery charger, which supplies power to the batteries. The load does not sense any normal power interruptions unless both the normal power and the emergency generator are out of operation and the battery charge drops below a certain point.

Cogeneration

Cogeneration is the production of more than one form of energy simultaneously; it usually refers to producing electricity and heat energy.

Cogeneration is discussed in detail in Chapter 46. The electrical concerns regarding the interconnection of cogeneration to the utility power grid are examined here.

When allowing interconnection of cogeneration, utilities are mainly concerned that the systems do not jeopardize the safety of utility personnel and the quality of service. During normal conditions, the utility needs to know if the power produced at the cogeneration site will be used entirely by the customer and, if not, how much of the power will be sold to the utility. Moreover, the utility wants to ensure that the harmonic voltage and frequency tolerances of the dispersed generation site meet the grid tolerances. During emergency conditions, network faults must be detected by the cogeneration device and isolated from the grid.

The utility electric distribution network is radial, so isolation of an area requires opening and locking a main circuit breaker. With cogeneration, the power network is not radial, but instead is a loop distribution system. Therefore, it is crucial for the utility to record the location of all cogeneration units and have access to a manual load-break disconnect at all times. The interconnection requirements of a cogeneration system depend on interconnection voltage, transformer configuration, protection scheme, and on-site load and generation capacity.

Electrical Protection for Cogeneration   In a utility distribution network, the overcurrent equipment is arranged in a series of overlapping zones to clear a fault on a prearranged sequence of primary devices and backups. This is achieved by coordinating the time-current characteristics of fuses, circuit breaker reclosers, sectionalizers, and relays from a substation. In a faulted condition, the available current drops as it moves from the substation to the customer site because of an increase in system impedance. Therefore, coordination is relatively simple. With cogeneration interconnection, a bidirectional power flow on the distribution system can continue to energize the part of the network separated from the utility system reference source. Moreover, a cogeneration site can contribute additional overcurrent during faults, which may cause protective systems to operate prematurely.

This high current level from the cogeneration site is over and above the available fault current from the utility, thus shortening the average melting time of the line fuses. In a 15-kV system, a small synchronous cogeneration unit of a few megawatts can reduce the fuse melting time by more than 30 percent; in an induction generator, the reduction in melting time is about one-third that of the synchronous generator.

Another problem lies with the utility's autoreclosures. The faults that occur with an overhead transmission system are usually momentary and self-clearing. After a fault, the autoreclosure closes the circuit a few cycles after the circuit is interrupted, and the customer downtime for such momentary faults is minimal. With cogeneration in the system, although the utility breaker has interrupted the circuit, the fault is fed by this unit and does not get a chance to clear. Therefore, when the circuit is closed by the autoreclosure, the fault has not cleared, and this increases downtime. The presence of cogeneration changes the available fault and the system coordination for in-house systems, as well as the utility grid.

Another concern utilities have with cogeneration is the problem of islanding. *Islanding* means that the cogeneration site is operating independently of the reference voltage and frequency of the utility power grid and is no longer in synchronism with it. Islanding can cause several problems. Utility personnel might assume that opening the line breaker will de-energize the circuit. The generator voltage and frequency variations might cause costly damage to the load. If the utility breaker is closed without synchronizing the cogeneration unit, serious damage can also be incurred by the generator and the breaker.

The harmonics generation from cogeneration sources must also be studied. For economic reasons, the magnetic core of in-house generators is not made of the same high-quality materials as the utility grade units, and the core nonlinearities of cogeneration units produce harmonics that cause problems with computers and other sensitive electronic equipment.

Minimum Protection Requirements   If an internal electrical fault occurs within the cogeneration unit, the available fault from the utility grid will cause major damage. Therefore, the electrical protection needs of a cogeneration system should not be taken lightly. The required protection depends on unit size, generator type, in-house load, and interconnection voltage. For small units where power is totally used in house, overcurrent, over- or undervoltage, and current directional relays are required. If power will also be provided to the utility grid, then in addition to the first two relays, overfrequency, underfrequency, and negative sequence relays will be needed. For larger units, the following additional protection relays are recommended:

- Differential protection
- Loss and excitation
- Overspeed
- Motoring protection
- Stator and rotor protection
- Overheating

For induction units, surge overspeed and internal short protection are recommended. It should be kept in mind that the protection levels suggested here are only guidelines; local utility requirements and site conditions must be taken into account.

To summarize, before the advent of cogeneration, facilities were only receivers of power; currently they are partners in the power grid with utilities. It is the responsibility of both sides to ensure that the reliability and safety standards of the network are not compromised when connecting cogeneration systems.

48.6 SYSTEM PROTECTION

Short-Circuit Faults

Electric current always follows the path of least resistance. What confines electricity in a conductor is the dielectric around the conductor. If the insulation between two conductors or a conductor and ground drops to zero, a large current is going to flow in the circuit. This is called *short-circuit current*, because the current has found a shorter path than the path through the load.

The short-circuit current can be as high as 10,000 times the rated current. Fault current can be destructive and cause equipment damage, fire, and personal injury. Short-circuit current magnitude is a function not of the load, but of the capacity of the power source and the length and size of the conductor. A water dam can serve as an analogy for potential short-circuit current. Normally, the water flow in a dam is dependent on the pipe size, but if the dam breaks, the water flow will depend only on the total water available in the dam, independent of the pipe size.

The available short-circuit current in an electrical system is explained in the following example. Consider a circuit in which a 500-V, 10-kVA load is connected to the utility through two possible transformers to the utility system. The transformer choices are a 10-kVA unit with an impedance of 0.2 ohms and a 10,000-kVA unit with 0.02 ohms impedance. The load impedance is 25 ohms. Thus, for both transformers the normal-load current is 20 amperes.

If there is a short-circuit at any point on the cable, the available current in each transformer will be different. Available fault current in the first transformer will be 2,500 amperes, whereas that in the second transformer will be 25,000 amperes. In the first case, the fuse must only be able to interrupt 2,500 amps, but in the second case the fuse must be able to interrupt 25,000 amps, since its available fault is higher.

There are four sources of short-circuit currents: the utility system, in-house synchronous generators, induction motors, and synchronous motors. The available fault from the utility is directly related to the size of the utility transformer. For a synchronous motor, the available fault current is four to five times the motor's full-load current, and for an induction motor, it is two to four times the motor's full-load current.

There are two types of faults: symmetrical and asymmetrical. A symmetrical fault is a three-phase fault, sometimes referred to as a *bolted fault*. Here it is assumed that all three-phase conductors are brought together simultaneously. About 5 percent of short-circuit failures are due to symmetrical faults. All other faults (e.g., line-to-ground, line-to-line, or line-to-line-to-ground faults) are referred to as *asymmetrical faults*. When the system is in a faulted condition, it can disrupt the transmission network in one or more of the following ways:

- Allowing large currents to flow, which can damage equipment
- Causing electrical arcing, which can start fires or damage equipment
- Raising or lowering system voltage outside acceptable ranges
- Causing a three-phase system to become unbalanced, which in turn causes three-phase equipment to operate improperly
- Interrupting the flow of power

The protection system of a high-voltage electrical system is designed to safeguard against these disruptions. It works to detect and isolate faults, it keeps as much of the system in operation as possible, it restores the system as soon as possible, and it discriminates between normal and abnormal system conditions so that protective devices will not operate unnecessarily.

There are three types of components in a protection system: fuses, relays, and circuit breakers. A fuse is a device that opens a circuit if an overload or short-circuit occurs. It consists of a short, fusible link held under tension. When the current is increased beyond a certain point, the link will melt, and the spring will pull the contacts further apart, thus interrupting the current in the circuit. The main selection criteria for fuses are voltage rating, ampacity, and interrupting rating, to which the following guidelines apply:

- The voltage rating of a fuse should always be equal to or greater than the system voltage.
- The ampacity of the fuse should be equal to the rating of the load.
- The interrupting capacity of the fuse should be equal to or greater than the available fault current.
- The time-current characteristics of the fuse should be such that system selectivity is ensured.

Protective relays are used to minimize damage to electrical equipment by interrupting the power circuit during a fault. There are four types of protective relays: electromagnetic attraction, electromagnetic induction, thermal induction, and electronic. Protective relays must have the following characteristics:

- *Reliability.* They may be idle for several years and then suddenly be required to operate quickly.
- *Selectivity.* They must not respond to abnormal but harmless system conditions, such as sudden changes in load.

- *Sensitivity.* They must be responsive enough to perform in every case required.
- *Speed.* They must make decisions and respond quickly.

Circuit breakers are mechanical devices that are capable of breaking and reclosing a circuit under all conditions, even when the system is faulted and currents are great. Circuit breaking occurs when a mechanical latch is released, which enables a coiled spring or a weight to open the contacts.

Selection of System Protective Devices

In institutional power systems, such as university campuses, circuit breakers have been used for applications requiring complex relaying schemes or high continuous currents. However, for most applications a choice of either circuit breakers or power fuses is available. Fuses have achieved widespread use in most such applications because of their simplicity, economy, fast response characteristics, and freedom from maintenance.

Circuit breakers and their associated relays are commonly used where the reclosing capability of the circuit breaker is an advantage, such as applications involving overhead lines, which have a relatively high incidence of transient or temporary faults. This reclosing feature is neither useful nor desirable in institutional power systems where the conductors are arranged in cable trays, enclosed in conduits or bus ducts, or are underground. The incidence of faults in these systems is low, and the rare faults that do occur are not transient and result in significant damage that would only be exacerbated by an automatic reclosing operation.

The relaying associated with circuit breakers is available in various degrees of sophistication and complexity. Systems requiring differential protection, reverse-power relaying, or non-current magnitude tripping of the protective device typically require circuit breakers. However, the size of transformers normally associated with institutional power systems generally does not warrant such sophisticated protection. Indeed, many users find that the complexity of such protective relaying, with its requirement for periodic testing and recalibration, is a distinct disadvantage.

Circuit breakers also are used in applications requiring a very high (above 720 amperes) continuous current-carrying capability. Although they may be an advantage in some cases, a higher degree of service continuity can be achieved with less expensive power fuses by subdividing the system into a number of discrete segments, with the result that a fault on one segment of the system will affect fewer loads. This high degree of segmentation also allows the use of smaller transformers located strategically throughout the university's electrical distribution system, eliminating the need for the long, high-ampacity secondary conductors that are required where fewer larger and widely separated transformers are used.

Where high continuous current-carrying capability is not required and reclosing or sophisticated relaying is not justified, as in medium-voltage and institutional power systems, power fuses offer a number of advantages. Power fuses are simple to install and require no maintenance of any kind; even after years of neglect, power fuses will operate properly. Recalibration is neither required nor possible; hence, elaborate testing procedures are not needed, eliminating the possibility that a carefully engineered coordination plan will be disturbed accidentally. Power fuses, unlike circuit breakers, provide fault protection for the system without depending on a source of control power, such as storage batteries and their chargers. Such batteries may be found to be completely discharged and thus incapable of tripping the circuit breaker should a fault occur. In addition, for high-magnitude faults, power fuses have inherently faster response characteristics than circuit breakers, permitting more rapid removal of faults from the system.

Types and Symptoms of Failures

The major cause of electrical failures is the breakdown of insulation. Insulation breakdown is caused by dirt, high ambient temperature, oil leakage, internal failure, overload, high-voltage surges, corona, ferroresonance, or flashover. Other causes are absorption of moisture and dust into the cores and excessive vibration and aging.

Dirt   Moisture or condensation of airborne chemicals causes electrical leakage, which in turn causes tracking and eventual flashover.

High Ambient Temperature   A 10°F to 15°F overheat above the rated temperature will cause insulation to embrittle, deteriorate, and shorten the useful life of equipment by half.

Oil Leakage   Excessive loss of oil or compound will result in equipment loss. Once the insulation material is lost, a void is created and dielectric values will be drastically reduced.

Internal Failure   Loose connections may result from mechanical forces that are created by surges, overloads, and vibration. Loosened terminals, fuse clips, and live part connections in the switch will create excessive heat and thereby accelerate further deterioration of the system.

Overload   Overload produces excessive heat that decreases the useful life of the equipment.

High-Voltage Surge   High-voltage surges are a serious problem for most utility companies. Surges create flexing and physical displacement of component parts, which in turn leads to loose connections and overheating. Surges also produce stability problems that may lead to resonant failures. Surges also can cascade into the secondary side and create failures.

Corona Corona is a discharge caused by electric stresses, which in turn can be produced by high electric fields, dirt, moisture, sharp bends in cable, severe weather conditions, and faulty design. It can be detected by its secondary symptoms: ozone odor, radio and television interference, visible pulsating of a blue or green color, crackling noises, and the production of a gray powder on the unshielded cable.

Ferroresonance Ferroresonance is usually caused by a single-phase opening where no secondary load exists on the transformer. The inductance of the transformer and the capacitance of the cable can form a series-resonant circuit and create instantaneous voltage up to fifty times the normal rating, which can give rise to a violent explosion in cables and transformers. The following are indications of ferroresonance:

- Loud humming and vibration of a transformer
- Spark-over of arrestors on open phases yet to be closed
- Overvoltage breakdown failure of cables, transformers, and arrestors
- Motors running backward

Ferroresonance can be prevented by the following:

- Grounding neutral on all transformer wye windings
- Energizing transformers with the same load
- Energizing cables first, then the transformer
- Installing fuses both at the cable entrance and at the transformer
- Energizing all three phases simultaneously

Flashover All of the failures mentioned thus far will eventually result in flashover if corrective action is not taken. The usual trigger for flashover is dirt and moisture over the insulation. As an arc is established, heat is generated and starts a cascade effect.

48.7 INSTRUMENTS

Test Instruments

Electrical test instruments are the tools used to perform maintenance on power systems. For low voltages, the multimeter and amprobe are used. Voltage and resistance are measured with a multimeter, whereas current is measured with an amprobe. For high-voltage systems, the following instruments are used:

- *Infrared Detector.* The use of infrared units can greatly enhance visual inspection, because problems such as overloads, imbalances, loose connections, and dirty cores in a dry transformer can be readily located.
- *Megger.* A megger, whether hand or motor driven, will give a quick analysis of the integrity of the insulation on a cable or in a transformer. The 2,500-V megger is effective for troubleshooting cables, motors, and transformers.
- *Hypot Tester.* A hypot tester normally is used when the condition of cable cannot be determined with a megger. Although the hypot tester has the capability to test up to 80 kV, tests that are up to two times the operational voltage are usually recommended. Great care must be taken with this instrument to avoid damaging the cable by imposing excessively high stress voltages.
- *Phase Meter.* A phase meter is used to test fuses or to phase two feeds to one another. It is also used for draining capacitance from a system during a shutdown and for proving that the system is deenergized prior to the attachment of ground connections.
- *Glow Stick.* A glow stick is an excellent way to test for fault potential on an unshielded cable. It is of no value for testing a blown fuse or for discharging a system.
- *Dielectric Tester.* A dielectric tester gives a quick analysis of the dielectric value of oil. Moisture, pH, and other tests also should be considered when using this instrument. A two-year test program on all liquid-filled apparatus is recommended.

Metering

The need to accurately measure electrical energy became critical after the energy crisis of the 1970s. The instrument for measuring electrical energy is the kilowatt hour (kWh) meter, which measures cumulative energy consumption over a period of time. Another useful measurement is kilowatt demand (kWD), which signifies the maximum power demand within a time period. Utilities use demand costs as part of the total electric charge, so by measuring power demand, the institution can analyze consumption patterns for possible reductions. In addition, the difference between peak demand and the substation rating indicates the available spare capacity, which is useful when considering future distribution expansion.

For low-voltage systems (less than 150 amperes), a kWh meter is connected directly to the service. For high-voltage systems and larger currents, potential transformers (PTs) and current transformers (CTs) are utilized. PTs have the same primary voltage as the system but have a secondary voltage of 120 V. CTs are shaped like doughnuts and are placed around the power conductor. Because CTs are constant current sources, if the CT circuit is opened when energized, an explosion can result from high voltages.

Electric meters are subject to drift, so they should be periodically tested and calibrated. The magnitude of service and the critical importance of the data will determine how often they should be calibrated.

Use of Capacitors for Power Factor Correction   Power factor is an important value in load consideration and measurement. Alternating current was adopted principally to take advantage of transformers that do not operate with direct current and also helped simplify motor design. At the same time, problems were introduced by the presence of inductive reactance in the circuit and reactive power required by motor loads. Because of the reactive power, principally in motors but to some extent in other loads, the current lags in time relative to the voltage. Therefore, more current is required to provide a given amount of power. The power factor is the quantity by which the apparent power must be multiplied to obtain the active power of the circuit. There is no way to eliminate this component of current, but it can be neutralized by adding another load to the circuit in the form of capacitors. Capacitors can be located at the loads, in the substations, or on the lines. Power factor correction on the lines generally is less costly.

Electric Power Quality

Alternating current electricity is a pure sinusoidal wave of one single frequency. More specifically, in the United States this frequency is 60 Hz. Ideally this is the shape of AC power at all times. In a real system, as long as the circuits have linear elements (resistors, capacitors, and unsaturated inductors), the wave shape will remain the same during steady-state conditions. However, as soon as nonlinear elements are introduced in the circuit (rectifiers, thyristors, and saturated inductors), the wave shape will become distorted. Therefore, some of the harmonic sources in a power system are saturated transformers, arc welders, voltage rectifiers, inverters, uninterruptible power sources, variable frequency drives, and self- and line-commutated converters. In addition to harmonics, electrical surges also introduce power glitches with values much higher than system voltages.

These harmonics and glitches can be a major nuisance for many types of sensitive electronic equipment, including personal computers. Usually the greatest challenge is finding the source of noise in the power system. Some common techniques for protecting devices from these problems are the use of isolation transformers, reactors, harmonic filters, uninterruptible power sources, and surge suppressors.

ADDITIONAL RESOURCES

Electrical Utility Engineering Reference Book—Distribution Systems. Pittsburgh: Westinghouse, 1965.

Fink, Donald G., and John M. Carroll. *Standard Handbook for Electrical Engineers,* tenth edition. New York: McGraw-Hill, 1968.

Glenn, D. J., and C. J. Cook. "A New Fault Interrupting Device for Improved Medium Voltage System and Equipment Protection." *Proceedings of the IEEE/IAS Annual Meeting.* Institute of Electrical and Electronic Engineers, October 1984.

Mason, C. R. *The Art and Science of Protective Relaying.* New York: John Wiley & Sons, 1967.

Miller, H. N. *DC Hypot Testing of Cables, Transformers, and Rotating Machinery.* Chicago: Associated Research, Inc., Manual 16086, 1990.

Qayoumi, Mohammad H. *Electrical Distribution and Maintenance.* Alexandria, Virginia: APPA, 1989.

Qayoumi, Mohammad H. *Electrical Systems.* New York: Upward Publishing, 1996.

Turley, S. Q. "Ferro-Resonance Oversimplified." *Transmission & Distribution,* October 1966.

Underground Systems Reference Book. New York: Edison Electric Institute, 1957.

Viermerster, P. *The Lightning Book.* New York: Doubleday, 1961.

SECTION III-C

OTHER UTILITIES

Editor:
Wayne Kjonaas
Purdue University

INTRODUCTION

Other Utilities

The chapters in this section deal with utilities that are less energy intensive such as water distribution systems, sewer and storm drainage systems, and telecommunications. Traditionally, these utilities received relatively less attention from facilities managers than other utilities because normally the water and sewer costs were a small percentage of the overall utilities costs. Moreover, until recently, telecommunication services were managed by the business office rather than the facilities department because the local telephone company provided all the necessary services.

With the divestiture of AT&T in the mid-1980s and the proliferation of PBX installations in many campuses, the role of the facilities department concerning telecommunications was redefined. Many university systems began to view telecommunications as an important utility and a capital asset rather than merely an operating expense. A number of other factors suggest an even more critical role for telecommunication systems at a university campus because of the strategic role they are beginning to play in meeting the institutional mission. For instance, almost all universities are under pressure to increase their involvement in distance education in which the technical feasibility of such an endeavor is directly tied to the telecommunication infrastructure of the organization.

Almost all students, faculty, and staff currently require high-speed, wide-band communication pathways to perform their jobs effectively and efficiently. The plethoric avalanche of technologies; the recent deregulation legislation; and the collapse of traditional differentiation between voice, data, and video add to the existing significant challenge. Therefore, facilities managers should have a general idea about the fundamental issues dealing with telecommunication systems and their current role in universities. In quite a few campuses, the telecommunication department may not functionally report to the facilities department, but the important role that facilities departments play in the design; installation; and management of the cable plant, switch rooms, and so forth cannot be overemphasized.

Chapters 50 and 51 address water distribution and sewer and storm drain systems. In the past several years, with the passage of the Clean Water Act and other legislation affecting water distribution, sewer, and storm drain systems, operation and maintenance issues have become complex. With the implementation of the National Pollution Discharge Elimination System (NPDES), the Clean Water Act has created a web of complicated waste water permitting systems both for point source as well as indirect discharge of all nondomestic sewage. As a result of these regulations, situations exist where universities must install and maintain pretreatment of sewage before it is discharged to public sewer systems.

The latest amendments of the Clean Water Act authorized local districts to increase their rates to meet the higher operational costs that result from chemical concentration of effluent. This authorization resulted in sizable rate increases, and in some instances the rates surged three or four times practically overnight, which negatively affected the utility budgets of institutions. Moreover, local authorities can charge universities not only for flow, but also for biochemical oxygen demand and total suspended solid. Similarly, the NPDES established requirements for storm water pollution prevention plans that contain drainage system maps, inventory of materials that could have been exposed, and a list of significant spills.

Operating the utilities discussed in this section has become more complicated in the past decade. Hopefully these three chapters will provide valuable information as well as stimulate enough interest to probe further.

—Mohammad H. Qayoumi

CHAPTER 49

Telecommunication Systems

Thomas E. Darragh
Indiana University

49.1 INTRODUCTION

Telecommunication systems, which to some are represented by wire and cable plants and telephone systems, must now be thought of more broadly to include data and video technologies. The digitizing of analog signals and the growth of fiber-optic networks are driving voice, data, and video technologies to the point of true convergency. This eventual convergence will support an institution's seemingly insatiable requirement for information delivery, both now and into the next century.

The planning for an institution's facilities organization, in collaboration with interested campus constituencies, to deliver the telecommunications services of the future will be complex. Consideration will have to be given to the abandonment of certain investments and the cost of new investments at a time when overall budgets may be shrinking.

If these factors do not seem to offer sufficient challenges, then consider the changes occurring within the information and telecommunications industries that can affect the choice of telecommunication services. Telephone companies want to deliver video, and cable TV firms want to handle voice calls. Government and industry groups are setting standards for the interoperability of systems, such as local area networks (LANs), video teleconferencing equipment, and wire and cable offering greater information carrying capacity.

The traditional role of the facilities organization, or a separate campus unit, as a provider of telecommunication services has evolved rapidly since 1984. At that point, the Bell Operating Companies (BOCs) were divested from AT&T as a result of a suit filed by the U.S. Department of

Justice. As the result of divestiture and the deregulation process, colleges and universities have assumed greater responsibility for their telecommunication and information systems and services.

Additional change will take place with the passage of the Telecommunications Act of 1996 and its far-ranging implications for the telecommunications industry and its customers. The enforcement of the Act will substantially increase competition among the suppliers of telecommunication goods and services. The development of this competition will stimulate the offering of new services while reducing the costs of existing goods and services. As with the 1984 divestiture and deregulation period, the Telecommunications Act of 1996 will provide challenges and opportunities to institutions managing their own systems.

The role of the campus manager of these services, in keeping pace with change, has evolved through the following stages:

1. *Facilitator:* Having responsibility for the coordination of basic telephone services. All technical services are typically provided by a third party, such as the local exchange carrier, AT&T, or a communications "interconnect" firm. Only basic support services such as centralized operator services and coordination with facilities trades are provided.
2. *Caretaker:* Assuming additional responsibility for budgeting, cost reallocation, and centralized record keeping.
3. *Service provider:* Providing most or all support for the procurement, installation, and maintenance of telephone system hardware and related services.
4. *Systems integrator:* Having responsibility for voice, data, and video communications. Various technologies are used to integrate all communications services, including conducting long-range strategic planning.

The events related to deregulation and divestiture presented a challenge to the campus manager who had responsibility for the telecommunications function. These developments caused many such administrators to initiate plans to acquire their own telephone systems, wire and cable plants, and long distance services in a single program to gain greater control of their telecommunications costs.

The changes of the recent past, in conjunction with the significant challenges of the future, have caused many colleges and universities to turn to the services of the professional telecommunications director. This is best evidenced by the increasing membership in professional organizations such as the Association of College and University Telecommunication Administrators (ACUTA) and user groups dealing with specific technologies and services, such as voice mail systems and private business exchange (PBX) systems.

This chapter is devoted to providing facilities staff with a better understanding of factors influencing the role of telecommunications in university life, modern telecommunication technologies, and future planning initiatives.

49.2 GOALS AND OBJECTIVES

APPA: The Association of Higher Education Facilities Officers has stated that the basic purpose of the facilities division is to 1) aid in the creation of a physical environment for education and research, 2) operate and maintain the facilities portion of this environment, and 3) provide services that enhance the use of facilities. The role of telecommunications, either within the facilities organization or separately, is that of a supporting service. This physical environment shall be used to assist the institution and its constituent organizations to achieve their primary goals and objectives related to education, research, and public service.

One responsibility of the facilities manager is communicating institutional goals to telecommunications personnel. It is not necessary that these goals be narrowly defined or limited to those to be accomplished in a short period of time. Rather, each goal should relate to the underlying mission of the institution and provide guidance to the telecommunications staff in setting appropriate objectives. Although all educational institutions share many common goals, different institutions generally have different priorities (e.g., improved classroom instruction, research, continuing education, cost containment, or higher student enrollment). Through effective planning, specific objectives can be developed that clearly define how telecommunications can enhance the attainment of these goals.

49.3 FACTORS INFLUENCING THE ROLE OF TELECOMMUNICATIONS

Telecommunications can enhance the ability of institutions to accomplish their missions in education, research, and public service. External factors or forces (e.g., divestiture and deregulation, the convergence of information delivery systems through the use of digitization and fiber-optic networks, other emerging technologies, and new services) have had a dramatic impact on institutional use of telecommunications. In addition, there are several factors within academia that have caused modern telecommunication systems and networks to be considered a college or university resource rather than the traditional utility. These internal factors, described below, are important in understanding the overall telecommunication needs of a college or university.

Planning

Significant capital investments in new telecommunications systems and associated infrastructure improvements by colleges and universities are a manifestation of the changing role of telecommunications. These investments represent commitments to the use of telecommunications technology by the highest levels of administration. Because of the magnitude of these investments, which can be tens of millions of dollars, it is important that planning for telecommunications improvements be closely coordinated with other university planning processes.

The financing of major telecommunications equipment and systems, such as the installation of a new campus telephone system, often requires special appropriations by state legislatures or private governing boards, the sale of bonds, or third-party financing. The development of a budget proposal for these expenditures, the evaluation of financing alternatives, and the associated approval processes can consume months and involve numerous university administrators. These expenditures must normally compete with other critical college or university requirements, so planning must be done with similar attention to detail, accuracy, and articulation of need.

It is important that the telecommunications plan be coordinated with other university capital improvement and land plans. New university buildings or major renovations of existing structures can substantially add to the line requirement and the need for outside plant improvements, (e.g., duct banks, conduits, and manholes) for new telephone systems. These possible future improvements should be identified in the planning of a new campus telephone system to ensure that sufficient switching capabilities are designed in the system at cut-over and adequate funding is provided for an appropriately sized telephone switch. After cut-over of a new system, it is necessary to continually evaluate the impact of new building projects on the configuration and cost of operating the telephone system.

Plans for changes or additions to academic and administrative computer systems and video delivery systems can have a significant impact on the utilization of campus telecommunications facilities. The implementation of computer networks or video networks can require the installation of separate fiber-optic, twisted-pair copper, or coaxial cable networks in existing underground telecommunications ducts. Because of the dependency of computer networks and video networks on telecommunications infrastructure, it is essential that these planning processes be carefully coordinated. The desired level of coordination may be more difficult to achieve at institutions with separate telecommunications, computing, and television administrative reporting structures. However, the integration of television, computer, and telecommunications planning is necessary to ensure that the appropriate services are available to all computer users.

Committees

The use of committees in the decision-making process of universities is traditional. Only in recent years have committees played a significant role in the formation of plans and recommendations for major telecommunications purchases. Today it is common for a university committee to conduct an exhaustive study of an institution's telecommunication needs and make recommendations regarding specific technologies that should be acquired. The composition of these committees should embody the diverse needs of the university, as the role of the committee often extends beyond the evaluation of a major system purchase. Committees also establish interface and protocol standards for campus networks and monitor and evaluate the effects of the changes in technology on campus telecommunications needs.

Network Infrastructure

Networks are common in our lives. A network ties things together. Trains operate over a network of tracks. Computer networks connect all types of computer and peripheral devices together. Control systems monitor door entry sensors and temperature devices and start and stop motors remotely. Video signals are delivered to the user via a network. Finally, there is the traditional telephone network.

Telecommunication networks operate over physical facilities—copper wire, coaxial cable, fiber-optic cable, and free space. Given the rapid growth of electronic information delivery requirements, colleges and universities need to continually address the viability of the campus telecommunications infrastructure. The use of structured wire plans, adherence to industry-developed standards for qualifying wire and cable information-carrying capacity, and adherence to industry-developed standards for installation of infrastructure are critical issues needing attention.

Special note must be given to the recent developments in copper wiring and the connecting hardware used in the horizontal distribution (station to floor closet) infrastructure. The Electronic Industries Association and the Telecommunications Industries Association (EIA/TIA), an industry standards development group, has promulgated the EIA/TIA-568 Standard, which gives the parameters for twisted copper pairs and connecting hardware.

All copper wiring is not manufactured to the same engineering standards, and recognizing that some applications (voice and data) may place less technical demand on the horizontal wiring, the EIA/TIA developed a classification system using "categories" as a grading index. The configuration of the cable—including its twist factor, its insulation, and its design—affects the speed and strength of the signal it can carry. In addition, connecting hardware and installation practices can add or detract from the performance of the cable system. To obtain the higher speeds for data applications, the horizontal cable must be designed and installed as a system.

The industry has recognized five classifications for twisted-pair cabling, each defining a certain category of performance. Figure 49-1 gives a description of each category and possible applications.

Persons having membership in the Building Industry Consulting Service International (BICSI) group will be familiar with the EIA/TIA-568 Standards and other standards that apply to telecommunications distribution design. These individuals may be found in departments such as telecommunications, facilities, and computer services.

Computers

One of the primary influences on the role of telecommunications at colleges and universities is the widespread use of microcomputers for administrative and academic applications. The move to microcomputer-based computing has been accelerating rapidly. This trend has been spurred by the declining cost of personal computers and workstations; growth in applications, especially multimedia applications; an increase in computer literacy; and the ability to network microcomputers through LANs and wide area networks. It is forecast that microcomputer growth will continue unabated well into the future, driven by new application developments and the availability of low-cost bandwidth capacity.

Figure 49-1

Performance Categories

Category	Description	Application
1	Voice	Minimal, for analog voice and 20-kbps data
2	ISDN/low-speed data	Supports up to 1-mbps data Useful for digital voice and ISDN
3	LAN/medium-speed data	Supports up to 16-mbps data
4	Extended distance/ medium speed	Supports up to 20-mbps data
5	High-speed LAN	Supports 100- to 155-mbps application, such as Copper Distributed Data Interface (CDDI) and Asynchronous Transfer Mode (ATM)

Video Communications

Video communications on university and college campuses are used for delivery of interactive instruction to remote classrooms, residence halls, and remote campuses; transmission of high-resolution images for clinical evaluation and research; delivery of entertainment television programming to residence halls; access to videotape or disc libraries; and teleconferencing.

There is a growing initiative for institutions to involve themselves, as part of their public service mission, in distance learning programs. This primarily involves the delivery of video signals, either one-way or two-way, to noninstitutional locations such as high schools or hospitals. The mode of transmission can be free space, using either satellite or microwave, coaxial cable leased from local cable television firms, or fiber-optic cable leased from telephone companies and others.

Whether video applications are to be delivered on campus or off campus, there is a requirement for the institution to provide large amounts of bandwidth to support these applications. This is true for either analog or digital video systems.

Voice Communications

The importance of basic voice telecommunication services has often been overshadowed by new demands for data and video communication services. The reliability of the telephone network may have resulted in an underestimation of its extreme importance as a basic means of communicating. The Centrex or PBX continues to be the communications workhorse for most institutions by processing millions of calls each year. Improvements to voice switching systems allow for the transmission and switching of high-speed data communications channels. The use of voice processing technology, such as interactive voice response (IVR) for student registration and voice mail for the storage and forwarding of messages, and the ability of the computer/telephone interface (CTI) to integrate the two systems for particular applications are growing elements in the voice services domain.

These relatively new uses have brought to institutional administrators a renewed sense of the importance of the telephone system.

Wireless Communications

There is a high degree of staff, faculty, and student mobility on campuses. This, coupled with a large land area, makes use of voice paging systems—whether tone or voice; cordless telephone; cellular telephone; or, in the future, the personal communicator—extremely attractive. At remote building locations, there may be an opportunity to use wireless systems to connect

LANs into the campus-wide computer system. The down-linking and/or up-linking of video signals for distance learning opportunities or, in the future, for the distribution of entertainment channels to residence halls also fall within the realm of wireless communications.

The key consideration in this area may eventually be the management of the frequencies used for each service to avoid signal influence.

49.4   TELECOMMUNICATIONS

Data Communications

Local Area Networks (LANs)   What is a LAN? Perhaps the definition used by the Institute of Electrical and Electronic Engineers (IEEE), the main body responsible for developing LAN standards, will provide the necessary answers:

> A LAN is distinguished from other types of data networks in that the communication is usually confined to a moderate-sized geographic area such as a single office building, a warehouse, or a campus, and can depend on a physical communications channel of moderate to high data rate which has a consistently low error rate.

LANs developed with the advent of desktop computing during the early to mid-1980s. The power resident within workstations and personal computers has continued to grow rapidly. Applications that run on these units, such as those in the multimedia field and computer-aided design, need access to vast quantities of information. This information may consist of video, still color pictures, or voice. LANs provide the means for users to access such information very quickly, often in less than one second, and to then communicate it to others equally as fast. The high-speed LAN is the most effective way to deal with these tasks.

All LANs can be described by five critical characteristics:

- The layout and logical structure of the network, called the *topology,* which includes the geometric arrangements of ring, bus, star, and associated hybrids
- The type of *communications medium,* such as copper wire, coaxial cable, fiber-optic cable, or wireless
- The manner in which a device (workstation or personal computer) accesses the network for the sending or receiving of information. This is called the *access method* and falls into two broad categories: deterministic and random or contention.
- Base-band or broad-band signaling defines the *transmission method.*
- The *speed* of information movement can range from 1 to 16 megabits per second (mbps) and, in the near future, to 100 mbps and beyond.

The IEEE, mentioned earlier in this section, has done a great deal of standardization work for LANs. The 802 Committee of the IEEE is directly responsible for the development of the standards. Three specifications of particular note are the following:

1. IEEE 802.3, a contention arrangement operating as base-band, on a bus topology, using coaxial cable or copper wire and running at 10 mbps
2. IEEE 802.4, a deterministic arrangement operating as broad-band, on a bus topology, using coaxial cable and running at between 5 and 10 mbps
3. IEEE 802.5, a deterministic arrangement operating as base-band, on a ring topology, using copper wire and running at 4 to 16 mbps

At least two new standards are emerging that will push speeds at the desktop to between 100 and 155 mbps.

LANs become more valuable when they are interconnected by high-speed backbone networks using bridges, routers, and gateways to move information between users.

Several books that offer more specific information on LANs are listed at the end of this chapter.

Wide Area Networks (WANs)   This term is used to describe the means of connecting local data networks at one premise to local data networks at one or more distant locations. The term *internetworking,* used widely by practitioners, is equivalent in meaning to WAN. However, in the broader sense, any network connecting distant geographical points into an operating whole for the exchange of voice, data, and/or video can be considered a WAN.

Given the scope of this subject, it can be covered only superficially in this section. For those readers requiring a greater knowledge of wide area networking, the books mentioned at the end of the chapter are good reference works.

When a college or university makes a determination that there is a specific requirement to develop a WAN architecture, it will need to select between several scenarios (e.g., dedicated vs. public network, fixed vs. variable cost, digital vs. analog transmission facilities) and decide whether to share the networks through the use of multiplexing for voice, data, and video services. WAN services, either dedicated or public, are provided by a common carrier and the local telephone company.

Private internetworking is usually deployed using a dedicated digital circuit between the sites. Based on the information traffic to be handled, a circuit can be ordered to operate at 56 kilobits per second (kbps) or 1.544 mbps or 45 mbps. These latter two speeds are commonly called T-1 and T-3 service, respectively. All of these offerings are fixed speed (bandwidth) and are available to the customer 24 hours per day, 7 days per week, with the cost based on the amount of fixed bandwidth provided by the common carrier.

Public network offerings are generally based on some form of usage-sensitive pricing. The cost of a typical telephone call is based on a time and distance formula. ISDN, the integrated service data network, at its "basic rate interface" level is a switched service, with charges based on call holding time.

Other public network services that handle traffic in a "packet" format, rather than the circuit switched method of ISDN, charge by the number of packets delivered for the subscriber. The most typical of these networks is one known as X.25, which is a world-recognized standard.

The common carrier industry will be offering to its customers public network services, such as frame relay, switched multimegabit data services (SMDS), broad-band ISDN (BISDN), and asynchronous transfer mode.

What the WAN should look like really comes down to the volume of information to be delivered, the time-criticalness of the information, and the cost of the network options. A hybrid dedicated/public network may be the most cost-effective alternative.

Before leaving the subject of WANs, one must note that most colleges and universities have recognized the value of being part of the Internet, which is a worldwide collection of networks. Any institution that is part of the Internet is a member of the world's largest WAN.

Voice Services

The most comprehensive telecommunications application currently deployed at colleges and universities is voice service. Because of its long history, the general familiarity of form and function, and the industry's reliability, telephone service is often taken for granted. Providing telephone service is assumed to be easy, that it manages itself, and—most frightening of all—that "the telephone company does it all."

The importance of the basic voice telecommunications services has often been overshadowed by new demands for data and video communications services. The historic reliability of the telephone network may have resulted in a lack of realization of its extreme importance as a critical means of communicating.

While the focus of this section is voice services, it should be remembered that these same fundamental tools also support other circuit-switched services that can be used for data and compressed video applications.

Campus Facilities

The primary elements of the campus telecommunications system are switching and related peripherals, public network connections, intracampus transport, and telephone station equipment. Intracampus wire and cable systems were discussed previously in Section 49.3.

Voice Switch

Centrex and PBX systems have been the primary voice communications switching systems for colleges and universities. Key systems are often used in conjunction with Centrex and PBX equipment in larger applications and may be used as the primary telephone equipment at smaller campuses or at extension sites. PBXs are owned or leased equipment that is typically located on university property. Centrex service is typically provided by the local exchange company, and the equipment is located in the telephone company's central office. Centrex services typically require smaller capital investments and less need for space and support services, but they are considered to be less flexible than a university-owned PBX. In some cases, custom Centrex contracts can eliminate most or all of the limitations of traditional Centrex offerings.

Switching systems can be deployed as a central resource, with all wiring concentrated into one main facility, or the switching can be distributed to modules that are located closer to densely populated service areas. The economics of each approach should be fully evaluated prior to any major telecommunication system renovations.

Most campus switches have been converted to digital capability. Equipment from a few manufacturers converts the analog voice signal to a digital signal at the user's telephone set and then transports and switches the digital signal. More common is the less costly approach of using analog telephones, transporting an analog signal to the switch, and converting to a digital signal at that point. The internal switching is then handled in a digital format at 56 kbps. Currently the primary technology used for voice and circuit switched telephony is time division multiplexing (TDM). Some equipment is capable of switching at 64 kbps, which is commonly referred to as *clear channel.*

The basic elements of the PBX and Centrex switch are common control, software, and the switching matrix. The level of redundancy in the common control equipment is usually a function of price and the relative level of risk that the purchaser is willing to assume. The software on every modern switch is extremely complex and requires routine patches and periodic updates. Both of these issues should be dealt with in the installation and operations plans. The switching matrix can be of a blocking or nonblocking design. In a blocking design, the size of the matrix in the system is based on assumptions of the amount of traffic that the campus switch must support. Operationally, it is also necessary to "traffic balance" the system to make sure that the appropriate number of high- and low-usage stations contend for a set percentage of the switching matrix.

Station Lines and Equipment

Station lines in the telephone switch are connected to end user telephones by a dedicated pair of wires. The connections between switch and station utilize combinations of 26-, 24-, and 22-gauge twisted-pair wires. Each service type has its own set of distance limitations for reliable service. Most telephones require one set of twisted-pair wire for basic voice services. Advanced-feature telephones, however, may require additional pairs. Electrical power is required for telephone sets that provide advanced functions. The power requirement can be supplied by a desk-side transformer, or it can be powered by a central power supply in the telephone equipment room. Central power supplies can be more easily provided with a backup source, and these may be less costly, but they require the use of twisted-pair wire to deliver the power and are more difficult to administer during station moves and rearrangements.

Telephone sets are the most visible portion of any telephone system. The telephones must meet the varying needs of students, faculty, and staff on campus. Their visibility and functionality make them key factors in the selection of a telephone system.

Trunks

The local switch is connected to other parts of the public switching network by trunks. Trunks provide interswitch connections. The local switch establishes connections between two lines on the same switch or between a line and a trunk for off-campus calling. Trunk-to-trunk connections are also supported for remote services. Trunks may be provided as analog facilities that support one voice channel each, or digital facilities, commonly known as T-1s, which provide voice channels in multiples of 24, may be used. Signaling between switches for call setup and control can be accomplished by in-band or out-of-band techniques. ISDN Primary Rate Interface (PRI) and Signaling System #7 (SS7) are the current out-of-band signaling technologies. Asynchronous Transfer Mode (ATM) is an emerging technology aimed at high-bandwidth applications for integrated video, voice, and data.

Public Switched Network

Campus telecommunications facilities are connected to the public switched network at the local exchange and, in some cases, by dedicated trunks that bypass the local exchange and make direct connections with interexchange carriers. Competitive local exchange companies currently exist only in large metropolitan areas. The activities of the local exchange companies are regulated by state public service commissions. Interexchange companies (e.g., AT&T, MCI, and Sprint) have competed openly since 1984. Their activities are regulated by the Federal Communications Commission.

Local Exchange

The local exchange provides flat rate and/or measured switching services for completing calls to the "local" area. Measured service, sometimes called *message units service,* implies a cost per call or cost per minute of connection time. The measured service charges are typically billed as a lump sum based on units used rather than on a per-call basis, as is the case with long distance service. The extent of the "local" area is determined by the local exchange company and the appropriate regulatory authority. Larger "local" calling areas bring a higher cost for lines and trunks from the local exchange company.

In addition to costs for lines and trunks, the local exchange company also charges for access to the wider public network. The access charges are a flat rate charged per trunk or per line.

Interexchange

Interexchange, or long distance, companies can be accessed through the switching services of the local exchange company or by dedicated access facilities. Dedicated access facilities are costly and are generally justified only in high calling volume situations or for redundancy requirements. Dedicated facilities must connect the campus facilities and the interexchange company switch, which may be located in a distant city.

The reliability of an interexchange carrier is influenced by the redundancy and diverse routing that are designed into the carrier's network structure. The distance between campus facilities and the interexchange switching site influences both the cost and the reliability of the network. The complexity of today's networks can make it difficult to assess the structure of the network used by a prospective interexchange carrier. A few interexchange carriers own and control their own interswitch transmission facilities, whereas most other carriers procure transmission bandwidth from third-party providers. A thorough review of the primary and backup arrangements should be conducted, in addition to reviewing the price and terms of the services offered.

Enhanced Voice Services

Paging One of the first, and still the most widely used, mobile telecommunications services was paging. Current paging options include tone and voice paging, call back number display units, and full alpha-numeric scrollable text paging. These services are available from several commercial suppliers. The interface is standardized and is compatible with all current telecommunications systems.

Voice Processing   Voice processing combines elements of voice telephony and information processing. It uses voice systems to convey or collect computer-based information. Voice processing is provided by one or more peripherals to the campus voice switch. Current voice processing systems can support most of the following applications and are currently available in systems based on industry standards that allow interoperability.

Voice Mail. Voice mail is the most common voice processing application currently in use. A voice mail system digitizes; compresses; stores; and then, upon request, retrieves, decompresses, and plays back the stored message. A user's voice mailbox is a confidential storage mechanism that also provides forwarding, preprogrammed distribution lists, and interfaces to paging and e-mail systems for notification of voice mail delivery.

Integrated Voice Response. An integrated voice response translates spoken requests or touch-tone key entries into computer commands that interact with computer applications to retrieve the requested information. The requested information is relayed to the caller in the form of a digitized voice. Typical uses of integrated voice response at a college or university include account balances, grade information, loan application status, touch-tone registration, and automated attendants. Touch-tone registration is a key application allowing students to select class schedules, drop classes, and enter class wait-list requests. It is based on a well-designed script that requests specific identification information from the caller, provides context-sensitive information, and deposits the resulting requests into a central database.

Fax Mail. Fax mail, or fax store and forward, consists of a digitized and compressed representation of an original analog fax modem signal. Upon request, just as with voice mail, the digitized record can be recalled, decompressed, and converted back to an analog signal. The signal is then sent out over telephone lines to another fax machine. The digitized record can be retrieved many times, sent to distribution lists, or stored for future reference. The primary use of fax mail is as a shared resource for repetitive distribution, upon user request, of written documentation.

Student Services

Student services generally fall into two categories. Residence services enhance the student living experience and often generate revenue. Administrative services enhance and improve administrative and educational interaction between the students and the university.

Residence services have traditionally included the provision of dial tone to student rooms and the sale of long distance services, but increasingly they include data services, video services, enhanced voice feature services, and a variety of other services that are specific to the individual campus residential environment. Residence services are valuable to the university; they can generate substantial outside funds, as they make residence halls a more attractive housing option.

Student telephone services, however, can require substantial administrative support and attention. Billing systems, complex staffing demands, cash accounting, and taxes are some of the issues that must be confronted to develop an effective student services operation.

49.5 TRENDS IN TELECOMMUNICATIONS

Trends in telecommunications are changing so rapidly that much of what is said here may be irrelevant by the time it is read. James Martin, in his 1990 book, *Telecommunications and the Computer,* spoke about moving into the symbiotic age, an age of the human–machine interface where the limited brain of humans is supplemented by the vast data banks and logic power of distant machines. He went on to say that in the near future, "All the professions will have their own data banks and, sometimes, their own languages. The nonprofessional or the mass public will use machines for doing calculations, for working out tax returns, for computer dating, for planning vacations, or just for sheer entertainment."[1]

Much of this forecast has become reality, along with his projection that these systems would grow, multiply, and interlink. In addition, humans have developed and continues to refine "navigation systems" that aid in the search for and location of specific data housed in multiple worldwide systems.

Our experiences, whether as a part of the information delivery equation or as a consumer of information, can validate the significant growth of voice, data, and video services at institutions. Much of this growth is due to factors beyond the bounds of any single department's responsibilities. Growth lies in the client's demand for new or additional information delivered faster. The information can be in any format—voice, data, image, or multimedia.

Clients want more control over data, so there is a move from centralized mainframe computing to client/server computing. Distance education and outreach programs are of growing interest to many institutions. Federal and state governments are pursuing initiatives to fund networks that will eventually interconnect higher educational institutions with K–12 schools, libraries, and other public agencies. The list goes on and on, making specific predictions, beyond saying that bandwidth requirements to the desktop will quickly reach 155 mbps, a real "guesstimation."

It is recommended that APPA members at institutions develop a solid relationship with those campus organizations responsible for computer telecommunications, and video services to understand emerging trends that may have an impact on the facilities organization. Furthermore, planning for the physical telecommunication pathways and cabling infrastructure must include these organizations.

NOTE

1. Martin, James. *Telecommunications and the Computer,* third edition. Englewood Cliffs, New Jersey: Prentice Hall, 1990, p. 20.

ADDITIONAL RESOURCES

Association of College and University Telecommunications Administrators. *Campus Telecommunications Systems: Managing Change.* Lexington, Kentucky: ACUTA, 1995.

Martin, James. *Local Area Networks.* Englewood Cliffs, New Jersey: Prentice Hall, 1989.

Slone, John P., and Ann Drinan. *Handbook of Local Area Networks.* New York: Auerbach Publications, 1991.

CHAPTER 50

Water Supply and Distribution Systems

Kavous Emami, P.E.
ORSA Consulting Engineers, Inc.

50.1 INTRODUCTION

Water is one of the most essential and basic necessities of life. One of the basic criteria for human settlement is the availability of water and the availability of farm land, which requires a large supply of water. As populations have grown and settlements have concentrated where water is available, inevitably the sources of water have begun to deplete, while the chances for water contamination have increased.

The effects of water on the environment are beyond one person's imagination. Although water has a simple chemical formula, it is so powerful that it can dissolve more substances in greater quantity than any other liquid; it is one of the sources of electricity (hydroelectricity) available to humans; and it is a major source of recreation. Yet, water is often undervalued and taken for granted. A great deal of money and resources are spent on the development and treatment of water sources to make it safe for drinking and household use. However, when it reaches the tap humans mistakenly treat it as an overabundant, cheap commodity. Requirements for drinking water standards are making drinking water more expensive to achieve, and individuals pay for this cost through increased water bills.

50.2 ELEMENTS OF A SUPPLY AND DISTRIBUTION SYSTEM

College and university water supply and distribution systems consist of the following elements: 1) a water source, 2) a distribution system, 3) pumping, 4) storage, and 5) fire protection.

Water Source

The two major sources of drinking water supply are surface water and groundwater. Surface waters are runoff from snowmelts at the mountain tops or rainfall collecting into lakes or rivers. These waters are transported to the cities by natural rivers or artificial aqueducts. They are considered raw waters and are exposed to the atmosphere, where they are subject to contamination. In addition, surface water is subject to receiving surface runoff along its route and thus can become contaminated from various sources with a variety of contaminants. Water purveyors receiving untreated surface water are required to provide multibarrier treatment to reliably protect users from microbiological contaminants prior to water being used for drinking (Figure 50-1).

Several sources contribute to groundwater; some of these are rainfall, rivers, lakes, and human recharge of the groundwater. One of the most abundant sources of groundwater is calcium in sea water. Calcium becomes so abundant in sea water that it precipitates out, forming crystals of the mineral calcite. So much calcite is precipitated that a thick layer of a sedimentary rock, called *limestone,* forms on the ocean floor. This rock may later be uplifted by large-scale geological forces to form part of the land areas of the world. If conditions are just right, the limestone may in time provide huge reservoirs for underground water resources (Figure 50-2).[1]

Groundwater pumped from wells that are constructed in accordance with the state department of health services and are deeper than 100 ft., is generally considered not at risk. Usually groundwater does not have to be treated, except by chlorination in some cases, to meet drinking standards.

Water sources for campuses are normally provided by a water purveyor in the area in which the campus is located. Water purveyors may be a private company, a public company, or a company run by a municipal government. These companies normally provide their customers with a combination of blended well water and treated surface water. The advantage of having a water purveyor providing the domestic water is that the purveyor is responsible and obligated by law to deliver safe drinking water to the point of connection with the campus. In addition, there are some initial capital investments, such as water treatment, storage, and operation and maintenance, that make it cost-prohibitive for some campuses to have their own water source.

Distribution System

A campus water distribution system is much like a small city with a different type of clientele. Water services to most buildings on the campus are not metered or charged directly to the users, and thus, there is little incentive for

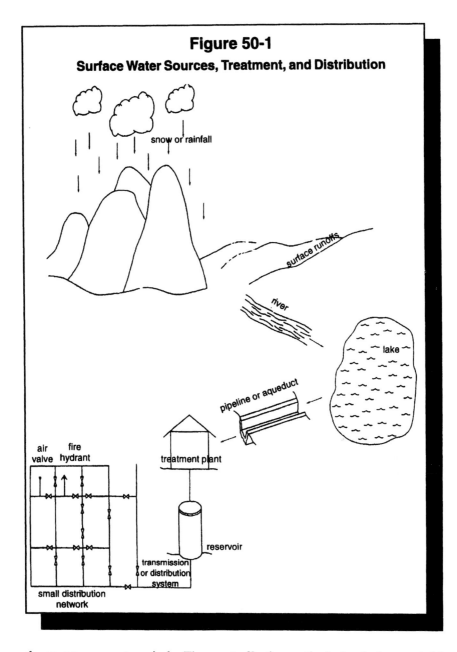

Figure 50-1

Surface Water Sources, Treatment, and Distribution

the user to use water wisely. The most effective method of reducing wasteful use of water on campus is by campaign and education.

The water distribution system consists of underground and above-ground piping, reservoirs, mainline water valves, fire hydrant assemblies, air vacuum and air release valves, metering vaults, pressure-regulating

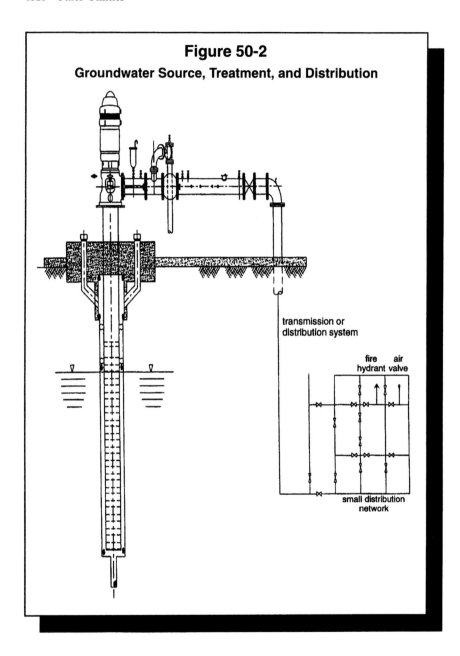

Figure 50-2

Groundwater Source, Treatment, and Distribution

stations, and backflow prevention assemblies. A campus water distribution system is considered a public water system and must meet all standards set by the state department of health services. A properly designed water distribution system should deliver the maximum required flow to all areas of the campus with adequate pressure at all times. In addition, the distribution system should be designed to prevent water interruption when a section of the pipeline is taken out of service.

Pumping

A reliable and cost-effective water distribution system is one that requires minimal pumping. When the available water pressure at the point of connection to a system is sufficient, the system can provide adequate flow and pressure throughout the distribution area during high-demand periods. However, it may become necessary to increase water pressure to high-rise buildings or areas of higher elevations by pumping.

Water pressures of 75 to 80 psi at static condition are considered adequate water pressures. As long as the distribution system is sized and looped properly, water at these pressures will not need any pumping during high water demand. Water pressure in any distribution system should not be higher than 130 psi, as higher pressure in a distribution system may cause frequent waterline ruptures and wear and tear on the valve seats and requires installation of special pipelines and related facilities. In accordance with the *Uniform Plumbing Code,*[2] the building water pressure should not exceed 80 psi. Water pressures higher than 80 psi are lowered before the water enters the building by installing pressure-regulating valves. A water pressure below 60 psi at static condition is considered weak and has limited flexibility. A minimum available pressure of 20 psi is required to operate the majority of plumbing fixtures. This level of available pressure should occur only during emergency periods and must not be a standard practice of system delivery.

Pumping is often inevitable in a system where the ground topography changes drastically, thus requiring multiple pressure zones within a system.

Storage

Water storage facilities and their capacities are integral parts of any water system and can greatly improve a system's reliability. Water supply lines, although intended for continuous operation, can be and are taken out of service for routine maintenance or emergency repairs. Adequate storage capacity can be used as a standby water source to ensure continuous operation when the water source is cut off from the system. In addition, having a water storage tank provides the flexibility to install pumps of various sizes to operate based on the water demand required for higher water pressure zones. Lack of a water storage tank combined with the need to increase water pressure requires installation of a large in-line variable frequency drive (VFD) to meet the highest peak, which may occur only 10 percent of the time, thus increasing energy and pumping costs.

Water storage provides a great deal of flexibility to a distribution system. Determining the water storage capacity needed should be based on the water demand, fire protection demand, and number of available water sources to a system. Water reservoirs are of reinforced concrete (generally square or rectangular tanks), prestressed concrete (circular tanks), or steel. The size of reservoir needed, construction cost, and site constraints often affect the decision as to the type of reservoir chosen. Steel tanks in 1-million-gallon capacity or smaller are the most common. However, steel tanks require more maintenance, cannot be buried, and are aesthetically less desirable than those of reinforced concrete. Reinforced concrete reservoirs can be fully or partially buried and last longer than other reservoirs; in addition, the top surface of these reservoirs can be designed to accommodate tennis courts, office buildings, or water-related control rooms.

Fire Protection

Campus fire protection is generally part of the domestic water distribution system. Fire flow requirements for each building within a campus include many factors, among which are the occupancy load, size of the building, construction materials, and usage. The state fire marshal or local fire department set fire flow requirements or fire protection measures for each building on the campus. Typically, fire flow requirements for campus facilities generally vary from 1,500 gallons per minute (gpm) to 3,500 gpm at 20 psi residual pressure.

On campuses that provide fire protection as part of their distribution system, the system should be designed to deliver the highest required fire flow and the maximum day water demand while maintaining a minimum of 20 psi residual pressure throughout the system at worst conditions.

50.3   OPERATIONS AND MAINTENANCE

Proper operation and maintenance of the water distribution system are the responsibilities of campus authorities, and trained personnel must be used to operate the system and deliver safe drinking water throughout the campus.

It is important for the campus to maintain an accurate record of repairs, water quality reports, backflow prevention programs, and modifications of the distribution system. An emergency plan and program must be drawn up in advance and implemented in response to a disaster. The location of valves and the type and size of underground pipelines should be accurately recorded and updated as necessary. Records of water pressure, water demand, and water production must be kept and maintained. Dead ends in the distribution system should be flushed on a regular basis. All mainline valves should be tested at least once every year and replaced with new ones when not working. When an addition to or a replacement of a section of a distribution system must be made, that section must be completely isolated from the remainder of the system; after repairs have been made, the section must be chlorinated and flushed thoroughly prior to putting it back in service.

Flushing the Distribution System

Flushing waterlines is an important part of the system operation. There is always some sediment in any water distribution system. Sources of these sediments include buildups in the reservoir, turbidity in the source, internal corrosion, and rusting of the metallic pipelines. If waterlines are not flushed at least once a year, these sediments may cause changes in water color and taste and odor problems, and may prevent chlorination in the distribution system. To properly flush a water distribution system, the velocity of the moving water in the pipeline must be 2.5 ft./sec. (scouring velocity) or higher. Therefore, the flushing outlet must be large enough to create that velocity.

Figure 50-3 provides a guideline for the size of the outlets required to have a velocity of approximately 2.5 ft./sec. for proper flushing.

As can be seen, to properly flush a distribution system, the flushing must be done through fire hydrants or blow-off valves that have large enough outlet nozzles to move the required volume of flow.

Figure 50-3
Size of Outlets Required for a Velocity of 2.5 ft./sec.

Pipe size (in.)	Flow rate (gpm)	Velocity (ft./sec.)
4	100	2.55
6	220	2.50
8	400	2.60
10	650	2.65
12	900	2.56

Emergency Planning

Disasters such as earthquakes, floods, fires, tornadoes, extreme weather conditions, threat of poisoning, and power outages are realities of life. If the operational staff is not prepared to take necessary action to mini-mize the effects of such disasters, these problems may cause a greater impact in terms of loss of life and property. Some of the most critical elements of a water distribution system during a disaster are storage, pumping, and the ability to deliver safe drinking water from alternative sources. Earthquake-related emergencies are often followed by fire and power outages. Therefore, if a distribution system relies heavily on pump-ing, a lack of electricity and a shortage of storage capacity could curtail or reduce the ability to fight a fire. It is very important to have either diesel or natural gas generators to run engines as a backup to electricity.

50.4 DISINFECTION

Most commonly, water is disinfected by chloramination or chlorination. Chloramine is a mixture of chlorine and ammonia. It reacts very slowly; however, it is quite effective. One of the advantages of chloramine is that it lasts longer in water, thus providing longer periods of disinfection. Chlo-rination is less expensive in comparison with other methods of disinfec-tion and is both effective and acceptable. Liquid or gaseous chlorine by itself is very poisonous and will cause serious injury if it comes in contact with skin. Most animals are killed in a short time at 0.1 percent volume of chlorine gas in air. Two cubic feet of pure chlorine are equivalent to 2,000 cu. ft. of chlorine at 0.1 percent concentration.

Chlorination is a process in which pathogenic bacteria are inacti-vated. Handling of pure chlorine in liquid or gas form requires many safety measures that make it nearly impossible to store pure chlorine on a campus. However, campuses using well water for drinking are re-quired to disinfect the water prior to delivering it into the distribution system. Sodium hypochlorite (laundry bleach) in a concentration of approximately 12 percent is an alternative to pure chlorine. Sodium hypochlorite can be stored in most places, and as long as it is not mixed with acid or any low pH chemical, it is not dangerous. Mixing sodium hypochlorite with low pH chemicals can release chlorine gas.

Water in a distribution system should have traces of chlorine residual at all times. The presence of chlorine in water is normally an indication that the water is free of pathogenic bacteria. A chlorine residual of 0.1 to 0.3 mg/L in water is common.

One of the concerns over the use of chlorine or chloramine in disinfect-ing water is the end user, such as people with kidney disease who have to use a hemodialysis machine (artificial kidney machine) several times a week.

This treatment may take place at a hospital or at home. Some of the chemicals used in the water treatment process, including both chlorine and chloramine, have a negative effect on the hemodialysis process. Campuses with hospitals must be aware of these patients, and hospitals must be informed when chlorination or chloramination is introduced to or removed from the treatment process.

50.5 FEDERAL LEGISLATION ON WATER QUALITY

Many of America's waterways that serve as drinking water sources have been polluted with toxins and other harmful industrial wastes. This led to the passage of the Clean Water Act and the Safe Drinking Water Act (SDWA) in 1974 to protect the environment and the quality of drinking water in the United States. These acts authorize the U.S. Environmental Protection Agency (EPA) to establish regulations and standards for all public waterways and water systems. The 1986 amendments to the SDWA increased the number of regulated contaminants. This number has since grown to nearly 100 and will likely continue to rise.

The EPA has developed water quality standards for water delivered by public water systems. "Public water system" means a system, regardless of type of ownership, for the provision of piped water to the public for domestic use, if such system has at least fifteen service connections or regularly serves an average of at least twenty-five individuals daily at least 60 days of the year. "Community water system" means a public water system that serves at least fifteen service connections used by yearlong residents or regularly serves at least twenty-five yearlong residents.[3]

The SDWA requires two types of standards: primary and secondary. Primary drinking water standards are those that regulate potential or adverse health affects. Secondary drinking water standards are those that regulate things affecting the aesthetic qualities of drinking water, such as taste, odor, color, and general appearance of the drinking water. Regulations for primary and secondary drinking water standards and maximum contaminant levels are established in the following sequence: interim primary drinking water regulations; revised national primary drinking water regulations; national secondary drinking water regulations; and periodic review, with updates of the regulations. All regulations proposed by the EPA are published in the *Federal Register* and promulgated following public hearings.

National Primary Drinking Water Regulations

The National Primary Drinking Water Regulations set the maximum contaminant levels for organic and inorganic chemicals. In the community water supply, the maximum level allowed for the inorganic chemical arsenic is

0.05 mg/L. The nitrogen (N) level should not exceed 10 mg/L. In the event that the nitrogen level exceeds 10 mg/L, local and state health authorities must be notified. Note that 1 mg/L nitrogen (N) equals 4.5 mg/L nitrate (NO_3). Nitrate is known to be harmful to pregnant women and infants under six months of age. Nitrate cannot be removed from the water by boiling. Reverse osmosis is one of the methods which effectively removes nitrate from water.

The maximum contaminant level for organic chemicals for community water (serving a population of 10,000 or more individuals) for the total trihalomethanes (THM) is set at 0.1 mg/L.

Turbidity   The turbidity in water is a measure of clarity of water that indicates the presence of solids and organic matter that do not settle out of water. In the past, turbidity was measured by projecting a candle flame to a depth of water until it disappeared. Turbidity is currently measured by a turbidimeter, which measures the interference to the passage of light through a sample of water. The light is measured in nephelometric turbidity units (NTU). Turbidity measurement plays an important role in the quality of water because the presence of solids and organic matter interfere with disinfection. Furthermore, these solids and organic matter may harbor pathogens. The maximum contaminant level for turbidity in drinking water, measured at the representative entry point(s) to the distribution system is one turbidity unit (TU), as determined by a monthly average. Five or fewer turbidity units may be allowed if the supplier of water can demonstrate to the state that the higher turbidity unit does not interfere with disinfection or maintenance of an effective disinfection throughout the distribution system and that it does not interfere with microbiological determination.

Total Coliforms   The public water system must collect coliform samples at regular time intervals throughout the month except in a system that uses only ground water and where that ground water is not under the influence of surface water. If any routine or repeat sample shows positive in total coliform, the system must determine whether fecal coliforms or *Escherichia coli* are present. In the event that a system is notified of a positive result, the state must be notified by the end of the day.

Total coliform monitoring frequency for community water systems is shown in Figure 50-4.

Lead and Copper Action Levels   The action level of lead should not exceed 0.015 mg/L in more than 10 percent of all tap water samples. Similarly, the action level of copper should not exceed 1.3 mg/L in more than 10 percent of all tap water samples.

Figure 50-4
Total Coliform Monitoring Frequency for Community Water Systems

Population Served	Minimum Number of Samples per Month
25 to 1,000	1
1,001 to 2,500	2
2,501 to 3,300	3
3,301 to 4,100	4
4,101 to 4,900	5
4,901 to 5,800	6
5,801 to 6,700	7
6,701 to 7,600	8
7,601 to 8,500	9
8,501 to 12,900	10
12,901 to 17,200	15
17,201 to 21,500	20
21,501 to 25,000	25
25,001 to 33,000	30
33,001 to 41,000	40
41,001 to 50,000	50

Source: Protection of Environment (40 CFR 141.21); revised as of July 1, 1995.

Maximum Contaminant Level Goals for Organic Contaminants The maximum contaminant level goals for organic contaminants are shown in Figure 50-5.

National Secondary Drinking Water Regulations

The most recent contaminant levels for the National Secondary Drinking Water Regulations as of July 1, 1995, are shown in Figure 50-6.

Fluoride The presence of fluoride in drinking water at moderate levels (0.5 mg/L to 1 mg/L) reduces dental cavities in children. However, increased levels of fluoride (greater than 2 mg/L) in children's drinking water may lead to the development of dental fluorosis, which causes pitting

Figure 50-5

Maximum Contaminant Level Goals (MCLG) for Organic Contaminants

Contaminant	MCLG (mg/L)
Benzene	0.0
Vinyl chloride	0.0
Carbon tetrachloride	0.0
1,2-Dichloroethane	0.0
Trichloroethylene	0.0
Acrylamide	0.0
Alachlor	0.0
Chlordane	0.0
Dibromochloropropane	0.0
1,2-Dichloropropane	0.0
Epichlorohydrin	0.0
Ethylene dibromide	0.0
Heptachlor	0.0
Heptachlor epoxide	0.0
Pentachlorophenol	0.0
Polychlorinated biphenyls (PCBs)	0.0
Tetrachloroethylene	0.0
Toxaphene	0.0
Benzo[a]pyrene	0.0
Dichloromethane (methylene chloride)	0.0
Di(2-ethylhexyl) phthalate	0.0
Hexachlorobenzene	0.0
2,3,7,8-TCDD (Dioxin)	0.0
1,1-Dichloroethylene	0.007
1,1,1-Trichloroethane	0.20
para-Dichlorobenzene	0.075
Aldicarb	0.001
Aldicarb sulfoxide	0.001
Aldicarb sulfone	0.001
Atrazine	0.003
Carbofuran	0.04
o-Dichlorobenzene	0.6

cis-1,2-Dichloroethylene	0.07
trans-1,2-Dichloroethylene	0.1
2,4-D	0.07
Ethylbenzene	0.7
Lindane	0.0002
Methoxychlor	0.04
Monochlorobenzene	0.1
Styrene	0.1
Toluene	1
2,4,5-TP	0.05
Xylenes (total)	10
Dalapon	0.2
Di(2-ethylhexyl)adipate	0.4
Dinoseb	0.007
Diquat	0.02
Endothall	0.1
Endrin	0.002
Glyphosate	0.7
Hexachlorocyclopentadiene	0.05
Oxamyl (Vydate)	0.2
Picloram	0.5
Simazine	0.004
1, 2, 4-Trichlorobenzene	0.07
1,1,2-Trichloroethane	0.003

Source: Protection of Environment (40 CFR 141.50); revised as of July 1, 1995.

and/or brown staining of the permanent teeth. The fluoride level in drinking water should not exceed 4 mg/L. Long-term exposure to a high concentration of fluoride can cause crippling skeletal fluorosis, which is a serious bone disorder.

Enforcement Responsibility

The EPA gives the individual states the primary enforcement responsibility for water quality. State and local governing agencies must adopt regulations that are at least as stringent as those set forth by the EPA, but their requirements may exceed those in the EPA's codes.

Figure 50-6

National Secondary Drinking Water Regulations
Maximum Contaminant Levels

Contaminant	Level
Aluminum	0.05–0.2 mg/L
Chloride	250 mg/L
Color	15 color units
Copper	1.0 mg/L
Corrosivity	Noncorrosive
Fluoride	2.0 mg/L
Foaming agents	0.5 mg/L
Iron	0.3 mg/L
Manganese	0.05 mg/L
Odor	3 threshold odor number
pH	6.5–8.5
Silver	0.1 mg/L
Sulfate	250 mg/L
Total dissolved solids	500 mg/L
Zinc	5 mg/L

Source: Protection of Environment. (40 CFR 143.3); revised as of July 1, 1995.

50.6 CROSS-CONNECTION

One of the major responsibilities of operating a safe drinking water distribution system is having an aggressive cross-connection control program on the campus.

Cross-connection is the potential for an undesirable substance or contaminant to enter the domestic water distribution system. Contaminants often enter the drinking water distribution system in an unexpected way. Nevertheless, it happens on a regular basis, and case histories are reported regularly by various water agencies. Three such case histories are presented in this chapter. These case histories were randomly selected from the EPA's *Cross-Connection Control Manual*.[6] Individual state public water supply agencies require public water systems to have an active cross-connection control program. State agencies usually have model plans available to guide water system managers in implementation of the cross-connection control program.

Case Histories

The following case histories are from the U.S. Environmental Protection Agency, Office of Water, *Cross Connection Control Manual,* June 1989.

Burned in the Shower

A resident of a small town in Alabama jumped in the shower at 5 am one morning in October 1986, and when he got out his body was covered with tiny blisters. "The more I rubbed it, the worse it got," the 60-year-old resident said. "It looked like someone took a blow torch and singed me." He and several other residents received medical treatment at the emergency room of the local hospital after the water system was contaminated with sodium hydroxide, a strong caustic solution.

Other residents claimed that, "It (the water) bubbled up and looked like Alka Seltzer. I stuck my hand under the faucet and some blisters came up." One neighbor's head was covered with blisters after she washed her hair and others complained of burned throats or mouths after drinking the water.

The incident began after an 8-in. water main that fed the town broke and was repaired. While repairing the water main, one workman suffered leg burns from a chemical in the water and required medical treatment. Measurements of the pH of the water were as high as 13 in some sections of the pipe. Investigation into the cause of the problem led to a possible source of the contamination from a nearby chemical company that distributes chemicals such as sodium hydroxide. The sodium hydroxide is brought to the plant in liquid form in bulk tanker trucks and is transferred to a holding tank and then pumped into 55-gallon drums. When the water main broke, a truck driver was adding the water from the bottom of the tank truck instead of the top, and sodium hydroxide back-siphoned into the water main (Figure 50-7).

Pesticide in Drinking Water

A pesticide contaminated a North Carolina water system in April 1986, prompting the town to warn residents of twenty-three households not to drink the water. The residents in the affected area were supplied drinking water from a tank truck parked in the parking lot of a downtown office building until the condition could be cleared up. Residents complained of foul smelling water but there were no reports of illness from ingesting the water that had been contaminated with a pesticide containing chlordane and heptachlor.

Authorities stated that the problem occurred when a water main broke at the same time that a pest control service was filling a pesticide truck

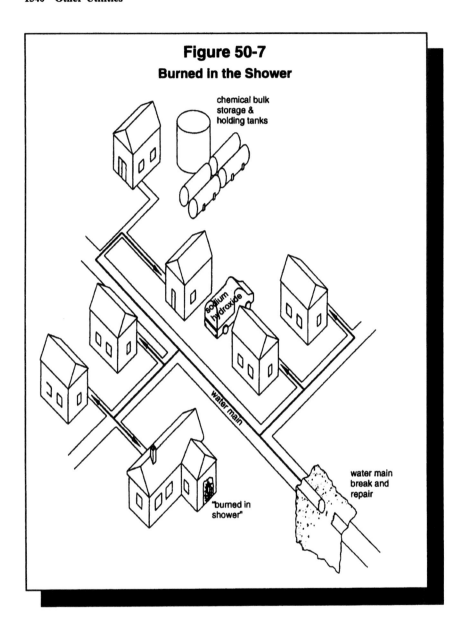

Figure 50-7

Burned in the Shower

with water. The reduction in pressure caused the pesticide from inside the tank to be sucked into the building's water main. The pesticide contaminated the potable water supply of the office building and neighborhood area (Figure 50-8).

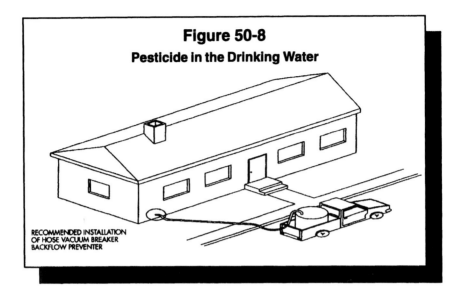

Figure 50-8

Pesticide in the Drinking Water

RECOMMENDED INSTALLATION
OF HOSE VACUUM BREAKER
BACKFLOW PREVENTER

Boiler Water Enters High School Drinking Water

A high school in New Mexico was closed for several days in June 1984 when a home economics teacher noticed the water in the potable system was yellow. City chemists determined that samples taken contained levels of chromium as high as 700 parts per million, "astronomically higher than the accepted levels of .05 parts per million."[6] The head chemist said that it was miraculous that no one was seriously injured or killed by the high levels of chromium. The chemical was identified as sodium dichromate, a toxic form of chromium used in heating system boilers to inhibit corrosion of the metal parts.

No students or faculty were known to have consumed any of the water; however, area physicians and hospitals advised that if anyone had consumed those high levels of chromium, the symptoms would be nausea, diarrhea, and burning of the mouth and throat. Fortunately, the home economics teacher who first saw the discolored water before school started immediately covered all water fountains with towels so that no one would drink the water.

Investigation disclosed that chromium used in the heating system boilers to inhibit corrosion of metal parts entered the potable water supply system as a result of backflow through leaking check valves on the boiler feed lines (Figure 50-9).

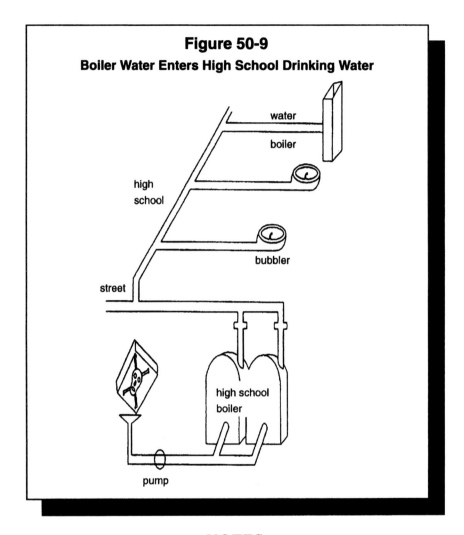

Figure 50-9

Boiler Water Enters High School Drinking Water

NOTES

1. Driscoll, Fletcher G. *Groundwater and Wells,* second edition. St. Paul, Minnesota: Johnson Filtration Systems Inc., 1986.
2. International Association of Plumbing and Mechanical Officials. *Uniform Plumbing Code,* 20th edition. Walnut, California: International Association of Plumbing and Mechanical Officials, 1994.
3. Protection of Environment (40 CFR 141.2); revised as of July 1, 1995.
4. Protection of Environment (40 CFR 143.3); revised as of July 1, 1995.
5. Protection of Environment (40 CFR 141.50); revised as of July 1, 1995.
6. U.S. Environmental Protection Agency, Office of Water. *Cross-Connection Control Manual.* June 1989.

CHAPTER 51

Sewer and Storm Drain Systems

Robert Charbonneau
University of California System

51.1 INTRODUCTION

Federal regulations promulgated by the Environmental Protection Agency (EPA) under the Clean Water Act apply to both wastewater and stormwater discharges to either sanitary or storm sewer systems, and to direct discharges to receiving water bodies such as rivers, lakes, bays, and the ocean. These regulations are implemented through the National Pollutant Discharge Elimination System (NPDES) wastewater permitting program. As of 1996, all but ten states and one territory had been delegated federal NPDES permitting authority by the EPA, so most states administer this regulatory program through their respective state water pollution control agencies. Regional EPA offices still directly administer the NPDES programs in Alaska, Arizona, Idaho, Louisiana, Maine, Massachusetts, New Hampshire, New Mexico, Oklahoma, and Texas, as well as the District of Columbia and Puerto Rico.

State and local regulatory agencies have the authority to promulgate additional wastewater and stormwater regulations as they see fit, as long as the regulations are not less stringent than the federal requirements. This chapter provides an overview of federal regulations. It is essential that each manager contact the local sanitary district or agency as well as the state water pollution permitting authority for comprehensive information on wastewater and stormwater regulations pertaining to his or her specific campus.

Federal wastewater regulations are broadly separated into two categories: those dealing with direct discharges and those dealing with indirect discharges. Direct discharges of sanitary sewage by campus-operated wastewater treatment plants into receiving water bodies are subject to effluent limitations and standards and must have NPDES wastewater permits. Indirect discharges of campus sewage into sanitary sewer systems that are ultimately treated off site at local wastewater treatment plants are governed by pretreatment standards and are often regulated by industrial wastewater discharge permits issued to campuses by the publicly owned treatment works. Most campuses are regulated as indirect dischargers and are therefore governed by pretreatment regulations.

There is an increasing trend toward heightened regulation and enforcement of all wastewater and stormwater discharges, especially at the state and local level. Complex state and federal hazardous waste disposal regulations will continue to restrict wastewater disposal practices in the future. Compliance with current and future wastewater and stormwater regulations will require closer cooperation, coordination, and communication between campus environmental resources and facilities management personnel.

51.2 FEDERAL WASTEWATER DISCHARGE REGULATIONS

Regulatory Background

Wastewater discharge into surface waters of the United States is regulated under the federal Water Pollution Control Act, as amended by the Clean Water Act of 1977. Wastewater regulations promulgated by the EPA under the Clean Water Act can be found in the Code of Federal Regulations (CFR), Title 40, Part 400 et seq. and in Title 40, Part 122 et seq. The CFR is revised constantly through daily issues of the *Federal Register.* A complete edition of the CFR is published annually that incorporates all the revisions of the previous year.

The Clean Water Act and its accompanying EPA regulations control direct point source wastewater discharges to surface waters as well as indirect discharges of all nondomestic sewage into publicly owned treatment works, commonly referred to as the local sewage or wastewater treatment plant.

Direct Point Source Dischargers

Direct point source dischargers must obtain and comply with the conditions of an NPDES permit, which is usually administered by state water pollution control agencies under authority delegated by the EPA (except for the twelve states and one territory listed earlier). A *point source* is defined as "a discernible, confined, and discrete conveyance, including but not limited to any pipe, ditch, channel, conduit, well. . . from which pollutants are or may be discharged" (40 CFR 122.2). Return flows from irrigated agriculture and agricultural stormwater runoff are excluded from the definition of point sources. In practical terms, point sources are discrete facility-oriented pipe outfalls.

Many states have their own water pollution control regulations with corresponding permitting requirements and wastewater effluent discharge limitations that are more stringent than federal NPDES requirements.

NPDES Permit Conditions Existing point sources, new point sources and new discharges, and nonprocess wastewater discharges (e.g., cooling towers) all have separate NPDES permit application requirements. Although the terms of NPDES permits vary depending on the type of discharger and the nature of the wastewater effluent, certain minimum standards are required of all permittees, as noted in Figure 51-1. The regulations set forth limited circumstances under which the NPDES permit may be modified, revoked and reissued, or terminated, as well as the conditions under which the permittee may be excused from a water quality violation caused by an unanticipated breakdown of any wastewater pretreatment equipment.

Figure 51-1
Minimum NPDES Permit Conditions and Requirements

1. Comply with all conditions of the permit, including effluent standards or prohibitions.
2. Take all reasonable steps to minimize or prevent any discharge in violation of the permit that has a reasonable likelihood of adversely affecting human health or the environment.
3. Properly maintain and operate all treatment facilities and systems.
4. Furnish the permitting authority with any information requested to determine whether to modify, revoke and reissue, or terminate the permit, or to determine compliance with the permit.
5. Allow the permitting authority or an authorized representative to enter and inspect the facilities, equipment, or operations; review any records; and sample or monitor at reasonable times any substances or parameters at any location.
6. Conduct representative compliance monitoring according to approved procedures and keep complete records for at least three years.
7. Submit periodic discharge monitoring reports and notify the permitting authority of specified physical alterations in the facility or its discharges.
8. Report any noncompliance that may endanger health or the environment within 24 hours of the time the permittee becomes aware of it.
9. Do not bypass or intentionally divert waste streams from any portion of the treatment facility except under specified circumstances.

Source: Clean Water Act (40 CFR 122.41); July 1, 1994.

Effluent Limitations and Standards   Certain categories of direct point source dischargers are subject to wastewater effluent limitations and standards requiring the application of various levels of pretreatment technologies. Federal regulations (40 CFR 405 et seq.) list a number of industrial categories subject to effluent limitations and standards (Figure 51-2). It is unlikely that any college or university would have one of these industrial operations that discharges wastewater directly into a receiving water body, making it subject to the effluent limitation regulations. If this does apply to a campus facility, the facilities manager should refer to the applicable 40 CFR section and part number for more details and should contact the appropriate state or federal NPDES permitting authority for additional information.

Effluent limitations are based in part on allowable chemical-specific concentrations. These standards are revised periodically, and the newer, more stringent chemical-specific standards are incorporated into the NPDES permit at the time the permit is revised and reissued. Generally local discharge limits are reviewed and updated every five years. In addition to the specific chemical limits, there is also increasing use of "whole effluent" testing that requires effluent to be tested using bioassays to determine if the composite effluent is toxic to aquatic life. Because of synergistic and other effects, an effluent may fail a whole effluent bioassay, even if it otherwise meets all chemical-specific limitations.

Indirect Dischargers

Most campuses discharge their wastewater into sanitary sewer systems that lead to publicly owned treatment works, rather than to campus-operated sewage treatment plants that discharge directly into surface waters. All "nondomestic" indirect dischargers into sanitary sewer systems must comply with EPA general pretreatment regulations as well as local pretreatment standards promulgated and enforced by local publicly owned treatment works.

Federal Pretreatment Standards   Pretreatment standards serve three basic functions for indirect discharges into sanitary sewer systems. First, the standards prevent the discharge of materials that could cause interference with the operation of the publicly owned treatment works. Second, they impose pretreatment standards for certain toxic pollutants associated with specific industrial categories (see Figure 51-2). Finally, the pretreatment standards require monitoring and reporting to ensure that industrial dischargers comply with the respective standards for toxic pollutants, and that all other indirect dischargers comply with any and all other effluent prohibitions, as deemed necessary by the local treatment works authority.

Figure 51-3 summarizes the general and specific effluent prohibitions applicable to all indirect dischargers into a publicly owned treatment

Figure 51-2

Industrial Categories Subject to Effluent Limitations and Standards

Industrial Category	40 CFR Part Number
Aluminum forming	467
Asbestos manufacturing	427
Battery manufacturing	461
Builders' paper and board mills	431
Carbon black manufacturing	458
Cement manufacturing	411
Coal mining	434
Coil coating	465
Copper forming	468
Dairy products processing	405
Electroplating	413
Electrical and electronics components	469
Explosives manufacturing	457
Feedlots	412
Ferroalloy manufacturing	424
Fertilizer manufacturing	418
Fruits and vegetables canned processing	407
Glass manufacturing	426
Grain mills	406
Gum and wood chemicals manufacturing	454
Hospitals	460
Ink formulating	447
Inorganic chemicals manufacturing	415
Iron and steel manufacturing	420
Leather tanning and finishing	425
Meat products processing	432
Metal finishing	433
Metal molding and casting	464
Mineral mining	436
Nonferrous metals forming	471
Nonferrous metals manufacturing	421
Oil and gas extraction	435
Organic chemicals, plastics, and synthetic fibers	414
Paint formulating	446
Paving and roofing materials (tars and asphalt)	443
Pesticide chemicals	455
Petroleum refining	419

(Figure continues)

Pharmaceutical manufacturing	439
Phosphate manufacturing	422
Photographic processing	459
Plastics molding and forming	463
Porcelain enameling	466
Pulp, paper, and paperboard	430
Rubber processing	428
Seafood canned processing	408
Soaps and detergents manufacturing	417
Steam electric power generating	423
Sugar processing	409
Timber products processing	429
Textile mills	410

works, regardless of any other pretreatment standards or requirements that may apply. These pretreatment requirements apply to all campus wastewaters. Most colleges and universities are not engaged in any of the industrial activities subject to categorical pretreatment standards (see Figure 51-2), which restrict the quantity, rate, or concentration of specific chemical, physical, or biological constituents of wastewater effluent. Effluent limitations are often based on conventional pollution control technologies and are monitored by compliance with performance standards.

Local Pretreatment Programs   The national pretreatment standards require most publicly owned treatment works to develop local pretreatment programs pursuant to federal guidelines. The local program must include wastewater influent limitations to prevent disruptions or interference with treatment processes, as well as a compliance program to enforce those limitations to ensure that the treatment works can meet its own wastewater discharge NPDES requirements. Publicly owned treatment works that are not required to develop their own pretreatment programs must still develop local pretreatment standards (influent limitations) if the treatment plant would otherwise have recurring problems.

Local pretreatment standards vary among publicly owned treatment works depending on the plant's capacity and condition and on any NPDES wastewater discharge limitations placed on the plant for it to meet local water quality standards. Managers should refer to the local sanitary district for specific information on applicable local requirements.

Publicly owned treatment works enforce both federal pretreatment standards and local pretreatment limitations through local ordinances.

Figure 51-3

General and Specific Pretreatment Requirements

I. General prohibitions

Dischargers shall not introduce into a publicly owned treatment works any pollutant(s) that, alone or in conjunction with a discharge or discharges from other sources, causes Interference or pass-through, defined as follows:

(1) Inhibits or disrupts the publicly owned treatment works, its treatment processes or operations, or its sludge processes, use, or disposal; and

(2) Therefore is a cause of a violation of any requirement of the publicly owned treatment works' NPDES permit (including an increase in the magnitude or duration of a violation) or of the prevention of sewage sludge use or disposal in compliance with all federal statutory provisions and regulations or permits issued thereunder (or more stringent state or local regulations) [Interference]; or

(3) Exits the publicly owned treatment works into waters of the United States in quantities or concentrations causing a violation of any requirement of the publicly owned treatment works's NPDES permit (including an increase in the magnitude or duration of a violation) [pass-through].

II. Specific prohibitions

In addition, the following pollutants shall not be introduced into a publicly owned treatment works:

(1) Pollutants that create a fire or explosion hazard;

(2) Pollutants that will cause corrosive structural damage to the publicly owned treatment works, but in no case discharges with pH lower than 5.0, unless the works is specifically designed to accommodate such discharges;

(3) Solid or viscous pollutants in amounts that will cause obstruction to the flow in the publicly owned treatment works resulting in Interference;

(4) Any pollutant, including oxygen-demanding pollutants (biochemical oxygen demand, etc.), released in a discharge at a flow rate and/or pollutant concentration that will cause Interference with the publicly owned treatment works;

(5) Heat in amounts that will inhibit biological activity in the publicly owned treatment works, resulting in Interference, but in no case heat in such quantities that the temperature at the publicly owned treatment works plant exceeds 40°C, unless alternative temperature limits are approved;

(6) Petroleum oil, nonbiodegradable cutting oil, or products of mineral oil origin in amounts that will cause interference or pass through;

(7) Pollutants that result in the presence of toxic gases, vapors, or fumes within the publicly owned treatment works in a quantity that may cause acute worker health and safety problems; and

(8) Any trucked or hauled pollutants, except at discharge points designated by the publicly owned treatment works.

Source: Clean Water Act (40 CFR 403.3 and 403.5); July 1, 1994.

The treatment works issues nondomestic dischargers an industrial wastewater discharge permit that contains specific limitations. These permits are required for all industrial dischargers subject to EPA categorical standards (see Figure 50-2). In addition, publicly owned treatment works may require permits from other dischargers who have the potential to interfere with the treatment plant's operation or who may cause the treatment works to violate its own NPDES permit. Dischargers deemed to be "significant" by the publicly owned treatment works may also require a wastewater discharge permit. Federal regulations (40 CFR 403.3) define "significant industrial users" as including all facilities that 1) discharge an average of 25,000 gallons per day (gpd) or more of process wastewater (this excludes sanitary sewage, noncontact cooling water, and boiler blowdown); 2) contribute process wastewater that makes up five percent or more of the treatment works' capacity; or 3) have a reasonable potential for violating any pretreatment standard or requirement.

Laboratory Wastewater Discharges

Many campuses have teaching, research, or clinical laboratories that discharge various wastewaters. Because of the presence of hazardous materials in these laboratories, wastewater disposal is regulated not only by pretreatment requirements, but also by federal and state hazardous waste regulations. The Resource Conservation and Recovery Act (RCRA), the main federal law governing hazardous waste, contains special provisions [40 CFR 261.3(a)(2)(iv)] for laboratory wastewaters that may contain certain specified hazardous wastes. These provisions exclude wastewater generated from laboratory operations from regulation as hazardous wastes only if a number of different conditions have been met. These conditions include limitations on wastewater chemical constituents and chemical concentrations. However, state and local hazardous waste regulations may not contain similar exemptions. Any wastewater discharges that may contain regulated hazardous wastes must be carefully evaluated in terms of all pretreatment requirements, as well as all applicable federal, state, and local hazardous waste regulations. In general, disposal of hazardous chemical constituents in wastewater is becoming more difficult and restricted.

Rate Determination Criteria

Federal regulations (40 CFR 35.2140) authorize local sanitary districts to charge sewage dischargers a user fee to cover operation and maintenance (including replacement) of sewer facilities. The user fee is structured to charge users for discharges of pollutants that increase the operational costs of effluent treatment and sludge disposal. User fees are based on actual use, ad valorem taxes (percentage rate), or a combination of both fee systems.

Generally, campuses fall under the actual use system, in which dischargers pay a proportionate share of operation and maintenance costs based on their contribution to the total wastewater loading from all users to the treatment plant.

In practical terms, a somewhat standard formula is used to determine large nonresidential discharger fees; these fees are based on sewage flow rates as well as the organic strength and total solids content of the sewage effluent. These factors are either added or multiplied together, depending on the manner in which charges are determined. The four common components of the formula are:

1. Sewage effluent volume
2. Biochemical oxygen demand (BOD) or chemical oxygen demand (COD)
3. Total suspended solids (TSS)
4. Dollar per pound treatment costs associated with both BOD or COD and TSS

The volume of sewage effluent discharged by a facility may be metered, estimated based on water supplied, or assigned an average value according to the facility's industry classification. Mass balance estimates of wastewater effluent based on metered water supplied to the facility must take into account water losses owing to irrigation, evaporation (swimming pools and cooling towers), and any other diversions from the sewer system. Similar to effluent volume calculations, BOD or COD concentrations (measures of effluent organic strength) and solids concentrations are seldom actually measured, but rather are estimated based on the discharger's industrial classification. There is usually some sort of appeals process that allows a discharger to conduct effluent sampling and submit actual water quality data if the discharger believes its pollutant concentrations are being overestimated by the standard formula.

The BOD or COD and TSS concentrations are multiplied by sewage volume to obtain mass loading estimates (in pounds) of these general pollutant measures. These mass loadings are then multiplied by a cost factor (dollars per pound) to estimate total costs for treatment based on effluent characteristics. Commonly, total estimated treatment costs (sum of costs for BOD or COD and TSS) for a facility's effluent are multiplied by (or added to) the facility's sewage volume to determine the discharger's sewage charges. For example:

Sewage $ Rate = Volume x [(BOD mass loading x $/lb. cost) + TSS mass loading x $/lb. cost)]

Future Regulations

Publicly owned treatment works must often update their wastewater ordinances and permit conditions in response to ever-changing federal, state, or local regulations. Stricter pretreatment requirements are often imposed on nondomestic wastewater dischargers to comply with the new regulations. The federal Clean Air Act and state air pollution control laws are becoming much more stringent, especially in the control of volatile organic compound (VOC) emissions. These new regulations will likely force publicly owned treatment works to further restrict the types and amounts of volatile compounds, such as solvents, that are permitted to be discharged to the sewer. It is also quite likely that hospitals will be subject to much more stringent pretreatment requirements within a few years.

Publicly owned treatment works' pretreatment requirements are also affected by regulations concerning the disposal of sewer sludge, or "biosolids." Federal regulations (40 CFR 503) passed in 1993 set numerical standards for certain metals that define "clean" sludge for the purposes of land application, surface disposal, and incineration. Future regulations will place further limits on toxic organics in sludge, ultimately resulting in more stringent pretreatment standards for these pollutants.

Enforcement

The Clean Water Act authorizes the EPA to impose administrative compliance orders, levy both administrative and civil fines of up to $25,000 per day, and bring civil actions against violators. There is an increasing trend of federal enforcement of pretreatment requirements against both publicly owned treatment works and individual nondomestic wastewater dischargers. The EPA has formally announced a policy of increased enforcement of treatment works' permit requirements, but the EPA will also consider taking action directly against individual facilities that consistently violate their wastewater pretreatment requirements.

State water pollution control agencies also conduct publicly owned treatment works inspections and compliance monitoring and have enforcement authority. The EPA will rarely take action if a state agency is taking enforcement action or if a large fine has already been levied by state or local authorities. State and local pretreatment requirements are often more stringent than federal standards. All this translates into increased public treatment works enforcement of pretreatment limitations on nondomestic wastewater dischargers. In situations where publicly owned treatment works can assess substantial fines for violations, there is a great monetary incentive for publicly owned treatment works to increase wastewater discharge permit compliance monitoring activity.

51.3 FEDERAL STORMWATER DISCHARGE REGULATIONS

Regulatory Background

The Water Quality Act of 1987 added Section 402(p) to the Clean Water Act, which required the EPA to establish phased NPDES permitting requirements for stormwater discharges associated with industrial activity and municipal storm sewer systems serving populations of 100,000 or more. This came about because all major wastewater dischargers have been regulated under NPDES since 1972, resulting in effective pollution control, whereas "nonpoint sources" of pollution remained unregulated and became the leading cause of water quality impairment in the United States. The EPA issued final rules on NPDES stormwater regulations in the *Federal Register* on November 16, 1990, and April 2, 1992, modifying 40 CFR parts 122, 123, and 124. States with authorized NPDES programs administer this permitting program, whereas the EPA directly administers the program in the ten unauthorized states and in Puerto Rico, and Washington, D.C.

Facilities and Construction Activity Permit Requirements

Phase I stormwater permitting regulations govern not only municipalities with populations of more than 100,000, but also eleven major categories of facilities. Figure 51-4 presents a list of the different industrial categories currently subject to federal regulations [40 CFR 122.26 (b)(14)]. Note that some categories are defined by Standard Industrial Classification (SIC) codes found in the *Standard Industrial Classification Manual* published by the federal Office of Management and Budget (OMB). Colleges and universities are listed under SIC code 8221, which is not specifically covered by any of the industrial facility categories. However, some authorized NPDES permitting states, such as California, have ruled that the permitting requirements extend to all auxiliary facilities defined in Figure 51-4, regardless of the primary SIC code of the owner or operator of the overall facility. This means that, in some states, if a college or university has any of the facilities listed in Figure 51-4, a stormwater discharge permit may be required for that particular facility. Common facilities that may require a permit include landfills, wastewater treatment plants, steam electric power generating facilities, bus maintenance facilities, and construction sites over five acres in size.

As a result of litigation, the EPA will be required to reevaluate two major exemptions from the Phase I stormwater permitting regulations. Both

Figure 51-4

Facilities Subject to Stormwater Permitting Regulations

Category (I): Facilities subject to stormwater effluent guidelines, new source performance standards, or toxic pollutant effluent standards under 40 CFR Subchapter N (this covers nearly all of the industries listed in Figure 50-2).

Category (II): Manufacturing facilities defined as Standard Industrial Classifications (SICs) 24 (except 2411 and 2434), 26 (except 265 and 267), 28 (except 283), 29, 311, 32 (except 323), 33, 3441, and 373.

Category (III): Oil and gas/mining facilities (SICs 10–14).

Category (IV): Hazardous waste treatment, storage, or disposal facilities operating under interim status or permit under Resource Conservation and Recovery Act (RCRA) Subtitle C.

Category (V): Landfills, land application sites, and open dumps that receive or have received any industrial wastes from facilities described in 40 CFR 122.26, including those subject to regulation under RCRA Subtitle D.

Category (VI): Recycling facilities, including metal scrapyards, battery reclaimers, salvage yards, and auto junkyards (SICs 5015 and 5093).

Category (VII): Steam electric power generating facilities.

Category (VIII): Transportation facilities with SICs 40, 41, 42 (except 4221–4225), 43, 44, 45, and 5171, which have vehicle maintenance shops, equipment cleaning operations, or airport deicing operations.

Category (IX): Sewage or wastewater treatment works used in the storage, treatment, recycling, and reclamation of municipal or domestic sewage, including land dedicated to the disposal of sewage sludge that are located within the confines of the facility, with a design flow of 1.0 million gallons per day or more, or required to have an approved pretreatment program under 40 CFR 403.

Category (X): Construction activity, including clearing, grading, and excavation activities resulting in the disturbance of five acres or more, or sites less than five acres if they are part of a larger common plan of development or sale.

Category (XI): Light manufacturing facilities where materials are exposed to stormwater as defined by SICs 20, 21, 22, 23, 2434, 25, 265, 267, 27, 283, 285, 30, 31 (except 311), 323, 34 (except 3441), 35, 36, 37 (except 373), 38, 39, and 4221–4225.

Source: Clean Water Act [40 CFR 122.26(b)(14)]; July 1, 1994.

exemptions—the five-acre size cutoff on construction activity and the requirement that light manufacturing facilities (Figure 51-4, Category XI) obtain a permit only if materials are actually exposed to stormwater—must be addressed in EPA's Phase II stormwater regulations. At this time, draft Phase II regulations are anticipated to be issued in 1997 with final regulations scheduled to be published in 1999. All construction sites and all light manufacturing facilities may be required to apply for stormwater permits in 2001, if the Phase II regulations mandate it.

Permitting Options

The EPA allows facilities covered under federal regulations to obtain permits in one of three different ways. First, the EPA or the authorized NPDES state can issue a general permit for stormwater discharges associated with industrial activity. This is the most common and simplest method and is typically satisfied by submitting a notice of intent to be covered by a general permit. Usually there is a separate general permit for construction activity. Some authorized states accept only this general permit option. Another option is to submit an individual or facility-specific permit application; this alternative is intended for special circumstances or facilities. Finally, a group application option is available for facilities with similar stormwater discharge characteristics, such as a number of different facilities with the same SIC code.

If a facility already has an NPDES permit for wastewater discharge, it is not necessary to obtain another permit if stormwater provisions are included in the original NPDES permit. Otherwise, a separate stormwater NPDES permit will likely be required. For most existing facilities, the permit application deadline was October 1, 1992. A stormwater permit is required prior to the start of construction for construction activity on sites that are five acres or more in size.

Permit Conditions

Under federal stormwater regulations, permitted facilities and construction sites are prohibited from discharging anything to the storm drain system except stormwater runoff. There is a list of exemptions, however, for discharges that are not feasible to eliminate. These include waterline/hydrant flushing, irrigation runoff, uncontaminated groundwater, runoff from washdowns and dust control, and dewatering runoff. The federal permits also require reporting the release of any hazardous substances or petroleum products pursuant to the reportable quantities set forth in 40 CFR 110-117-302. Permit conditions also include monitoring and record-keeping requirements, as well as the preparation of a site-specific stormwater pollution prevention plan.

The latest federal regulations (57 FR 11394; April 4, 1992) set forth minimum monitoring requirements for stormwater discharges, modifying 40 CFR 122.44; there is no federal requirement for actually sampling stormwater runoff. Facilities must conduct annual site inspections to identify areas that contribute to stormwater runoff and evaluate whether measures to reduce pollutant loadings, as identified in a stormwater pollution prevention plan, are adequate and properly implemented in accordance with the terms of the NPDES permit and the plan, or whether additional control measures are needed. Construction sites must be inspected once a week (or once a month in arid areas during the dry season) and within 24 hours after any rainfall greater than $1/2$ in. Specific areas of the site that must be inspected include disturbed areas, exposed building material storage areas, structural erosion controls, and vehicle entry/exit areas.

A stormwater pollution prevention plan (SWPPP) is required for all permitted sites. Requirements for the plan differ depending on whether the stormwater permit is issued for a facility or a construction site. For facilities, a SWPPP must contain a storm drainage system map, an inventory of exposed materials, a list of significant spills and leaks over the preceding three years, and an evaluation of all nonstormwater discharges to the storm drain system. Facility SWPPPs must also contain an evaluation and description of best management practices and other controls that will be implemented at the facility. Finally, an evaluation based on inspection records is included to determine the effectiveness of the SWPPP and to assess compliance with the permit conditions. Construction site SWPPPs must have a site description that identifies all potential sources of pollution, as well as a description of the nature and sequence of the construction activity. In addition, the SWPPP must include a description of and an implementation plan for erosion and sediment controls and other stormwater management practices. An inspection and maintenance program for construction site controls is also required.

The permit holder must keep facility inspection records for three years and certify that the facility is in compliance with the plan and NPDES permit. States with authorized NPDES programs will likely have more stringent monitoring requirements than these minimum federal requirements. In addition, local jurisdictions may promulgate any stormwater regulations that they choose, as long as they are not less stringent than any state or federal regulations. Colleges and universities located in municipalities with populations of more than 100,000 will likely be indirectly affected by stormwater regulations promulgated by local jurisdictions in response to their own new NPDES stormwater permits. State and EPA enforcement actions are focused on nonfilers at this time.

Best Management Practices

Control of stormwater runoff pollution is based on the selection and implementation of best management practices (BMPs). In general, BMPs are a practice or combination of practices determined to be the most effective and feasible means to prevent or reduce water quality degradation. BMPs must be determined on a site-specific basis. Selection of BMPs will depend on site operations, layout, materials and areas in contact with stormwater, cost, and industry standards.

BMPs fit into the following general categories: scheduling/timing of activities, elimination or prohibition of discharges or practices, operation and maintenance procedures, control measures, and pretreatment/treatment facilities. Nonstormwater discharges and cross-connections to the storm drain system must be identified and eliminated. After potential sources of stormwater pollution are identified in the SWPPP, options to eliminate or reduce the pollution sources should be evaluated. Training and education of personnel and modification of standard operating procedures should be considered when developing BMPs for the site. Structural modifications such as berming and pretreatment measures such as the installation of oil and grease traps are other examples of common BMPs. An outline of construction site erosion and sediment control principles is presented in Figure 51-5. These principles can be used as a conceptual guide for the selection of site-specific erosion and sediment controls. Many state water pollution control agencies have published handbooks that provide facility owners and site developers with specific guidance on selecting BMPs, as well as design criteria for various applications.

51.4 SEWER SYSTEM EVALUATION AND REHABILITATION

Sewer systems must be evaluated for financial planning (e.g., system operations budget as well as capital budgeting for improvements and replacement). As existing systems expand, the demands on infrastructure continue to grow, and the capacity and condition of facilities must be continually evaluated. Because sewer systems are designed for service lifetimes of 30 to 50 years or more, planning of these systems does not include replacement costs. Future expansion and development of campus facilities must take into account the cost of this replacement. Because of the high cost of increasing interceptor and collection system capacity, especially in fully developed areas, it is important that infiltration/inflow (I/I) be minimized and that the necessary investment be made over the lifetime of existing facilities to preserve the system's condition and capacity. Timely rehabilitation can extend the service lifetime of sewer systems and save campuses the

Figure 51-5

Erosion and Sediment Control Principles

1. Plan development to fit the site topography (soils, vegetation, waterways).
   - Limit the length and steepness of slopes; leave steep slopes undisturbed if possible.
   - Long, steep slopes should be broken by benching or terracing or through diversion devices.
   - Retain existing vegetation whenever possible.
2. Minimize amount and duration of exposed soils.
   - Phase approach to site development to minimize exposure.
   - Complete site grading as soon as possible.
   - Vegetation (temporary or permanent) with mulching should be in place before rains.
3. Apply soil erosion control practices for *source control.*
   - Protect exposed soils with vegetation and/or mulches.
   - Divert hill slope runoff away from steep or exposed areas.
   - Use grade control and stabilization structures to control surface water.
   - Source control is less difficult and less expensive than sediment control.
4. Apply sediment controls around perimeter to prevent off-site sedimentation.
   - Filter runoff as it moves through site.
   - Impound water to allow sediment to settle out.
5. Implement a comprehensive operations and maintenance program to maintain controls.
   - This is essential for effective erosion and sediment control.
   - Specify inspection, maintenance, and repair procedures and responsibilities.

large expenditures required to replace deteriorated sewers. This chapter provides only an overview of sewer system evaluation and rehabilitation (Figure 51-6). Much of this information was taken from the EPA's *Sewer System Infrastructure Analysis and Rehabilitation Handbook.* Readers should refer to the list of resources at the end of this chapter for more information.

Preliminary Analysis

A preliminary sewer system analysis should be performed first to quickly and easily determine if there are serious I/I problems and to evaluate the extent of these problems to select the approach for further analysis and investigation. For systems that have not been previously evaluated, the following occurrences indicate the need for a preliminary analysis:

- Greater than anticipated flows measured in the system or at Wastewater treatment plant (WWTP)
- Flooded basements during periods of intensive rainfall

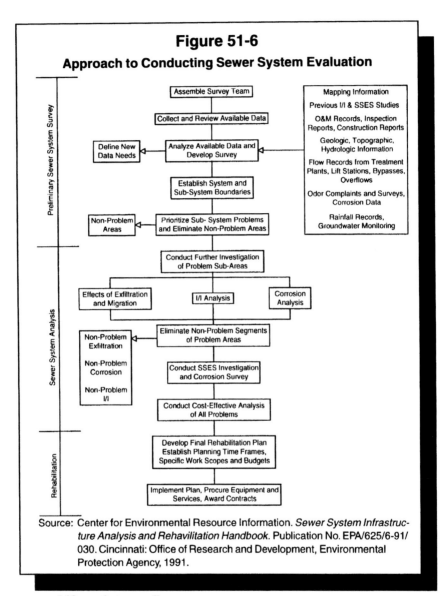

Figure 51-6

Approach to Conducting Sewer System Evaluation

Source: Center for Environmental Resource Information. *Sewer System Infrastructure Analysis and Rehavilitation Handbook.* Publication No. EPA/625/6-91/ 030. Cincinnati: Office of Research and Development, Environmental Protection Agency, 1991.

- Lift station overflows
- Sewer system overflows or bypasses
- Excessive power costs for pumping stations
- Overtaxing of lift station facilities, often resulting in frequent electric motor replacements
- Hydraulic overloading of facilities
- Excessive costs of sewage treatment, including meter charges levied by local sanitary district

- Aesthetic and water quality problems associated with bypassing of raw sewage
- Surcharging of manholes and eventual settlement or collapse
- Odor complaints
- Structural failure
- Corrosion

The scope of the preliminary sewer system analysis depends on the size of the system and the amount of information available. A flow diagram outlining the major steps included in a preliminary survey is presented as part of Figure 51-6. The survey can usually be conducted by campus engineering and maintenance personnel, rather than by outside consultants. The major purposes for conducting the survey are to identify, localize, and prioritize those areas of the sewer system subareas with the greatest potential problems and to scope out subsequent investigations. The preliminary survey is a forerunner to traditional I/I and sewer system evaluation survey (SSES) procedures and includes flow monitoring at critical junctions, limited physical surveys, preliminary corrosion surveys, and information to correlate flows with rainfall and groundwater information.

Infiltration and Inflow Analysis

Infiltration is extraneous groundwater flow that enters sewers and sewer connections through foundation drains, defective joints, broken or cracked pipes, deteriorated manholes, or faulty connections. *Inflow* is surface water that is discharged into existing sewer lines from such sources as roof leaders, sumps, floor and yard drains, and storm drains. I/I is the major deterrent to the successful performance of a wastewater conveyance and treatment system. I/I problems develop when infiltration and inflow become excessive, leading to sewer surcharging, overflows, and backups. Furthermore, I/I problems can lead to public health hazards, nuisance situations, and increased operations and maintenance costs. Control of I/I is an essential part of sewer system maintenance and an integral part of overall system rehabilitation. Preventive maintenance programs must be established to monitor and control excessive I/I.

I/I analysis is conducted according to a standard sequence of tasks, as outlined in Figure 51-7. If this analysis indicates that I/I is excessive, the next phase should be a full SSES that determines the specific locations of inflow, flow rates, and rehabilitation costs for each I/I source. The main goals of the I/I analysis report are as follows:

- To identify which sewers have reliable available data to determine whether excessive I/I exists

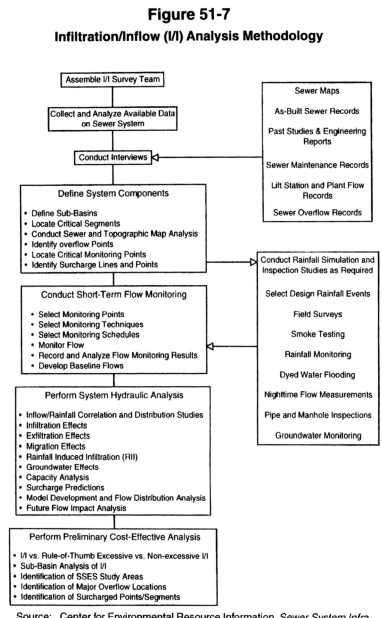

Figure 51-7
Infiltration/Inflow (I/I) Analysis Methodology

Assemble I/I Survey Team

Collect and Analyze Available Data on Sewer System

Conduct Interviews

Sewer Maps

As-Built Sewer Records

Past Studies & Engineering Reports

Sewer Maintenance Records

Lift Station and Plant Flow Records

Sewer Overflow Records

Define System Components

- Define Sub-Basins
- Locate Critical Segments
- Conduct Sewer and Topographic Map Analysis
- Identify overflow Points
- Locate Critical Monitoring Points
- Identify Surcharge Lines and Points

Conduct Short-Term Flow Monitoring

- Select Monitoring Points
- Select Monitoring Techniques
- Select Monitoring Schedules
- Monitor Flow
- Record and Analyze Flow Monitoring Results
- Develop Baseline Flows

Conduct Rainfall Simulation and Inspection Studies as Required

Select Design Rainfall Events

Field Surveys

Smoke Testing

Rainfall Monitoring

Dyed Water Flooding

Nighttime Flow Measurements

Pipe and Manhole Inspections

Groundwater Monitoring

Perform System Hydraulic Analysis

- Inflow/Rainfall Correlation and Distribution Studies
- Infiltration Effects
- Exfiltration Effects
- Migration Effects
- Rainfall Induced Infiltration (RII)
- Groundwater Effects
- Capacity Analysis
- Surcharge Predictions
- Model Development and Flow Distribution Analysis
- Future Flow Impact Analysis

Perform Preliminary Cost-Effective Analysis

- I/I vs. Rule-of-Thumb Excessive vs. Non-excessive I/I
- Sub-Basin Analysis of I/I
- Identification of SSES Study Areas
- Identification of Major Overflow Locations
- Identification of Surcharged Points/Segments

Source: Center for Environmental Resource Information. *Sewer System Infrastructure Analysis and Rehabilitation Handbook.* Publication No. EPA-625-6-91-030. Cincinnati: Office of Research and Development, Environmental Protection Agency, 1991.

- To generate sufficient flow data and to define system characteristics to enable sound engineering decisions regarding excessive
  flows
- To obtain realistic cost estimates for rehabilitation of sewers with
  excessive I/I
- To determine the scope of additional investigations needed for the
  SSES in excessive I/I areas

Sewer System Evaluation Survey

The purpose of the SSES is to quantify the amount of I/I, rainfall-induced
infiltration, and inflow that can be reduced and the cost of such reduction
on a source-by-source basis. The SSES confirms and refines the overall findings of the I/I analysis. The findings of the SSES should be sufficiently
specific to describe the corrective actions needed and to accurately account
for the amount of I/I, rainfall-induced infiltration, and inflow that will be
eliminated from each major sewer segment or source. The SSES must separately define the cost-effectiveness of infiltration and inflow removal. The
following tasks are usually included in the SSES:

- Survey planning and cost estimating
- Physical survey
- Rainfall simulation
- Preparatory cleaning
- Internal inspection
- Corrosion survey
- Report preparation and cost analysis

A flow diagram showing the overall approach for evaluating sewer
systems is shown in Figure 51-6. Figure 51-8 presents a diagram of the
methodology for conducting a SSES. The physical survey is performed to
isolate the obvious problem areas and to determine the general condition
of the sewer sections selected for further study. Rainfall simulation is conducted to locate the rainfall-associated I/I sources in the sewer lines and
may not be required, depending on the results of the I/I analysis report,
the smoke test, and the physical inspection. Preparatory cleaning of the
sewers is required prior to internal inspection. Debris in sewer inverts,
grease accumulation, and heavy root infestations not only obstruct visual or video inspection, but also may hide or mask actual infiltration
sources. Internal inspection locates the I/I sources, the flow rate from
each source, and the structural defects in the pipe. Inspections are conducted by closed-circuit television or regular cameras or by physical inspection. The corrosion survey identifies the most likely locations for
corrosion to occur and is followed up by visual inspection. Finally, the
survey report summarizes the results obtained during the survey, and

Figure 51-8

Sewer System Evaluation Survey (SSES) Methodology

Assemble SSES Team

Review I/I Report
and Results Study

Develop Specific SSES Study Plan

- Develop Project Study Scope, Budget, and Schedule
- Identify Sub-Basins and Analyze to Minimize Migration Effects
- Develop Physical Survey and Inspection Plan Budget
- Develop Cleaning Plan and Budget
- Develop Physical Survey Plan and Budget
- Select Internal Inspection Methodology
- Identify Need for Rainfall Simulation and Additional Flow Monitoring

Conduct Physical Survey

- Conduct Aboveground Inspections
- Verify Adequacy of I/I Monitoring
- Select Flow Monitoring Equipment
- Conduct Manhole Inspections
- Conduct Rainfall Simulation, If Required
- Conduct Flow Monitoring Studies

Conduct Corrosion Survey

- Collect Data
- Visual Inspection

Conduct Sewer
Cleaning Program

Conduct Internal Inspection

- T.V. Inspection
- Photographic Inspection
- Physical Inspection (large Sewer)

Conduct Cost-Effectiveness Analysis of I/I
by Sub-System and for Total Study Area

- Develop Costs for Infiltration as a Function of Infiltration Removed
- Array Costs and Develop Cumulative Cost vs. Infiltration Removed Curve
- Develop Cost for Transportation and Treatment
- Develop Total Cumulative Rehabilitation, Transport, and Treatment Costs and Choose Optimum Point
- Develop Costs for Inflow as a Function of Inflow Removed
- Array Costs and Develop Cumulative Cost vs. Inflow Removed Curve
- Develop Cost for Transport and Treatment
- Develop Total Cumulative Rehabilitation plus Transport and Treatment Cost and Choose Optimum Point

Summarize All Recommended
Rehabilitation Activities

Source: Center for Environmental Resource Information. *Sewer System Infra-structure Analysis and Rehabilitation Handbook.* Publication No. EPA-625-91-030. Cincinnati: Office of Research and Development, Environmental Protection Agency, 1991.

presents a cost-effectiveness analysis of the I/I sources that can be economically corrected.

The SSES cost-effectiveness analysis provides a detailed and thorough analysis of the sewer system, including the I/I flow rates from each source and the best method for rehabilitation of each source. For an effective cost analysis, the cost of correction for infiltration, inflow, rainfall-induced infiltration, and groundwater migration must be considered. Subarea SSES analysis, including migration effects, is an improved approach to the traditional point source method for evaluating sewer systems. Flow adjustments for infiltration should be performed before the cost-effectiveness analysis is conducted. Costs for rehabilitation should be based on the actual physical conditions observed. Costs for infiltration and inflow correction must be separately estimated.

Sewer System Rehabilitation

Many different methods of sewer system rehabilitation are currently available. This section provides a general description of these methods. Readers should refer to the resources at the end of this chapter for more information. The following methods are most commonly used:

- Excavation and replacement
- Chemical grouting
- Sliplining (also known as insertion)
- Fold-and-formed process
- Inversion lining
- Specialty concrete
- Liners
- Coatings

Some techniques for rehabilitating manholes and service laterals will also be described.

Excavation and Replacement

This standard practice is currently used less often owing to the widespread use of trenchless technologies. Excavation and replacement of defective piping are usually necessary under the following conditions:

- Structural integrity of the pipe has deteriorated severely (e.g., pieces of pipe are missing, crushed, or collapsed or pipe has large longitudinal cracks).
- Pipe is significantly misaligned.
- Additional pipeline capacity is needed.
- Trenchless rehabilitation methods would produce an unacceptable reduction in capacity.

- Point repair is needed for short lengths of pipeline that are too seriously damaged to be effectively rehabilitated by any other methods.
- Entire reaches of pipeline are too seriously damaged to be rehabilitated.
- Removal and replacement are more cost-effective than other methods.

Disadvantages of pipeline removal and replacement include high costs, disruption of traffic and access to buildings, and threat of damage or interruption of other underground utilities.

Pipeline replacement can be done in either of two general ways. Excavation and replacement can be done in the same alignment as the former pipeline, or the existing pipeline can be abandoned in place and the new pipeline placed in a parallel alignment. The parallel alignment can be either immediately adjacent to the existing line or parallel to it along a different route. Pipeline replacement materials include reinforced concrete, clay, ductile iron, and a variety of plastics.

Problems unique to removal and replacement projects along existing alignments include the following:

- Maintaining tributary systems, service flows, or both during construction
- Removal and disposal of old pipes
- Filling up abandoned pipes with structurally sound material to prevent collapse
- Working around utilities overlying or closely parallel to the pipeline

The following universal problems occur both in removal and replacement as well as in new construction along a new alignment:

- Disruption of surface street traffic
- Disruption of access to buildings and properties
- Temporary loss of on-street parking
- Trench shoring requirements
- Dewatering excavations in areas of high groundwater
- Uncharted live and abandoned in-place utilities

Chemical Grouting

Grouting is a joint sealing technique used on joints that fail the initial leakage test. It is normally used to control groundwater infiltration in unpressurized pipelines where infiltration is caused by leaking pipe joints or circumferential cracking of pipe walls. The most common chemical grouts currently available are acrylamide gel, acrylic gel, urethane gel, and polyurethane foam.

Chemical grouting of sewer lines is used mainly to seal leaking joints and circumferential cracks, although small holes and radial cracks can also be sealed. Grouts can be applied to pipeline joints, manhole walls, wet wells in pump stations, and other leaking structures using special tools and techniques. All chemical grouts are applied under pressure after appropriate cleaning and testing of the joint.

Prior to selection of chemical grouting for joint rehabilitation, the pipeline should be inspected to determine pregrouting cleaning needs and the extent of root intrusion. For effective grouting, the pipeline must be relatively clear of sand, sediment, and other deposits. Cleaning should be performed immediately prior to grouting. Crushed or broken pipeline sections should also be identified for replacement. Deformed or longitudinally cracked pipe sections should not be grouted.

Chemical grouting can be used on precast concrete brick, vitrified clay pipe, and other pipe materials to fill voids in backfill outside the sewer line wall. Backfill voids can reduce lateral support of the pipe wall, resulting in rapid deterioration of structural integrity. Chemical grouting adds no external structural properties to the pipe where joints or circumferential cracking problems are due to ongoing settlement or shifting of the pipeline. It is not effective in sealing longitudinal cracks or joints where the pipe near the joint is longitudinally cracked. Chemical grouting does not improve the structural strength of the pipeline and therefore should not be used when the pipe is severely cracked, crushed, or broken. Chemical grouts may also dehydrate and shrink if the groundwater drops below the pipeline and the moisture content of surrounding soil is significantly reduced. Large joints and cracks may be difficult to seal because of the large quantity of grout required. Large cracks, badly offset joints, and misaligned pipes may not be sealable.

Sliplining

Sliplining is used to rehabilitate pipelines that have severe structural problems. It can be used in lines with extensive cracks, lines located in unstable soils or deteriorated pipes in corrosive environments, pipes with massive and destructive root intrusion problems, and pipes with relatively flat grades. One of the advantages of sliplining is that it requires minimal excavation of an access pit, which limits traffic disruption and minimizes interference with surface structures and other underground utilities. Sliplining can also be used to avoid extensive dewatering and in pipelines having moderate horizontal or vertical deflection or severe corrosion. In addition, for most sliplining projects it is not necessary to eliminate the entire flow within the existing pipeline, as the rapid insertion process can often be completed during periods of low flow. On the other hand, sliplining may reduce pipe capacity and requires removal of all internal obstructions. It is less applicable in pipelines with numerous curves or bends because multiple access pits would be required.

The most popular materials used to slipline sewer pipes are polyolefins, fiberglass-reinforced polyesters (FRPs), reinforced thermosetting resins (RTRs), polyvinyl chloride (PVC), and ductile iron (cement-lined or polyvinyl-lined). Polyethylene is the most common polyolefin material used and is available in low, medium, and high density. High-density polyethylene compounds are best suited for rehabilitation applications because they are hard, strong, tough, and corrosion resistant and have good stiffness. Polybutylene is similar to medium-density polyethylene pipe in stiffness and chemical resistance but has better continued stress loading characteristics and good temperature resistance as well. FRP pipe is frequently specified as an acceptable alternative to polyethylene because it has good chemical and corrosion resistance and is suitable for use over a wide pH range. RTR pipe has high strength and elasticity and good corrosion, erosion, and abrasion resistance. Flexible PVC is highly resistant to acidic corrosion and is very smooth, exhibiting good hydraulics. Grouting of the annular space is required to give strength to the PVC pipe.

Prior to sliplining, sewer lines must be thoroughly cleaned and inspected to identify all obstructions such as displaced joints, crushed pipes, and protruding service laterals. Television inspection should also locate all service connections that will need to be connected to the new liner pipe. It may be necessary to proof-test the existing pipe by pulling a short piece of liner through a segment. Sliplining is performed by either a push or pull technique. Once the liner has been inserted, it is grouted in place. Grouting at manhole connections is required, but grouting of the entire length of pipe is not needed if the liner is strong enough to support loads in the event of collapse of the original pipe. This is determined after evaluating the severity of structural deterioration and anticipated hydrostatic and structural loadings.

Fold-and-Formed Process

This method, in use since about 1988, can be considered as an improved version of sliplining. The process uses a folded thermoplastic (polyethylene or PVC) pipe that is pulled into place and then rounded to conform to the internal diameter of the existing pipe. Excavation is not required for installation when there are existing manhole access points, and lateral reopening is done internally. The finished pipe has no joints and fits moderately tightly against the existing pipe wall. The plastic piping has excellent corrosion resistance. This method is less versatile than inversion lining in terms of pipe diameter range and installation lengths, and only slight offsets and bends can be negotiated.

There are currently two fold-and-formed processes commercially available in the United States: U-Liner and NuPipe. The U-Liner technology uses a high-density polyethylene resin U-shaped pipe wound onto spools ready for installation. After cleaning and television inspection and analysis to identify defects and determine the applicability of this method, a preengineered seamless coil of precut pipe is winched into place. The pipe is pulled off a spool at ambient temperature, fed through an existing manhole, and winched through the existing pipe to the terminal point. Once the pipe is in place, steam is fed through the inside of the folded pipe, softening the plastic to allow for reforming inside the existing pipe. After the plastic has been heated, pressure is used to reround the pipe. Sufficient time must be allowed for the system to stabilize before the end treatment is finished and the laterals are reopened utilizing a remote-controlled cutter head.

The NuPipe product is made of PVC and extruded in a folded shape onto spools while still pliable. Installation includes cleaning of existing pipe along with a television inspection to determine the extent of deterioration and to verify the applicability of this method. A flexible reinforced liner called a heat containment tube (HCT) is inserted into the existing pipeline to provide a closed environment for installation and processing. After the HCT has been strung through the existing pipeline, the folded PVC is heated while on a spool and is pulled through the pipeline. Once the NuPipe has reached the termination point, steam is introduced both through the interior and around the exterior of the folded pipe. After the PVC becomes pliable, a rounding device is introduced into one end of the pipe and propelled through the folded pipe, moving standing water out while expanding the plastic tightly against the existing pipe wall, creating a mechanical lock at the joints and laterals. Cold water is then injected into the NuPipe to solidify the plastic.

Inversion Lining

The pliable nature of the resin-saturated tubing used in inversion lining allows it to be installed around curves and maneuvered through pipe defects. Inversion lining is successful in dealing with a number of structural problems, particularly in sewers requiring minor structural reinforcement. However, caution must be used in applying this method to pipelines with major loss of sidewall. Inversion lining can be done relatively quickly and does not require excavation, making it especially suitable for repairing pipelines around structures, in congested areas, and in areas where traffic disruption must be minimized. It can be used in noncircular pipes and pipes with irregular cross-sections. This method is also effective in correcting minor corrosion problems and can be used to bridge gaps and misaligned joints. The new lining has no joints or seams and has a smooth interior surface, which may actually improve flow capacity despite slightly decreasing pipe diameter.

Inversion lining is formed by inserting a resin-impregnated fabric tube (turned inside out) into the existing pipeline and inverting it as it progresses inside the pipeline. It is then cured in place through the use of heated water or steam. Prior to installation of the liner, the pipeline section must be cleaned to remove loose debris, roots, protruding service connections, and excessive solids. The pipeline segment must be isolated from the system and requires bypassing of flows during installation of the inversion lining. The liner is usually inserted via existing manholes. After the lining system has been installed and cured, a special cutting device is used with a closed-circuit television camera to reopen service connections identified prior to installation.

Two resin types (polyester and epoxy) are widely used in this method of pipe rehabilitation. Both are liquid thermosetting resins that have excellent resistance to domestic wastewater. Chemical resistance tests should be performed for applications other than domestic sewage. Vinyl ester resins can be used if superior corrosion resistance is required at higher temperatures. There are currently three cured-in-place processes in use in the United States: Insituform, the most widely used process; Paltem (Pipeline Automatic Lining System); and KM Inliner.

Specialty Concrete

Specialty concretes containing sulfate resistant additives are used to reinforce weakened concrete pipes and manhole structures through application of an acid-resistant coating over the original surface. Specialty cements can resist attack by many substances, including mineral salts, mild solutions of organic and mineral acids, sugar solutions, fats, and oils. Applicability of this method depends on the degree of corrosion-related deterioration and the structural integrity of the sewer. Thin film specialty concrete is applicable to mildly deteriorated pipes or manholes, whereas an elastic membrane concrete system is more versatile. After curing, the specialty concrete bonds firmly to the original surface. The new acid-resistant layer extends the service life of the pipe or manhole.

Specialty concretes are available in three types: cement mortar, gunite (shotcrete), and cast concrete. All these techniques require prior sewer cleaning to remove oils and greases, foreign objects, and loose materials. Wastewater must be bypassed during application and initial curing. Mortar lining is applied using a centrifugal lining machine and is a successful rehabilitation technique for sewer lines, manholes, and other structures. Reinforcement can also be added to the mortar with a reinforcing spiral-wound rod that is inserted into the mortar, with a second coat applied over it. Gunite, or shotcrete, is a low-moisture, high-density mixture of fine aggregate, cement, and water. It is used on man-entry-size (32-in.) or bigger sewers and on manholes. Gunite bonding with the original surface is usually stronger than the base material itself, with better adhesion on more deteriorated and irregular piping. The gunite is applied under pressure by a self-propelled, operator-controlled lining machine after reinforcing steel is set into place. Cast concrete is silicate-bonded, poured, or cast-in-place structural concrete with about half the density or strength of gunite. It is poured over prefabricated or hand-built interior pipe forms that can be removed and reused. Reinforcing steel is added prior to application.

Liners

Rehabilitation techniques using liners entail the installation of segmented prefabricated panels or flexible sheets inside man-entry-size sewers. They are fixed in place either with anchor bolts or concrete-penetrating nails. Although the liner materials are relatively inexpensive, labor costs for installation may prove to be prohibitively expensive. Liner failure can occur if leaking joints allow hydrogen sulfide gas or sulfuric acid to penetrate the liner materials and attack the underlying concrete substrate. Surface preparation and prolonged wastewater bypass are required prior and during installation.

Liner materials include PVC, polyethylene, or segmented fiberglass-reinforced plastic or cement. The PVC liners are acid resistant, have better hydraulic characteristics than concrete, and form an effective barrier to gaseous penetration. Polyethylene liners are similar to PVC but are made of polyethylene resins that are tough, rigid, acid resistant, smooth, and inexpensive. Polyethylene is not recommended in areas of turbulent flow, as cracks may develop. Fiberglass-reinforced plastic liners are acid resistant and have high mechanical and impact strength and good abrasion resistance. None of these liners provide any structural support, but they do provide an adequate corrosive barrier and smooth interior surface for structurally sound sewers. These liners have little absorption ability and no apparent permeability.

Fiberglass-reinforced cement liners have high mechanical and impact strength and good acid and alkaline resistance. They are also highly resistant to abrasion, with negligible absorption and permeability. These liners are not designed to support earth loads and should be used only in structurally sound sewers. They can be easily assembled to fit variations in grades, slopes, and cross-sections and provide a smooth surface that improves hydraulics. Segmented plastic and fiberglass-reinforced cement liners are installed so that they overlap at the joints. Space is left between the existing surface and the liners for grouting purposes. Joints are coated with an adhesive to better connect the panels and are sealed with an acid-resistant resin. After all the panels are set into place, the entire section is cement pressure grouted to prevent sagging and deformation.

Coatings

Coatings are used to form an acid-resistant layer that protects concrete surfaces from corrosion. They can be quickly and economically applied, especially to uneven surfaces. Coatings are applicable only to man-entry-size sewers and manholes and may exhibit poor bonding to vertical or overhead surfaces. It is recommended that new coatings be field tested prior to use because of problems with these products in the past. The coatings include a variety of proprietary materials, including coal tar epoxy, concrete sealants, epoxy, polyester, silicone, urethane, and vinyl ester that can be applied by spray machines or brushed onto concrete surfaces.

Surface cleaning, preparation, and repairs as well as wastewater bypassing are required prior to application. Concrete surfaces must be allowed to dry before the coating is applied and must be allowed to cure before removing the bypass. High-pressure spraying is excellent for coating uneven surfaces and is much faster than brush application for some products.

Manhole Rehabilitation Techniques

Sewer manholes may require rehabilitation to prevent surface water inflow or groundwater infiltration, repair structural damage, or protect surfaces from corrosion. Manhole replacement should be considered if rehabilitation is not cost-effective. When selecting a rehabilitation method, the manager should consider the following factors: nature of the problems, physical characteristics of the manhole structure, location, condition, and the age and type of original construction. Manhole rehabilitation methods focus on either the frame and cover, or the sidewall and base.

Manhole frame and cover rehabilitation prevents surface runoff from flowing into the manhole through holes in the cover lid, into the annular space around the lid and framed cover, or under the frame if it is improperly sealed. Techniques to rehabilitate manhole frames and covers include the following:

- Installation of stainless steel bolts with caulking compound and neoprene washers or corks to plug holes in the cover. This is simple to perform but restricts natural venting.
- Installation of a prefabricated lid insert between the frame and cover to prevent water, sand, and grit from entering the manhole. Plastic lids are resistant to corrosion and damage by sulfuric acid and road oils and come with gas relief and vacuum relief valves to allow gas escape. The lids are easy to install and can fit any manhole, but require perfect fit and periodic maintenance to function properly.
- Installation of resin-based joint sealing tape between the metal frame and cover to seal imperfectly fitting surfaces and provide flexibility for shifting ground. Sealing tapes can be used on all types of manholes.

- Application of hydraulic cement and waterproofing epoxy to seal cracks and openings on manhole frames. This is a labor-intensive method, and the freeze-thaw cycle may reduce patch life.
- Raising manhole frames to minimize flows through the frame covers in areas outside of street right-of-ways.

Manhole sidewall and base rehabilitation is done primarily to prevent infiltration of groundwater. Casting or patching can be used to rehabilitate structurally sound sidewalls. Complete replacement should be done if manholes and bases are severely deteriorated. Techniques for manhole sidewall and base rehabilitation are as follows:

- Application of waterproof and corrosion-resistant epoxy, acrylic, or polyurethane-based coatings to interior manhole walls. These can be applied by towel brush or sprayer to brick, block, or precast concrete manholes and bases. Prior to coating application, manhole wall surfaces should be clean and dry and all leaks plugged using patching or grouting materials. The manhole must be structurally sound.
- Application of chemical grout from the interior walls to the exterior walls to stop infiltration through cracks and holes. This is an inexpensive method but has a short service life.
- Insertion of fiberglass-reinforced polyester structural liners inside manholes to provide structural restoration. This has a longer service life than coatings, but installation may be costly.
- Insertion of preformed polyethylene liners that are grouted in place. These require removal of the manhole cone or top for insertions.

Service Lateral Rehabilitation Techniques

Service laterals connect buildings to main sewer lines and can be a significant source of infiltration through defects such as cracked, broken, or open-jointed pipes. Service connections may also carry water from inflow sources such as roof and foundation drains, basement sump pumps and floor drains, and various stormwater runoff sources. The most common rehabilitation methods for service laterals are chemical grouting and inversion lining.

The following three chemical grouting methods are commonly utilized: Pump Full, Sewer Sausage, and Camera-Packer. In the Pump Full method, chemical grout is injected through a conventional sealing packer from the sewer main into the service connection to be grouted. The forced grout surrounds the pipe, and a seal is formed after the gel has set. Excessive grout is augured from the building connection, and the lateral is returned to service after the sealing has been accomplished. The Sewer Sausage method is similar to the Pump Full method, except that a tube is inverted into the service connection before sealing to reduce the quantity of grout used and to minimize the amount of cleaning required after completion of the sealing. The Camera-Packer method uses a miniature television camera in conjunction with a specialized sealing packer that is pulled through the lateral, repairing faults viewed through the camera. The service connection can be returned to service after the repairs are completed.

Inversion lining is similar to main sewer installation and involves the insertion of a resin-impregnated flexible polyester felt liner into the service lateral. No annular space is created between the liner and the existing pipe that could result in infiltration migration. No prior excavations are required to repair slight offsets. An access point is needed on the upstream side of the service connection line. A variation from regular sewer main installation is the use of a special pressure chamber to provide the pressure needed to invert the fabric liner through the service lateral. After completion of the curing process, the downstream end of the liner is cut manually or with a remote-controlled cutting device placed in the sewer main. The upstream end is trimmed at the access point prior to restoration of the service connection.

ADDITIONAL RESOURCES

American Consulting Services, Inc. *Sewer System Evaluation for Infiltration/Inflow.* Paper prepared for Technology Transfer Program, Environmental Protection Agency. Minneapolis: American Consulting Services, Inc., 1973.

American Public Works Association. *Control of Infiltration and Inflow into Sewer Systems.* Publication No. 11022 EFF 12/70; NTIS Publication No. PB200827. Washington, D.C.: Water Quality Office, Environmental Protection Agency, and Thirty-nine Local Government Jurisdictions, 1970.

American Public Works Association. *Prevention and Correction of Excessive Infiltration and Inflow into Sewer Systems—Manual of Practice.* NTIS publication No. PB-203208. Washington, D.C.: Water Quality Office, Environmental Protection Agency, and Thirty-nine Local Government Jurisdictions, 1971.

American Public Works Association. *Sewer System Evaluation, Rehabilitation, and New Construction—A Manual of Practice.* Publication No. EPA/600/2-77/017d. NTIS Publication No. PB-279248. Cincinnati: Municipal Environmental Research Laboratory, Office of Research and Development, Environmental Protection Agency, December 1977.

Brown and Caldwell, Inc. *Utility Infrastructure Rehabilitation.* HUD Report No. HUD-0004113. Washington, D.C.: Department of Housing and Urban Development, 1984.

California Best Management Practice Handbooks, Volumes 1–3. Prepared by Camp Dresser and McKee et al. for the Stormwater Quality Task Force, March 1993.

Carter, William C., A. J. Hollenbeck, and R. J. Nogaj. "Cost Effectiveness and Sewer Rehabilitation." *Public Works*, Vol. 17, 1986, pp. 64–67.

Center for Environmental Research Information. *Sewer System Infrastructure Analysis and Rehabilitation Handbook*. Publication No. EPA/625/6-91/ 030. Cincinnati: Office of Research and Development, Environmental Protection Agency, 1991.

Center for Environmental Research Information, Office of Research and Development. *Odor and Corrosion Control in Sanitary Sewerage System and Treatment Plants*. Publication No. EPA/625/1-85/018. Cincinnati: Environmental Protection Agency, 1985.

Collection Systems Digest (compendium of articles published in *Water Environment & Technology* or presented at WEF annual conference). Publication No. P0036GA. Alexandria, Virginia: Water Environment Federation, 1993.

Collection Systems Operation and Maintenance. Publication No. TT044GA. Proceedings of Water Environment Federation Conference, Tucson, Arizona, June 1993. Alexandria, Virginia: Water Environment Federation, 1993.

Collection Systems Symposia. Publication No. C2006GA. Proceedings from 65th Annual WEF Conference in New Orleans, Louisiana, September 1992. Alexandria, Virginia: Water Environment Federation, 1992.

Darnell, Paul E. "Conducting Sewer System Evaluations for Small Systems." *Water & Sewage Works*, Vol. 123, 1976, pp. 68–71.

"Deciding to Rehabilitate, Repair, or Replace." *Water Engineering & Management*, Vol. 132, 1985, pp. 50–53. Condensed from Brown and Caldwell, Inc. "Deciding to Rehabilitate, Repair, or Replace." *Utility Infrastructure Rehabilitation*. Washington, D.C.: Department of Housing and Urban Development, 1985.

"Evaluating Utility System Conditions." *Water Engineering & Management*, Vol. 132, 1985, pp. 43–49. Condensed from Brown and Caldwell, Inc. "Evaluating Utility System Conditions." In *Utility Infrastructure Rehabilitation*. Washington, D.C.: Department of Housing and Urban Development, 1985.

Existing Sewer Evaluation and Rehabilitation—Manual of Practice #FD-6. WPCF Publication No. MFD6GA. ASCE Manuals and Reports on Engineering Practice No. 62. Alexandria, Virginia: American Society of Civil Engineers/Water Pollution Control Federation, 1983.

Fernandez, R. B. "Sewer Rehab Using a New Subarea Method." *Water Engineering & Management*, Vol. 133, 1986, pp. 28–30.

Handbook for Sewer System Evaluation and Rehabilitation. Publication No. EPA/ 430/9-75-021. Washington, D.C.: Municipal Construction Division, Office of Water Program Operations, Environmental Protection Agency, 1975.

Heinecke, T. L., and C. H. Steketee. "The Key to Effective I/I Control." *Public Works*, Vol. 115, 1984.

Hollenbeck, A. J. "Designing for Removal of Sanitary Sewer Cross Connections." *Water Engineering & Management*, Vol. 131, 1984, pp. 29–31.

Infiltration/Inflow Collection System Management: Challenge of the 80's. Hyattsville, Maryland: I/I Evaluation and Control Division, Department of Maintenance and Operations, Washington Suburban Sanitary Commission, 1982.

Joint Committee of American Society of Civil Engineers and Water Pollution Control Federation. *Design and Construction of Sanitary and Storm Sewers—Manual of Practice #9.* Publication No. M0010GA. Alexandria, Virginia: American Society of Civil Engineers/Water Pollution Control Federation, 1969.

National Association of Sewer Service Companies (NASSCO). *Recommended Specifications for Sewer Collection System Rehabilitation*, fifth edition. Altamonte, Florida: National Association of Sewer Service Companies (NASSCO), August 1987.

National Water Well Association, RJN Environmental Associates, Inc., and Washington Suburban Sanitary Commission. *Impact of Groundwater Migration on Rehabilitation of Sanitary Sewers.* Hyattsville, Maryland: Washington Suburban Sanitary Commission, 1984.

Office of Water. *NPDES Stormwater Sampling Guidance Document.* Publication No. EPA 833-B-92-001. Environmental Protection Agency, July 1992.

Office of Water Program Operations. *Guidance for Sewer System Evaluation.* Washington, D.C.: Environmental Protection Agency, March 1974.

Recommended Standards for Sewage Works. Policies for the Review and Approval of Plans and Specifications for Sewage Collection and Treatment. A Report of the Committee of the Great Lakes Upper Mississippi River Board of State Sanitary Engineers (Ten-States Standards), 1978.

RJN Environmental Associates, Inc. *National Alternative Methodology for Sewer System Evaluation.* Hyattsville, Maryland: Washington Suburban Sanitary Commission, 1988.

Roy F. Weston, Inc. *Determination of Excessive/Nonexcessive Inflow Rates.* Study conducted under EPA Contract No. 68-01-6737. Washington, D.C.: Municipal Construction Division, Office of Water Program Operations, Environmental Protection Agency, 1984.

Smith, J. M., and Associates. *Analysis of Acceptable Ranges for Infiltration and Inflow Reduction in Sewer System Rehabilitation Projects.* Study conducted under EPA Contract No. 68-01-6737. Office of Municipal Pollution Control, Environmental Protection Agency, 1984.

Smith, J. M. and Associates, HydroQual, Inc. *Report to Congress: Hydrogen Sulfide Corrosion in Wastewater Collection and Treatment Systems.* Publication No. EPA/430/9-91/009. Washington, D.C.: Office of Water, Environmental Protection Agency, 1991.

Task Force on Alternative Sewer Systems. *Alternative Sewer Systems—Manual of Practice #FD-12.* Publication No. MDF12GA. Alexandria, Virginia: Water Pollution Control Federation, 1986.

Urban Water Resources Research Council of American Society of Civil Engineers and Water Environment Federation. *Design and Construction of*

Urban Stormwater Management Systems—Manual of Practice #FD-20. Publication No. MFD20GA. Alexandria, Virginia: American Society of Civil Engineers/Water Environment Federation, 1992.

Water Environment Federation Technical Practice Committee. *Wastewater Collection Systems Management—Manual of Practice #7.* Publication No. M0007RGA. Alexandria, Virginia: Water Environment Federation, 1992.

Water Pollution Control Federation. *Sewer Charges for Wastewater Collection and Treatment—A Survey.* Publication No. M0035GA. Alexandria, Virginia: Water Pollution Control Federation, 1982.